Prophets of Prosperity

PROPHETS OF

PROSPERITY

America's First
Political Economists

Paul K. Conkin

INDIANA UNIVERSITY PRESS
BLOOMINGTON

Library of Congress Cataloging in Publication Data

Conkin, Paul Keith.
Prophets of Prosperity.

Includes bibliographical references and index.
1. Economics—United States—History.   2. Economists
—United States—Biography.   I. Title.
HB119.A2C59   330′.0973   79-3251
ISBN 0-253-30843-7   1 2 3 4 5 84 83 82 81 80

CONTENTS

PREFACE

OVER the last several years I have enjoyed the company of the first generation of American political economists. Now I want to introduce these economists to a contemporary audience. This takes a bit of courage or possibly even a bit of arrogance. After all, who today cares a whit about the intricacies of Ricardian rent theory? Yet, swayed perhaps by earlier claims of its enormous importance, I think a great many people ought to be very concerned not only with rent theory but with the whole range of issues, practical as well as theoretical, debated by our first professional social scientists.

By 1815 Americans had achieved stable political institutions. Only a mature two-party system awaited full development. The earlier deluge of political literature now subsided. Those most concerned with policy issues increasingly turned from what John Adams called the science of government to the fledgling science of political economy. Between 1820 and 1860 dozens of economic texts and treatises poured from American presses. Economic issues dominated congressional debates and helped shape our evolving two-party system, as contending political factions, tied to industrial sectors or geographical sections, struggled to realize competing economic ideals. Almost every conceivable economic option still seemed open in America. This gave special urgency to policy debates, for it seemed certain that economic decisions once made and implemented would lead to entrenched economic arrangements. These would permanently dictate the direction of the American economy. Both soaring hopes and deep anxieties about the American economic future helped dignify the role of professed economic experts and provided a limited but eager market for their writings. The political economists shared as many anxieties as hopes. They were prophets in the Hebraic sense. They did not so much predict a future as calculate all the hazards or pitfalls that lay in the way of a prosperous and equitable society. Precautionary warnings, often tinged with laments over a lost innocence, dominated their analysis.

Alas, the experts could never agree with one another. Their differing theories provided solace and effective rationalizations for all sides of every controverted policy. This embarrassing diversity of viewpoints challenged the central claim of most political economists—that they were developing a true science. Since the exact implications of that claim often occasioned debates among American economists, I can only roughly suggest the issues. From Adam Smith on, analytical economists assumed some constants in the human situation. Surely certain needs were so basic to human existence as to transcend cultural differences. All men needed food, clothing, and shelter from the elements; all had the ability through language to coordinate the production and exchange of goods. Other constants pertained to man's environment, to those limited resources of nature capable of fulfilling man's essential needs. It seemed obvious that from such constants it should be possible to formulate some invariant propositions or principles. For example, any growing population in a limited environment must develop more efficient means of satisfying basic needs or face starvation. By careful analysis, one could discover the factors that would support a more efficient production and exchange of goods. One could also chart the invariant relationships between these factors.

Given such constant factors and relationships, then one should be able to relate them unequivocally to culturally conditioned institutions. No able economist ever denied the critical economic role of culture, of linguistically conditioned preferences or tastes. But if an economist could take into account the particularities of a reasonably stable cultural environment, or for analytical purposes simply stipulate such an institutional context, then he could construct a very reliable economic model. To the extent that an economist could have exact and continuous knowledge of variable economic factors, he could draw upon his knowledge of invariant relationships to predict the future course of economic development. This was one of the goals of nineteenth-century American political economists, and the goal most consistent with their scientific claim.

Economists here and abroad repeatedly pointed out certain obvious hazards in economic analysis, such as imprecision of language, incomplete or ambiguous propositions, and logical fallacies. They had recourse to these hazards to explain the immaturity of their science and to account for their failure to reach anything close to a consensus. Besides these formal problems, they confronted the problems posed by cultural differences. If, as in the Ricardian tradition, one simply stipulated the institutional context, then one risked a model so abstracted from any existing national economy as to be virtually useless to policy makers. But if one tried to avoid irrelevance by tying the model to the particularities of an existing society, then one faced a completely unmanageable complexity. Moreover, such a model was vulnerable wherever it rested upon empirical ignorance, and this was at almost every point in an age when economists always suffered from a dearth of reliable data.

The effort to develop a true science did not preclude a humanistic conception of political economy. In fact, by a quite general understanding, political economy still constituted a branch of moral philosophy. Not only Adam Smith but many later economists moved from early work in general moral theory to the narrower discipline of political economy. The logical tie between class and subclass involved two assumptions that might be challenged today but seemed unarguable to early nineteenth-century moralists, particularly those in the Scottish tradition. The primary linking assumption was their belief in knowable and universal moral principles, tied to certain common human characteristics and needs. Their second assumption involved the utility of political economy; only by applying its principles could mankind achieve a fulfilling and humane society. To come to know the principles of political economy was, therefore, to gain needed instruction about one's duties and obligations. It was also to grasp in one practical area some of the implications of a broader moral science. Of course, any scientific knowledge could be useful. What distinguished political economists from physicists was the fact that they studied a special and distinctive subject—man. This brought political economy into the universe of moral philosophy, into those empirical and descriptive disciplines that have as their subject intelligent and morally responsible beings, whereas the physical sciences remained in the partially overlapping but quite distinct universe of natural philosophy.

The word *political* in *political economy* did not refer to the policy implications of economic theory or to the interaction of economic analysis and governmental action. Rather, *political* designated a universe of discourse. Political economy included those universal principles applicable to a national economy, to a single sovereign entity. It set off the public scope of political economy from the more limited field of domestic economy, and thus from those principles applicable only to a single household or firm.

Because of its purported scientific status, its presumed empirical validity, and its universal scope, political economy seemed supremely useful. Had it not been scientific, it would not have seemed so worthy of study. Early American economists were rarely humble when promoting their discipline. They believed they dealt in a kind of knowledge that was indispensable for enlightened political choice, a knowledge essential to any long-term prospects of human happiness. Intense moral commitment undergirded their search for reliable knowledge. They not only celebrated the utility of their science but often tried to speed the implementation of policies that seemed clearly indicated by a correct understanding of political economy. Many became advocates of particular policies. Of course, such advocacy reflected their own tastes and preferences as well as their economic theories. But except for narrow and often single-minded advocacy on such issues as the tariff, the inevitable mingling of analytical and normative concerns scarcely threatened the scientific claim. If a medical researcher announces a new cure for cancer, the policy implications are surely clear. When a political economist predicted that existing policies would soon lead, by the operation of what he believed to be invariant regularities or laws, to much suffering and even starvation in large segments of a nation's population, he scarcely needed to dwell on the policy implications of his prediction. Unless one were willing to repudiate all the seemingly humane consequences of a more efficient production of material goods, or a fairer distribution of such goods, then one could do no other than applaud the moral significance of verified axioms in political economy.

It is with some trepidation that I refer to these political economists as our first professional social scientists. One can only be intimidated by the recent and often brilliant scholarship on professions in America and, above all, by the evident pitfalls of definition. What is a profession? If professionalism requires a highly specialized type of inquiry, a scholarly organization with its own journals or other official publications, and some formal means of certifying those with expert knowledge, then our early political economists did not yet participate in a profession. But most of these political economists held academic positions, professed a special and acquired competence, dealt with a body of esoteric and technical information, already had their distinguishing jargon, and used as a common resource a standard array of classic books and articles. They wrote critical reviews of one another's books in journals of opinion, generally dealt with the same questions (often in the same conventional order), rallied together in defense of their discipline, and tried, often with small success, to maintain a valid distinction between their expert labors and the work of mere laymen. They were aware of themselves as constituting an intellectual community, one that I gladly acknowledge as a profession.

My goals for this book are limited and simple. I have tried to describe the beliefs of approximately twenty nineteenth-century American economists. I have tried to achieve clarity without oversimplifying and technical accuracy without using economic jargon. I simply want the reader to meet these men, to hear their best arguments, to develop an appropriate appreciation for their brilliance or their moral urgency. In a sense, mine is a rescue operation. No other group of American intellectuals comparable in the scope and brilliance of their ideas or in their influence on their own contemporaries has received so little attention from scholars. Despite the recent proliferation of reprints of older works from all disciplines, at least half of the most important books or articles written by these economists are still available only in the original editions, and thus only in a few major libraries.

American economists did not live in a vacuum. They all tried to understand American economic institutions, some in order to celebrate them, some to criticize. In an all too brief and summary first chapter, I have tried to fill in a bit of this institutional background. Our early economists also worked with a common but borrowed intellectual heritage—the tradition in political economy launched by Adam Smith and variously developed by his English and French successors. In my second chapter, I have tried to identify the major doctrines within this intellectual heritage.

A theme that pervades the writings of these economists touches on some very personal memories and concerns. In noting this, I come as close as I can to some of the motives that ultimately led me to write this book. Our first generation of economists wrote during the infancy of associated modes of production in America. The success of our early textile mills, the course of development in England, and much economic analysis all suggested an irreversible trend toward larger productive units, more centralized management, greater economic interdependence, and more wage labor. In brief, the path of development in America already seemed to lead from the still normative proprietary ideal toward some type of collectivism. Sooner or later most independent American workers would have to give up entrepreneurial roles and become employees. This happened to my father in the depression thirties. For him, as for so many native-born Americans before him, the move from farm to factory was a very painful, grudging surrender to economic necessity. He had to alter his self-image, give up earlier fortifications of self-respect, and confess the failure of a noble American dream—that all men could be free. His family, beleaguered by depression debts, benefited enormously from that sacrifice. Without it I would never have been in a position to write this book.

The selection of economists proved very difficult. I tried to include representatives of each distinctive point of view. To do this, I had to include a few relatively obscure economists, ones who made little or no original contribution to economic theory. In this category are early and slavish Ricardian disciples, and some of the radicals, or agrarians. I have tried to describe the beliefs of these men fairly but briefly, without extensive analysis or attention to detail. On the other hand, I allocated most space to these economists whom I consider more able or more influential, those who contributed to political economy either new doctrines or a greater precision in analysis. This means that the length of my essay on each economist rather closely correlates with my estimate of his ability or significance. Thus, I allocated two chapters to Henry C. Carey, one each to John Taylor and Daniel Raymond, and one-half of a very long chapter to George Tucker. I believe Carey was the most original and most broadly influential American economist before the Civil War. In analytic ability, I rank Tucker highest; on sheer originality, Raymond. Taylor was not nearly so able an economist as the others, but he was a more influential and significant intellectual. He first began the shift among American intellectuals from largely political to economic issues, and also became the prototypical spokesman for a body of economic beliefs and attitudes that remained more broadly pervasive in America than any others up until the Civil War.

In no sense have I explored new territory. As early as 1925, Edwin R. A. Seligman identified almost all of the economists who appear in this book and also provided a detailed bibliography of their writings. ["Economics in the United States: An Historical Sketch," in his *Essays in Economics* (New York: Macmillan, 1925)]. Joao F. Normano wrote the first detailed survey of early American economic theory; he gave special attention to anti-Ricardians or nationalists and assessed their influence in Europe. [*The Spirit of American Economics* (New York: John Day Co., 1943)]. Michael J. L. O'Connor wrote what remains the definitive book on early textbooks, and in it he offered a brief synopsis of the theories of most leading American economists. [*Origins of Academic Economics in the United States* (New York: Columbia University Press, 1944)]. In addition to monographs or articles on most individual economists, two topical studies involve most of "my" economists. As early as 1921, John R. Turner carefully surveyed the fate of Ricardian rent doctrines in America [*The Ricardian Rent Theory in Early American Economics* (New York: New York University Press, 1921)]. Gary Hull has written an excellent dissertation [*The Prospect for Man in Early American Economic Thought* (University of Maryland, 1968)]. I owe him very special thanks, for it was he who first whetted my interest in American economists.

All these acknowledgments lead to Joseph Dorfman, and to his two-volume work, *The Economic Mind in American Civilization, 1606–1865* (New York: Viking, 1946). We are all indebted to Dorfman. No one has done so much to discover, and to bring appreciation to, all those Americans who have written on economic issues. His original two volumes, as well as three subsequent ones, are encyclopedic. He missed no one. His volumes were constant companions to my own research; if it were not pointless to do so, I could footnote him in each chapter. Yet I would not have written this book if I had not found serious deficiencies in Dorfman's first two volumes—deficiencies in organization, style, and content. Some of these problems are inevitable in pioneer efforts; some derive from Dorfman's controlling purpose, which was not so much to provide a coherent and sympathetic summary of the doctrines of major economists as to place even the most technical economic analysis within a broad social and cultural context. I feel that I do him honor, not by threshing out all our differences of approach and understanding, but simply by writing my own very different book.

Prophets of Prosperity

PART ONE

BACKGROUND

I

The American Economy
in 1815

BY 1815 Americans already enjoyed the highest living standards in the world. They had developed a sophisticated, household-based economy, with comparatively high per capita returns in all economic sectors—in the direct extraction of natural resources, in cultivation and husbandry, in the further processing of such produce, in exchange, and in personal services. Most of the economic product ended up in private consumption. Americans enjoyed inexpensive governments. They lacked the public wealth enjoyed by the English—great buildings, venerable universities, ornate cathedrals and museums—but few Americans knew the privation, the meager returns, of the mass of English tenants and wage laborers.

Past economic achievements provided the point of departure for American political economists. Some warned of all the future pitfalls; others celebrated future possibilities. But quantitative attainments made up only a part of the perceived achievement. The glory of the American economy was not so much prosperity as freedom. The idealized American producer was free and independent, without an economic master. He owned his own land or shop or tools, commanded his own labor, reaped his own returns, all without any obligation to anyone else. The idealized American was always a proprietor, whether a farmer, mechanic, or merchant. The dominant productive unit in America was the household. Such independent households existed in complex horizontal, rather than hierarchical, relationships. Never before, it seemed, had such a degree of freedom and independence been joined with such productive efficiency.

Why had Americans done so well economically? Not primarily because of rich resources, but because of the cultural attributes of European colonists and the energizing economic policies adopted first by British and then by American governments. Englishmen migrated to America; they did not colonize in the sense of using a native population as a reservoir of cheap labor. They brought developed skills and accumulated capital. At least in Puritan New England, emigration screened in behalf of exceptional ambition and talent. English and Protestant beliefs and values, as well as English legal institutions, favored work, saving, and high achievement. But most important, Britain had to entice settlers by a very generous land policy, and then, by default as much as intent, it permitted such settlers almost complete entrepreneurial freedom. Investment returns were simply too low to justify absentee direction by British companies, and even local proprietors like William Penn found it nearly impossible to control economic activity, or even collect rents, in "their" provinces. Except in a few areas, such as the Hudson Valley, an English style of tenancy never flourished in the colonies. Most heads of households gained full and clear possession of land in perpetuity.

The most basic economic policy in any society is that which determines the conditions of access to nature. All consumable or potentially consumable goods come from nature. Some goods are ready for human consumption as gathered or harvested; most require additional labor in order to transform them into useful items or to exchange them at distances. But without access to nature, one has nothing to consume or to transform or to exchange. Thus, in any economic system, the extractive and agricultural industries are most basic, for all else depends on them. If they are inefficient, if they require almost all available labor, then the overall standard of living is necessarily low. Land or resource policies are the first determinants of the performance of these essential industries. Beyond that, easy access to nature has enormous political implications. Unless a person has a protected right to use a portion of nature, he cannot control his own economic destiny. He is compelled to bargain with those who "own" nature, and thus to some extent he must accept a dependent or even a servile status.

In one sense, Britain offered American colonists very little. The land they received was almost worthless in its undeveloped state. Recipients gained little more than the substance of a dream, the foundation of a great hope. That was enough. From this beginning all the way through the early disposition of United States public lands, the cost of access rights was always small compared with the cost of bringing land into production. Clearing and fencing land, building houses and barns, acquiring draft animals and tools—all required considerable savings or credit plus enormous expenditures of labor. Except in the better financed and organized adventures, like that at Massachusetts Bay, new settlers had to suffer an extended and often enormous diminution of their accustomed standard of living. They lived for years in unimaginably crude houses, lacked all social amenities, and were exposed to new diseases. But for those who paid their own way to America, the future promise surely redeemed much of the early hardship. From the beginning they worked to acquire, and then to improve, their own small kingdom, and they eventually gained a type of economic independence that they could never have aspired to in England, which was already fully owned, mostly by a small elite, and in which access to land came at an ever dearer price.

Americans procured land not only to use but often to sell. Farmers realistically hoped to gain the increment of value occasioned by denser settlement; it was their reward for coming first. The typical proprietor combined the outlook of a peasant and a gambler. He wanted not only a secure homestead, a place of work and fulfillment, but also capital gains should he decide to sell and move on. To some extent, all landowners were speculators, with a gambler's hope for good fortune. The typical proprietor welcomed immigrants, rejoiced in population growth and the rise of cities, and boosted his local community. By so doing he stood to increase his own wealth. Soon, Americans who spoke of the "right" to own land meant the right to get as much as one could and to collect the largest possible capital gains from it much more often than they meant the right of each person to gain his share of nature. In fact, by the 1830s those who voiced the aspirations of outsiders, of the dispossesed, and who sought easier access to land, gained the reputation of being dangerous "agrarians."

In 1815 independent household units still dominated all sectors of the American economy. The heads of such households enjoyed almost complete entrepreneurial freedom. They managed productive tools and directed subordinate laborers. For success, such entrepreneurs required what could be called cultural capital—a body of aspirations, values, and acquired skills. Those with such assets were able to develop a productive farm or shop and thereby acquire the necessities and the few comforts that characterized established American families. The losers lacked these assets—they were unable to innovate, to find new efficiencies, to limit consumption, to gain needed tools, to apply, or inspire others to apply, disciplined work. Pride, intense ambition, even a morbid or obsessive fascination with efficiency and acquisition helped assure success.

The American economy was never static. But contrary to all the myths, the United States never experienced an industrial *revolution*. In certain industries spectacular innovations did trigger very dramatic and rapid increases in production (witness the changes brought about by the cotton gin, the power loom, steam-powered river boats, and the reaper), but these never coincided with one another. For the economy as a whole, growth in per capita income accelerated only slightly from one decade to the next throughout the nineteenth century. Structural changes (in the form of ownership, in degrees of specialization, in the size of productive units, in the relation of management to labor) also occurred gradually, and at quite different times or at different rates in various industries.

Even a description of the general characteristics of the American economy after 1815 conceals as much as it reveals. Most Americans lived in rural areas or in villages (only 5 percent of the total population lived in cities in 1776, only 9 percent in 1830, and less than 20 percent as late as 1860). In 1815 approximately four out of every five workers considered agriculture as their primary occupation; from then until 1860 a steadily larger proportion found primary employment in other fields, but even at the end of the Civil War slightly over half of all American workers remained in agriculture. Because of varied criteria of judgment as well as inadequate data, employment status is very difficult to estimate, but it seems that as late as 1815 at least 80 percent of white adult males were self-employed, a percentage that dropped only slowly throughout the nineteenth century.

But such figures are deceptive; they have the effect of exaggerating both the commitment to agriculture and the independence of most workers. Behind the vague label *farming* hid many forms of production. Well into the nineteenth century, most American artisans, even those in the larger cities, grew gardens and kept cows, hogs, or chickens. Likewise, most workers in rural areas, even those on the more specialized farms, engaged in nonagricultural tasks, in various types of processing, in local commercial exchange, and in the providing of services. Wives, for example, spent more time in first-stage manufacturing (cooking, canning, churning, spinning, weaving, sewing) and in services (nursing, cleaning, grooming, laundering, ironing, waiting table) than in such agricultural tasks as milking cows or gardening. Men spent up to half of their time in manufacturing (as part-time blacksmiths, millers, carpenters, masons, butchers, tanners) or in commercial activities (transporting goods to a market, swapping or buying and selling, borrowing and lending). In fact, I suspect Americans as a whole devoted more of their total time to manufacturing in 1815 then they did in 1860, and a great deal more than they do today.

In spite of occupational versatility, most households in America were not self-sufficient. Most families grew and preserved basic foods and cut their own wood for fuel. This assured only a minimal security; any degree of comfort depended on forms of specialized production and on market exchange. In 1815 the specialization and exchange was largely local, but supplemented almost everywhere by foreign trade. Primary exchange occurred within neighborhoods and created complex, overlapping networks of contact, since neighborhood boundaries seldom matched political or religious ones. Town or county lines might send next-door neighbors to different voting places, just as church membership might lead two neighbors into quite divergent patterns of group loyalty. Yet such neighbors might exchange work, swap hogs, carry their grist to the same mill, go to the same blacksmith, call in the same midwife, and take their surplus goods to market in the same yearly communal trip.

With exchange went specialized skills. Every woman learned to cook and to spin and sew, but only some operated looms or became midwives. Every man in a rural area learned to work oxen or horses and mastered the indispensable skills of cultivation and harvest, but only a few became expert (even if unlicensed) veterinarians, or highly valued carpenters, or part-time merchants, or expert butchers. Every neighborhood had its specialists. In fact, even as late as the mid-nineteenth century a close look at any rural economy would have revealed that every adult was a specialist or expert in one area or another. Yet, at this primary level, few people were able to work at their specialty full-time. The most likely candidates were the miller and the blacksmith, but usually even they did some farming, as did most carpenters and masons, and even preachers, to give due recognition to the most esteemed person in the local service sector. Thus the standard of living attained by rural Americans still depended upon a high degree of cooperative interchange, or a complex swapping of specialized skills, products, and services.

To note this specialization is not to idealize it. It gave exceptional opportunities to those who had badly needed and scarce skills, and often further enhanced the benefits of wealth or past privilege. In fact, with growing populations and more complex and extensive patterns of exchange, higher and higher rewards went to the able. Thus, through almost all of American history the rate of overall economic growth correlated with greater inequalities of wealth and income, or with enlarged returns to intelligence, political acumen, cultivated skills, and past accumulation, and smaller returns to unskilled physical labor. By 1815 the economic distance between the wealthiest households and the poorest was often dramatic, particularly in the cities and in the tidewater South, least so in backcountry areas. Increasing numbers of rural families, perhaps varying regionally from one-fourth to one-half, either owned no land at all or lived on land so poor that it barely yielded minimal subsistence.

Household production was not only consistent with specialization but also with communal work. Many farm tasks required cooperative labor, and even when optional shared work facilitated companionship. Households were often large and everyone worked, the women and children of the family as well as servants and slaves. Thus, most actual household workers (at least four out of five even in nonslave areas) were always of a subordinate or dependent type. The later growth of factory production did not drastically increase the number of dependent workers, since few farm proprietors ever chose or had to accept wage labor. Work patterns varied both seasonally and according to the drive or ambition of owners. New homesteads meant endless work—clearing land, fencing, erecting buildings. Women, in particular, had continuous chores. But developed farms allowed leisurely work in season. The household pattern permitted child abuse—in overwork or in neglected nutrition or education. Yet most youngsters were eager to become more involved in the communal work, to earn adult status, to share in the companionship of group efforts.

The independent household prevailed, not just in rural America, but also in villages and cities. Full-time mechanics or artisans also worked in household shops. Most merchandise firms were family-owned and had few employees. Most city workers had relationships with employers that went well beyond simple wage payments. But by 1815 a few large southern plantations, those with more than a hundred slaves, had attained a scale and an impersonality in labor management that probed the limits of the household model, and so had a few large merchandising companies, a few shippers, and a few urban shops.

Given a degree of local specialization and cooperation, the household unit could be very efficient. It gained even greater efficiency as better transportation and communication expanded the geographical size of markets, and allowed greater specialization within households. This meant not only that farmers could devote a greater portion of their land and effort to cash crops but also that women could profitably specialize in household forms of manufacturing. In some industries, including most agricultural industries and several types of retail merchandising, the household has remained the dominant mode of economic organization in America. Such household production is not inimical to the use of very refined tools or to sophisticated management—witness the enormous leaps of productivity on American farms since World War II. In fact, if one wants to find an industrial revolution in America (that is, rapid gains in productivity over a brief period of time), perhaps the best place to look for it would be in agriculture in the 1950s and 1960s, and this largely within the same household structures that dominated all sectors of the American economy in 1815.

But in some industries (including a few agricultural ones), the household mode of production presents nearly insuperable human or technological limitations. Some types of production, to reach the highest attainable levels of efficiency, require very talented managerial skills or very technical types of expert knowledge. It is all but impossible to develop such human assets for the head of every household unit. Thus, today, the awesome education or training requirements for success in agriculture have finally jeopardized the family farm. Equally critical, some capital-intensive forms of production, either to occur at all or to be efficient, require large concentrations of plants and machines or large clusters of narrowly specialized workers. Here economies of scale exclude house-holds. Few household heads can accumulate the required capital or pay the required workers. As late as 1815 (and for a majority of industries even as late as 1860), existing productive tools were not so sophisticated or costly, nor laborers so narrowly specialized or so available in America, as to give any clear edge to the large-scale, factory mode of production. But even by 1815, the textile industry had already clearly demonstrated the limitations of household production in that industry and the possible efficiencies of collective or centralized productive units.

As late as 1815, the exchange of goods and services, and the specializa-tion this supported, largely involved the local neighborhood. This meant that people frequently exchanged goods with nearby neighbors and by direct contact. No middlemen facilitated such exchange. But always some more distant exchange supplemented and in subtle ways affected the local market (it secured the type of money used locally), and for the commodi-ty areas of the South such distant exchange challenged the primacy of local neighborhoods. It required the services of middlemen, created economic ties between complete strangers, and often involved complex credit arrangements. In 1815 the main focus of distant exchange remained foreign markets. The goods of commerce flowed to coastal ports, and then largely to Europe, Africa, or the West Indies, and not to other sections or regions of the United States.

Economic development after 1815 in much of the South simply ex-panded this older, semi-colonial pattern. The South exploited the great international boom in cotton textiles. It furnished the raw materials for numerous English factories and for the emerging New England factories. At both ends—the plantation and the mill—the cotton boom produced very high profits. By the 1830s the most successful entrepreneurs in Amer-ica were those who had cotton plantations on the newly opened lush delta soils of Mississippi and Louisiana (a few counties here had the highest per capita income in the United States) and those who owned integrated spinning and weaving mills in New England. Planters had a large and stable work force in their slaves. Whether they reaped economies of scale or not (this remains a controverted issue) they did accumulate a highly mobile and marketable form of human capital, and were able to bear the risk of a very specialized form of agriculture. When not working cotton, slaves could grow foodstuffs or carry out various types of home processing or manufacturing. Small cotton-belt farmers could not risk as great a degree of specialization, but they too made cotton their primary money crop. Slave-owning cotton planters, large and small, constituted the most powerful, self-conscious, aggressive economic interest in pre–Civil War America. They tried to secure all possible political advantages for their exported money crop. Although with each passing decade they realized a larger home market for cotton (but never one to rival England) and increasingly used northeastern financiers or shippers (New York eventually rivaled New Orleans even in the cotton trade), they never formed a political alliance with New England manufacturers, and they fought such manufacturers on most policy issues. In a sense, one cotton industry battled another. This conflict between commodity agriculture and factory manufacturing, between free trade and protection, between black slavery and wage dependence, forced most American political economists to take sides in what became our principal sectoral, as well as sectional, conflict.

Less than half the South was congenial to cotton culture. On the older plantations of the Southeast, whose soil was in many cases exhausted, cotton never supported inflated profits and rarely led to great riches. Older commodities—tobacco, rice, and sugar—were more profitable—in the case of sugar, because of tariff protection. Except in the Mississippi delta, parts of the black belt, and, later on, in the black prairies of Texas, returns to capital and labor in the agricultural South never matched those in commercial or manufacturing enterprises in the Northeast. Yet southerners rarely converted labor and capital to specialized manufacturing. Economic historians still debate the reasons why, but southerners of the time believed, correctly or incorrectly, that profitable factory production was impossible with slave labor. Thus the South contained the whole economic spectrum, from the greatest wealth and highest incomes in the delta and commercial New Orleans to the lowest incomes on depleted piedmont soils and in the Appalachian highlands. Overall, after 1815 wealth and income in the antebellum South lagged behind those in New England, but remained higher than those in what was then called the West, now the Midwest. Until the Civil War, the South showed that commodity agriculture, although largely tied to foreign markets, could nonetheless be very profitable, provided that the commodity enjoyed a great and rapidly growing demand, that its producers could exploit the deposited fertility of new land without renewing it, and that they could continue to use a slave labor force.

After 1815 economic growth outside the South largely depended not on increased foreign trade, but on larger and better-integrated domestic markets. Slowly the immediate, face-to-face exchange of local neighborhoods yielded, at least in part, to regional trade. Local patterns of exchange atrophied, only to revive briefly in times of depression. In New England, even before 1815, fairly dense settlement and reasonably good internal roads had facilitated regional interchange. This allowed more specialization in both farming and manufacturing, and required more full-time middlemen. Full-time artisans readily gathered in cities and towns, while rural families slowly relinquished many inefficient forms of processing. New England and the Middle Atlantic States soon enjoyed a cosmopolitan economy. Manufacturing and commercial services clustered in dominant cities, each surrounded by its hinterland of specialized agriculture (truck farms near town and farms growing durable grains on the outer perimeter). A series of dramatic improvements in transportation (steam-powered river boats, new canals, better turnpikes, and the beginnings of a network of railroads) facilitated such regional specialization. Local neighbors had offered only a small market for most artisans, thus limiting the degree of specialization. Now, drawing customers from forty and fifty miles around, artisans in the market towns could work full-time. Those whose goods or services were everywhere needed set up in every county seat; those who catered to special needs or manufactured luxury goods (silverware, clocks) clustered in the larger commercial cities of Boston, New York, Philadelphia, and Baltimore.

Regional trade required not only an increased commitment to transportation but to other commercial services. Those engaged in commerce or related fiscal services had suffered, or felt that they had suffered, the most from the restrictions of British colonial policy and later from the insecurity and lack of contractual guarantees under the Articles of Confederation. To a disproportionate extent, merchants and bankers helped shape the struggle for independence and lead the movement for a federal constitution. They secured most of their goals in the federal Constitution, which created a national common market, with federal controls over interstate commerce, tariffs, foreign trade, coinage, and bankruptcy. The Constitution prohibited states from impeding obligations and contracts, and assured a protected national market for the recipients of special economic favors from state governments. But farmers and manufacturers alike remained jealous of shippers, merchants, and bankers. Such jealousy led to incessant policy conflicts—over internal improvements or other subsidies to shippers; over tariffs or other restrictions on the free flow of trade; over monetary and banking policies; and, less constantly, over bankruptcy legislation.

In the commodity areas of the South, prosperity depended on foreign markets and foreign prices. In the more integrated mixed farming and manufacturing areas of the Northeast, prosperity depended upon home production and regional exchange, plus returns from commercial services provided to both the South and the West (the present Midwest). Incomes remained lowest in the West despite lush soils and more efficient agriculture. In areas of new settlement, enormous amounts of human energy had to go into capital development. Transportation costs also hurt. The West never developed any dependable export commodity (wheat sales varied immensely according to the fortunes of European agriculture), nor did the cotton South provide a large market for Western grain or meat. Thus, the Northeast provided the largest external market for western agricultural products. Lower transportation costs eventually helped cement an economic alliance between commercial and manufacturing interests in the Northeast and Western farmers.

Even regional exchange and specialization altered the role of households. Urbanized artisans slowly gave up their gardens and their cows and became dependent on produce from surrounding farms. Farmers shifted toward full-time agricultural production and toward one or a few profitable crops. Wives gladly gave up a whole range of home manufacturing, but in some areas profitably specialized in one form of efficient home manufacturing, such as in weaving before the wide use of the power loom. Finally, more people worked full-time in industries associated with exchange, transportation in particular. Such specialization made production more efficient but it also made the producers vulnerable to fluctuations in demand in distant markets, which now had a great deal more to do with local welfare. City artisans, especially, became completely dependent on the demand for their products. Few had alternative skills or any way to fall back on the family farm in lean times. Depression for them meant no work, no income, no way to grow food, and utter dependence on savings or on private or public charity. Thus, from the 1820s on, beginning in Philadelphia and New York, vulnerable and beleaguered mechanics organized effective protest against their often adversely changing fortunes, and in the process formulated wide-ranging schemes for basic structural changes in an economic system that, from their perspective, seemed increasingly unjust and exploitative.

Broader horizontal integration also increased the role and the power of middlemen. They were often in an enviable position to anticipate, and respond quickly to, shifts in supply or demand. Merchants also effectively used various credit instruments, thus enormously increasing their working inventories and, unless overwhelmed by unexpected calamities, their profit potential as well. Position and accumulating wealth (both profits and risks were high in commerce) gave the large merchants needed power over other producers. As a result, the merchants slowly moved from their functional contribution to the horizontal integration of households, to an early form of vertical or hierarchical integration of artisans. Detailed studies of the shoe and tanning industries have revealed the complex process by which merchant-capitalists slowly subordinated and eventually came to dominate certain household industries. The lines of dependence slowly grew—the process might begin with a merchant's simply buying an artisan's product for distribution to more distant markets and progress to the merchant's supplying credit or market information, and then to his gathering and supplying raw materials to the artisan and making large contractual purchases, and culminate in his direct intervention in the management of the shop. The independence of both masters and journeymen was diminished, until the master in effect became a crew foreman and the journeyman a mere wage employee, with both men working under the overarching supervision of a merchant house, which meanwhile had the same relationship to other manufacturers and to suppliers of raw materials. The cost to artisans was not always economic; those whose skills remained essential usually received the highest wages offered. What they lost was economic security and status, their earlier sense of independence and dignity. This loss underlay much of their protest in the first workingmen's movements in the 1820s and early 1830s.

The other emerging form of vertical integration involved not households but solitary workers. The "factory system" (to use the imprecise label that has come to designate it), instead of making use of the household, threatened to supplant it as the primary productive unit. Unfortunately, the word *factory* almost defies precise definition, and no firm conventions yet guide its use. Thus, no one can conclusively identify the first American factory or even clearly trace the growth of factories. It is easy to distinguish between a household, headed by a father or a master craftsmen and encompassing a limited number of dependent workers either within the immediate family or clearly bonded to it by other than economic ties, and a large New England textile mill, with a managerial hierarchy and two hundred wage employees gathered from one hundred households spread over three states. But there were fewer than a dozen mills of that size in all America in 1815. As late as 1811 all the cotton mills (87) in the United States together employed only about four thousand people, mainly women and children. What existed in most manufacturing industries was a continuum ranging from small household shops up to a few extremely large firms with twenty or thirty employees, with only a handful larger than that. In 1811 Tench Coxe and Albert Gallatin, in the first extended survey of American manufacturers, found one hat factory with two hundred employees and another with 150, which along with two or three large cotton mills, were the largest factories in the country, and by their very size a marvel to everyone who visited them.

In defining a factory, size may not be the primary issue, but rather the nature of economic relationships. These are not easy to gauge. Was an enterprising tanner, who built larger vats and seasonally hired up to ten employees, thereby creating a new type of production? It depends. If he pulled workers outside the household context, out of the paternal bonds of such a household, and hired them strictly for their output, and if work took place apart from other routine activities, apart from where workers lived and formed primary relationships and ate and slept, then their labor functioned as a commodity, with its price competitively determined. By these standards, a shop with ten workers might conclusively break from the household pattern and another of forty workers not do so, just as a large cotton plantation with up to two hundred slaves might still retain most of the features of a household.

Given such structural distinctions, then one has to look carefully at the relationships of different people in any productive unit, however large or small. And when we do so, we find that all along in America there had been a small proportion of dependent and often quite mobile laborers working outside households. The people nominally in the household system whose status is the hardest to define were journeymen, farmhands, and nonindentured household servants or domestics. In some cases they might be fully integrated into the household system of reciprocal duties and obligations, their status being rather like that of children. But in other cases the bonds might slacken to the extent that they functioned merely as contractual wage employees. Of course, at a household level, such contractual employment could be much more personal and even intimate than in large firms, but the relationship could also be more tyrannical because of the complete absence of group scrutiny or accepted and enforced rules of fairness.

Not at all ambiguous was the status of those clearly outside the household system. Proportionately, their numbers were small, possibly not more than 3 or 4 percent of the work force in 1815. Who were they? Sailors on large ships (not the small family-owned fishing boats of New England); public servants, including the military; urban day laborers, best represented by dockhands and construction workers; and employees of the new, hierarchically organized textile mills, tanneries, ironworks, hat and shoe factories, and large ship-building firms. For household heads who chose, or were forced to seek, such outside employment, the shift meant a clear loss of freedom and independence, of entrepreneurial status, whatever the advantages of income and consumption. In fact, the shift of free workers to dependent status is one of the continuing and poignant stories in American economic history. But for subordinate members of households—and it is well to remember that they made up four-fifths of American workers— the transition was often more liberating than enslaving. At least in a time of labor scarcity, the conditions of contractual wage employment often yielded higher benefits than work at home—more personal income, less-arbitrary supervision, the quite desirable option of changing jobs or place of residence according to fancy, and a richer social life in villages or cities. It was not poverty or economic compulsion that lured the first New England farm girls into the early cotton mills. Nor was it economic compulsion alone that lured a smaller proportion of young men, increasingly precluded from proprietary opportunities in local agriculture, to the better-paying jobs (and for the most able, eventual managerial roles) in factories. This choice was often more appealing than the hazards and uncertainties of moving to new farms farther west.

The first surge of factory growth, which came after 1815, involved a widespread and often creative use of corporate privileges. Textiles clearly led the way, just as earlier spinning mills had begun a factory tradition in Rhode Island as early as 1791. By 1830 the power loom made possible integrated cotton and woolen mills (that is, mills that did both spinning and weaving). These, along with growing numbers of hat and shoe factories, provided the best outlet for investment as well as a rapidly growing demand for wage labor in Rhode Island and in parts of Connecticut, New Hampshire, and Massachusetts. Smaller mills were locally important in the diversified manufacturing city of Philadelphia, in growing Cincinnati, and even in parts of the upper South. In their early development such factories pooled workers from rural households without displacing such households. Until 1840 most wage employees in the textile mills were women and children. And even after 1840, most male operatives were immigrants, not displaced farmers. Everywhere except in New England, the farm population continued to grow. The large firm replaced household manufacturers (dramatically so in the case of household weavers) simply by moving them from the home context into more efficient or capital-intensive factories. Farmers concentrated more thoroughly on cash crops and shifted production to supply the changing demands and new markets created by concentrated urban populations. Thus, the growth of New England factory manufacturing was not all a growth in the *amount* of labor devoted to manufacturing. This fact was not apparent to contemporaries, and thus was rarely recognized in publicized debates in Congress. At the time few people realized that structural changes were taking place in all sectors as a result of the dramatic and highly visible factory growth, which also diverted attention from the continuation of older forms of work dependence. Only the plight of the slave caused the same degree of widespread concern as was expressed for the fate of factory workers.

The early and quite limited growth of factory manufacturing, plus the growth of attendant commercial and financial services, raised the perennial problem of government favoritism for one sector as against another. Intense competition between sectors became a major motif of congressional debates after 1815. The most intense debate had to do with the status, privileges, and dangers of highly integrated, concentrated, collectivized, politically powerful, and usually corporate forms of manufacturing or commerce; such sectoral conflict centered on a few intensely controversial issues, especially protective tariffs. In the midst of such conflict, the first American political economists began to offer their purportedly expert advice to policy makers. Their claim to expert knowledge was largely based on their analytic tools, most of which they borrowed from established European economists. But they continuously struggled to adapt those tools to American realities.

II

European Sources

TWO documents of world-shaking significance date from 1776—the American Declaration of Independence and Adam Smith's *Wealth of Nations*. Both announced new beginnings. Both assayed great human possibilities. The Declaration expressed the dominant concerns of American political and intellectual leaders: to win independence from Europe and to achieve distinctive political institutions. These enormous tasks required all their talents. Meanwhile, in England and France, Smith's masterpiece quickly became the point of departure for a revitalized discipline of political economy. Only after 1815, when conflicts over economic policy began to dominate American politics, did our most brilliant moral theorists take up the issues posed by the new economic doctrines. As latecomers, Americans inherited from European political economists their controlling issues, analytical concepts, challenging models, and even ritualized language. This did not foreclose all options. Americans delighted in refuting one or another European master and soon charted new paths in a growing discipline. But they could not ignore their predecessors, could not create their own universe of discourse. They came to school after the first recess.

Adam Smith neither originated political economy nor provided Americans with their first instruction in the intricacies of economic analysis. The French Economists or Physiocrats, many of whom were personal friends of Franklin and Jefferson, first introduced Americans to the new discipline. But *Wealth of Nations* quickly established itself in America as a work of tremendous authority. More than anyone else, Smith helped make political economy the first well-developed social science during its first critical period of growth, from 1776 to about 1850.

Both Adam Smith and the Physiocrats repudiated a reigning economic theory called "mercantilism." Unfortunately, the label is far from precise. Few economists or economic advisers, not even the great Colbert, ever matched the straw man that Adam Smith so mercilessly ridiculed. "Mercantilism," as Smith caricatured it, identified one clear policy—that a nation sell more abroad than it imported, in order to accumulate money in the form of gold and silver. To gain favorable trade balances, it had to favor its own merchants and manufacturers, acquire foreign colonies as protected markets or sources of raw materials, charter specially favored trading companies, and regulate its domestic economy in behalf of overall national priorities. This outlook meant policies that ignored or penalized domestic agriculture, invited foreign adventure and the possibility of wars, and shackled nonfavored domestic producers with all manner of distorting state regulations. In the ugliest caricatures, "mercantilists" even endorsed the lowest possible wages for domestic workers, justified slave labor in foreign colonies, and only sought the wealth and happiness of a small commercial elite. So defined, mercantilism scarcely required any detailed refutation. Needless to say, certain mercantilist goals— favorable trade balances, increased supplies of money, an overall coordination of domestic producers, and great national strength and glory—had enduring appeal and lent themselves to nonpejorative descriptions. But it was the caricature that engaged the French Physiocrats.

The Physiocrats celebrated agriculture. This, along with their defense of complete economic freedom, endeared them to Americans. The Physiocrats professed to be scientific in their approach; their adored mentor, François Quesney, backed this up with his elaborate economic tables. The Physiocrats focused on the annual productive cycle of a nation, distinguished between productive and unproductive labor, and traced the threefold distribution of the product to wages, rents, and profits (Adam Smith would develop all these themes.) But the Physiocrats became famous, or among their critics infamous, for one doctrine—that agricultural labor alone leads to a surplus product, and that in this sense it alone is productive. This thesis involved both truisms and sophistries. Obviously, all consumer goods come from nature. In agriculture, in contrast with extractive industries, processes of organic growth join with human labor. The Physiocrats believed a farmer could normally produce more than he needed for his own consumption and the maintenance of his land and tools. This surplus underwrote rents to landlords. They earned such rent only to the extent that they improved the soil. Otherwise, the Physiocrats desired a single tax on land, the ownership of which they saw as a kind of private monopoly over access rights to an unimproved nature.

In manufacturing and commerce, the Physiocrats contended that human industry created no surplus. Here, workers added a value equal only to the cost of raw materials, their own subsistence during their period of work, and payments of ordinary profits to utilized capital. Although the Physiocrats used pejorative language for such work("barren,""unproductive"), they never denied the usefulness of manufacturing and commerce. Changing the form or place of an object made it available to more consumers, freed farmers for full-time agricultural work (enabling them to create an even larger surplus by the only kind of truly productive work), and increased the total industry of a country. But the larger product derived directly from the work of farmers, and only indirectly from that in the other two sectors. This made manufacturing and commerce servants of agriculture. The Physiocrats used these agruments, not to justify restrictions on manufacturing or trade, but to argue for their free and natural development upon a strong agricultural base. They particularly repudiated mercantilistic bounties to these nonproductive sectors, for such bounties penalized agriculture and retarded economic growth.

Adam Smith celebrated Physiocratic policies and, much more than he acknowledged, incorporated aspects of their analysis into his work. He denied that agricultural labor alone was productive, but he conceded that farmers could produce larger surpluses than other workers, and he often shared Physiocratic suspicions of the motives of manufacturers. Above all, he joined the Physiocrats in their desire to free human industry from all artificial government restraints and privileges. Smith developed his political economy during the golden era of Scottish university life, out of a sophisticated, morally serious, responsible Calvinist intellectual environment. He acknowledged the influence of several eminent eighteenth-century Scottish philosophers, including David Hume, Dugald Stewart, and above all his mentor, Francis Hutcheson. Smith began his academic career at Glasgow in logic and moral philosophy and wrote a perceptive book on moral sentiments. He first developed his views on political economy while still lecturing to students.

It would be hard to overestimate the influence of Smith. His masterpiece was beguiling in 1776 and remains so today. Smith was a comprehensive, thoughtful, original moral theorist. His prestige soon required every political economist and almost every politician to deal with his theories. Unlike many of his English successors, Smith had a message of cheer. In the normal and natural course of events, people in civilized nations inevitably realize ever higher levels of consumption. And, most flattering to Americans, only free societies sustain this normal progression toward greater wealth.

Smith began with a "law of progress." His law was neither normative, as in the laws of a state, nor descriptive, as in the laws of physics. It neither prescribed conduct nor identified any structural regularities. In effect, Smith identified a number of human traits that provide sufficient conditions for increased productivity. These traits include an all but unlimited human desire for consumer goods and an instinct for trade, or a love of bargaining, for self-advantage and possibly even for sheer enjoyment. Such economic exchange involves man's self-conscious estimate of his own interests. Self-regard, or the pursuit of self-interest (not selfishness) is the basis of a morally beneficial form of interdependence, that which makes possible a division of labor. This, in turn, allows a high degree of specialization, rewards skill, and encourages invention. Smith's "law of progress" was identical in form with one later made famous by Charles Darwin. Darwin showed how certain existing factors—reproductive fecundity, normal hereditary variations, and environmental pressures— alone insured the evolution not only of new species, but of "higher" species. A god did not have to intrude into such purely natural events in order to secure such progressive outcomes. In the same sense, Smith tried to show that economic progress requires no guiding hand, no external contrivances, and particularly no detailed direction from the state. The process is self-motivating and self-regulating.

A minimal legal order is necessary for Smith's law to work. Governments must not only protect individuals and their honestly acquired possessions from external and internal enemies, but also uphold all the voluntary contracts that people enter into, for otherwise no one could afford to take the risk of specialization. Just as laws must undergird any economic progress, so they can delay or prevent it by adding restrictions on free choice, by imbalancing the types of equilibrium that emerge from individual choice, by giving unfair advantages to one side in contractual relationships.

Smith not only explained the causes of economic evolution, but he also indicated a typical pattern of economic development. From one perspective, this meant a shift from narrow, local networks of exchange. He called such networks *markets*, a word whose meaning in Smith's writing and in that of most subsequent economists is very elusive. He soon reified the word and talked as if the word *market* referred not to a dynamic process but to a causal agent. The broader the network, the greater the degree of possible specialization and the more complex the interdependence. Ultimately, with ocean transport and the aid of money, the whole world could become one market, and everyone could benefit from almost infinitely specialized production and from the various skills and complex tools called forth by such specialization. This evolution from narrow to broad markets paralleled a steady extension of human labor from agriculture to intricate manufacturing and complex forms of commerce. Each sector built upon the other, with agriculture the most important. Smith believed that, in any society, agriculture offered the first and most profitable investment, as well as such noneconomic returns as independence and tranquility. He accepted the Physiocratic doctrine of a natural increase. Labor in agriculture alone gains an added increment, which usually goes to landlords in the form of rent.

Fortunately, an efficient agriculture can meet the national need for raw produce without using all potential labor, thus freeing industry and skill for commerce and manufacturing. These bear a symbiotic relationship to agriculture, since they offer a market for agricultural produce, free farmers for full-time agricultural production, and provide them with ever cheaper manufactured goods. In Europe, a free and productive agriculture developed late, after the breakdown of feudal restraints. A better, more natural evolution was occurring in America. Here, a nonfeudal, free, but commercial agriculture first developed, as it properly should. Such agriculture reflected the best expression of self-interest. In America no land monopolies or high rents impeded agricultural profits. Heavy manufacturing would develop later, and naturally, when surplus labor and capital found in it more profitable returns than in agriculture. The highest level of wealth, he believed, required sophisticated production in all sectors, at least within a market if not within a country. He described manufacturing as a final key to prosperity, for here a higher degree of specialization was possible than in agriculture.

Smith tried to set a new standard of rigor in economic analysis. He often failed, but he defined most of the problems faced by subsequent English and French economists. Smith opened his analytic section with the issue (or issues) of value. Many objects have value to people. They meet human needs. Smith was primarily interested not in such plentiful goods as water or air but in goods that have a value in exchange. He began with a very narrow issue—the best measure of value. His simple answer—the amount of labor an object will command. Smith wanted to find a constant in the flux of relative values. He believed that labor was the only universal and accurate measure, by which he seemed to mean that over time and at any place on earth people place an equal value on their own labor, given needed qualifications for levels of skill and difficulty. In this sense, the value of labor is constant, and so an accurate measure of the shifting value of commodities through the centuries. In prosperous countries, where productivity is increasing, the labor that objects can command steadily decreases. Stated alternatively, real wages rise. Given a completely stable medium of exchange (there are none), economic progress means that the money price of goods goes down even as money wages go up.

Most later economists would eventually give up trying to find a constant measure of value. Instead they would explore the determinants of exchange values or, given some constant standard, prices. Smith explored this issue, but rather sketchily. In a very primitive yet free economy, he argued, the quantity and quality of labor is the only conponent that goes into prices. Even here, Smith did not mean that labor immediately determines prices. Shifts in supply and demand do that. At times one hour of labor may exchange for two. But over time, prices in such an economy would gravitate toward the level dictated by inputs of labor, or what Smith called their natural level. At times with Smith, as with such predecessors as John Locke or such successors as Karl Marx, such a labor theory of value had moral as well as descriptive content. It embodied the principle of fairness or justice. Such a theory also clarified an all but magical regulator in a free economy. As shifts in supply or demand push prices out of line with their natural level, rational producers are motivated to shift to other industries. Such shifts not only restore natural prices, but help insure the best allocation of labor. But such a regulator cannot work except in an atmosphere of free choice. This means that political freedom is a prerequisite of economic justice.

Prices reflect more complex determinants in any developed society. There people own land and tools of production. The prices of most products reflect payments of rent and profit. In such a society natural prices are those sufficient to cover the natural returns to labor, land, and capital. But what determines natural levels of wages, rents, and profits? Smith gave only partial answers. He pointed to such determinants of rent as location and soil fertility, but admitted that rent went to a type of political monopoly. He often confused rent as access costs with rent as payment for improvements and sometimes even with rent as payment for managerial wisdom. Finally, he acknowledged that rent did not help determine prices, but was itself price determined. As for profits, he refused to concede that they were proportionate payments for past labor. Had he done so, he could have argued that rent was a monopoly payment, and that, beyond it, workers and capitalists shared the remaining product according to how much labor, direct or indirect, they had contributed. Failing such an argument, he could only talk of that level of profit needed to secure investment and growth, or a variable and elusive proportion of the economic product. For the same reason, natural wages were difficult to define in any precise way. What Smith ended up with was a cost-of-production theory of prices, and the barest outline of a distributive theory that assured, over the long term, natural and presumably fair returns to each sector.

Smith's primary economic goal was high real wages, by which he meant high levels of attained consumption. He assumed that most men in developed societies will have to work for wages, and that for most of mankind work is so onerous as to be avoided if at all possible. It seemed to him that not one in twenty workers in Europe owned land or tools or raw materials, or could accumulate enough food to support themselves during a growing season or a manufacturing process. The main body of people, the "inferior sorts,"were dependent workers, scarcely able to survive for a week without employment by a master. In poor countries, many lived at a minimal level, but Smith backed away from any morbid analysis of what constituted a minimal wage. He never envisioned such a minimum as a necessity, and only casually noted natural limits to population growth. If people did live at a subsistence level, then human institutions were at fault. He noted the exploited situation of wage laborers even in enlightened England. Masters had all advantages on their side. They misused apprenticeship contracts. They combined to resist high wages, but used the political process to prevent worker combinations and to put down labor protests, which were often conducted with the violence borne of desperation. But with all this said, Smith still revealed a mixture of equal parts of concern and contempt for the mass of working people, urban and rural. He wanted them to have higher wages, a greater degree of independence, even a public educational system. Yet, seemingly, he expected that very few of them would ever achieve a true political role, one that would enable them to understand and look out for their own interests. In no sense did he address his writings on political economy to them, even though he directed much of his thought toward their welfare

Although Smith celebrated savings and capital investment as the source of economic growth, he disapproved of high profits and was suspicious of those who lived only on investments. By saving from their existing production, and commiting such savings to new tools of production, people assured more specialization, greater efficiency, and future prosperity. Increasing capital meant a healthy competition for labor and thus high wages. But so long as owners of capital competed with each other, growth meant lower rates of profit on investments. Smith used this somewhat oversimplified analysis to identify the constructive classes in a society. The heroes of his analysis supported growth; the villains opposed it. If they understood their own interests, workers would obviously favor growth. Not so capitalists, for growth meant lower rates of profit. Here Smith failed to note that investors may be more concerned with the total amount of profits received than with the rate of return. Growth may so increase the value of capital goods, or the volume of them, as to compensate for lowered rates. Since he did not acknowledge this, Smith argued that it was in the self-interest (here a truly selfish interest) of investors to oppose growth policies, or to try to circumvent the effects of growth by monopolistic privileges of one type or another. Thus, capitalists, and particularly those who had large amounts of capital invested in heavy manufacturing, became the devils in his system.

Ironically, Smith's self-serving capitalists at least used their savings to futher economic growth. The seeming parasites in his economic analysis were landlords, who collected rents, not for labor rendered, but on their monopolistic control over land. Yet Smith applauded the social role of landowners. Even if monopolists, they still supported growth. For, according to his analysis, rents rose in a growing economy. Smith linked high rents to high wages, a position David Ricardo would later completely invert. A high demand for labor, particularly in manufacturing and commerce, means a growing demand for subsistence. This means higher agricultural prices and higher returns either to agricultural labor, capital, or land. Because the demand for land rises during such growth, Smith assumed that the rate of rent would rise. This meant that rational land-lords would support growth policies, which would free human energy by removing mercantilistic privileges and restrictions.

This does not mean Smith wanted high food costs. These obviously would cancel out the benefits of any increase in monetary wages. But growth and high agricultural demand would, he assumed, mean higher levels of investment in agriculture. Agricultural capital would suffer lower rates of return, or rates comparable to those in other sectors. But this higher capital investment promised greater efficiency in production and a gradual lowering of food prices. Landlords might also be agricul-tural capitalists, and thus suffer a lower rate of profit along with their higher rents. This accounts for Smith's overall formula: during economic growth farm wages and rents both go up, farm profits go down. Changes in wages and profits both affected Smith's beloved leaseholders. Fortu-nately for such yeomen, their higher wages easily canceled any losses they suffered from lowered returns to their limited capital. Meanwhile, absen-tee landlords reaped higher rents.

Smith defined any medium of exchange as money. He certainly valued its role; greater specialization and expanded markets required it. But what he valued money for was its role in exchange. In itself money is not properly a part of the wealth of a nation, for it is neither consumable nor productive. Value inheres, not in money, but in what it commands. A nation needs enough money to facilitate all needed exchange and not a particle more. To accumulate beyond this need is foolish, for excess money takes the place of consumer and productive goods and retards growth. This was Smith's most telling argument against mercantilists. His definition of money encompassed not only the precious metals, but various circulating credit instruments. Gold and silver, when not coined, are consumable products whose value is determined by the cost of pro-duction. But when coined they are no longer consumable, although their monetary value is normally equivalent to their commodity value. If it is, then they make an especially sound form of money. Credit instruments like bank notes lack such intrinsic value, but in the best of situations serve as well as or better than gold. They are less costly to keep in circulation. The substitution of paper for specie frees gold and silver for consumptive uses or allows them to flow abroad to pay for extra consumer goods or, if wisdom prevails, for capital goods. With his endorsement of paper notes, and of the types of sound banking necessary to circulate it safely, Smith included many warnings about possible abuses in private banking, which later anti-banking spokesmen in America found useful.

Because of his concern for the growth of productive resources, for putting more people to work and helping them work more efficiently, Smith emphasized a beguiling distinction between productive and unproductive labor. He used the terms quite literally. *Productive labor* eventuates in a product, either a tangible consumer product or a capital good. *Unproductive labor* encompasses various human services, from the professions and the civil service all the way down to household domestics. Smith did not always intend *unproductive* as a pejorative term. After all, he saw some form of fulfilling experience as the ultimate end or payoff for all labor. Eating food or using an efficient tool might not rival the satisfaction of having a physician ease one's pain. But it seemed clear to Smith that most services are luxuries, usually enjoyed only by the affluent even in prosperous societies. Many involve sheer, wasteful indulgence on the part of those who reap large profits and rents. The more national wealth used up in such services, the less potential for economic growth. Actually, Smith might more usefully have distinguished three kinds of labor: labor that produces capital goods, labor that produces consumer goods, and labor that provides personal services, the last being least supportive of growth. Above all, he wanted to encourage savings and productive investment, for only this use of accumulated wealth steadily expands the demand for labor, raises wages, and improves the lot of the masses. Thus, he hoped taxes could be diverted from the pay of court servants or from military waste and into such public capital as roads and canals.

Smith ended *Wealth of Nations* with a series of policy recommendations, generally tailored to the English context but instructive for policy makers in other countries. He offered a devastating critique of mercantilistic policies, particularly trade-surplus theories and the resulting restrictions on commerce. He was in favor of a slightly qualified free-trade position. He denounced all protective tariffs except retaliatory ones, all restrictive apprenticeship laws, all privileges for trading companies, all bounties to favored exports, nearly all bounties to domestic manufacturing (he favored only patents and copyrights), and all economic restrictions on the American colonies. By reducing the direct economic role of government, he hoped to reduce taxes. Given the public privileges involved in land ownership, he favored land taxes over all other kinds.

Taxes on wages and profits end up penalizing all consumers. Excise taxes on luxuries, specially allocated revenue tariffs, or taxes on certain high salaries or fees, are all fairer. Smith accepted the necessity of a public debt during war. He also noted the often convenient use of debt instruments as a type of money. But, in warnings long taken to heart in America, he predicted that the long-term funding of a national debt would eventually bankrupt a country. Almost no government, it seemed, was ever able to reduce funded debts. The interest payments became a permanent and growing drag on private investment, and thus on the potential for growth, although Smith admitted that a productive use of such funds by governments lessened their dire economic consequences.

Despite his overall optimism, even Smith occasionally plumbed the darker, somberer implications of economic growth, although he did not relish doing so. Specialization, the key catalyst of growth, tended to destroy the variety, the imaginative challenge, the inventive inducements, the broad and liberating role of work. The undesirable effects of specialization were most evident in the factories. The boring and routine duties of the operatives tended to make them ever more ignorant and stupid even when they realized higher levels of consumption. Such dehumanizing labor made men unfit even to be soldiers. More and more of the laboring poor seemed destined to live such stultified lives, while the affluent lived more varied and stimulating lives than ever before because of intellectual and scientific advances and the growing leisure that came with prosperity. The poor had little contact with a literate and refined culture; since their long hours of work allowed them no time for education, they inevitably became dull and stupid people.

Given these realities, Smith even had kind words for the more zealous religious sects and the type of caring community they offered the most alienated and unhappy workers. Certainly the established churches had ignored the plight of the workers. But the ultimate answer had to go beyond superstition and enthusiasm. For "the middling sorts," for artisans and yeomen, he hoped a popularized science would serve as an antidote for religious enthusiasm. Perhaps the effect of scientific knowledge would rub off even on "the inferior sorts." Beyond this, he talked vaguely of public diversions, of poetry, painting, music, dance, exhibitions, as ways to lift the melancholy gloom that so typified the lower classes. Finally, he proposed a scheme of practical education, partially tax-supported, for all laboring-class children. But none of his remedies seemed more than mildly palliative. Smith's glorious scheme of inevitable economic progress seemed to promise new levels of degradation for a majority of mankind.

Thomas Robert Malthus added the next somber reservation to Smith's vision of unending growth. He gained an undying reputation for his 1798 *Essay on the Principles of Population*. The *Essay* provoked endless controversies and many angry denunciations of Malthus. Soon, *Malthusianism* was a stereotype. Malthus subsequently revised his theory and considerably modified its more pessimistic implications. Unfortunately, Malthus's language in the original *Essay*, his message, and the very context in which he wrote, gave a very false impression of the man. Malthus was neither gloomy nor deeply pessimistic. A learned mathematician, an Anglican vicar, and later a gentle professor of political economy, he was by all accounts unusually gentle, kind, and unassuming.

Malthus wrote his *Essay* to refute the wild anticipations of utopian theorists, particularly William Godwin and Condorcet. His now famous thesis was neither original, profound, nor very clear. Man, along with all other animals, has an astonishing reproductive potential. Accepting some observations by Benjamin Franklin about natural population increases in America, where resources were abundant, Malthus guessed that unchecked natural fertility would double a population every twenty-five years. Obviously, in only a few centuries such a geometrical increase would lead to a scarcity of food. Malthus argued that, at best, food can only increase incrementally or arithmetically (five to six to seven to eight). Sooner or later, mankind must run up against nature's limits. Except in favored areas like America, where much unused fertile land awaited development, natural checks on growth already assured near-stable populations. Any sudden improvement in agricultural production, any new frontier windfall offered only an interim relief from such checks, for Malthus assumed that a surge of new babies would soon bring the population back into balance. The great regulator of population was need and misery, either reflected in war and violence or in high mortality rates caused by privation. At first, Malthus saw only one other alternative— vice, either in the form of unnatural and sinful modes of birth control or in such perversions as homosexuality.

The unrelieved pessimism of the *Essay* haunted even Malthus. In a second edition he enormously fortified the historical arguments for his thesis, but modified its impact. He increasingly emphasized the cultural factors that determine minimal levels of subsistence; a psychological variable enters into the check of need and misery. He also recommended a possible escape route through moral restraint. By self-discipline, by marrying late, prudent men could reduce birth rates without vice, avoid the effects of the ultimate check, and maintain living standards well above those needed for survival. The English middle classes already exhibited such prudence, and for the rest of his life Malthus tried to persuade the laboring classes to adopt such a rational and responsible mode of domestic behavior. He believed such prudence was terribly undercut by the existing poor laws of England, which encouraged irresponsible reproduction and which degraded and brutalized the recipients.

Even in his later writing, Malthus never allowed his optimism to go too far. He remained a Christain moralist. When confronting utopian dreams, he resorted to a balancing realism. Man is born in sin. Suffering and misery are his lot. In fact, Malthus erected a theodicy around this fact. For it is only in the midst of the frustrations and challenges of life, including hard economic realities, that man rises above the brutes, learns to act with foresight and reason, and slowly creates the adornments of civilization. The very law of population served a godly purpose. Still, Malthus wanted to avoid as much misery as possible, and not just celebrate the cunning reason of God. In his later writings he was very much concerned with education and political reform, with such policies as could bring middle-class virtues and rewards to all Englishmen. Generally, he drew less pessimistic and fatalistic conclusions from his law of population than did Ricardo. The later Malthus was not very "Malthusian," according to the popular use of that word.

Jean Baptiste Say of France published his remarkably clear and systematic *Treatise on Political Economy* in 1803. Since he was a declared disciple of Adam Smith's, a personal friend of Franklin's, and an admirer of the United States, it is not surprising that the first English translation of his book, published in 1821, had an enormous impact. This version of the *Treatise* dominated the United States textbook market until after 1837. Several of Say's distinctive doctrines directly influenced Henry C. Carey and helped shape the first completely original theoretical system developed by an American.

Say tried to extract the key doctrines of the *Wealth of Nations* from the midst of Smith's many digressions and present them in a tightly organized text. Although he rarely disagreed openly with Smith, he rejected his mentor's animus toward unproductive labor and placed greater stress on managerial talents and on applied science. He rejected the Physiocratic carryover in Smith's emphasis upon nature's unique contribution in agriculture. Say discounted organic growth and thus argued that nature cooperates with man in all forms of production. Every form of productive labor adds equally to the total national product. Here he came close to generalizing the concept of rent, anticipating a position that Jacob Cardozo in America would soon develop.

Today Say is known primarily for his famous "law." Few issues in economic theory have led to more semantic confusion than Say's Law. Say kept updating and revising his own version. In the simplest version of his law, Say stipulated that production creates its own demand. The key challenge in a national economy is increased production, not increased demand. A person produces an object either to consume it or to exchange it for another product of equal value. Either way, the effective demand in an economy goes up just so much as people add to the total product. This suggests a tautology, a mere play on words. A common identity seems to unite supply and demand, making them simply two sides of one coin. But Say intended a causal argument, and developed his law in the context of a complex international debate over general gluts, or what we now call depressions. Say and his disciples denied the possibility of a general glut in a free economy, for in such an economy an overall deficiency of demand was inconceivable. Yet business cycles were already common. Say acknowledged that there were temporary, self-correcting distortions in the market. In fact, such imbalances played an essential role in forcing shifts of labor and capital to meet changing human desires. What he denied was the possibility of any general or universal lack of demand, of a situation in which all consumer goods would not sell at the level of their productive costs. To him, a surplus of one product had to mean a scarcity in others. When such local or partial gluts occurred, the proper response was not cuts in investment, some artificially created scarcity, or subsidies to encourage demand. Since demand takes care of itself, a local glut demanded shifts of capital into areas of scarcity, and an overall increase in capital formation and in production.

Even Say eventually qualified his position on gluts. His critics pointed out that general gluts had occurred. We now know that individuals who live above a subsistence level have considerable leeway in the disposition of their income. Individuals may postpone purchases, defer the use of available credit, or even hoard money. If a great many people do this at the same time, they in effect sharply reduce the national supply of money, which may cause a rapid drop-off in demand for all products and services. But even such suggestions point to a need for a very precise definition of different types of demand, and to analytical subtleties still unavailable to Say. In America, the policy implications that Say drew from his "law" had as great an impact as his theories about gluts. Say emphasized the harmony of interests in a society. He deplored the invidious sectoral comparisons made by Smith and the Physiocrats. He had an optimistic, positive prescription for economic prosperity—that all sectors cooperate, that all people join together, that they realize that desirable economic competition is allocative, not eliminative. It forces such needed market shifts as contribute to a higher form of mutuality. He wanted to show how all sectors are complementary and interdependent. He favored economic balance, discounted the more atomistic assumptions and class themes of British economists, and was a bit more open to state regulation and guidance than Smith had been.

Say never found Malthusian population theories threatening. He saw no diminishing returns in the near future. He seemed to envision more and more people inhabiting limited areas, but prospering from highly specialized, efficient, integrated agriculture and manufacturing. He shared many of the preferences of a later Henry C. Carey, and joined

Carey in lamenting the special burdens of a colonial economy tied to foreign exports. Neither did Say see any problem in distributive justice, given a free market. In a growing economy, everyone gained. Workers realized higher wages, landowners could increase their rents, and capitalists gained larger gross profits (not higher rates of profit). Like Smith, he anticipated no major distortions or injustices because of rising rents. He apparently expected new agricultural improvements to so increase productivity as to neutralize the social costs of high rents. In all these sanguine hopes, he most clearly disagreed with his eminent contemporary, David Ricardo.

Of all nineteenth-century European economists, David Ricardo had the greatest impact on Americans. After 1825, every American economist felt compelled to affirm Ricardian doctrines, to revise them appropriately, or to refute them. Of all Ricardo's technical contributions, it was his theory of rent that received the most continuous and most rigorous attention in America. Ricardo, a lay economist with enormous influence in Britain, combined business interests (he was a banker and a landowner) with effective advocacy. No one fought more effectively against the British corn laws than he did or engaged in more stimulating dialogues with leading public figures and other political economists. His own political analysis was not of a piece. He was always qualifying or revising key doctrines. But this was not usually apparent to Americans, who knew him either through his late and exceptionally abstract *Principles* (1817), or through the work of such doctrinaire disciples as John R. McCulloch. In his final synthesis, Ricardo created a slightly blurred but internally consistent economic model, the first of the genre. He was all but incapable of conceptual clarity or clear prose, and thus ever in need of literary help. But what he lost in richness and subtlety he gained in generality, simplicity, and abstractness. His model was internally coherent and even at times truistic. His system proved very persuasive, even when it turned out to be irrelevant to many policy issues or ambiguous in its practical implications.

A few assumptions about the economic universe and about the characteristics of its members underlay Ricardo's economic model. Much more than had his predecessors, Ricardo worked at an abstract level; he stipulated his universe, described the actors, and defined the rules of his economic game. His universe was a single, stable, economically developed, populous nation, with a body of secure laws but with necessarily limited natural resources. The laws protected all categories of private possessions, allowed all types of private economic effort (except obviously criminal kinds), and under a code of contractual fairness permitted virtually unlimited exchanges of goods and services. From the perspective of government, of the rule makers, these laws were calculated to foster national prosperity, wealth, and power. The people involved in this economic game were thoroughly acquisitive in their preferences, sexually active, fully mobile within the national boundaries, and at least usually well-informed although not necessarily wise. That is, each of them understood many of the circumstances that momentarily shaped the conditions of exchange, and each consistently sought to maximize his own economic position. This was the object of the game from an individual perspective. Finally, although the Ricardian game did not require it, it was less confusing and made much better sense when each actor played a single role. Each person in a perfect game was either an unpropertied worker who lived entirely on wages, a nonworking landlord who lived on rents, or a capitalist who lived on profits.

What Ricardo tried to do was demonstrate how this contrived game would proceed, what would happen to individuals and to the nation if the actors made certain choices. He tried to identify certain necessary economic constants in any such game and certain invariant relationships among such constants (for example, the determinants of rent, wages, and profits). He was interested in long-term trends, in averages, and not in momentary, unpredictable eventualities occasioned by "accidents" which, fortunately, fell so randomly as never to distort the more basic trends. Thus, critics often accused Ricardo of adhering to an unrealistically static model, a criticism that often embraced both methods and content. Unlike Malthus or other dissenters from his key doctrines, Ricardo often adopted what is now a very conventional method of analysis. He attended to only one variable, such as improved agricultural techniques, and then calculated the effects of the economic system as if everything else remained unchanged. Also, his presuppositions pointed to an end-game for any developed economy—to a form of static equilibrium.

It is impossible to clarify Ricardo's chief doctrines in brief compass. Fortunately, many of them will become clearer as I develop the critical response to Ricardo by Americans. In many areas, Ricardo adopted the viewpoint of his predecessors. He was as emphatically committed to a free market and to free trade as Smith. He incorporated Say's law into his system, and with both Say and Smith emphasized the essential role of investment and capital formation in stimulating growth. He attended even more carefully to problems of taxation than had Smith, and generally saw high taxes as a direct threat to capital accumulation. With Malthus, he opposed the dole or other direct forms of poor relief. Not that he was heartless or unconcerned with human suffering. Just the opposite. For example, he eventually expressed his concern with the short-term hardships suffered by workers in industries transformed by a rapid introduction of new machines. Two distinctive doctrines—a labor theory of value and a theory of rent—had the greatest impact on early American economists; these alone justify fuller explication.

Ricardo argued that, at least in his stipulated economic universe, inputs of labor fully determined natural prices, those toward which an economy gravitated over time. But he so qualified his labor theory as to bring it very close to Smith's earlier cost-of-production theory. Ricardo granted qualitative differences in labor; a product of one hour of highly skilled labor may exchange for the product of two hours of common labor. Later Ricardians tried to make even this consistent with a simple, quantitative formula, for they argued that added payments for skill represented delayed payments for the earlier, noncompensated work that went into the acquisition of such skills. In effect, they made skill a form of capital. Ricardo, in his clearest break with Adam Smith on problems of value, considered capital simply as a form of stored-up labor. Thus, wages and profits are both returns to labor. Over the long run, beyond the momentary shifts of value occasioned by supply and demand, stored-up labor realizes the same returns as immediate labor. Thus, for Ricardo, the labor theory of value did serve a moral end—distributive justice. The only complication in such a consistent and appealing theory involved rent.

Malthus made an indispensable contribution to Ricardian rent theory, although the two economists ultimately disagreed on this vital issue. Malthus, in his *Essay*, first emphasized a finite nature and ultimate limits on population growth. Although he did not formulate it in so many words, he provided the needed support for a concept of diminishing returns. A finite nature can yield only so much to the application of human labor and tools. As population presses against natural scarcities, the returns from added inputs of labor and capital in agriculture will necessarily diminish. At some point, the added returns will not be enough to justify the effort or the investment. Unless there is control of the birthrate, expansion in new territiories, or dramatic new means of getting more out of an existing environment, the masses of people in any mature economy face a most dismal prospect. Ricardo's rent theories simply reflected some logical, although not always crystal-clear, inferences drawn from such Malthusian insights.

Rent is a confusing word in the English language. Ricardo tried, with only limited success, to adhere to a narrow and precise definition. Formally, he defined rent as that portion of farm production paid to a landlord for use of the "original and indestructible powers of the soil." This was too narrow—it excluded rents on nonagricultural lands—and also confusing—no powers of the soil are really indestructible. In various discussions of rent, including that for mines, Ricardo considerably broadened his definition. In effect, he treated rent as any payment for access to, and normal (even if depletive) use of, an unimproved nature, with location as well as inherent fertility affecting rent values. But unlike Smith, Ricardo usually distinguished between rent and payments for improvements to land (profit) and payments for managerial decisions made by landlords (wages). Thus, rent was always an unearned return. It did not compensate for labor expended, and by this very fact alone could not go into the determination of prices, given Ricardo's labor theory of value. Rent was a payment for a form of monopoly, but like Smith, Ricardo accepted the legitimacy of private land ownership. Yet his theories about rent opened the door for a series of socialist or agrarian radicals, culminating in Henry George, who would all challenge the legitimacy of private ownership of raw nature and thus the legitimacy of any private rents.

Since rent is payment for a monopolized scarcity, even the best land can command rent only when land is scarce, when other equally fertile or accessible land is not available for the taking. This clarifies one of Ricardo's determinants of rent. So long as a nation has unused land available to farmers, the natural rent that a landlord can charge a tenant is always the difference between what his land can produce for given inputs of labor and capital, and what was produced on the last land taken into production. This last land, or land on the productive margin, pays no rent at all, for it is only fertile enough or accessible enough to return competitive profits. Should a farmer (that is, a capitalist) have to pay rent to use such land, his profits would sink below the national level and he would ordinarily move his investment elsewhere. As food prices rise, existing land commands more and more rent. The price of food is determined by labor and capital costs alone, or really by the only costs paid by a capitalist at the margin of agricultural production. Ricardo saw rent as a payment for the productive contribution of better agricultural lands; this view was very close to the Physiocratic idea of rent.

Perhaps because of the American context—expanding frontiers and endless debates over land policies—almost all American economists focused on levels of fertility as a determinant of rent. They usually ignored Ricardo's second determinant. Even should all the land of a nation be cultivated, or should all land be of the same quality, landlords could still collect rents. Here Ricardo appealed not to diminishing returns based on recourse to worse soil but to diminishing returns to capital on existing land. In the absence of new ground to break, leaseholders could only expand production to meet new needs by applying more capital to existing land. Yet, beyond a point, additional manure or added tools would have less and less impact on production. The capital, or intensive, margin is that point at which a final increment of capital will barely realize a competitive level of profits, with no payment at all to a landlord. But landlords can collect, as rent, the difference between what the first applications of capital earned, and what the last or marginal application earned.

As population grows, as natural scarcities become more threatening, rents go up. The proportion of the total national product going to landlords increases with every necessary resort to less fertile soil or more intensive use of existing land. Nationally, diminishing agricultural returns mean that a nation has to commit more and more of its labor force, and its capital, to the securing of raw produce, leaving less for manufacturing and commerce. Perversely, landlords profit from such national misfortune. Whereas Smith cast capitalists as the devils in the economic game, Ricardo cast landowners. Their self-interest dictated that they oppose technological improvements in agriculture, and that they seek tariff protection against needed imports of cheaper food. In these calculations Ricardo assumed an all but fixed demand for agricultural products. As productivity went up, production would cease on the last marginal lands plowed, and some of the last increments of capital would move into other sectors. Landlords would fight such changes, but capitalists had every reason to applaud them (to Ricardo, an excellent example of a capitalist was the farm operator, the one who furnished tools and hired farm laborers).

Not only did diminishing returns in agriculture penalize workers and capitalists to the advantage of landowners, but at a certain point they began to distort normal distributive returns to labor and capital. Here Ricardo began to explore his endgame and the dismal prospects it revealed for even a growth economy if a nation found no way of controlling population. As rents absorb more and more of the national product, wages and profits shrink. But the shrinkage has clear limits in the case of wages. Ricardo defined a natural wage as a minimum wage—enough to maintain a worker, a wife, and two children according not to sheer physical need but culturally conditioned expectations or standards. Capitalists, at a certain point in a developing natural scarcity, would no longer be able to keep passing the burden of ever higher rents along to workers. They would have to pay the minimum wage or risk an early shortage of workers from higher mortality rates. This would mean severe pressures on profits as an economy moves toward its ultimate growth potential. Squeezed profits would eventually reach such a low level that they could not induce any further savings. In the endgame, a type of horrible equilibrium would prevail. Profits would be so low as barely to maintain existing tools, wages would be at a subsistence level, and only landlords would enjoy any comforts or luxuries, if the state still allowed them to collect rents. Several strategies—improvements in agricultural technology, colonial expansion, large exports of food from less crowded parts of the world—might postpone this final equilibrium, but, given finite resources, only controls over population could permanently avert it.

Ricardo's model had enormous impact in Britain. His major doctrines became the heart of an orthodox tradition, one now often called "classical." The famous John Stuart Mill gave a final endorsement to this orthodoxy in an 1848 textbook. But all along it faced major dissenters.

The most able of these was none other than Malthus, who has a very anomalous position in political economy. On almost every issue, he contributed to the orthodox model, and not just through his population theories. But as he matured his final system, he came to disagree with Ricardo on so many critical doctrines that it is appropriate to identify his as a distinct economic tradition. Yet Malthus remained in many respects a disciple of Adam Smith, and was always a respectful critic of his good friend, Ricardo. Other critics broke more decisively with the whole orthodox tradition. For Americans, the most influential of these was Lord Lauderdale (James Maitland). He offered an early criticism of Adam Smith, yet without going back to a stereotyped mercantilist position. In even more aggressive language, Daniel Raymond began a tradition of economic analysis in America with doctrines almost identical with Lauderdale's (see chapter 4).

The older Malthus continued to reinforce his early reputation for gloom. He continued to oppose utopian schemes, to fight for a repeal of the poor laws, and to insist that no institutional reforms could rescue the bulk of mankind from adversity and suffering. He believed that most people were sensual, lazy, and selfish. Not that he was an ascetic. He denounced celibacy and self-denial, and always praised the joys of virtuous marriage and comfortable living arrangements. He believed that all forms of private property, including land ownership, were justified, for he believed everyone would starve to death without the energizing incentives to work offered by ownership. Protected property means unequal shares, often for accidental reasons. So be it. Some men are destined to be proprietors, but most of those who in "the great lottery of life, have drawn a blank" are fated to be mere laborers. Their divergent fortunes reflect not poor or correctible policies but necessities tied to the nature of man, to his competitive struggle in a finite world. These hard realities all set strict limits on the possibility of reform, but the very competition is the mother of invention. It leads to new productive techniques, which in turn support all the arts and graces of life. Given his acknowledgment of such realities, Malthus was a moderate reformer himself. He sought to foster steady economic growth, higher wages, and a type of middle-class gentility and comfort for all English workers. He rejected the gloomy rent theories of Ricardo, and as much as Say sought social harmony.

Malthus was always more attuned than Ricardo to history and to immediate facts. He was more sensitive to cultural and institutional differences, and often more concerned with short-term eventualities than with some distant endgame. He lacked Ricardo's ability for abstract analysis, and on many points of logic came up the loser. If he had one controlling thesis, it was his insistence on the need for public policies that would sustain a high level of effectual demand for goods. He rejected

Say's law. More than any of his predecessors, he was aware of the subtleties in the word *demand*, and explored some of the psychological meanings of the word.

Unlike Ricardo, Malthus had no one prescription for economic growth, such as increased savings and more capital growth. Under certain circumstances, he argued that too much parsimony, too rapid capital growth, could lead to a glut and even to a stagnating economy. He looked with favor upon certain mercantilist policies—government fiscal incentives, growth-inducing subsidies and regulations, and deliberately increased supplies of money. But in his sentimental loyalties he remained closest to the Physiocrats and to Smith. He trusted and admired the English gentry, sought agricultural improvements above all others, and developed a considerable distrust for the new manufacturing capitalists who were coming to dominate the English economy. Manufacturing was indeed productive, but too often factories created luxury goods for the wealthy, or for export, whereas farmers added to the national fund of basic necessities. Wealthy manufacturers competed in an often brutal international market, and often did all in their power to depress wages and maintain high profits. He deplored England's growing commitment to manufacturing, to becoming rich "by running a race for low wages."

For years Malthus debated Ricardo on rent. He had the last word, since he lived longer. But Ricardo persuaded most economists. Malthus, like so many later American economists, found that Ricardo's abstract formula did not match historical realities. Rents had risen along with wages and profits. Landowners had always favored new agricultural improvements, and such improvements had accompanied higher, not lower, rents. Exceptions in Ricardo's theory could account for most of these observations. More critically, Malthus could never find the logical tools he needed to support empirical observations. Malthus often confused landowners with estate managers, and thus obscured the behavior of true rents. More important, he confused short- and long-term effects. By Ricardo's formula, major agricultural improvements might increase the potential for rent on good lands, but landlords could not realize these until population increases expanded the productive margins back beyond their earlier locations. In the interim, rents had to fall if, as Ricardo assumed, the demand for food remained constant. Malthus knew that nothing remains constant, but he did not explore the complex variations in the demand for food that could indeed prove that his landlords were rational and not just benevolent. George Tucker of Virginia would later offer the first internally consistent revision of Ricardo's rent theories. Malthus lamely fell back on distinctive English institutions—such as lifetime leases—to explain the behavior of his beloved landlords.

Every economist wanted high wages for workers, but not high wages at the expense of profits. Malthus and Ricardo accepted a truistic wage-fund theory. Wages have to come out of the annual product of a country. Other shares of this product pay rents and profits. Neither wanted to socialize the returns to rent, and thus challenge sacred property. Workers who wanted higher wages had only one real alternative—to produce more. Failing that, they had to compete with one another for shares of the fund committed each year to wages, or they had to conspire to gain a share of normal profits. To do the latter was against their own best interests, for diminished capital growth would threaten their future wages. The only difference between Ricardo and Malthus was a subtle but critical one. Ricardo believed that capital growth, stimulated by healthy profits, was both a necessary and sufficient condition of growth and ever higher wages. Malthus believed it was a necessary but far from sufficient condition, and this qualification struck at the heart of Ricardian orthodoxy.

Whether new capital abetted growth or not was a cultural, as well as an economic, issue to Malthus. New tools of production may go unused and undeveloped in a culture of poverty, as in despotic countries in which passive people acquiesce in low levels of gratification. In such cultures, those with savings have compelling reasons to invest them abroad or use them up in added consumption. Growth requires, not just parsimony among those with high incomes, but a rising demand for goods among the general population. New capital goods, such as a new factory building, do not necessarily lead to an increased demand for workers or to a higher level of demand in the society as a whole. For example, an ambitious manufacturer might move his former menial servants into his new factory and pay them the same wages as before. Here Malthus probed what was a central theme in his later writings—the extent to which the mix of productive and service workers affected the behavior of a whole economy. When demand slackened for a particular manufactured item, workers faced unemployment unless other industries could absorb them. Often they could not. Then only a shift of workers into the service sector could avert unemployment, a lower demand for goods, and possibly a national glut.

Such complexities led Malthus to his own tentative analysis of the causes of economic growth. At the heart of these was an ever-rising level of consumer demand. None of the conventional prescriptions for growth were sufficient. A growing population, within limits, can promote national prosperity and greatness, but whether it serves this end or not depends upon the habits of the people. A passive, servile, unimaginative people may aspire to little more than bare subsistence, and eschew both work and saving. Without a keen desire for goods, for the products of the labor of other producers, new people may be a drag on an economy. Not that the later Malthus agonized much over population explosions. He did not believe an economy normally let alone necessarily moved toward Ricardo's dismal endgame. He hoped that workers, at least in enlightened countries, could learn prudence, check births, and gain a strong competitive position as against capitalists. Sexual prudence, joined with education, might provide them the condition of endless wage increases. In a growing, secure economy, workers would not only gain from the larger product, but would be able to compete for a larger share of the whole, for in such an economy the demand for labor would remain high while profit rates were low yet sufficient to stimulate needed investment. This all meant that the most basic conditions of growth were moral and political—honest, industrious, literate citizens in a free country under equal laws.

As I earlier suggested, Malthus also denied the sufficiency of capital accumulation. This insures growth only if it involves added industry, and not just a shift of workers from services. It has to accompany a higher level of effectual demand. Austere capitalists are not likely to indulge in new luxuries; the new demand has to come from increased work and wages among the general population. Malthus even conceived of the possibility of a stingy society, one in which almost everyone wanted to save and invest, and in which almost everyone was willing to live at a near-subsistence level in order to make money.

New technology does not insure growth. It increases the consumption potential of a society. But it also increases the potential for leisure, and some people will choose the leisure (Malthus clearly did not believe that increased leisure would have any economic value). If new machines are not accompanied by an increased demand for cheaper goods, then drastic problems in distribution arise. People cannot easily shift employments. Farmers confront a very inelastic, short-term demand. When sudden technological improvements create surpluses, farmers receive low wages and low profits. The ramifying effects of their discomfort—lower rents for landowners, lower demand for manufactured goods—may propel a whole country into depression. Malthus carried such analysis on and on. No factor insured growth unless it was accompanied by higher demand. This was the critical condition of growth, which Say and Ricardo had ignored. Too much parsimony means too little demand, hence gluts; too much consumption eats away at needed capital growth. One must consider both sides of the equation. People had to develop "an adequate passion for consumption," which was something that an economist could never safely assume. (Ricardo simply stipulated such a passion in his model).

Malthus had no magical prescription for growth. But he did emphasize the importance of three factors, all keyed to the problem of demand. First was a wide (not universal) distribution of land. A free system of ownership had an important energizing effect on the economy, which would be threatened by either feudal monopolies or some artificial distribution of land to every family. Malthus assumed that only a minority of a population had the abilities needed to manage estates. Although he applauded the land system in America, he still supported the English system, including its primogeniture laws. It somehow supported a responsible gentry and provided incentives for actual farmers.

His second prescription for growth was a lively domestic and foreign commerce. In itself this duplicated prescriptions by both Smith and Ricardo. But in this context Malthus introduced his countercyclical fiscal policies, policies that largely account for his present reputation as an economist. Broad markets and narrow specialization, although needed for growth, create a vulnerable form of interdependence and a danger of business cycles. Government policies, Malthus believed, can prevent or minimize gluts. When depression threatens, a government should increase the national debt in ways calculated to spur the private demand for goods. Certainly a government should not try to pay off debts in a period of incipient depression (he condemned such policies in Britain after 1815).

Malthus also wanted nations to increase monetary supplies as a defense against impending gluts. To do this, a government might have to place controls on foreign commerce. He believed mild monetary inflation desirable at all times. This was a return to one mercantilist position—policies to insure that there was more specie imported than exported. Increased supplies of money helped assure a rising level of consumer demand. The corn laws had this effect. Contrary to what Ricardo argued, these tariff laws actually aided workers as well as landlords, for they helped maintain the needed demand for goods that lay behind high wages.

Malthus's other countercyclical policy—expanded government employment through public works—joined his third general prescription for economic growth: a periodic diversion of workers into services. Everyone applauded certain services, such as in education, the ministry, or medicine, but few economists other than Malthus had kind words for domestic servants and government employees. Service workers, he believed, have a vital role in a growth economy. They consume as much as other workers but do not add to the sum of material products. They thus act as a regulator. They were part of the great "body of demanders" that Malthus loved so much. In England, he believed, most capitalists were too busy making money to consume their share of newly created goods. Manufacturing laborers might take up this slack, but to divert more wages to them meant lowered profits and a threat to the very accumulation of capital necessary to keep people at work. Thus, in times of threatened depression, service employment offered the best answer. Even menials in rich households not only expended their own wages but also helped create extra demand, as for livery, coaches, and extra housing. Increased numbers of tax-supported government workers directly increased demand, production, and wealth. Their employment entailed an economically stimulating and demand-creating redistribution of national wealth, although "sacred property" kept Malthus from recommending any overt leveling. But he at least hoped the government would never suddenly decrease its employees. In the post-1815 glut, England clearly suffered from a redundancy of capital, a deficiency of demand. It was time to spend, not to save. Malthus then had only contempt for such Ricardian policies as governmental economy and new incentives to capital formation.

Even this oversimplified summary of the views of the greatest early masters of political economy shows the richness and diversity present in an emerging discipline. Early American economists inherited, not a rigid and monistic system, but an array of technical arguments with quite divergent policy implications. Unfortunately, such brilliant innovators as Malthus and Ricardo soon gained a reputation as callous and insensitive prophets of doom. No image could have been more unfair to them. Intensely moral men, they did their best to discover how to insure continued economic growth and higher living standards for all. They certainly appreciated all the difficulties that lay ahead, but believed that only the fullest understanding of them could make economic progress a possibility rather than only a beguiling illusion.

Ahead within the English analytic tradition lay fascinating new economic options. None of these were available to pre-Civil War American political economists. One line of development involved refinements in the Ricardian system, embodied in the new precision and mathematical exactitude of late nineteenth century neo-classical theory. Karl Marx eventually perfected a much more radical alternative, the basis of another line of development. But even his intensely moral critique was still tied at several points to Ricardian analysis. Like Ricardo, Marx held an extreme labor theory of value and celebrated the possibilities of capital growth. He even retained Ricardo's definition of a natural wage as an essentially subsistence wage. But he found behind the Ricardian model some very exploitative social institutions, which allowed an ever smaller owning class, a class that used political power to monopolize land and capital, to appropriate all the surpluses (all value beyond that required for subsistence wages) created by the new, more efficient collective forms of production. Another line of development only came to full flower in the twentieth century. This involved the revision of neo-classic economic theory to include Malthusian demand theories in a much more sophisticated mathematical guise. We now loosely label this revision as *Keynesian*.

PART TWO

——

FIRST FRUITS

III

John Taylor

EVEN in the perspective of time, John Taylor retains an austere, fore-boding visage. He still challenges our easiest assumptions and casts dark shadows over our illusioned hopes. He punctured the orthodoxies of his day. With tireless energy and a maddening consistency, he cast his impre-cations against practically every innovation in American life from 1787 until his death in 1824. He died with warnings of impending doom still on his lips. He was our first Jeremiah.

Taylor marked a transition in interest among public-spirited American intellectuals. The Revolutionary generation, which he knew as a young man, had directed its energies to political theory and to problems of government. But as he moved to middle age, Taylor recognized that economic questions posed the most pressing issues for Americans. We had established a consensus on political institutions. The last major debate over basic political alternatives occurred in the election of 1800. Now we had to come to terms with closely related economic institutions. Taylor considered our economic options in a series of books. In them he tried to adopt Adam Smith's ideas to American particularities, and thus to initiate a major American debate on the more technical issues of political economy. No one more loved American particularities than Taylor, but no one else offered such a gloomy critique of developing American economic policies.

Taylor's intimations of doom departed from an impossibly high esti-mate of American possibilities and a disturbingly acute sensitivity to every compromise or political failure. Taylor believed a fortunate set of circumstances, and a series of enlightened political choices, had resulted

43

by 1787 in a near-perfect union of nation-states. Whatever the weaknesses of local government, the early federal union reflected the most sagacious of political principles, the wisest possible precautions against tyranny. But no sooner had the new federal government assembled in New York City than a body of clever, "capitalist"conspirators began to undermine it and turn it into a centralized instrument of special economic privilege. Taylor reluctantly took upon himself the task of righteous exposure and fervent, if usually futile, efforts to stimulate popular awareness of evil and, with it, the political exertions necessary to escape an impending bondage. The urgency of his mission grew with the passing years, for Taylor knew that free men may avert slavery, but that slaves are forever helpless. Every increment of special privilege, whatever the deceptive propaganda of the oppressors, draws tighter the bonds and makes more difficult any possible redemption.

At the heart of all Taylor's criticism was a very ancient and a very simple belief: that the main end of organized society is to protect men in their labors, to secure for each person the fullest possible returns to his ability and honest industry. In a just society, made up of free or autonomous men, work and skills alone divide up property. The ever-present pitfall in any society is special privilege, which is a form of political robbery in which the power of the state sanctions a transfer of the fruits of honest labor to a parasitic leisure class. Taylor wrote five books to expose the numerous and complex political and legal strategies by which a few men robbed the many. If those few were expert enough at political robbery, they could do it with the blessing of the exploited.[1]

Taylor was never a self-revealing writer. He frequently mentioned his occupation as a farmer and often displayed his thorough knowledge of law but commented only infrequently on politics in his home state of Virginia. One can read his books and get almost no sense of his family or his personal finances. He rarely alluded to his political career or noted the source of his ideas. He celebrated his provincial loyalties, particularly to his nation of Virginia, but still wrote as a disinterested gentleman, concerned above all with truth and right. This stance accentuated the prophetic tone, the sense of a detached intellect, rather like the impersonal voice of a god. Yet the tone could be deceptive; Taylor was a brilliant polemicist, who often took unfair advantage of his opponents, using the camouflage of universal principles to indulge some intense political animosities.

Both of Taylor's parents died shortly after his birth in 1753. His cousin, Edmund Pendleton, took the child into his home and reared him as a son. Pendleton, a close friend of Thomas Jefferson's, was a distinguished lawyer and judge, a delegate to the First Continental Congress, and one of the small circle of politically powerful first citizens of Virginia. Taylor received an exceptional education—from tutors, in a private academy, at

William and Mary, and in Pendleton's law office. He began law practice in
1774, on the very eve of the Revolution. The next year he joined the
Virginia Militia. In 1776 he became major of his own local unit and
afterward went north to command a unit of the Continental Army. His
horror at the conditions in that army reinforced his lifelong belief in the
importance of local militia and his deep aversion to militarism. After
taking part in the unsuccessful invasion of Canada, he resigned his com-
mission in 1779. Back in his home state, now more beloved to him than
ever, he served in the Virginia Legislature and then as a Lieutenant
Colonel in the Virginia Militia during the siege of Virginia and the climax
of the war at Yorktown.

In 1783 Taylor married Lucy Penn, the daughter and heiress of another
prosperous farmer and politician (John Penn had signed the Declaration
of Independence and had served in the Continental Congress). Financial-
ly favored by a large inheritance, and by the size of the fees he earned as a
lawyer, Taylor began buying land. He built his home plantation at Hazelwood, in Caroline County, on the Rappahannock below Fredericksburg.
By 1798, when he moved to Hazelwood, he owned a 2,245-acre farm, a
large house, and more than sixty slaves. By then he was the county's
leading citizen, a member of the Episcopal Church, and renowned both
for his hospitality and for the fertility and beauty of his fields. At Hazelwood he developed what became a lifelong interest in agricultural reform. Much later, in his second published book, *Arator*, he would advocate dramatic new farming techniques to save the depleted soil and
declining agriculture of tidewater Virginia. He was an enemy of one-crop
tobacco farming, of the land-depleting overseer system, of overcropping
followed by fallow fields; he extolled the virtues of animal and vegetative
manures (particularly red clover), of mixed cropping dominated by corn
(maize), of better tools, and of fenced fields to allow the growth of organic
cover crops. More important, he illustrated these improved methods on
his home plantation and, to a lesser extent, on several other outlying
farms that he eventually acquired.[2]

Like many another wealthy country gentleman, Taylor frequently
accepted public office. He did not enjoy the experience and became
increasingly suspicious of politicians and of political parties. His two most
intense periods of political involvement were during the ratification of the
federal constitution and during the presidential election campaign of
1800. Taylor at first feared the consolidationist and antilibertarian potential of the federal constitution and opposed its ratification. After its
adoption, and after the tenth amendment had lessened its centralizing
potential, he became a staunch defender of what he considered its pure,
early, uncorrupted form. In 1792 he served the first of three abbreviated
terms in the federal Senate, and there began his lifelong crusade against
the corruption of the constitution and against a "capitalist" aristocracy

based on political privilege. He resigned after two years, disgusted with party bickering and glad to go home, where he began writing his first constitutional essays. Periodically, he served in the Virginia Assembly (a job requiring only brief absences from home), there favoring a new state constitution with fairer legislative apportionment and an expanded franchise, both of which threatened his own personal interests as a politically favored tidewater planter.

By 1800 Taylor was a firm supporter of Jefferson. He fought the Alien and Sedition Acts, developed a temporary distaste for John Adams that undoubtedly colored his later, unfair criticism of Adam's political views, introduced the Virginia Resolutions in the Virginia Assembly, and slowly matured his own consistent conceptions of the constitution and the federal union. During Jefferson's administration Taylor supported a group of "purifying" amendments to the federal constitution, and slowly came to be the intellectual spokesman for a group of "orthodox" Republicans in Virginia (his views very much influenced both Jefferson and James Monroe). But he had the scholar's fear of partisan advocacy, the intellectual's horror of an enduring solidarity with any party. All men in power, he believed, would compromise their principles, even Jefferson. Taylor opposed the embargo, feared war with England and France, and eventually repudiated Madison as a crypto-Federalist because he supported or accepted so many of Taylor's prime devils—a war that enriched those already wealthy, a subsidized bank, internal improvements for favored states, and special bounties for manufacturers. Disillusioned with partisan politics, Taylor turned to letters. Although he would later serve two brief terms in the United States Senate, the pen became his principal weapon against developing national evils.

Except for his remedial prescriptions for agriculture, Taylor devoted his writing to matters of public policy. Even in *Arator*, he prefaced his agricultural recommendations with a long list of the political evils that blocked reforms in husbandry. Policy was always most basic, and in his eyes policy always reflected hard economic realities. Taylor restricted most of his political and economic analysis to a few problems; over half of his writing concerned banks, tariffs, and constitutional review. But he explored these issues from many perspectives and supported his own positions with abundant examples and with a plethora of sharp, biting, even bitter denunciations of opponents. In fact, his overflowing indignation and his penchant for taking unfair polemical advantage often obscured his positive recommendations, as did his terribly eccentric vocabulary and his awkward, convoluted prose style. He was explicit in exposing evils, too often vague in suggesting remedies. As a polemicist, he was overtly civil, complimenting his foes and disingenuously apologizing for his rusticity and ignorance. Yet as much as any writer of his era, he caricatured his opponents unmercifully, and often completely distorted their views or chose to discuss only a few of their weakest arguments, which he then ridiculed or refuted.

Taylor merged his economic theories with strongly held political and constitutional principles. Unfortunately, his complex views about government suffer from any brief summation, but some acquaintance with them is necessary in order to understand his economic thought.

Taylor rejected the political formalism that he found in John Adams. He wrote his most comprehensive treatise, the *Inquiry*, to refute what he saw as the major themes of Adams's seldom-read three-volume *Defence of the Constitutions of the United States*. But even though Taylor rejected much of what he found in Adams—a confining image of human nature and certain universal guidelines about the form of government—his beliefs were in the end much closer to Adams's than he ever admitted. Adams tried to correct Taylor's misapprehensions about the *Defence* in a series of detailed letters, but to no avail. Taylor believed, with Adams, that men are normally generous and humane but that they frequently suffer from ignorance and bad judgment. When vested with great power, they are always tempted to self-aggrandizement. The virtue of individuals cannot be depended on to secure good government, and is, as Adams had always argued, more nearly a product of good laws than a cause of them. Although Taylor stressed the necessary relationship between the form of government and local circumstances, he still believed that only a frugal, limited, and just government would allow human fulfillment and encourage individual magnanimity. Beyond language, or ill-formed modes of expression, his only substantial disagreement with Adams involved his rejection of Adams's dearest preference, mixed government, and his distaste for either the British or classical precedents that informed Adams's analysis. Taylor believed that most historical examples were irrelevant in America, which had launched a new era in the history of government. He denied the existence of a natural hierarchy among men and therefore of any necessary aristocratic principle that mandated a mixed system. Any aristocrat was a creature of privilege. In America we had no social orders, and we had no reason to create them in order to attain some fragile balance. He claimed that the real problem of government was how it functioned and not its form. Any government could become tyrannical, as was proved by the fact that the new federal government in America had quickly tended in that direction. As an ironic comment on his feud with the puritanical John Adams, Taylor once described himself as the political Puritan, fighting to preserve civil liberty and "republicanism" against the growing corruption that threatened so soon to sully our great political reformation.

Taylor was consistently an unabashed apologist for everything American. No people had ever had as many advantages: immense resources, expanses of fertile soil, insulation from foreign invasions, a common language in each of the several nations, no fixed social orders or exclusive privileges, no dominant or established religion. It seemed a miracle that so much here conduced to liberty. For that very reason, Americans had an awesome responsibility to all of mankind. If we could not show the world how to maintain fair and free governments, if we misused all the benefactions of God, then we would consign endless generations everywhere to the tyranny of expensive and dictatorial governments. And we might fail. In fact, Taylor felt, if we continued along the early paths of federal policy, we were sure to fail. The first American governments had been founded by free men, but they could so easily lose that freedom. By free, Taylor referred in part to religious toleration and to such expressive liberties as freedom of speech and of the press. But the primary mark of a free man was a secure right to productive property and to the products of one's own labor, or an absence of economic dependence on other people. Expressive freedoms meant little to economic slaves. If a parasitic party of privilege destroyed proprietary opportunity in America, or took from working men an ever larger share of their product, then even expressive freedoms would not long survive. Already such economic exploitation followed in the wake of new forms of subtle political privilege. These privileges were already reducing free farmers and mechanics to dependent wage employees. Taylor valued education and the franchise, but he feared that the new aristocracy would monopolize learning and subvert partisan elections to its own ends.

Even while Taylor explored the corruptible potential of party politics and federal elections, he continued to value local, nonpartisan elections and directly responsive legislative assemblies. But he valued even more two ultimate safeguards of good government—popular sovereignty and a complex division of powers. By popular sovereignty, Taylor meant the ultimate power of a people to create and revise their governments as they saw fit, a power that they had exercised in America by constitutional conventions and through amendment procedures. A cherished constitution is the most enduring symbol of popular government. If adhered to, constitutions insured Americans against the forms of governmental sovereignty still prevailing in Europe. Obviously, if a people are sovereign, they alone have the power to decide all constitutional conflicts. All branches of government, including the courts, are free to act only in areas prescribed by a constitution. Nothing horrified Taylor more than the claim that a government, or some branch of government, had the power to determine what a constitution means. Any such power in a government meant a regression to European patterns—government as master and people as subjects.

Just as Americans were the first people to realize popular sovereignty in their perfected constitutional processes, so they were the first to have implemented a thorough division of powers. Here we had divided the people from their government, divided the branches of government, and divided government responsibility among several state governments and one federal government. All such divisions served to restrict those who governed to their only reason for holding power—the protection of property, of all honest labor, and of such expressive freedoms as those of religion, speech, press, and assembly. If fully realized, division could prevent those who governed from falling into the most beguiling temptation of power—the arbitrary taking of property and the fruits of honest labor for their own gratification or to reward specially favored supporters. Only such division insured limited, austere, and simple governments. Expensive and aggressive governments subvert freedom and easily become the tools of special privilege. Taylor deplored strong executives, long terms in office, extensive patronage, and life-tenured appointments. He had no fears of governmental ineffectiveness in times of emergency, for any compelling and clear need would insure both cooperation among all branches and the necessary popular support. Besides, until Americans had a broad array of economic privileges to defend, or imperialistic wars to fight, they had no need for strong governments. And any such felt need would only be evidence of their failure to maintain freedom.

By 1800, Taylor believed the principle of division was in deep jeopardy at the federal level. Even at Philadelphia in 1787, the proponents of a federal union of sovereign states had met formidable opposition from consolidationists, those who wanted to create one unified nation. The true federalists ultimately prevailed, as the Preamble and the Tenth Amendment showed, but the nationalists simply shifted their effort to the new federal government, and tried to invest it with nonconstitutional powers that would achieve their nationalist goals by indirection. Taylor set himself the task of understanding the spirit and true purpose of the original constitution (he never advocated a strict literalism in interpreting it), and became America's most subtle and penetrating constitutional theorist before Calhoun.

From the surviving historical record and his analysis of the resulting document, Taylor concluded that a clear majority of the delegates at Philadelphia had approved a tighter and more perfect union of sovereign states. By their ratification of the Constitution the people of each state (this was the meaning of "we the people") had delegated new but carefully defined general powers to a common government and had deprived their existing state governments of certain former powers. The ratification of the federal constitution thus entailed a major revision of each state constitution, for in specified areas the new federal government was ascendant over state governments. In all nonspecified areas of jurisdiction, the existing state governments remained supreme, subject of course to state constitutions. The centralizers or nationalists, led by Alexander Hamilton and James Wilson, lost at Philadelphia but subsequently gained many of their ends through an unending flow of nationalizing legislation and court decisions. The subversion came by degrees, its true purpose and future effects concealed by logical sophistry or appeals to temporary political exigencies, but its effect was to serve the narrow and avaricious economic interests of an emerging aristocracy of paper and patronage. Each nonconstitutional expansion of federal power took us a step closer to what Europe had long suffered—sovereign governments. Each accession of power was a benchmark of the scope of special interest legislation, of the invidious means the central government had found to transfer an ever larger share of the products of honest labor to a parasitic class at the top.

Taylor pleaded for greater popular awareness of how special interests had subverted the constitution. He developed several strategies to disarm the consolidationists. He supported constitutional amendments to restrain congressional power (shorter senatorial terms, lower congressional pay, rigid prohibitions against federal jobs for ex-congressmen, and limited terms of office) and to restrict the even more dangerous power of the president (he wanted to strip the president of most patronage, beginning with the appointment of judges, to forbid more than one term in office, to eliminate all executive secrecy, to reduce executive war-making power by requiring a two-thirds majority in both houses of Congress to declare war, to offset presidential control over the military by strong state militia units, and to limit presidential adventuring in foreign affairs by allowing treaties to go into effect only after senatorial approval). To prevent the presidency from becoming a powerful popular office, subject to party factionalism and the vulgarity of electioneering, Taylor urged all states to choose their electors in their state legislatures, and he wanted an amendment to settle presidential runoff elections in the electoral college and out of the Congress. But above all, Taylor fought against the expanding power of federal judges. His greatest nemesis was John Marshall. Federal judges not only abetted power grabs by Congress and the President, but by claiming an ultimate right to interpret the meaning of the federal constitution, they had violated the principle of popular sovereignty. They, not the people, determined what the constitution meant.

How could Americans check this judicial omnipotence? The Congress and President had no reason to check it so long as compliant judges endorsed their usurpation of powers. The greatest threat to the constitution lay, not in the competition of the branches, but in their consensus. Since the answer had to be outside the system of balances, Taylor had what seemed even then a radical answer. He admitted that judges had to interpret the federal constitution in their adjudication of conflict; in fact, they were sworn to uphold it. So were legislators and the president. Thus, every federal official had a sworn duty to uphold the constitution within his sphere of delegated power. This duty entailed his responsibility for trying to determine what the constitutions really mandated. Judges rightly stopped the enforcement of any laws they interpreted as unconstitutional, but the judges could not speak for other federal officials, who had in each case to make their own judgment about the enabling document. If the branches of government disagreed on the meaning of the constitution, then they might end up checking each other into near-inactivity. Congress might keep enacting laws that the executive would not enforce or the courts would not sustain. But the people of each state are sovereign; they own the constitution. They alone have the power to determine its meaning. A constitutional impasse should lead quickly to clarifying amendments.

In order to force the people to assume their full constitutional responsibility, Taylor advocated the extreme doctrine of mutual interposition. His constitutional theory clearly implied the ultimate right of secession, but Taylor never endorsed it and clearly sought a milder expedient; he often chided New Englanders for their secessionist gestures during the War of 1812. But he did believe that state officials and state judges had their own duty to uphold the federal constitution (the people of their state had ratified it), and in order to uphold it, they had to interpret it. They should abide by that interpretation rather than bow to the mistaken interpretations of federal officials. If state and federal officials disagreed on some provision of the constitution, and this was most likely to occur on the critical but often disputed boundaries between state and federal jurisdiction, then both were obligated to act according to their understanding. This meant that state courts might try to stop the implementation of federal laws (Taylor encouraged this in the aftermath of the *Marbury* v. *Madison* decision, when he urged the state of Maryland to collect taxes despite the decision), or that federal officials might disregard or evade what they saw as usurping state legislation. Such possibilities threatened confrontation and even conflict. Taylor preferred this to tyranny, and he believed tyranny was almost inevitable without several checking devices. He believed the people in the states would intrude before violence erupted and either call a new constitutional convention or amend the existing document. His purpose was to activate the constituent process as often as possible, and to keep the people constantly alert to governmental aggrandizement.

When Taylor died in 1824, he was sure that he had failed in his effort to alert and activate the public. His fears for America, whose future had seemed so bright in 1776 and again in 1787, increased as the powers of the federal government increased. The agonies of the Missouri Compromise, the signs of solidifying regional parties, and the growth of nationalistic feeling all deepened his gloom about the future of America. His disappointment at various constitutional, political, and economic developments was all of a piece; they all symbolized decline.

Taylor's detailed analysis of American economic issues, guided by the wisdom of a congenial and much more sanguine Scottish gentleman, Adam Smith, began the serious and systematic study of political economy by Americans. Taylor began and ended his economic analysis with a carefully developed concept of property. For Taylor, the desire for property was both the reason for government and the most frequent source of its corruption. The need for government springs from human greed; the hope for good government rests in human self-interest, in man's desire for a secure enjoyment of the manifold blessings that nature offers as a reward for expended labor. The joys of social intercourse, the desire for commerce and trade, the pleasures of consumption, the social arts and all the refinements of civilization—all depend upon a love of property, a "passion to which mankind are indebted for the most perfect state of society and its blessings."

Taylor, perhaps informed by his knowledge of American Indians, was willing to admit that primitive tribes might lack a love of property, but it was apparent to him that a love of wealth was common to all civilized men. This very love was the undoing of just societies. Those who govern share the passion for wealth, and in most governments they are abundantly tempted to gain wealth by law rather than by work. In past societies, and particularly those cursed with feudal institutions, governments had either owned, or had had complete power over, all wealth. That alone insured that governments, not the people, were sovereign. In America the greatest danger was that our governments would seek not to protect property but to control it and redistribute it to favorites. This would mean a tyranny of the same order as that which led us to fight for independence from Britain—the power of the strong or the ambitious over the weak and the honest.[3]

Taylor defined what he called *authentic* (or legitimate or natural) *property* in a quite conventional way. It is the possessions one gains by talents and industry, the reward for labor. The word *property*, he believed, should not attach to possessions gained in any other way, particularly not to those gained either wholly or partly by theft, fraud, or that modern, sophisticated combination of the two: special interest legislation. Such politically acquired possessions he called *artificial property*, and he stressed the absolute opposition between the two forms of property, which to him were as different as good and evil.

Since man's labor alone legitimizes property, a person is free to convert his labor into any subclass of property he pleases—into money, productive capital, land, or consumer goods. In the long run the end of labor is human happiness. Taylor was an unabashed hedonist. He wanted people to enjoy the products of their labor, including such ancillary benefits as status or power. A beautiful and happy life, he assumed, depends upon material plenty, for even the most admired social graces rest upon economic competency. Thus, both money and the means of production are largely instrumental forms of property, vindicated by the forms of fulfillment they make possible—freedom from want, political and social status, challenging and intrinsically rewarding work, and all kinds of consumer pleasures.[4]

Land (or nature as a whole) had a special status in Taylor's model of legitimate property. It is a given. Man does not create it; he can abuse or improve it. Unlike other means of production, land is never a creation of law and never subsists on other interests. He believed that abuse of the land was a sin, a form of blasphemy, and censored American farmers for despoiling the land and landscape. Only in America was unimproved land more valuable than "improved" (if that word could be used to describe treatment of the land that usually resulted in early and rapid depletion of its fertility). Ownership of land entailed a moral, almost a religious, responsibility to take loving care of it and to improve it; it needed the commitment of the serious farmer, not the irresponsibility of the speculator.

In a society without special privileges, Taylor believed, there would be no danger of land monopoly. Defined as property, land is simply one product on the market. He favored no limits on individual acquisition, so long as possession represented the disposition of honest labor. He assumed that serious abuses of land ownership always derived from special political favors, such as bank paper, which supported speculation, or entail and primogeniture laws, which supported a feudal monopoly. He stressed that land and other forms of productive wealth had to be widely, although far from equally, distributed in order to maintain a democratic republic, for wealth always rules. Taylor believed that, so long as wise policies prevented the rise of a new paper aristocracy, land monopoly could not develop in America. Our elimination of entail and primogeniture laws precluded it. He assumed that, generation after generation, the gifts of talent and wisdom would shift from family to family, that equal inheritance would continually divide land, and that a completely free market would insure a fair price for land.[5]

The problem with the word *property*, as with so many other abstract terms Taylor sooner or later had to define, was that few people made his distinction between natural and artificial forms. Even land gained by theft or political favoritism was artificial by his standards. The ambiguities in the word *property* invited deceit, as Taylor continuously argued. In England (always the prime source from which Taylor drew examples of evil practices) the paper aristocracy had fooled the working classes by appeals to the rights of "private property," when in fact they used their political power to destroy all natural or authentic property. Clever and ambitious men were always happy to label as private property their very pillages of true property, to wrap in its sanctity such artificial and enslaving instruments as titles, tithes, feudal obligations, speculative gains, funding, corporate stock, sinecure offices, and every other imaginable species of fraud, monopoly, and corruption. And they were usually able to fool the working people, most of whom lacked political sophistication: "We farmers and mechanicks have been political slaves in all countries, because we are political fools. We know how to convert a wilderness into a paradise, and a forest into palaces and elegant furniture; but we have been taught by those whose object is to monopolize the sweets of life, which we sweat for, that politics are without our province, and in us a ridiculous affectation. . . ."[6]

Consistent with his emphasis upon nature and labor as the ultimate sources of all wealth, and labor as the only legitimate basis of any exclusive claim to wealth, Taylor wanted government to leave labor free in every sense of the term. Like Adam Smith, he believed the state should never help or hinder any industry or individual producer. The only economic role that could be safely allowed to the state was the protection of legitimate property and honest labor against theft or fraud. The framers of the federal constitution had accepted this wisdom and had therefore given the federal government almost no economic role beyond a carefully circumscribed taxing power. It had received no right to reward or retard any sector of the economy. In fact, to reward one industry is eventually to penalize another, for the government has to take what it gives (a subsidy to Peter is a penalty to Paul). As soon as a government begins to distribute favors, various local interests organize and compete for all they can get, insuring parties, factionalism, and a need for more and more governmental coercion. It is a process that, once well advanced, leads on to centralized tyranny. In the long run, only a minority can benefit from such subsidies, for the workers of the country are the source of all wealth and it is they who have to pay for all privileges given. However disguised, a subsidy is a tax on honest labor. Workers pay; clients of the state receive. Even if a government could take all wealth produced, and then distribute it in some just, impartial way, almost everyone would feel cheated. Taylor knew that such a just distribution was impossible, for a government that possessed all wealth would be a sovereign government, able to do as it would with property. Those who governed, or their special cronies, would extract a disproportionate share.[7]

One distortion of the proper economic role of government would be radical egalitarian laws, which are political strategies for taking property from the rich to give to the poor. If great wealth was a product of ability and labor (even over several generations), Taylor believed it was legitimate and rightly protected by government. If it reflected special privilege, it was illegitimate and fair game for expropriation through taxes or any other measure a government could devise. But recovered subsidies should go into general funds, which would finance the minimal needs of government (which include, on the local level, humane care for the truly destitute or disabled), and not into new subsidies for some newly favored group, not even the poorer classes. Like Adam Smith, he argued that schemes to level all property, or to do away with private property, strike at the very roots of society—a desire for abundant subsistence, for creature comforts, even for luxuries. Out of pecuniary destress (usually the result of an unjust distribution of property), some desperate people may celebrate a community of goods and disclaim any love for private possessions, any respect for the possessions of others, and all respect for contracts and laws that order and protect property. They violate all the rules of society, which they correctly perceive as based on property, but so far from being the metaphysical saints they claim to be, they are malignant misanthropes and unprincipled demagogues.

Taylor believed that anyone who recklessly dissipated his property, who abused or disowned his land and possessions, also dissipated his honor and virtue. But he never really feared such perverted idealism in America, at least not until privilege and oppression had advanced much further. As a whole, Americans loved their property; even the poorest farmers and mechanics feared egalitarian schemes. Yet Americans often seemed to prefer fraud over forced equality, for they avidly acclaimed several forms of privilege. Thus Taylor believed that egalitarian ideas were not realistic options in America; moreover, those who tried to amass wealth by means of special privilege used egalitarian proposals as demagogic strawmen. In this way they diverted attention from their own clever forms of theft by appealing to popular prejudice and fear of agrarianism or communism. Thus, of two hated extremes of tyranny—egalitarian leveling and oligarchic exploitation—Taylor preferred the former. He despised aristocrats more than mobs.[8]

Taylor, a professional farmer, had a deep affinity for agricultural pursuits. He placed husbandry above all other arts. Like Jefferson, he praised agriculture as an intellectually challenging science, productive of the highest physical and moral qualities in its devotees. But in his economic views he was as close to Ricardo as to the French Physiocrats. He applauded a growth economy, with higher and higher levels of consumption. He denied that luxuries, in any invidious sense of the word, exist, for "God saw that all his works were good." He acknowledged that economic growth required an increased specialization of labor, capital growth, an increased exchange of goods between both industries and nations, and more manufacturing. He commended a mixture of agriculture, commerce, and manufacturing, and always tried to appeal to all three sectors in his economic analysis.

As a declared disciple of Smith's, as a fervent advocate of free trade and national specialization, Taylor offered an economic, and not a sentimental, defense of agricultural primacy in America. Farming was, and should long continue to be, America's largest industry not because of its noneconomic rewards (they were an incidental blessing) but primarily because American resources and location insured that farming offered the most profitable returns from capital and labor. If these circumstances changed in the future, Taylor conceded, it would be necessary to channel more labor into manufacturing. It is important to remember that the agriculture he knew and commended was already highly commercialized and specialized and quite dependent upon a European market. For people of wealth like him a free agriculture seemed a prudent and profitable area of investment, not just a favored way of life. If discriminatory policies destroyed this investment potential, he knew that American agriculture would decline and new forms of favored enterprise absorb much of its capital and labor supply. He deplored such a diversion of labor and capital in part because it was unnatural, necessarily founded on subsidies or privileged charters. Although a favored few would benefit, it would mean an overall loss of economic returns and a decline in the average living standards of the people.[9]

Of course, Taylor's love for agriculture influenced his economic analysis. But most of his praise of farming appears in *Arator*, which he addressed to fellow farmers. In his four "heavy" books he at least muted his preference, and was most forceful in his effort to win the political support of mechanics (laborers). Taylor wanted to form an alliance of all workers against what he called "capitalist" privilege. His idealized American was not just the farmer, but any proprietor or free worker, whether he labored in his shop or in the fields. What he feared was dependent wage workers in any industry, including agriculture. He condemned the English landlord system as fervently as the English factory system, for they both reflected political privilege and economic oppression.[10]

Taylor stressed agriculture's special economic status. It satisfies man's most basic needs. Taylor, in a rare dissent from Adam Smith, adopted a key Physiocratic idea—that commerce and manufacturing change the place or the form of goods but do not add to the total value of goods. All real growth is natural, and only those who cultivate the land or domesticate animals facilitate this natural increase. This was not to denigrate the processing industries, which Taylor believed were necessary for prosperity and high living standards. But, like Adam Smith, he often noted the logical and chronological priority of agriculture. Until man so masters the art of husbandry as to produce a surplus, then all have to live at a subsistence level. All the luxuries possible in a mixed economy rest upon successful agricultural techniques that free laborers for other tasks. Farming thus "suckles" all industries.

This prior status also made agriculture vulnerable. Commerce and manufacturing, which move or transform natural produce, can easily pass the whole burden of taxes back to the farmer or miner, where the burden has to stop. Workers ultimately produce all goods and pay all taxes; in America this meant that agricultural workers paid most taxes. An impecuniary federal government, and particularly one that favored other industries, could quickly damage American agriculture and drive small farmers either into tenancy or into factories. As he evaluated data on the American economy, Taylor concluded that agricultural profits had steadily declined from their peak just after the Revolution. Most American land was not permanently fertile (he did not know the lush soil of the Midwest); it needed continual replenishing. Agricultural profits were low partly because the federal government took an ever larger share of the national income and used much of this to enrich a few "capitalists." Even prosperous farmers had stopped making agricultural improvements and had invested their savings in bank stock, which clearly offered them higher returns. Because of this, the best talent was leaving the farms for the cities. Few farmers received true profits, for they drew their meager returns from an ever more depleted soil. This meant, after a time, deserted farms and declining rural villages, as the base of agricultural prosperity eroded beneath retreating feet.[11]

Taylor's ideal economy included the merchant. The exchange of products is a necessity of civilization. Commerce permits specialization, the accrual of tools, the honing of new skills. It stimulates new wants, multiplies human relationships, raises horizons of expectation, liberates human energies, and thus underwrites economic growth (all arguments from Adam Smith). A nation profits by trade when it can undersell others, yet still swap less labor for more. If one hour of labor growing wheat in Virginia could purchase two hours of specialized factory labor from Britain, Virginia was the gainer. Taylor had no doubt of the ability of the united American states to compete with other countries on a free basis. Our workers were the freest and most talented in the world— proud, inventive, industrious. We even profited from European distresses. British policies, at home and abroad, had served to depress factory wages and lower prices on manufactured goods, to our advantage as well as to the advantage of a few English capitalists. We enjoyed the cheap products of a virtual slave-labor system. The corn laws had distorted

British agriculture, creating artificially high prices and making peasants of the yeomanry. Here was the market for our efficient production. The imperial wars of Europe also increased our market. But our advantage would remain only so long as America avoided both war and the European system of special privileges.[12]

Taylor applauded manufacturing, although here again semantic questions arose. Labor is the only manufacturer, and all workers—upon the land, in factories, even in the professions—give new form or place to some article of nature. In this sense, every worker is a manufacturer, and each is entitled to complete freedom. Taylor often used the word *manufacturer* as a synonym for mechanic, or what we might today call a craftsman or skilled laborer. But in his somewhat eccentric vocabulary, *manufacturers* always meant the actual producers, not the financiers or managers or owners. Manufacturer was a good word, capitalist a bad word, and the interests of the two were diametrically opposed at every point. Taylor was proud of the mechanics of America, and welcomed a natural growth in their numbers. They were blessed in America, for they enjoyed high wages and public esteem, and thus were in no sense servile. Mechanics voted, held political office (a son of a mechanic had been president), and served as militia officers. The virtual slave labor of Britain, which boosted our agricultural markets, lowered the economic prospects for heavy or factory-style manufacturing in America. Unless subsidized our factories could not compete with low English prices. But American manufacturers did enjoy a 20 percent transport cost advantage over England, and with this margin Taylor expected that there would be continued growth in light manufacturing and in those crafts directly related to agriculture. So long as such growth involved no subsidies, he welcomed it.[13]

For Taylor, the source of industrial progress, of new techniques and tools, was not only saving or capital accumulation but inventive intelligence, which flourished only in freedom. Unwilling to concede anything to English capitalists, he suggested that the original source of British preeminence in manufacturing had been Huguenot immigrants who brought the needed skills. Britain adopted them and, by a forced-labor system, squeezed all they could out of the advantage. But, in the long run, such oppressive conditions of labor would discourage the initiative and effort needed to make further improvements in productive techniques. Growth, in England, would continue to come out of the hides of driven workers. Taylor would never concede that the whip was as productive as self-interest in stimulating invention. Coercion can create only well-trained robots. Only in freedom does the productivity of labor increase, both through inventions and a more efficient management of capital and labor. The few directing minds at the top of English mercenary combinations were actuated by greed, and would not long provide the types of industrial intelligence displayed by free laborers. Above all, Taylor refused to accept the prevalent argument that the cultural achievements of a parasitic leisure class justified the oppression at the bottom. Even in this area he believed free laborers were the most likely source of both new ideas and new forms of beauty. In a free economy, many among those who work could, like Taylor, acquire a competence and then enjoy the leisurely pursuits of a gentleman. He expected America's philosophers to come from free workers and individual entrepreneurs.[14]

The picture Taylor painted of the British economy was as gloomy as that of any critic before Emerson or Henry C. Carey. In Britain the wealthy landowners had joined with finance capitalists to squeeze the laboring class into poverty, to crucify them on the cross of avarice. Formerly free artisans had become wage slaves without social status or political rights. England had also developed all the necessary accouterments of a centralized capitalist system—soldiers to maintain order, laws to confine workers to long hours and their "factory chains," frequent wars to excuse new privileges, a colonial empire to fatten the profits, and even a minimal amount of what we today call redistributive welfare (poor rates, workhouses, hospitals) to keep alive those who had been forced into penury. Even capitalists conceded the right of the poor to remain alive. But the poor factory worker had to spend all his wages for subsistence. He had no security for unemployment or disability. His dependency and despair often drove him to crime or into pauperism, two ever present afflictions of factory towns. The poverty of the workers, combined with the usual human frailty, rendered them especially susceptible to all sorts of temptations. Such workers lost all respect for government and remained a fertile source of insurrectionary sentiments. The state had to provide more and more police to control the incipient disorder. Most workers in England had no political role, held no offices, and in their misery could hardly be considered citizens. They had no legal recourse, for the capitalists fashioned laws to make mechanical combinations (unions) illegal. With no check on capitalist greed, the producing classes were "reimbursed by penalties for the loss of hope."[15]

The horrible fate of Britain already threatened America. Taylor sincerely believed that farmers and mechanics and small merchants were all on the brink of slavery without realizing it, much closer to that awful fate than they had been in 1776. Three minority groups would escape the coming hell and gain all the benefits of the new age—large planters with extensive holdings and accumulated wealth (or men like Taylor), large merchants with surplus funds, and the bankers and financiers who now plotted the victory of privilege over honest work. Taylor, who had to resist the temptation to join the privileged, at times feigned the role of a martyr. Already his own finances had suffered from the diminution of agricultural profits, and he believed that he could invest his wealth more profitably in corporate stock or commercial schemes. What was at stake for him was not his livelihood but a valued way of life. He would not desert his calling. His commitment to agriculture, to individual entre-preneurship, overrode his own desire for acquisition.

Taylor resisted a simple conspiratorial theory. He professed at least compassion for the seeming oppressors. In the developing system of privilege, in the great grab bag of government favors, men of virtue and talent would go along, either because they did not understand what was really happening or because they had few alternatives. Taylor tried to place the major blame on a political system, not on the individuals who took advantage of it. The voting majority had endorsed the system, even though they stood to lose from its operation. It was too much to expect tempted individuals to refrain from taking advantage of it. The need was for a different system, not for more virtuous men. Even the hated capital-ists were often men of ability and integrity, as were such political enemies as Hamilton and Madison. Taylor felt that they supported immoral policies but not always, or even usually, out of immoral motives.

Obviously, Taylor used the word *capitalist* in a very eccentric way. It was his preferred synonym for *evil*, and despite all his disclaimers he at times used it to designate evil men and not just evil policies. Yet, even in this, his most polemical use of language, he occasionally paused for semantic clarification. In economic contexts, Taylor used the word *capital* (never a bad word to him) to designate both the tools of production (except for land) and also the monetary wealth that could command such tools or provide subsistence for laborers. Such capital is a necessity both in agriculture and manufacturing, for it is growth in capital that increases the amount and the efficiency of labor and thus the living standards of a society. But Taylor never used *capitalist* to designate those men who eschewed consumption in order to accumulate capital for productive purposes. To him such men were simply inventive and able workers. All men who work bring some capital to bear upon production, for labor and developed skills are also a form of capital. Men of superior ability bring the most capital. Those who contribute a large accumulation of monetary wealth to productive processes or those who have or invent new tools and techniques are the most useful people in a society. But they were never *capitalists* in Taylor's vocabulary. To deserve this odious label a person must have acquired his capital not by talent and work but by theft or political scheming. The term *capitalist* thus applied only to some men with capital, since it referred to a mode of acquisition and not just to the nature of the possession, although some types of property (paper wealth) neces-sarily rested on privilege. This distinction, like his subtle distinction between authentic and artificial property, was not always easy to make. Taylor often was incapable of identifying a capitalist until he knew how a person had acquired his otherwise legitimate property (a shop or a farm). More loosely, he once defined a capitalist as one who followed the maxim: "Get money, fairly if you can, but get money." Since Taylor always applauded economic ambition, consumptive goals, and profits as high as one could earn by honest labor and fair exchange, this is evidence once again that he identified a capitalist by his tactics, not his goals.[16]

Taylor's conception of capitalists as politically favored oligarchs led him into some dubious economic analysis. He assumed that only earned capital really benefited a country or led to higher production and consumption. Yet if one steals capital (say a carpenter's tools), there seems to be no economic gain for the country but also no necessary economic loss, provided the thief uses the tools as effectively as the former owner. Taylor assumed he would not. Only free and honorable men, with a protected right to their own earning, work with zest and imagination. Those who gain money or productive capital by cheating are much less likely to put that capital to productive uses. They usually gamble with it, or seek nonlaborious paths to more wealth. Conversely, the free worker, when robbed of his capital, may continue to work out of economic necessity (perhaps as the wage slave of the one who robbed him), but his servile labor will usually be inefficient and unimaginative. This means that all strategies by speculators or political manipulators to siphon off some of the earned profits of workers in order to pool capital never increase the total production in a society for long, and will eventually decrease it. Special privilege, or legal means of stealing wealth from those who produce it, retards economic growth.

Taylor had no difficulty with his moral contentions—robbery is robbery and slavery is slavery. But in certain circumstances, robbery and even slavery can surely increase capital accumulation and at least support a short-term increase in production. Legally entrenched methods (such as regressive taxes) of stripping laborers of a large share of their production, at a high cost to their consumption, can divert a larger share of wealth into capital goods and, at least, into new productive capacity. But Taylor still believed that even though such a strategy might build more factories (he feared it would), it would not increase either long-range production or consumption, both of which depend on work output. Thus, unlike Malthus, he stressed not the effect on demand, but the long-term impact on production. Over the long haul, slaves would not produce as much as free workers, however cleverly managed they were or however efficient the tools they used. Thus, he always attributed economic as well as moral costs to any type of special privilege.

These assumptions supported Taylor's image of all capitalists as

parasitic recipients of governmental subsidies. They make up a nonproductive leisure class. To pass any income to them was to send it down the
drain of excessive and luxurious consumption. But this view left un-
answered questions about the avenues of choice open to beneficiaries of
special legislation. In Taylor's view, if they had used their cleverness in
productive work rather than political scheming, they would have made a
net addition to national wealth. Here Taylor assumed that those who
became rich through political favors, such as the hated bank owners of
America, provided no needed service. It is almost as if he believed all
capitalists took their inflated and subsidized profits, consumed a normal
amount of American-produced necessities, and then either hid the re-
mainder of their wealth in a shoe, invested it abroad, used it to secure
even more privileges, or wasted it on European-produced luxuries. But
Taylor, so replete with facts and figures on the extent of privilege, never
produced any evidence at all about the disposition of unearned wealth.
This, more than anything else, weakened his case against the dire economic consequences of privilege, not just for special sectors (he supported with evidence many of his contentions about its effect on agriculture) but for the total economy.

In a loose way, Taylor placed his analysis of developing economic evils
in a historical perspective. Since greed is universal, the potential for a
privileged aristocracy always exists. Some of that potential is in all of us.
In Western history, this aristocracy has taken three forms. The first, an
aristocracy of priests based on superstition and ignorance, gave way to a
feudal aristocracy based on military prowess, conquest, and a rigid class
system. Remnants of these two still existed in Europe, but not in an
enlightened America. The third aristocratic age reached maturity in
Britain and was well under way in America. It rested on paper and
patronage, on politically acquired economic favors. It was in all ways the
most sinister. The priests took a tithe of only 10 percent (paper already
took 40 percent in America, and would eventually take all profits), and in
partial return for such theft bestowed some knowledge and tried to
improve public morals. The feudal nobility of Europe monopolized land
(a horrible crime), but entertained their serfs with feasts and pageantry
and at least had the courage to fight their own wars and provide a minimal
level of military security. Fear and the dangers of battle both restricted
the number of wars and their severity. But an aristocracy of paper
entertained the people only with high taxes, hard labor, and penal laws.
Such aristocrats never fight in wars. Instead they plot wars and imperial
adventure and hire others to fight them, using even victory as an excuse to
increase taxes and their unearned profits. The people always lose. Aristocrats of paper had the most enviable of positions. Their plunder was
legal, they were rarely even conscious of wrongdoing, and a gullible

public, busy congratulating themselves on having escaped established churches and feudal titles, had greeted the modern exploiters with gratitude and rewarded them with public offices.[17]

Taylor's forecast was gloomy. If the paper aristocracy continued for fifty years in America, all productive workers would be wage employees, and thus virtual slaves. The system, at maturity, would allow only two economic classes, creditors and debtors, masters and slaves. He could not understand public apathy, particularly after the zeal of the revolutionary struggle against a lesser tyranny. The explanation had to be the clever propaganda of the paper aristocrats, their soothing platitudes and wondrous promises. The people thus took their assassins to their bosom, blinded by their surface appearance, by their appeals to national honor and greatness or to the sacredness of property and charters. Even little people were enticed by a promise of future riches. Taylor had to refute the sophistic rationalizations and unearth the hidden realities, particularly for three critical beachheads of privilege in America: debt funding; chartered corporations, particularly banks; and bounties to favored interests, particularly the protective tariff. All too often he was unable to balance his thunderous indictments with equally telling economic arguments.[18]

Taylor's theories on the evils of debt funding were so subtle, and so poorly expressed, that probably only a very few readers grasped his position. Taylor distinguished two forms of borrowing. In one, a person buys the use of some value, such as a farm or the money to buy a farm. The interest paid is simply a form of rent, and one who borrows on a farm is a special type of tenant, paying his rent to the mortgage holder. Such a borrower converts the principle into a form of productive wealth that normally retains its value. This form of borrowing passes no burden on to future generations. The person who borrows to buy a farm may indeed leave his heir with a debt, but the farm can be sold and in normal times will more than redeem the loan. The son may continue the interest payments as a form of rent, but even in that case gains the value of payments made by his father.

A second form of borrowing is more reckless. One may borrow to pay for a richer consumption, thereby dissipating his estate. The children suffer. A farmer who mortgages his farm to buy European silks and wines leaves his son only a debt, for the wine and silk no longer exist. This was the form of improvident borrowing that Taylor condemned, for it often forced the next generation into a life of unremitting toil. Government borrowing had the same effect, and he objected to it for the same reason. Almost all government debts buy ephemeral goods or services, not productive property. Thus, our Revolutionary War debts paid for guns and soldiers' salaries. One exception, and one which Taylor defended at the cost of some stretching of his constitutional theory, was the Louisiana Purchase. A nation that borrows for present needs literally mortgages away its wealth to private individuals. It has to pay back both interest and principal through taxes assessed on labor or through the indirect tax of a depreciated currency. The most honorable solution to necessary debts of this type (Taylor almost conceded the necessity in the Revolution) is for the generation that contracts the debts to pay them off in full, as Thomas Jefferson had often argued.

In one sense governmental borrowing is economically useless and even deceitful. In war a nation has to gather the needed materials from the production of its citizens. One cannot get guns out of futurity. Borrowing is thus a political and not an economic strategy; it is a form of bribery. The sacrificing generation receives claims on the future production of a country, and may therefore be more willing to exert intense efforts in the present. They may even feel that future generations should join them in the sacrifice, since they may collect most of the fruits of victory. Taylor wanted Americans to rise above such bribes, to let patriotism alone do the persuading. The future is unpredictable. Any easy technique for passing the burden along invites fiscal irresponsibility and casual wars. Another, more telling objection to government borrowing is the obvious fact that such claims on the future are rarely, if ever, evenly distributed or fairly paid. Here Taylor cited the extreme case of the settlement of Revolutionary War debts. Those common people who held government debt paper lost because of severe depreciation, sold their claims to speculators out of sheer necessity, and then paid heavy taxes to pay off these claims at their face value after Hamilton won support for his funding scheme.

Taylor did not expect such blatantly unjust schemes for debt retirement in the future, but he still saw any federal debt as a perilous agent of privilege. As a governmental debt increases, repayment becomes more and more difficult, and the annual interest becomes a larger and larger claim upon the returns of labor. Taylor noted that the interest rate on government bonds, held by a small minority of bankers and men of wealth, was higher than the average profit margin of farmers and manufacturers. Should the governmental debt approach the total value of productive capital, the interest alone, collected as taxes, would absorb all profits by producers, drive wage rates down to a bare subsistence level, and slowly force desperate farmers to further erode our major national resource—a fertile soil. The debt in America was still far from such a level (not so in Britain), but Taylor believed a very persuasive body of capitalists would try to push it ever higher. As the workers of America foundered under a heavy burden of taxes, the financiers would bask in prosperity, living in idle luxury on the high returns from their notes and bonds. They would resist any retirement of the debt and, because of the growing sacrifice required to retire it, they would easily win that battle. The government would adopt a permanent policy of refinancing, thus maintaining the existing debt. Under such a permanent funding system, each generation would pay taxes (300 percent interest over an average lifetime) to profit capitalists. Since the original reason for the borrowing (to win a war) no longer existed, and no productive resources remained to compensate for the interest, the debt was a permanent excuse for extortion. Those enriched by it formed a powerful political faction, for they held one of the most lucrative forms of wealth in the society. With a virtual monopoly on profits, they would soon gain the political power to maintain both the debt and high interest rates. Anyone who gained new wealth would find every economic reason to join this aristocracy of government creditors.[19]

By such convoluted logic Taylor converted the seemingly innocuous policy of debt funding into the sinister threat of fiscal monopoly by government creditors. He saw a body of eager financiers waiting like wolves to fatten upon each new, more nearly enslaved generation of working people whose private property, if they still held title, was an empty mockery, since it could not yield any profits because of high taxes. Meanwhile the debt holders would become the great defenders of a sacred "property," even as they successfully resisted taxes on their ill-gotten gains.

A funding system anchored a heavy burden on all taxpayers. Chartered banks added to this burden, for bankers gained the right to levy taxes for their own benefit. Funding promised slavery in several generations; bank paper insured it in one. But bank paper was only a peculiarly virulent example of a more general evil—chartered corporations.

Taylor used either British precedents or the Bank of the United States as his horrible examples of the evils of charters. He traced chartered corporations back to medieval times, when sovereign princes granted a degree of autonomy and certain liberties and privileges to towns or to mercantile associations. A corporation was thus a "body politick,"a mini-government, an artificial entity that never died but which possessed the attributes of sovereignty. Because of its legal privileges, a corporation was an instrument for transferring public rights and property into private hands. Because of continued adherence to antiquated feudal laws, a corporate charter could hide behind the sacredness of contract and thus long outlive its original purpose. As Taylor understood popular sovereignty, no American government had a constitutional right to establish corporations, for only the people of a state could set up governments and bestow governmental prerogatives. He thus implied that each charter should derive from constituent and never mere legislative action. He paralleled corporations with established churches, and warned against both in America. We needed neither an episcopate nor an East India Company. If governments had the power to charter corporations to carry out constitutional functions, then we could eventually be besieged with hundreds of privileged federal corporations not even taxable by state governments and virtually beyond public control. To ask individuals to shift for themselves before such privileged organizations was to exclude them from the benefits of government and society, or even to deny them the status of free men. His advice, expressed in a typically vivid but crude metaphor: "Throw away the law charter tubes, contrived for sucking subsistence from those at work, as the vampire sucks blood from those asleep."[20]

The all-important charter privilege enjoyed by both the Bank of the United States and most state banks was the right of taxation, concealed in the privilege of issuing bank notes. Taylor was a persistent enemy of American banks and easily gave the impression that he hated banking. In fact, he opposed only their one crucial role of note issue. He had no animus against places of deposit, or facilities for exchange (checks, bills of exchange), or even lending institutions, so long as they loaned specie or government notes and not their own credit instruments. Moreover, his distaste for bank paper was not, under all circumstances, a repugnance for paper money. Because of these qualifications, his attack upon bank paper has to be prefaced by his overall monetary theory.

Taylor believed a free country had to have a permanent, stable standard of exchange. Property, and thus individual freedom, is insecure if a country had an arbitrary or rapidly fluctuating monetary standard or one easily manipulated by special interests. In such fluctuations some group is always hurt and that group will almost certainly not be the bankers. The existing metallic standard for international exchange, based on gold and silver, served well, and Taylor no doubt loved his "innocent and patriotic specie." But, again under the influence of Adam Smith, he was not inseparably wed to metallic currency. Money has one indispensable function—to facilitate exchange. It is not a kind of capital or a consumer item. It does represent both capital and goods. Given free international trade, specie flows to where it is needed. That is, Americans always had the privilege of importing gold rather than consumer products in exchange for their exports. If a local currency shortage raised the value of gold (and depressed prices for goods), then importers would buy gold. In a free world market the total supply of specie remains in equilibrium with economic activity and need. The fact that the United States did not mine gold and silver was irrelevant, for it did produce goods efficiently and could sell them easily on the world market. The existing form of specie had only two hazards—that it become so plentiful as to lose most of its intrinsic value (this destroys its utility as a standard) or that it fail to increase in proportion to production and new exchange requirements (the standard units would then appreciate in value, causing severe hardships for many groups, and particularly for debtors). Taylor apparently assumed a natural increase in specie, and hoped to persuade the United States, or any other nations that would listen, to avoid the types of artificial tampering (tariffs, paper currencies) that would wreck the natural equilibrium system that automatically adjusted currency to need.[21]

The supply of money, in conjunction with the supply of and demand for goods, determines price levels in monetary terms. But "real" prices are ratios of exchange. Exchange values, Taylor believed, reflected far too many variables for any full understanding of their mechanics. He eschewed the endless debates over theories of value by English economists. Perhaps, in a dream world, exchange should reflect equivalents of labor. In the real world, effective demand reflects all manner of human passions and fashions, and supply reflects great variations in skills and efficiency. In this real world, the mark of successful exchange is to give less labor for more. Money plays a crucial role. Within a national economy, any circulating medium of exchange makes up a part of the total supply of money (he included as money not only government and bank paper but the stock of chartered corporations), and therefore helps determine monetary prices. After an adjustment process, paper issues raise monetary prices on the international market. Domestic paper issues usually free specie for export, and by increasing the supply of specie in international trade raise the effective world monetary supply. Although this inflation of prices does not permanently alter real prices or exchange positions, the short-term effect is quite distorting. If a country made it a policy to issue large amounts of paper money at frequent intervals, then these temporary distortions would become the rule. The resulting instability would destroy the self-correcting features of the international currency market, and erode the property-securing function of a stable standard.[22]

Taylor conceded that there were rare occasions when a country had to have additional currency even to sustain domestic commerce. Apart from an unlikely possibility that world supplies of gold and silver might dry up, the most likely occasion for a paper issue is during war. In the Revolution the United States had to use all or most of their specie and all their exports to buy military necessities. For such occasions, Taylor suggested governmental issues. The specie that supports such paper is the taxing power, and behind that the productive wealth of the country. He wanted a constitutional amendment to restrict such issues to the yearly amount of taxes collected by the federal government, and with each state responsible for redeeming its portion as based on the distribution of taxes. He wanted such notes, if not made legal tender, at least to be acceptable for at least one-half of the federal tax payments. This carefully qualified scheme was Taylor's way of avoiding any possible excuse for bank notes.[23]

When a private bank issues notes, it in effect borrows money. It asks those who hold its notes to trust its credit and reliability, and to assume any risk that the note will not in fact be redeemable in specie at some future time. Yet, to the horror of Taylor and many of his contemporaries, bankers did not pay the holders of its notes any interest for the trust given. Note that the holders could be anyone in the society, since bank notes were negotiable under the terms of state or federal charters. To compound their exploitation of special privilege, banks normally issued notes as loans. They, in effect, exchanged notes with private individuals, discounting the paper received at up to 8 percent (the interest charged), but paying no interest on the paper given. This dramatically illustrated the magnitude of the privilege enjoyed by bankers and not by ordinary citizens. In comparison with the total of outstanding paper, the bank undoubtedly had less security for its borrowing than the individual who borrowed on the security of a farm or other concrete values. But the bank had its magical charter that allowed it to collect profits for no clear service rendered. The advertisement and solicitation of note sales (under the ruse of making loans) was certainly no service to the people. Here, as so often, Taylor ignored the often pressing need for credit, and the expansionary effect of credit used for productive purposes. He only conceded that banks did provide a convenience to government in the collection and disbursement of funds, but noted that even here the banks primarily facilitated that other devil of government—debt funding. The same capitalists who owned bank stock also held the national debt.

The profit of bankers (Taylor estimated it at $10 million in 1814) had to come from the production of laborers. Again, Taylor assumed that these were fully parasitic profits, that banks performed no public service. These profits simply defined the cash value of the subsidy given to bank stock by the government. This was not the total cost of banking to the economy. If borrowers paid the whole bill, banks would not deserve as much resentment. People do not have to borrow, and they know the interest they pay. But society pays most of the cost. One minor but hidden cost of banking is the number of people withdrawn from productive labor to staff the banks or to live in idleness on the earnings of bank stock. More important, bank paper drives out specie and becomes the circulating medium. The banks hold the supply of specie in the country as inadequate security for their notes. The paper creates an excess or redundancy of currency (that is, more than needed for ordinary market transactions), a redundancy proved by the disappearance of specie from circulation. This currency expansion raises the quantitative price of every article, even as real prices retain the same ratios. Those who hold real property (a farm, a ship, a store of wine) neither gain nor lose from the rise of stated prices, for everything, including wages, will go up at about the same rate. But price inflation does hurt those who own currency, or who have obligations defined in currency (a loan to be collected). The frugal people with savings, and creditors, really pay the cost of bank stock, and not the borrower. He may do well. Not only can he use his borrowed funds for productive purposes, but the continuing inflation of monetary values helps lower the effective interest he pays. If inflation is rapid, he may repay less than he borrowed in real values. Taylor did not note that this inflation also threatened the profits of banks, the largest creditors of all. He apparently assumed that, during inflation, they would speed up their presses, and sell more and more of their one marketable product—notes. Bank notes, easy credit, and inflated monetary values could lead to rampant land speculation or even to a speculative mania that insured a panic and depression. But Taylor did not dwell on the possibilities of over-extended issues, insufficient specie and a sudden collapse of our whole credit system. Banking was bad enough even in its normal and prudent operations.[24]

Taylor yearned for the past, when private holders of specie arranged loans at low interest. Before they succumbed to the lures of paper, the affluent were willing to loan at modest rates, for they confidently expected to collect as much value as they loaned (no fears of inflation) and had no other more profitable market for their savings. Such low-interest loans of specie offered an excellent incentive for young men who needed capital. Such loans had no distorting effect on prices. Under the new paper system, affluent men like Taylor had to charge a high rate of interest on loans, and still they received lower returns than if they had invested in bank stock. Part of the interest they had to charge reflected rent on their money, but over half represented the likely amount of future inflation, the concealed cost of bank paper. Bank profits thus represented a heavy tax on all lending. Bankers collected these taxes at the time they issued bank notes, but the whole monetary system had to absorb the tax burden. Whether the borrower paid most of the tax (in the form of excessive interest rates) or private creditors (in the hidden cost of inflation, which might cancel all their returns on money loaned), the bankers still received a large unearned increment.[25]

Not only did the paper interests founded on banking easily ally themselves with the holders of governmental debt, but they also merged with those advocating protective tariffs. The worst forms of privilege, instead of checking one another, coalesced in one powerful aristocracy. As always, the collusive relationships were too subtle for most people to understand until too late.

Remember that Taylor believed that the world supply of specie moved to meet local needs, insuring a form of equilibrium. If the United States somehow found themselves with an excess of specie, then the redundancy would raise domestic prices (as stated in monetary terms) and temporarily lower the relative prices of foreign products. Unless checked by import duties, Americans would buy those cheaper foreign products, exporting specie along with products to pay for them. Soon the export of specie would elevate world prices even as the diversion of specie from home purchases lowered domestic prices, restoring the equilibrium and a normal balance of trade in goods. Since bank notes add to the currency supply at home, and thus create a redundancy of specie available for export, such issues serve to raise domestic prices and to depress the relative price of foreign products. These results of bank policy eventually threaten bankers. Importers demand additional specie for payments abroad. This lowers the demand for bank notes and also erodes bank reserves, threatening an end to redemption and with it a monetary crash. Thus, bankers have a compelling reason to restrict imports, which translates into support for protective tariffs. Only behind such tariff walls can they continue, over a long period, to reap the fullest rewards of credit expansion based on their own notes.

Bank paper also burdened American workers, particularly when combined with tariff duties. Bank note issues temporarily made American products more expensive and less competitive on the world market. If continued issues, or tariffs, or both, prevented the restoration of an equilibrium through the operation of a free market, then someone in the production-distribution system had to suffer the loss occasioned by a noncompetitive international position. By the very logic of the case, producers absorbed the loss, although a loss often cleverly concealed by an inflated currency (monetary returns remained the same even as real returns went down). Since almost all American exports were agricultural, the farmer faced the greatest loss of markets. The merchant could not stay in the export-import business without a small margin of profit, and thus had to pass the burden on to producers, who had no real alternative but to pay it in the form of reduced profits or even losses. The farmer had only one possible compensation for lower returns on his exports—the temporary cheapening of imports, mainly manufactured goods.

Taylor knew that even this temporary advantage was an anathema to capitalists. Cheaper foreign goods threatened not only the specie reserves of bankers but the profits of those who owned domestic manufacturing firms that competed with foreign producers. Particularly threatened were the new, large-scale New England textile mills. Who owned these early manufacturing corporations? Usually the same capitalists who held the government debt and subscribed to bank stock, including many who lived in Europe. Thus, the final keystone to the system of paper and patronage had to be a protective tariff: it would reduce imports and thus relieve the specie drain for bankers; it would protect a profitable market for American factories; and it would insure that the whole burden of a developing and infinitely clever system of privilege fell on the proper shoulders—those of American workers. Since these workers were still a good way from complete slavery and subsistence incomes, a lot of fat remained to be rendered. The tariff was the final, perfect tool for doing just that.[26]

Taylor held to Adam Smith's classic free-trade position. He idealized international trade as much as domestic exchange. The more the better, for the larger the economic market the broader the diversity of talents and resources. Trade spurred new consumption (for example, men of northern climes acquire a taste for tropical fruits), while the new demand led to a growing expenditure of human energy to cater to it. The very diversity allowed different peoples an opportunity to exploit their varied talents and advantages. Barriers against international trade reduced living standards in all countries, and marked a beginning move back toward the meager, self-sufficient, nonspecialized economies of savage tribes.

Taylor never considered what options Americans would have if foreign trade barriers cut off all our exports. Such an eventuality was unthinkable to a Virginia planter, for permanent barriers would have forced Americans to devise a mixed economy. As late as 1824 this possibility still seemed farfetched to Taylor. Britain simply could not feed her people and her factories. Whatever the impediments, she would continue to buy American products, and to a lesser extent so would other countries. In these circumstances the United States should continue to exploit their peculiar economic advantages, which were still largely in agriculture and basic raw materials. If we did this, European wars, instead of threatening our economic position, would always enhance it. He saw no military threat from Europe. The only real threat to maximum profits for the American economy conceived as a whole came from governmental policies. If the govenment indulged in a frenzied nationalism, waging frequent foreign wars or undertaking imperial adventures, we could lose our trading advantages by cutting ourselves off from European markets. A more likely eventuality, with equally undesirable effects, was the creation of an artificial national economy by means of subsidies and trade barriers; such an economy would be necessarily more impoverished as a whole although enormously more profitable to a favored few.

Protective tariffs tax both industry and consumption. Taylor saw them as typical of strategies for transferring wealth by law rather than by industry. Not that he objected to all tariff duties. He always preferred low import duties, assessed on a tonnage basis, as the best means of raising federal revenues. He conceived of such duties as a sales tax mostly on luxuries, and thus on the playthings of the wealthy, whereas most excise taxes amounted to a sales tax on the necessities of the poor. But when unequally applied, duties constituted a concealed bounty to favored interests, as did subsidies for internal improvements. At bottom, all such subsidies constitute a form of economic privilege. As such privileges accumulate, they create bitterness on the part of those penalized, a bitterness that leads to violence unless one of two political expedients arrests it. The only good expedient to Taylor was the restoration of a free economy and the abolition af all special bounties. The other expedient was a completely centralized police state that used coercion to maintain order. Taylor never doubted that the rich in such a centralized state would get the largest share. But those on the bottom would of course get something—just enough to keep them alive, enough to train them for orderly work (under the pretense of educating them), or just enough to keep them from dying or exploding in revolution.

Most of the proposals for tariff protection in America related to manufacturing, not to farming. To Taylor, the effect of this was not only bounties for one small sector of the economy, but because of regional economic interests a bonus for the North (the Northeast of today) and a costly burden for the agricultural South and West. The South would pay a triple tax. Retaliatory tariffs on agricultural commodities abroad would curtail the existing market for staple crops, the tariff would represent a high sales tax on the imported articles received in exchange, and the dwindling of foreign commerce would soon erode the existing source of federal income, forcing higher excise taxes to the detriment of all consumers. Farmers in the West who grew nonexport crops for domestic consumption faced higher costs for manufactured products, new excise taxes, and a possible loss of markets for foodstuffs in an impoverished South, which might have to convert from staples to subsistence.

Taylor never accepted the argument that, in the future, a prosperous manufacturing sector would provide a lucrative market for domestic agricultural production. Obviously, it would provide a market. But the farmers, increasingly cut off from world markets, would be at the mercy of domestic purchasers. Because of surpluses, low prices, and the concealed sales tax on manufactured goods, farmers would face bankruptcy. Thus, tariff protection was a concealed technique for driving workers off the land and creating a pool of subservient wage laborers for our factories. High tariffs would make America like England: we would have an artificial economy, high profits for a few managers, and subsistence wages for everyone else.[27]

Above all, Taylor tried to prove that protective tariffs had a destructive effect on free mechanics. A bounty system would make factories more profitable in America, and thus enrich financiers. Whatever the level of wages, Taylor believed American craftsmen would be fools to exchange their entrepreneurial prerogatives for wage labor in an impersonal factory. But wages would not go up. None of the subsidy for manufacturing would reach the workers. The market, not abstract considerations of justice, determined wage rates, even as a bare subsistence established their minimum. If competition and policy allowed, capitalists would push wages to that minimum, collecting all the profits they could. In America, the past secret of its comparatively high salaries for mechanics had been inexpensive land and a ready market for agricultural products, which made homesteading always a tempting possibility. Since a protective tariff would mean diminished agricultural profits and opportunities and a redundance of agricultural labor, it would insure lower, not higher, wages in the growing factories and crowded cities. A few wealthy and ambitious farmers might beat the system by securing tariff protection for certain agricultural products and by investing much of their wealth in corporate stock. But small farmers and laborers would have no such alternatives.[28]

With high protective tariffs, the paper oligarchy would have its insurance policy for ever growing profits, and American workers would soon be slaves in a capitalist system. A privileged leisure class would eventually gain all its goals. Taylor could only appeal to Americans to reverse the process before it was too late, and at times he suspected it was too late already. His prescription was simple in concept, almost impossible to achieve—to elect new representatives willing to pay off the national debt, repudiate all corporate charters, and go back to a revenue tariff. Then the states should pass a series of constitutional amendments that would preclude a political system that could ever again fall into such privileged and unconstitutional legislation.

In one respect, all Taylor's admonitions had a hollow ring. No man ever analyzed more thoroughly the pathways to slavery. Yet the same man eventually owned hundreds of slaves. How reconcile the contradiction? Taylor never tried. He admitted his own dilemma. On no other issue was he so defensive and touchy. Negro slavery was an evil. He never denied this. It exacted some horrible penalties, one of which was unease of conscience. Another was the manifest suffering of many Negroes. He stressed that the white population of the world was not justified in using the labor of Africa because of any assumed superiority of intellect. Negroes could only gain in intelligence through their own free labor in their own homeland. Taylor never speculated on the intellectual potential of the Negro, even as he avoided any clearly racial arguments in characterizing them. All of his firsthand experience proved their inferiority in their existing station, and it was to the existing circumstance that he directed most of his analysis. In the present, he believed that mass emancipation meant disaster for both races. He foresaw only bitter racial warfare, with up to two million casualties. This, he believed, was a horrible solution to a terrible problem that lent itself to no immediate answers.

Taylor tried to generalize the guilt. The hated English had introduced slavery in order to get higher profits from tobacco and to prevent the growth of colonial manufacturing (they assumed Negroes could not be used in factories). Now a self-righteous North used the southern labor system as an excuse for exacting tribute, as they tried to force the South to subsidize northern factories. Because of slavery, the South was moving close to a restored colonial position. Taylor could comprehend abolitionist crusades only as a cover for northern economic imperialism. If fervent moralists wanted to attack the evils of slavery, they might best turn away from the southern states within the Union and concentrate on those without, such as Brazil or Cuba. Then their moral fire would not end by consuming even themselves. Besides, northerners should look at the mote in their own eye. Paper slavery was worse than Negro slavery, although both were forms of tyranny. The southern owner (not the callous overseer, whom Taylor identified as an unmitigated evil in southern agriculture) moderated his treatment out of his own economic interest in healthy slaves, out of deference to community opinion, if not out of benevolent impulses. Factory slaves had less security, worked longer hours, were forced to eventual penury, and lived in worse housing.[29]

Taylor criticized Jefferson for presenting such a horrible image of the effects of slavery on southern whites. Jefferson wrote his *Notes on Virginia* in the heat of a war for liberty, and thus indulged hyperbole. If all his extreme charges were true, if southerners had become barbarous because of their relationships with slaves, then Taylor admitted that southern whites should go ahead and liberate blacks and fight them to a mutual death rather than be abhorred by God and hated by man. But as he examined himself, as he looked at other southerners, as he surveyed the slave systems of ancient Greece and Rome, he could not believe such an extreme indictment. Men of good character owned slaves. Blacks did not, in all cases, inspire furious passions or sexual exploitation, but rather induced benevolence and pity. The children of owners learned more than the art of tyranny from their contact with blacks. Taylor in *Arator* tried to analyze the psychological implications of black-white, slave-free relationships, and found them to be infinitely complex. He even speculated that God had allowed the institution to arise in order to reveal the wonders of civil liberty, and to heighten white Americans' awareness of a worse form of impending slavery. Negro slavery had a providential role if it led white Americans to effective resistance against a paper aristocracy.[30]

What was the answer for Negroes? For the present, only more humane treatment by masters. Gradual emancipation and colonization were the final answers. Taylor believed emancipation was proceeding as fast as circumstances allowed. In fact, emancipated Negroes presented numerous problems. They were neither slave nor free, without opportunity to work, and quickly driven to crime. They could only transfer their bitterness to slaves and further erode a weak labor system. He wanted Congress to purchase land in a free state, and give free blacks the option of settling there or emigrating from the country. His final proposal was for joint British-American (those most responsible for the affliction) efforts to settle blacks in a fertile part of Africa, where there might be a reinvigoration of the virtue, religion, and liberties of Negroes.[31]

Slavery was the ultimate test of the American Union. Taylor saw no possibility of any consensus on the slave issue. Northerners and southerners argued from different evidence and different experience. Reverse their position, and each would soon think like the other. He had no fear of the moral and religious aspects of the problem. These issues had to contend by persuasion. But with the Missouri question slavery became a potent political issue. It was the one local issue, reserved to the states by the federal constitution as a necessity of its adoption, which would certainly shatter the Union if it became a federal issue. If the federal government proceeded against slavery, then it would by that act become a consolidated and sovereign government exercising a form of tyranny over the South. Let Americans but accept the idea of consolidation, of one nation, of one superior government, and slavery would inevitably be the issue of all issues. Abstracted from local circumstances, slavery was certainly prejudicial to the welfare of the United States, an embarrassment to the whole. Like Lincoln later, he acknowledged that one "nation" could not survive, half-free and half-slave. Unlike Lincoln, he believed the federal Union was not one nation but a limited alliance of many, some with slavery and some without.

The future was dark. Northerners, in a consolidated system, would try to use federal power to do what southerners knew to be visionary, to turn blacks into good patriots. Southerners would not and could not compromise on this issue. Suicide lurked in compromise, and thus they would fight back as if for their very lives. Only a preserved Union of free states, with slavery a state issue, could prevent the confrontation. Taylor thus pleaded with Americans. Let each nation in the Union solve its own internal problems. Do not try to coerce nations into being free and happy. Only restraint could preserve all we fought for against Britain. At his death in 1824, old John Taylor, to some already a souvenir of a past age, had profound doubts that the Union would ever survive the slavery issue.[32]

Taylor's economic views remained influential long after his death. They reflected one polar position in the policy conflicts of the Jacksonian era. Taylor had immense influence on contemporaries in Virginia and North Carolina. Congressmen were still quoting or paraphrasing him at the time of the Civil War. Many of the economic attitudes or policies later identified as Jacksonian derived directly from Taylor. Taylor obviously voiced beliefs widely shared in America, beliefs in the value of individual proprietorship, in the dangers of centralized government, in the threat of mobilized capital, in the dangers of special privilege or any expanded economic role for government. Since he also could refer nearly all his policy preferences to the great Adam Smith, it is surprising that the next serious American economist—Daniel Raymond—challenged almost all of Taylor's deepest commitments.

IV

Daniel Raymond

EVEN before John Taylor died, a New Englander living in Maryland wrote a treatise in political economy that rivaled Taylor's *Inquiry* for breadth and originality. Daniel Raymond, in his 1820 *Thoughts on Political Economy* (he entitled the expanded two-volume 1823 edition *Elements of Political Economy*), elaborately and often brilliantly defended governmental policies at the opposite extreme from Taylor's, yet he was as fully committed to a proprietary society as Taylor and often quite as hostile toward private banks. In his treatise, which was close to an academic text, he critically reviewed the by-then conventional topics established by European political economists, particularly Smith, Malthus, and Say. Although Raymond was unorthodox in his theories, his systematic approach later gained for him the reputation of being America's first economist. Like Taylor, he rarely attended carefully to the exact doctrines of European economists. But he developed and expanded, usually without express acknowledgment, the doctrines of Lord Lauderdale and the later beliefs of Malthus.

Raymond was descended from old Puritan families. Born in Montville, Connecticut, he attended the famous Litchfield Law School in the western part of his state. In 1814 he moved to Baltimore. There he took part in the defense of Fort McHenry and published his first pamphlet (on theology) in 1817. Apparently he was never very successful as a lawyer, and used his ample spare time to write his textbook on economic theory. He became a member of the local Colonization Society and in 1825 helped organize an Anti-Slavery Society. His textbook won him the admiration and patronage of Mathew Carey, a lay economist and protectionist.

Carey helped Raymond win an offer of a professorship from the proprietary University of Maryland, but the University refused to meet Raymond's salary demands. In 1830 he moved to western Maryland, and possibly lived briefly in nearby West Virginia. In any case, he suffered business losses in West Virginia, and by 1842 he had moved on to Cincinnati. Here he set up as an aggressive newspaper editor. In his columns, as in the first edition of his text, Raymond used very pungent language and roughly disposed of anticipated criticism. By the time he came to Cincinnati he had already published the fourth and final edition of his text (1840), the only edition that he extensively revised. After his newspaper failed, he spent the last years of his life practicing law, apparently without much financial success. He died in 1849, "reduced in circumstances."[1]

Raymond expressed in an unusually pure and consistent manner the economic imperatives one might expect from his New England Puritan heritage. His treatise was the perfect economic counterpart of John Adams's exclusively political *Defence* and a strong counterattack on Taylor's beliefs, which were already orthodox in much of the South. To a greater degree than any other early American economist, Raymond celebrated social solidarity, or communal unity, and called for a degree of individual commitment to the welfare of the whole that verged on self-sacrifice. Like Adams, he saw government as a disciplinary tool, a restraining check upon individual egotism and selfishness. But unlike Adams, Raymond was very much a nationalist. His personal history of mobility worked against provincial loyalties. His community was America. He had no interest in, no solicitude for, the individual states. In his early writings Raymond's nationalist views remained merely implicit. But in the final 1840 abridgment and revision of his text, he added an extended essay on constitutional theory. In it he defended some exceedingly novel theories, ones that were diametrically opposed to the constitutional beliefs of John Taylor.

All Raymond's constitutional theories arose out of one eccentric doctrine—that the federal constitution did not delegate any powers to any government. Outside a political community, each person is sovereign—that is, free to use his own faculties or powers as he wishes. When people enter into a political society, they constitute a collective sovereignty (the right to do anything they wish), but the exercise of this corporate sovereignty entails the principle of majority rule. A political community may exercise its sovereignty directly, as in a simple democracy, or it may appoint one, a few, or many from among its members to exercise it for the whole. They thus establish governments. The primary purpose of a constitution is to determine the form of such a government. Those who govern, themselves a part of the larger social organism, act for the whole, and have by logical presumption all the powers of the people they represent, unless the people specifically place limits on their power.

Raymond dismissed as redundant and superfluous all articles of the Federal Constitution that specified the powers of Congress. In relation to the actual power of Congress, they were as meaningless as the Tenth Amendment. He asked Congress and the courts to ignore all such articles. It made no sense for a people to grant powers to themselves or to their own agent. It is true that a constitutional government derives its powers from the people, but not in the sense of a restrictive list of revocable responsibilities, for such an illogical conception of a constitution would enervate any government and in effect place limits on the sovereign powers of the people. In this way Raymond expanded the implied powers doctrine to its ultimate limits—all powers are implied save those expressly denied.

Raymond seemed to view constitution making as largely a one-time affair. He simply ignored procedures for amendment. Evidently he believed that the people would need to amend the constitution only if they wished to change the basic form of their government. Seemingly, they would also have to resort to constitutional procedures to place new limits on governmental power, but Raymond usually assumed that they could accomplish this by a reinterpretation of existing articles. In effect he made the process by which a people interpret their constitution completely political. The American people, acting at the state level but not as states, were the sole parties to the Constitution. They had ratified it, and they alone now had the power to interpret it. Every citizen had the right, even the duty, to interpret it, but only the interpretation of a constitutional majority could prevail. The defeated minority had to abide by this interpretation or emigrate. The Congress interpreted the Constitution for the people, who endorsed or rejected such interpretations through the electoral process. What Congress declared to be constitutional at any one time was thereby constitutional. Raymond did not fear such an ample leeway for legislative interpretation, largely because Congress did not reflect a simple majority but a constitutional one. Because of our bicameral system, the ongoing interpretation of the Constitution as reflected in legislation always rested with both the majority of the whole people, as reflected in the House of Representatives, and a majority of the people in a majority of the states, as reflected in the Senate. One-fourth of the people could block legislation. Congressional action came close to consensus.[2]

Obviously, Raymond hoped the people would interpret the Federal Constitution as liberally and broadly as possible. This meant that they would drop all the nonsense involved in theories about limited delegation of powers and also interpret flexibly the specific limits on federal power.

Particularly in economic areas, he wanted the fullest possible scope for federal action. Why would a people so interpret their constitution as to limit their ability to promote their own welfare? Why would they deny government the power to enact needed tariffs or to make internal improvements? An illiberal and restrictive interpretation could only deprive each generation of a needed liberty of action. Raymond's views were in fact very close to those held by John Quincy Adams. The only stated limits that counted, that he wanted interpreted in a strict way, were those that protected freedom of speech and of the press, and ensured due process of law. If a continual expansion of power at the center meant consolidation, so be it. In ratifying the Constitution the people had opted for a high degree of consolidation. They had consolidated the states into one nation, but they had wisely stopped short of doing away with state governments. Since ratification they had so interpreted the Constitution (that is, so legislated) as to effect even greater consolidation. So much the better if this served their felt needs. Only in a few cases, for instance, federal bankruptcy laws, had the people turned against federal action and returned a responsibility to the states. Raymond felt that this was clearly an exceptional choice.[3]

Despite his nationalist loyalties, Raymond applauded the role of state governments. He never wanted to weaken them. He even acknowledged that the Constitution, although largely a national document that applied directly to the individuals that constituted our "one nation," was in a few cases also a federal document directly related to state governments. These federal sections scarcely extended beyond the militia provision and a mere handful of stipulated limitations on state governments. Otherwise, as a national document the Constitution established a central government whose powers transcended those of the states. State governments had to operate not only within the limits of a state constitution, but under the limits of both the Federal Constitution and all federal statutory law. He denied any possibility of jurisdictional conflict. Since the Federal Congress, by its legislative action, revealed the majority, and thus the true, interpretation of the constitution, any possible act of Congress automatically superseded state action. Federal supremacy was complete. The problem of a state government was when to act and not where. It could act *whenever* the federal government did not act. And here Raymond again appealed to the inherent and presumptive power of any people to govern themselves as they will. If the larger community did not speak, if the federal Congress refused to legislate on any issue not forbidden by the Constitution, a state government was completely free to act unless specifically prohibited by its state constitution. The useless list of congressional powers in the federal document no more set positive limits on state action than it implied any negative limit on federal action.

Instead of trying to limit state governments, Raymond wanted them to be more active and adventurous, particularly in economic areas.[4]

What about judicial review? Raymond of course denied any constitutional delegation of power to the courts. Their power was inherent in the very task of litigation. The United States Supreme Court had to uphold and enforce both the Constitution and federal law. When the two seemed to conflict, federal judges had to give priority to the Constitution. But Raymond feared an overly ambitious court. Like Felix Frankfurter in the twentieth century, he argued that judges should always defer as much as possible to the people's interpretation of their Constitution as reflected in legislation. They should strike down as unconstitutional only those laws that clearly violated the express limits written into the Constitution. They should overturn censorship laws, for example. It was in such morally sensitive areas that Raymond was most apt to distrust the short-term wisdom of the people, even three-fourths of them. In all other areas he hoped judges would follow the voice of the people, which on political and economic issues had the same authority as if it were the voice of god. In no case did judges have a right to interpret a constitution for the people. Again, the true Constitution is always what the constitutional majority (House and Senate) of the moment determines it to be. Given such a flexible document, Raymond denied any role at all for judicial precedent. What was completely unconstitutional in 1820 might be fully constitutional in 1840. Judges who refused to accept this, who tried to impose the dead hand of the past on a present generation, were flirting with a vicious form of minority tyranny.[5]

In these constitutional arguments Raymond, unlike John Taylor, showed little fear of government, or of special privilege as the inevitable product of positive government. Raymond always saw government as a tool, subject of course to misuse but usually open to beneficent uses. He wanted a righteous state, and he wanted the government, wherever wisdom and knowledge permitted, to expand its role in order to remedy inequities and to foster communal prosperity and happiness. He hoped that government would not only open up new areas of opportunity, but also exercise numerous restraints upon individual aspiration in both economic and moral areas. He still reflected the highest hopes of early Calvinists. Surely serious and responsible men can build a rough approximation of the City of God. Magistrates can govern well. Rich and poor, and all the gradations in between, can live together in mutual trust and pursue common goals. The task is difficult. It requires endless inquiry and unceasing effort. A righteous community does not spring miraculously from a near-anarchy of self-seeking individuals. Instead, it derives from a high sense of social responsibility and the support of strict laws.

Like his English predecessors, Raymond saw political economy as a

fledgling but supremely important science. Most of all, it was a science
that should be put to work. It was the intellectual armament needed for a
strong, positive, and righteous government. To have it and not use it was
sinful, a failing he freely attributed to advocates of extreme *laissez faire*.
Like his most able successors, Raymond understood all the pitfalls of any
economic science, beginning with confusions of language. Here the English had failed abysmally, using words ambiguously or imposing upon
them unexamined cultural assumptions. Most efforts at political economy
theretofore written had a distinctly provincial flavor. Even such great
pioneers as Adam Smith and Thomas Malthus had unwittingly assumed
as normal and universal characteristics that were peculiar to English
society. Raymond would use this insight with the greatest brilliance in his
discussion of property. He readily admitted that his was not the "true
science" of political economy, but no one else had developed such
either—therefore he felt free to try his hand. In a rare example of
chauvinism, he suggested that it was only to be expected that a mature
economic science should develop in America since America had already
furnished the highest attainments in civil government. He made this claim
not because Americans were brighter or essentially different from Europeans, but because Americans were not yet encumbered by so many
artificial institutions. "Here we can see the operation of the principles of
nature in their utmost purity.[6]

Raymond adhered as loyally as any of his eighteenth-century predecessors to the natural law tradition. Each man has a right to life, liberty, and a
fair share of earth's bounties. To the extent that a government fulfills its
moral purpose, it safeguards these individual rights to the limit of its
abilities. Not that most states originated with such moral ends in view.
According to Raymond, most societies began with a social compact
predicated on a single notion: "We will plunder our neighbors." The
typical goal was not a protected environment for honest labor but an
excuse to avoid labor. To illustrate this, Raymond cited the rapacious
behavior of Europeans in annihilating American Indians and in enslaving
African Negroes. Like John Adams, he liked to dwell on man's disposition to violence and plunder, or what he called the curse of Adam. In
diplomacy such selfish ends still governed the relation of states with each
other and, in the absence of any supervising international order,
Raymond accepted as inevitable the rule of national self-interest in
foreign policy.[7]

But within a nation under the rule of law, he believed, a moral order
was possible, and Americans had substantially achieved it. Such a moral
society is no easy attainment. Any organized society necessarily suffers
moral tensions, for the state is artificial. In order to exist at all it must
enforce conventional rules, beginning with rules pertaining to property.

These rules cannot be completely equivalent to natural justice. Some rules, directed to the welfare of the whole, necessarily conflict with those rights that one can deduce logically from a consideration of man in a natural state. Here, Raymond felt, was the greatest challenge to any organized society: to compromise the implications of natural rights no further than is absolutely necessary for the welfare of the whole. Such socially necessary restrictions on the realization of natural rights will best serve the long-term interests of all citizens, but obviously not always the interests of an individual (the soldier who is forced to sacrifice his life in battle does not live to reap the eventual rewards of victory).[7]

This emphasis on the community sharply distinguished Raymond's work not only from that of Taylor, who took individual hedonism for granted, but also from that of Ricardo, who assumed that each actor looks out for his own best interests. Raymond tried, without success, to draw a sharp distinction between his views and all European economic schools. In his first edition, he was downright nasty in his criticisms of other economists. He often showed contempt even for "Dr. Smith" and his "absurd theories"; at one point he referred to Smith's "singular aptitude for ambiguity," and at another, to his "incoherent, unintelligible non-sense." He thought he found in all English economists a major error—a failure to distinguish the very important differences between individual wealth and national wealth. His own distinctive doctrines were based on this vital distinction, although his attempt to sharpen the disagreement with Europeans often involved him in esoteric definitions or in unfair interpretations of his opponents' words.[8]

Raymond joined Adam Smith in rejecting the accumulation or surplus theories of mercantilists, but condemned theories of saving or parsimony, which he often incorrectly attributed to both Smith and Malthus. In fact, his counteremphasis on consumption and on the role of market demand expanded upon ideas already developed by Malthus. Raymond admittedly moved back toward the earlier mercantilists, particularly approving their emphasis on government incentives and regulations to foster national wealth, but he rejected their notion that national wealth depends on accumulation rather than home consumption. He repudiated what he saw, correctly, as Physiocratic elements in Smith: his agricultural bias and an undue emphasis on a completely free market. Raymond tried, much as Malthus had, to attain a correct blending of mercantilist and market economic ideas—the sense of social solidarity and government responsibility in mercantilism, and the emphasis on socially beneficial freedom and on capital growth in Smith and Say. In the attempt he anticipated several of the insights of American institutional economists and even several of Keynes's more salient doctrines.

Raymond borrowed his central concern from Smith: What policies best promote national wealth and happiness? The first issue, and Raymond believed it was the central one, was a useful definition of national wealth. He believed that the mercantilists and Smith had erroneously extrapolated from individual wealth to national wealth. For an individual, wealth means productive property—the land, money, and tools that will procure for him, even without his labor, the necessities and comforts of life. Thus, the rule for an individual seeking wealth is to save. The more land or money or tools one has the wealthier he is. Wealth is roughly synonymous with property, and it is a substitute for labor. But for a nation such accumulation, particularly of land and money, is not wealth, for it cannot sell or rent either in such a way as to support its citizens in idleness. And the sum of the private accumulations of individuals is not the same thing as national wealth (he accused Adam Smith of confusion on this score). A nation may contain many rich individuals and yet be very poor because of the ways that wealth is handled, just as a nation may have a vast hoard of uncirculated gold and still be desperately poor.

Raymond defined national wealth as a capacity for acquiring the necessities and comforts of life for its citizens. Today we might define it as the potential for assuring a high standard of living for all citizens. Superficially, this definition seems almost equivalent to his definition of individual wealth. But Raymond emphasized that an accumulation of land or money or tools by individuals or a government as a trustee of a community is not at all a sufficient condition of national wealth. The ability to put them to work is the major issue. Land and capital must be joined with an industrious citizenry having developed skills, with such opportunities for ownership as needed to stimulate labor, with the development of the arts and sciences, and above all with government policies that promote industry and consumption. Thus, Massachusetts lacked the natural resources and favorable climate of Virginia yet for other, largely institutional reasons was much more prosperous. Labor was the best clue to Raymond's distinction. For an individual, wealth removes the need for labor. For a nation, wealth means the widest possible range of opportunities and stimulants for labor, or those conditions that encourage work. A wealthy nation facilitates efficient labor, and with it enjoys an ever increasing amount of production and ever higher levels of consumption.[9]

Consistent with these distinctions was Raymond's argument that private wealth may or may not contribute to national wealth. A nation is more than the sum of its parts. It is a unity with ends of its own, ends that very often conflict with the goals of individuals. There is no logical equivalence between private preferences and national welfare, and no automatic harmonizing principle to make them equivalent. The wealth of individuals may, indeed, flow into the stream of national wealth, just as it may impede it (as Raymond believed the slave trade did). The end of public policy is to bring individual wealth into the stream and to channel it in a social direction, even if individuals have to give up the highest possible returns on their labor or investment. He saw this channeling as a complex task, and one too often shirked by economists, who usually had no larger prescription than freeing the individual to do what he wanted. This does not mean that Raymond wanted a vast, elaborate system of economic regulation. He believed that in most contexts this would impede national wealth by discouraging individual industry. However, he did want to control what he perceived as antisocial activity by individuals. Above all, concern for channeling individual wealth into the national stream meant government policies that would keep individual wealth working—land producing, skill being utilized, money circulating rapidly, and, above all, people consuming the whole product as fast as they produced it. Such policies would have to control the types of private property permitted, the overall distribution of property, the special incentives and aids given to needed types of enterprise, and the forms of welfare provided to families that unfairly suffered under the always artificial institutions that make up any society.[10]

Raymond's sympathy with natural rights and his constant concern with the common good directed him over and over again to what he believed was the most vulnerable, because least examined, assumption of all those made by the English economists—the legitimacy or even the necessity of existing forms of property. He realized that the word *property* is a lair of ambiguities. In the natural rights tradition the word had gained the same lofty status as life and liberty, and rightly so, given the meaning it had in that tradition. The issue was: What forms of *property* deserve that status? According to Raymond, only a person's interim right to use a portion of the earth to obtain food or other necessities. Raymond's restrictions on natural property (need, actual use, and only a temporary possession of one's fair share of the whole) closely followed those of Locke and the early Puritans. But unlike Locke and most of Locke's successors, Raymond saw no possible equivalence or even significant overlap between natural property and the forms of property allowed in any organized society. The types of property that receive protection in any nation, and the only types that concern political economy, cannot be "natural," since they deprive some men of free access to their "undefined" portion of nature. In fact, man's natural right to the earth is inconsistent with the very existence of an organized society, whatever the form of tenure recognized by that society. If citizens of a state claimed their natural right to property, then no land titles could be secure. A hungry man has a clear "natural" right to cultivate any unused land without any obligation of rent. In effect, Raymond denied that an individual has any inherent right to exclusive ownership of any part of nature.[11]

Raymond confronted the moral tension that is part of any social organization. Governmental rules, including those that define and protect property, are human contrivances even when directed toward moral ends. Such contrivances are necessary for human happiness, for they provide the only order within which human effort has much chance of success. Exclusive forms of real property, he believed, were the very cornerstone of any advanced society, even though they always infringe on some men's natural right of access to a portion of the earth (collective or government-owned property would be no exception to this rule). In this argument Raymond challenged a key presupposition of such extreme libertarians as John Taylor. He defined property in land, even as it existed in America, not as a natural right, but as the first and most basic form of special privilege. Such private property was rightly subject to all manner of social regulation and could even be taken away from its owners when the common good required it. Exclusive ownership of a portion of the earth means that one has already received an artificial benefice. This is true even when one buys the property with the returns from honest labor, for even then part of its value derives from state vestment and protection and from the security of tenure this assures.

Since forms of exclusive possession provided the very foundation of social order, Raymond accepted private property in land and productive tools as well as in consumer goods. But he always stressed that man's artificial modifications of natural rights, of a condition in which every man had rightful access to nature, should be carried no further than absolutely necessary to accomplish a social object. A state of nature, without any positive law, leaves each man with an equal moral claim to his heritage from God, but provides no coercive power to protect that moral claim. Practically, it is useless, for the strong collect all the benefits. Raymond saw no hope in any return to nature. His bent was in the opposite direction, toward more rules and more discipline. But most rules should discipline property owners, force private property into the "stream of national wealth," and protect the interests of those who have not gained exclusive possession of a part of nature.[12]

Raymond bitterly attacked Malthus. He lamented what he saw as an unquestioned and false Malthusian assumption—that the present proprietors of the earth's surface had a perfect, absolute, and exclusive right to their property, that they had no more than their just share, that their property involved no injustice to the poor. Malthus ignored the unequal laws that led to glaringly unequal divisions of land, and assumed that the poor were poor, not because of institutional distortions but because of some fault of their own or because of excessive reproduction. If Malthus were correct, if natural justice required that only one-half of mankind own the whole earth and divide it at their will, then indeed the poor should be left to starve and decrease. Anticipating some of the radical deductions later drawn from Ricardo's theories about rent, Raymond found in English property laws several unnecessary inequities. These laws went far beyond providing the minimal social order or protecting men in their honest labor in order to encourage national economic growth. Entail and primogeniture laws, as much as corporate charters, had supported an artificial inequality by steadily concentrating productive property in a few hands, and had foreclosed access to nature for millions of Englishmen who were now dependent on jobs and at the mercy of employers and of economic cycles.[13]

Raymond's practical prescriptions for a fair division of property were tame compared to his basic presuppositions. He felt that a wide distribution of property was morally obligatory and also conducive to the maximum economic effort by individuals. He wanted state protection of property titles only for a lifetime. Such restricted protection would serve the one main economic function of private property: to allow individual talents fully to express themselves and to provide a motive for continued and vigorous labor. Limiting accumulation to just one lifetime would militate against the amassing of great fortunes and the subsequent ill effects of great inequities in the distribution of wealth: the idleness, luxury, and dissipation of the wealthy few and the dejection, discouragement, moral degradation, and pauperism of the masses. He believed that governments should, if only it were possible, resolve all private wealth into the general mass every generation and redistribute it according to actual individual merit and effort (an anticipation of Thomas Skidmore's agrarian redistribution scheme of a decade later). But, somewhat lamely, Raymond merely advised laws requiring an equal inheritance for each surviving child as the best practical expedient. He believed that equal inheritance would somehow prevent extremes of wealth and poverty, and thus prevent in America all the social evils of Europe.[14]

The radical import of Raymond's views concerned not inheritance laws, but his recognition of the social origin of all exclusive claims to a portion of nature. Even in its most benign form, private property exacts a penalty from some people and in its more inequitable forms literally forces a large portion of mankind into servitude and grinding poverty. From this he drew a conclusion that his Puritan forebears would have applauded. Since those who own such property have received a benefice from society, they have a special responsibility toward those without property. If they are unwilling to assume this responsible stewardship, then the state that secures and protects their estates must either force them to be responsible or else take enough of their profits in taxes to provide for the welfare of the unpropertied and poor. After all, he insisted, the government is a "good shepherd," burdened to support and nourish the weak until they gain sufficient strength to take their chance with the strong. In line with this openness to economic regulation and to redistributive welfare, Raymond defended the poor laws of England. There, at least, poverty derived from all manner of special privileges to the rich, beginning with a highly artificial and unfair distribution of land. This created a class of able-bodied men who often could not find employment, not because of poor character, but because of poor institutions. Property owners had no legal obligation to employ all would-be workers, and the poor had no legal right to extract subsistence from the returns to owners of productive property. Raymond believed that most poor people in England were reluctant to receive aid under the poor laws, that they did not reproduce faster than other people, and that they were proud and desired jobs and independence. The few wretches who welcomed welfare and abused it rarely married or raised families.[15]

At least in England, poor laws were a humane necessity. It was no compliment to the moral sensitivity of English economists that they so easily overlooked the institutional causes of poverty and talked instead of all their gloomy expedients, even down to the need for celibacy among the poor. Raymond believed that redistributive welfare was not the best answer to human suffering. The need for poor laws only revealed the need for basic institutional changes, for a forced and more equitable division of property, and for an array of government policies directed at high consumption, the full employment of human talents, and more rapid economic growth. America, which was not yet burdened by the worst abuses of property concentration, not yet afflicted with other artificial and narrowly selective privileges, and still free to develop governmental policies conducive to economic expansion, needed no poor laws. This was an index of our economic health. If Americans accepted the wisest counsels in political economy, their welfare needs would remain minimal.[16]

For Raymond, the earth was the source of all wealth, labor the immediate cause of all wealth, and capital an instrument that improved the efficiency of labor. Capital in itself is not productive. However, labor, although it is the single immediate cause of wealth, is not the sole determinant of exchange values. Raymond ridiculed a simple labor theory of value, for the value of a product in the market depends on shifting wants, whims, and fancies. Not all men think alike or want the same things. Some articles, such as the precious metals, have a more stable value than others and are esteemed over most areas of the world, but even their value in exchange fluctuates. Of course, no significant theory of labor as an ultimate determinant of value ever precluded such short-term shifts. In effect, Raymond refused to enter the increasingly complex, and in his estimation artificial, debates over value theory, debates that so long absorbed British economists.[17]

Labor was nonetheless the key term in Raymond's political economy. The end of his economic policy was the stimulation of more labor and more efficient labor. Like so many later American economists, Raymond refused to join the Physiocrats and Adam Smith in distinguishing between productive and unproductive labor. All labor that contributes in some way, direct or indirect, to human happiness is productive, including most types of intellectual labor and most services. The only possible useful meaning for the term *unproductive labor* was either "unsuccessful labor" (labor expended in vain in behalf of some unachieved product), or "labor expended successfully but in behalf of some antisocial or harmful product" (labor expended in the slave trade). Yet he made a very fundamental distinction between labor directed at a consumable product or service (he often confusingly called this *productive labor*) and labor devoted to the improvement of production or to capital accumulation (to new plants, tools, methods), which he called *effective*, or later *permanent, labor*. This distinction led him into a few near-sophistic arguments. He attacked Adam Smith for emphasizing parsimony and the setting aside of part of the annual production as a path to national wealth. But for Smith, such saving simply referred to the diversion of labor from consumables to capital or, to use Raymond's terms, a shift of labor from productive to effective purposes. Smith joined Raymond in decrying a build-up of unconsumed goods even as he condemned a mere accumulation of uncirculated gold and silver.[18]

But without question, Raymond placed more emphasis on full consumption than any previous economist. Here his claim to originality holds good, for he went well beyond Malthus and Lauderdale. To Raymond, the engine of economic growth, of a full use of a nation's potential labor and talent, was full consumption and high demand. Not only does a market glut lead to the permanent loss of perishable goods, but it also lowers the demand for both kinds of labor, productive and effective, and thus results in a serious depression. Usually Raymond considered capital formation as a form of consumption. But apart from capital, all other production is for use, and use as quickly as possible. A surplus of consumer goods poses a dire threat to an economy. Legislators must try to get rid of it by stimulating more consumption or, if that is impossible, even by destroying the surplus. It is better to sacrifice the utility of goods than to leave them unused as a drag on the market. The ideal for a nation is a steadily increasing effective demand for goods, and at any one time a demand well beyond supplies. This insures full use of productive resources and labor. Without such high demand, growth slows, capital formation ceases, unemployment increases, wages fall, rents go up, and a nation faces economic decay. The source of gluts is not nature but poor public policy. Raymond assumed that there is an infinite range of human wants. A type of economic scarcity always exists in any society however productive it is, for there is no limit to how much people will consume if given the opportunity (Raymond never mentioned advertising or other artificial means of stimulating demand but surely would have applauded them). His emphasis on demand clarifies several other of his mandates: a broad distribution of productive property, laws to discourage hoarding or a slowed turnover of money, and a cultural climate that esteems comforts and even luxuries and reckless spending.[19]

As is by now obvious, Raymond gave a very optimistic slant to the "gloomy science." He foresaw an unlimited expansion in demand for goods, and predicted a hundredfold augmentation in primary produce from the earth, including that gained by husbandry. One need not contemplate the dismal prospect of most of mankind living at or near a subsistence level unless stupid policies prevailed. Raymond also rejected the implications that Malthus had early seen in population increase. A growth economy can accommodate large although not unlimited increases of population along with rising living standards. Raymond never foresaw a rate of economic growth equal to the potential fertility of mankind, but then mankind never realized this potential. Already, in every country, the birth rate was well below the natural maximum, and rarely was dire economic deprivation the limiting factor. A thousand cultural factors limited births and high among these was the prevailing living standard which raised a culturally determined desire for consumer goods above the desire for offspring. The very process of increasing human wants not only stimulated new technology and more production but also created new cultural impediments to population increase (like most economists of his day, Raymond discreetly avoided mentioning the methods of birth control). If legislators adopted growth policies, then the need for food need never at any time in the foreseeable future become a limit on population.[20]

Raymond's preoccupation with consumption helped shape many of his policy recommendations. Because he wanted government to stimulate demand, he supported market-expanding government expenditures and, until the final edition of his book, even saw beneficial results from a permanent government debt. He did not recommend wars of offense, but noted that wars are stimulants to national industry and, when their stimulating effects are not offset by devastation or by the violent fluctuations of reconversion, also a cause of rapid economic growth even in the civilian sectors. War can infuse a new level of energy into a body politic. War illustrated Raymond's daring thesis that even wasteful consumption may be a stimulus to increased national wealth. In many contexts, mindless and wasteful consumption could serve social ends.[21]

Public services and public works have the same stimulating effects as war, but without the waste and potential destruction. Thus, Raymond was a strong advocate of public education and internal improvements. Of course, a government has to draw taxes to pay for such benefits, but well-conceived improvements could easily stimulate enough additional economic activity and production to more than compensate for the taxes. Just as human wants are almost infinite, so Raymond assumed that labor is always in some sense in surplus supply. Usually some labor is unexpended, and always there is a potential for more efficient labor. Thus, public works schemes can, if correctly devised, utilize unused or underused labor rather than drawing from the sum of labor already expended in private production. At the same time the benefits of the improvements (such as better internal transportation) may expand markets and production in the private area. Public works may overcome lethargy and torpor in the economy as a whole and provide a badly needed stimulus. Raymond wanted continuous doses of such stimulants, and apparently saw no hazards at all in rapid growth; inflation was dangerous, but it was a product not of growth but of unwise policies. Raymond did concede to opponents of internal improvements that such expenditures could involve a significant redistribution of income. Those who paid the taxes, or the interest on a long-term debt, might not receive the direct benefits. Raymond had small sympathy with the losers, both because he expected individual sacrifice in behalf of national betterment but also because he thought the stimulating effects of such expenditures would, in the long run, benefit every producer. His view of private property justified a forced redistribution of wealth if this helped increase rather than reduce the number of owners. Public works, if carefully planned, could further a desirable form of redistribution.[22]

An equally potent source of economic growth is technology, the result of private invention. Public policy can stimulate such invention. Raymond was astounded that any economist (this time he singled out Ricardo for criticism) could see labor-saving machines as other than beneficial. Tools extend men's labor but do not, cannot, replace labor. Of course, if distorted institutions limit effective consumer demand, then new machines lead not, as they should, to a vastly increased production by the existing or even an expanding labor force, but to the same level of production by less labor, and thus to a greater redundancy of labor. The vice is then in the policies, not in the machines. They are the glory of man. Government should always encourage invention (Raymond defended patents as one of a very few desirable internal monopolies), but it has an equal obligation to stimulate the extra demand needed to absorb the new production they make possible. Raymond argued that the potential of machines meant that with a proper utilization of resources and a proper distribution of property and incentives, no able person should ever have to live without the means of subsistence and some comforts. Starvation or widespread poverty reflected either natural disabilities or some widespread abuse of law and justice. At the very least, smugly propertied men should be certain, before they abandoned the poor to the operation of a purported law of nature, that the poverty did not reflect "an unnecessary inequality in the division of property, produced by unequal and partial laws." The problem posed by growth through improved technology is not a diminished need for labor but the likelihood that through an improper division of the product, labor will not get its fair share. This, in turn, undercuts the increased market needed to absorb the growth in production, leading to greater wealth for a few but poverty for the many. In such a distorted system, machines do appear as a curse for the laboring classes.[23]

Neither in his original treatise nor in later revisions did Raymond react directly to Ricardo's enormously influential theories about rent. Raymond saw rent income as distinctive in only one sense—it depends upon the right, given in a social compact, to exclusive ownership of land. Tenure provisions and inheritance laws very much condition the rent value of land. Given certain institutional determinants, then rent varies according to supply and demand, and thus behaves much as other returns to investment. Raymond emphasized the usually inverse relationship between rent and wages. If good land is plentiful, rents are normally low and wages proportionately high. Unjust laws, such as entail, which foster large accumulation and artificial scarcity, lead to an undercultivation of land and excessively high rents. This excludes much labor from agriculture, lowers wage rates, and depresses a whole economy. But unlike Ricardo, Raymond did not foresee any inevitable and dangerous increase in population, any depletion of productive soils, and any increasing diversion of national wealth into higher and higher rents with a resulting impoverishment of both capitalists and workers. This would happen only when completely unjust tenure and inheritance laws prevailed, as they did in England. By this approach, Raymond anticipated some of the more radical disciples of Ricardo, later socialist and single-tax advocates who worked primarily for land reform. For Raymond, land scarcity was relative both to population and to agricultural technology. Since he foresaw an unlimited increase in agricultural productivity, a real land scarcity and appallingly high rents would only testify to completely unjust property laws. The squeeze of high rents is not at all inevitable, given the possibilities of major social controls over property and government incentives for agricultural technology. Growth is the solvent. In any rapidly growing economy with fair land laws, wages will be high and the amount of the total product going to rents proportionately low (even as money rents rise). If rents do impinge upon growth, then Raymond was clearly open to various redistribution strategies that could socialize part of the rent.[24]

For several reasons Raymond minimized distinctions between wages, rent, and profit. Since he refused to view capital as productive (only labor is, but much more so when armed with capital), he defined profit as an always somewhat arbitrary portion of wages designated as a return to capital. In agriculture the profit of a tenant is an unspecifiable portion of his wages attributed to the tools he brings to the production; the profit of the landlord is an unspecifiable portion of what he calls rent attributed to improvements to the land. In proprietary America, where the landlord was usually the tenant, even rents and wages remained practically indistinguishable. But Raymond granted that undue rents, based usually on a very distorted distribution of land ownership, threatened the one prime essential of national prosperity—high wages.[25]

Raymond desired a balanced as well as a growing economy. He accepted the rough, conventional classification of labor into three sectors—agriculture, commerce, and manufacturing—but also insisted that the three sectors made up one unified economic system. He believed it was silly, outside some specified context, to give priority to one sector over another (as silly, he said, as a farmer preferring sowing over reaping), and constantly berated the Physiocrats for favoring agriculture and mercantilists for favoring commerce. Yet he made several necessary concessions to agriculture. The earth is the source of all that is consumed. Thus, agriculture in its broadest sense is most basic in point of time, for raw produce is the prime necessity for life and the minimal foundation for any commerce or manufacturing. Even in a sophisticated and balanced economy, agriculture continues to provide most of the necessities of life, even as manufacturing provides most of the comforts and luxuries. Both sectors provide opportunities for technological advance. Agriculture ordinarily requires less skill and pays lower wages than commerce and manufacturing. But agricultural labor has compensating advantages. Raymond conceded that farmers, in contrast with merchants and mechanics, made up a superior class of men—superior in vigorous health, personal character, and in more "elevated and liberal minds." It is more congenial to man's nature to labor in fields, breathe pure air, and admire the works of creation and the beauties of nature, than to be confined to the unwholesome and impure air of a workshop. Farming "softens the heart and liberalizes the mind," while the workshop "hardens the heart, contracts the mind, and corrupts the passions."[26]

Such agricultural preferences never weakened Raymond's prescription of economic balance. For the welfare of the whole country, many Americans would have to travel the forest trails or the treacherous oceans or toil in a workshop or countinghouse. A balancing of sectors was necessary for the highest forms of civilization, which require exotic foods from distant climes, the luxuries of manufacturing, and the refinement of the arts and sciences. Localized agriculture by itself permits few of these refinements and luxuries. But, in theory, any one nation might channel all or most of its labor into its most profitable sector, just as English conditions favored manufacturing and trade to the detriment of agriculture. Which sector is more profitable depends on local circumstances and world markets. Raymond would probably have conceded to Taylor that America was best placed for efficient agricultural production. But such arguments did not persuade him to support an unbalanced economy. The insecurities of international trade, the threat of war and foreclosed markets dictated balance and domestic self-sufficiency. A nation should, for the good of the whole, often prevent individuals from pursuing what would be, for them, the most profitable line of activity. In the American context of 1820, this suggested public support for manufacturing, our most neglected and underdeveloped sector. For England, it dictated special aid for a lagging agriculture. It is manufacturing (at home or abroad) that provides new tools and a growing market for agriculture. In the long run American farmers would profit from thriving domestic manufacturers: Raymond did not oppose foreign trade but wanted no vital national dependence upon it, although the dependence was more threatening for a manufacturing country like England than for an agricultural country like the United States, where people could at least eat during a curtailment of trade.[27]

Commerce is the handmaiden of consumption, which in turn is the stimulus for production. Internally, trade has to keep pace with production and consumption. Raymond wanted federal support for the internal improvements necessary to develop a national market. But his desire for national self-sufficiency did not mean that he advocated trade surpluses or a favorable balance of trade. England had indeed become prosperous through the exploitation of international monopolies and the commercial development of her colonies, but in the very process had also become exceedingly vulnerable to international instability and a drop in foreign markets. She continually faced the dismal prospect of a glut in export items, a domestic depression, and massive unemployment. Trade balances did not help in such situations, and certainly an accumulation of gold or of international credits did not help. Raymond believed that a young country might have an unfavorable annual balance of trade for many years and still grow continuously in national wealth. In the United States, the trade balance was usually negative, for Americans continued to buy more abroad than they sold. But because of rapid growth, these annual deficits reflected little more than the ability of Americans to buy more foreign products on credit with each passing year. Even though the total of our foreign debts increased every year, our foreign debts expressed as a percentage of our national product did not increase. In one sense, such debts only reflected a wise use of credit to sustain growth. But by 1840, Raymond had become much more apprehensive about trade imbalances, and by then he advocated governmental policies to curtail credit-based imports. In particular, he favored a rigid regulation of private banks.[28]

Raymond obviously supported an expanded economic role for the federal government. Because of some of his policy preferences, particularly on internal improvements and a protective tariff, he later became an acknowledged ally of Henry Clay's American System and an intellectual pillar of the emerging Whig Party. But, as always, party politics involved too many intellectual compromises, reflected too many competing interests, for any detailed parallels between abstract theories and campaign platforms. In several areas, Raymond's views and prescriptions came closer to the avowed theories of the Jacksonians, although it is very difficult to characterize either Jacksonians or Whigs by clear policy profiles. Raymond was most alien to the Jacksonians in his advocacy of a positive state, in his incessant ridicule of laissez-faire, and in his aggressive nationalist and anti-state posture. At least at the time he first wrote his text, he agreed with the professed doctrines of Jacksonians on the evils of banks of issue, on the dangers of internal monopolies and chartered corporations, on the need for a wide distribution of property, and in his avowed commitment to the welfare of the working classes and in a clear antipathy to great wealth.

Raymond believed that extreme governmental restraint was an abdication of responsibility. In some cases, of course, a government rightly chooses inaction, but it *does choose*. Only no government at all would leave men solely to their own devices. The problem of government is not so much when to legislate as how. Wise laws are the problem. A government should pass and enforce all laws that promote national wealth, however much such laws restrict individual enterprise or profits. Raymond simply refused to set any theoretical limits to the degree of permissible government economic regulation or intervention. This openness to government action did not mean any insensitivity to individual rights. Raymond celebrated natural rights more than most economists in the nineteenth century. His acceptance of detailed government regulation was simply a corollary of his conception of all private property as an abridgment of natural rights. His focus was alway on the interests of the whole community, and on the vulnerable men of no property or small property who most suffered the penalties of exclusive and limited possession. Thus, it was the moral imperatives of natural justice that made detailed regulation necessary and which in extreme circumstances necessitated complete dispossession (he assumed fair compensation in ordinary cases). After all, society allows exclusive ownership for social ends.

This exclusivity is integral to existing economic arrangements, and therefore the society has a standing right, even an obligation, to make whatever modifications in conventional property arrangements it deems desirable.[29]

Raymond illustrated the practical implications of his theories on four issues that had provoked John Taylor and that figured prominently in the political debates of the Jacksonian era: government finances and debts, protective tariffs, banking and monetary policies, and monopolies and corporate privilege. With almost gleeful contempt for the conventional wisdom of his day, Raymond endorsed many of the consequences of governmental borrowing and long-term debt funding. When it creates debt, a government creates obligations that may serve as a needed circulating medium, even as they provide a safe investment for women, children, and others not able to manage property to advantage. The key issue in government indebtedness is the use made of borrowed funds. Borrowing for necessary military expenditures or to support education or internal improvements usually stimulates new economic activity without any dire consequences. Additional government spending puts men to work and speeds the circulation of money. Even the wisest governmental borrowing bestows on private creditors a draft on the future industry of a people, but a draft that may fall lightly on the people if it has in the meantime stimulated rapid economic growth. The growth can easily outweigh the interest costs, and leave even the most severely taxed individuals better off in the long run. Carefully chosen government debts illustrate a rare example of government policies that at one and the same time help enrich private creditors and still augment national wealth. Everyone gains. In certain contexts, Raymond recommended deliberate government borrowing, not so much to meet obligations as to provide a needed economic stimulant. He suggested the multiplying effects both of government spending and subsequent debt retirement (one dollar in debt payment by the government may help retire a hundred or thousand dollars' worth of private debts as it circulates from one person to another.)[30]

Raymond stressed that government expenditures are simply part of the total expenditures of a nation. They represent an alternate way of consuming, not some subtraction from national wealth. If government expenditures help create productive resources, it is absurd to talk of a national debt as a burden on posterity, for children inherit and use these resources even as they help pay for them. A government that borrows mainly from its own citizens (this analysis may not apply to debts owed to foreign governments) threatens national wealth only when it so uses its funds as to lower the total quantity of labor. Generally, Raymond acknowledged that it is better (economically more stimulating) for individuals to spend the returns of their own labor without detouring the expenditure through government. But only the empirical context can rightly apportion spending between individuals and governments.

To illustrate his heretical views, Raymond used hypothetical examples. A government may not only spend more than its tax revenue year after year, but may compile a national debt equal to all property in the country and which requires the full annual product in taxes to maintain its interest (this is the absolute limit of debt) without a necessary drop in national wealth and living standards. The same people who paid all their earnings in taxes could, in theory, hold the government debt and receive their taxes back again in interest or dividends. Even this ultimate debt does not, of necessity, curtail industry and reduce the total annual product. It only "alters the channels of circulation, and changes the mode of distributing the annual product of labor to consumers."[31] Such a complete debt would effectively collectivize all productive property (taxes take all the profits, rendering property of no value) and make all former landlords and capitalists public tenants. It meant a form of socialism. Taxes paid by individuals are a loss to them, but not necessarily to the whole community. It is at least conceivable, in certain cultural contexts, that a government will consume its tax income or borrowed income in a manner more conducive to capital growth and enlarged employment opportunities than would individuals. The lesson of all this is that the rate of taxes or of borrowing is never, in itself, a sure clue to the health of a national economy. High taxes to support needed government services, or borrowing to stimulate an active economy, are in line with all other wise uses of income. Again, the real issue is how fairly a government gains its funds and how wisely it uses them.[32]

And here Raymond's fears almost matched those of Adam Smith and John Taylor. Even when government taxing or borrowing increases the sum of national wealth, it still almost inevitably redistributes incomes and property. It takes from some and gives to others. Such redistributive effects offer an opportunity for a fairer and more just apportionment of national wealth, but in fact usually mean a less fair distribution. Fiscal policies in England had helped concentrate property in fewer hands and leave millions impoverished. England's large debts were evidence that rapid economic growth and large debts could accompany each other, but Raymond did not want the distributive injustices that went with England's large debts, for such injustices would impede continued growth. Even in America we needed some shifts in relative wealth, such as from agriculture to manufacturing, but even the wisest redistribution would invite warring private interests and political instability, as tariff battles already indicated. High taxes are expensive to collect and always vex citizens. Too many debt instruments may circulate and bring all the abuses possible with paper money. Privileged elites may use political tactics to manipulate the returns on government securities. Finally, debts and high taxes provide a perfect opening for political demagogues.

But all these hazards pale beside the probability of a less and less equal division of property, or of a monied oligarchy supported by government funding. Here Raymond agreed with Taylor. Those citizens who own the national debt have an interest in all the property and industry of a country, with almost no risk and no responsibility for laboring on or managing this unique form of property. Their debt paper diminishes the profits and value of all the land in a country, not only because of the taxes levied to pay the dividends but because government securities divert investment funds from land, thus depressing land prices. Landowners tend to suffer most from large public debts, a suffering justified only by compensatory gains for the whole nation. In actual fact, only the wealthy are able to buy debt paper. Funding thus facilitates their accumulation of more and more property. Raymond believed the Treasury of England had become "The Strong Box of the monied men of the nation. . . ."[33] with the government an obliging broker. The working class received little but grief from the debt system and from the idle wealthy class that profited from it.[34]

A fair tax system is only a partial safeguard against those hazards. Raymond wanted taxes based on wealth and ability to pay. He felt that duties on imports were an ideal tax, for they largely penalized the consumption of luxuries. Because of problems of assessment and apportionment, he ranked property taxes below selective excises, such as those on whiskey. As a good Puritan, he wanted taxes to function not only as a source of revenue but as a technique to channel private consumption into moral or socially beneficial areas.[35]

Raymond defended a protective tariff, although again with careful qualification. For the United States, selective protection could achieve two desirable goals: competitive advantages for Americans over foreigners, and a direct stimulus to additional economic activity. Good tariffs represented a form of limited monopoly but with all the penalties assessed against foreign producers. Whether there should be protective duties, on what products, and how high are not questions for a political economist. Answers here always depend on variable circumstances and national goals. If a government has reason to believe that protective duties will serve national goals, such as increasing national wealth, then that government should enact such tariffs with little regard for their detrimental economic effect on private individuals or on a particular industry or section of the country. Public interest, not private profit, should always determine policy. A nation is like an army. The goal of the whole army governs the deployment of units and the disproportionate sacrifice required of each. A part can enjoy only the degree of self-direction consistent with the interests of the whole. Government is oppressive only when it circumscribes such nonthreatening liberty, or when it fails to assess responsibilities and sacrifices as fairly as conditions allow.[36]

The justified end of a protective tariff is not a favorable balance of trade or the accumulation of gold or credits. Here Adam Smith and other free trade advocates were correct. Protection is justified only when it stimulates economic growth by adding new laborers to the work force, or when it redirects labor toward national military or diplomatic goals. Generally, if all American laborers were fully and profitably engaged in productive tasks, the United States should buy cheap luxuries from abroad. But if American workers were either idle or inefficiently employed, then the nation could profit from tariff restrictions even when the resulting American production was inefficient compared to foreign sources. This remained true even when such duties hurt one class of laborers to benefit another. The loss of export markets and profits for certain farmers would probably not match the addition to total production made by newly protected artisans.[37] This position was in line with Raymond's willingness to back even wasteful expenditures if this was necessary to employ heretofore idle people, and thus add to the total store of production without diminishing the sum of labor in other areas. In all his calculations, Raymond always made increased labor a positive value. A work ethic of some type ruled his assessments. He never once suggested that labor, beyond a certain point, is drudgery, or that inefficient labor devoted to comforts and luxuries might not be worth all the effort. He revealed no concern for the values of leisure, no recognition that economic growth may, in some contexts, be a lesser value than less work and less consumption. He believed that work was good for people, and thus to an extent an end in itself.

Raymond disagreed with Taylor and other free trade advocates, not so much in moral goals, as in his evaluation of the exact effect of tariff laws. He believed that future economic expansion in America would have to be in manufacturing (not necessarily in large factories, which Raymond rarely acknowledged or anticipated). A great advocate of agricultural technology, he foresaw a redundant labor supply in rural America and no domestic or foreign market large enough to absorb our potential production of food and fibers. A free trade policy amounted to a growing subsidy to existing landlords, for it steadily increased the value of land (a socially vested privilege), but threatened to squeeze more and more men from the economic system. These unemployed or underemployed men, with their low living standards, needed protection in order to develop new lines of economic endeavor. The nation needed their skills and their labor. His goals in political economy—more labor expended, more production, ever higher consumption—seemed inconsistent in America with free trade and a continued reliance on the economic advantages we enjoyed in agriculture. He conjoined tariff support with a frank demand for interim sacrifices by certain farmers, such as staple growers in the South, in aid of American mechanics, who needed more work, higher wages, and a higher level of consumption. When they could achieve this without protection, so much the better. Usually they required protection to launch new industries, and it was in the national interest to provide them a public subsidy.

High tariffs might mean temporarily lower returns for farmers but, unlike Taylor, Raymond never anticipated any shift of labor away from agriculture or any decline in agricultural production. The loss would be suffered only by individuals, not by the nation. And the economic growth that lay ahead would again minimize all the sacrifices. Everyone would eventually gain, although not to an equal extent.[38] Note that Raymond advocated tariffs as an aid to laborers or mechanics, not to financiers or speculators. He disliked both, even as he constantly applauded communal over against purely acquisitive goals. He seemed to expect American manufacturing to continue in the hands of individual craftsmen or in small cooperative shops. Even the word *profit* bothered him because of its selfish, individual connotation.[39]

Another apparent casualty of protective tariffs is the consumer. Raymond admitted the obvious: Tariffs do briefly raise consumer costs, with greatest impact on the poor. Every consumer helps pay the subsidy to new industry. But the costs are much less than generally assumed, and the benefits easily outweigh them. By protecting the home market, tariffs prevent foreign dumping and help stabilize demand and prices. Those farmers and manufacturers producing for a home market can more easily calculate demand and thus avoid gluts and depressions. Even work habits improve with the resulting stable employment. The incentives for home production create a demand for new skills, for new arts and sciences, for new inventions. In a later, more polemical defense of protective tariffs, Raymond even tried to minimize their effect upon consumers. Tariffs never for long add their full rate to domestic prices. A tariff of 25 percent on felt hats will mean a temporary increase in consumer prices of something close to that amount, provided all felt hats have been imported. But decreased demand, or altered consumer habits, will create a glut on the international market and force lowered retail prices. In this way, most of the cost of a tariff can be passed to the foreign producer. Since the growing domestic production also adds to the total international supply, the very growth of home production further helps drive down prices to consumers. Lower prices quickly reduce the amount of subsidy involved in tariffs. The real benefit to domestic manufacturers is a protected market, not high profits. In time, domestic prices will move lower than when the tariff was first applied. Meanwhile, a prosperous and efficient native industry has developed, with small cost to consumers or to other American producers.[40]

On the complex banking issue, Raymond used aggressive nationalist arguments to espouse goals quite similar to those of many later Jacksonians. He wanted strict federal controls over the supply of money, and damned the evils of chartered private banks as they functioned in America. Raymond restricted the term *money* to a legally certified standard of value, and refused to assign it to those forms of credit that also make up part of the circulating medium. They have no intrinsic value and thus only represent or "stand in for" a real standard. In actual fact, by long accepted and near universal consensus, gold and silver alone served as money in civilized countries. Money facilitated property transfers and allowed the easy fulfillment of contracts. For a private person, the accumulation of money meant wealth. At the national level, the mere accumulation of money was a sure sign of impending economic stagnation. Sufficiency and use are the proper monetary guidelines for a nation. A country needs a supply of money proportioned to its property and level of economic activity. But the amount of coined gold and silver is no more important than the rate of circulation. Consistent with his emphasis upon growth, Raymond usually emphasized policies to speed circulation, not to increase monetary supplies.[41]

Credit instruments, when negotiable and accepted in place of money, add to the volume of circulating medium and are much more convenient than coins in large transactions. When under direct governmental control, Raymond approved such paper issues. In certain contexts, he agreed with Adam Smith that such issues actually stimulate economic activity. But he feared large issues, for they drive specie from the country and produce wide fluctuations in prices. They inflate prices and hurt creditors, while a return to stable values penalizes debtors. Consumers often suffer unfairly, even as the value of contracts erodes. Raymond wanted only fully redeemable government issues. In line with his overall theories, he might have endorsed even deliberately inflationary paper issues during a depression or whenever prices moved rapidly downward. Then paper could help stabilized prices and stimulate economic activity. But he never made this type of analysis.[42]

Whether hard money or soft, Raymond insisted that the federal government provide it and control it. State-chartered banks horrified him with their irresponsible note issues. They assumed a governmental prerogative and usually botched it. Bank notes, at least beyond the value of bank capital, amounted to a private right of coinage and led to higher

prices and the defrauding of innocents. The private banks had left the
federal government with only a shell of its monetary prerogatives and
with little means to maintain stability in money supply and in prices.[43]

Raymond defined four functions of banks: a place of deposit, a discount office (bank not original creditor), a loan office (bank as original
creditor), and a source of circulating bank notes. Raymond found the first
two in all ways beneficial. People need a safe depository for their savings,
and the discount function is almost indispensable for commercial transactions (discounting enables a merchant to procure usable funds in place of
his bills of exchange, and thus finance new endeavors even as he awaits
final payment on past shipments). In Europe, private banks without
special charter privileges fulfilled these two functions, but in America
there was not enough available private wealth to subscribe such bank
stock. The special privileges bestowed by charters seemed to be a necessary inducement for such investment, at least outside a few large cities.[44]

Private borrowing may or may not be in the public interest. Need,
prospective use, and cumulative effect all help determine this. Private
banks, according to Raymond, did not make this determination, but
loaned all they could in hopes of maximizing profit. Here again he
expressed his aversion to any private profits that did not support communal goals. Some private loans further only the private goals of lenders
and borrowers, and frustrate national goals (as in loans to pay for vices).
Thus, the opportunities for credit needed careful social discipline, or
what private banks never supplied. Banks often loaned up to ten times the
amount of specie they held, and by such an expansion of credit underwrote a socially harmful speculative boom. Bank owners then grew rich
on profits that were inimical to the national interest, for the boom hurt
creditors and the inevitable collapse destroyed debtors. Raymond
wanted a more disciplined and responsible source of private credit to
replace profit-motivated banks that operated outside social controls.[45]

In 1820 note issues represented the normal form of bank loans.
Raymond accepted the whole spectrum of antinote arguments already
well summarized by Taylor. He stressed that chartered banks had the
exclusive right of charging interest, rather than paying it, on their own
credit instruments, and that they also charged usurious rates. Unlike
laissez-faire economists, he desired a rigid regulation of interest rates. As
in other areas, he believed private profit seekers should never be allowed
to capitalize on human weakness or interim shifts in demand. He could
find no public benefit in high-interest returns to private creditors, and at
least by implication supported direct controls over access to credit. He
was not friendly to the speculative possibilities of easy credit, and saw
enough human weaknesses to believe easy credit an evil temptation to
many. In effect, bank owners invested a very limited amount of capital,

and then by the magic of bank note issues (a chartered privilege) loaned several times as much in the form of bank credit and at legal rates. This meant a usurious return on invested capital, for their dividends often exceeded the legal rate of interest by several times. Everyone who held money assets paid the usury through price inflation. Even the legal rate of interest (usually 6 percent) was unfairly high for many types of loans. The risk on a mortgage was minimal. For such loans, a fair interest would be the rent value of the property, or what was usually well below bank rates. The fact that borrowers were willing to pay interest rates well above rents proved, to Raymond, that banks catered to speculative motives and thus helped create a selfish and morally insufferable approach to economic issues: Get as many profits as you can.[46]

Raymond offered a hard prescription for banking problems. He wanted to use laws to separate deposit and discount banking from loans and issue. If the government chose not to hold specie and issue all notes (this Raymond preferred), he recommended a careful governmental licensing of all banks of issue along with rigid reserve requirements. Another alternative was an excess profits tax to limit returns on bank investments to the legal interest rate, and thus remove all profit incentives for wild credit expansion.[47]

Even monopolies did not elicit from Raymond the absolute condemnation expected in America. He defended public monopolies in foreign trade and recognized the tariff as a partial monopoly. In defiance of all the hallowed myths of the American Revolution, Raymond even defended foreign colonies under restrictive trade regulations, so long as such colonial policies led to an increase in national wealth for the nation as a whole. He saw a colony much as he saw regions or individuals—part of a larger whole and under obligation to serve the larger interest whatever the sacrifice. Colonists, no more than individuals at home, have any moral right to view public issues from the vulgar perspective of local interest.[48]

But Raymond conceded that private monopolies within a nation almost always diminished national wealth. They usually epitomized the selfishness he deplored. The exceptions to this rule were patents and copyrights, which are necessary to stimulate new techniques or knowledge essential to the future wealth of a country. In all other cases, private monopolies are unjust and oppressive, with unearned rewards for the few, economic deprivation for the many, and a lower level of economic activity as a consequence of growing inequities in the distribution of wealth and the decreased demand for goods.[49]

In America, Raymond believed most forms of chartered corporations illustrated all the evils of private monopoly. Much like Taylor, he traced the medieval origins of the corporation, and still applauded its political uses (as in the revered towns of his boyhood New England). But in the first three editions of his treatise he condemned money corporations (limited liability, privately owned corporations dedicated to profit, including banks, insurance, road, and trading companies), for these existed to enrich members through artificial privileges while they only incidentally provided public benefits. The very object of such incorporation was the acquisition of unequal rights and, with them, greater inequities in the distribution of property.[50]

He argued that, "*prima facie*,. . . all money corporations are detrimental to national wealth. They are always created for the benefit of the rich, and never the poor," who have no money to invest.[51] The rich use incorporation to pool their already ascendent wealth. They thus best unchartered competitors, escape the personal liability assumed by private citizens, and inevitably contribute to a more and more unequal division of property. Incorporated banks can grow until they have enormous economic power over individuals, or become arbiters of national economic activity. As so often, Raymond used theories about property distribution and sustained demand to uphold ethical norms. He did not deny the greater productive potential of pooled capital under the relative safety of a corporate charter, but saw the long range distortions in distribution as more than offsetting the short term boost to production based on economies of scale.[52]

By 1840 Raymond had considerably revised his opinion of corporations. He then distinguished between public and private corporations. By public, he did not mean government ownership but rather private firms that received special privileges for effecting needed public services. Such public corporations received either special and exclusive franchises, as in the case of canals, railroads, and water and gas companies, or assumed governmental roles, as in the case of the virtual right of coinage assumed by note-issuing banks. Raymond continued to lambaste all the inherent abuses of such corporations, and for those few deemed absolutely necessary he advocated limited term, strictly qualified charters joined with continuous government supervision. On the other hand, he endorsed private corporations, a category that he had not even identified in his early editions. Such private, competitive firms, which usually engaged in needed manufacturing, received no special franchises but only the right to pool capital under advantageous circumstances, and thus to avoid the many legal entanglements of partnerships. Raymond saw such a right of incorporation, including limited liability, as a convenience to small investors and a benefit to the public. Such competitive firms might be indefinitely multiplied without public danger, at least so long as governments protected investors against stock jobbers. Even here Raymond feared the speculative mentality, the thirst for riches, and thus favored detailed government regulation, including charter provisions requiring annual reports and full public disclosure. He admitted that, up to 1840, most state-granted charters had failed to protect the public interest and had sanctioned selfish, speculative, and even criminal behavior.[53]

Here, as in all policy areas, Raymond sought a responsible national community, without extremes of wealth and poverty, and with economic policy always predicated on communal needs. He was particularly sensitive to the plight of the poor and to the needs of the mass of working people. He most feared a rampant speculative madness, or a vulgar enshrinement of private profits as the appropriate motive for individual effort. The government should be the patron of the industrious common people, a shield against the strategies of aggressive, wealth-seeking individuals. It should restrain private greed, particularly at the top, and stimulate industry and innovation among those who work. These commitments helped define his attitudes toward slavery.

Raymond began his public advocacy with an 1819 pamphlet on the Missouri issue. Then, as in his subsequent treatise on political economy, he eschewed moral and sentimental posturing in behalf of what he believed to be demonstrable economic and demographic truths. Writing from Baltimore, he tried to persuade both northerners and southerners that gradual manumission was in their own best, long-term interests. But such a practical appeal did not disguise Raymond's own repugnance at slavery, which he described as the greatest evil and curse of America, or as a poisonous plant of vigorous and rapid growth, devouring all in its path and slowly blasting away at the tree of liberty. He described the slave trade as the most atrocious of crimes against God and man. It violated the law of God written upon every heart.[54]

For Raymond, the long-range economic and demographic effects of slavery far outweighed its immediate harshness for Negroes. God, the moral governor of the universe, was wreaking horrible vengeance on the oppressors of blacks. Because of slavery, a naturally favored Southland was much worse off than a less favored New England. The South already exhibited the horrible accounting—a diminished white population, depleted fields, imperfect cultivation, idle and dissipated habits, and moral degradation. Still, slavery was profitable for owners, another example of how individual profits often opposed communal good.

The explanation of slavery's dire effects lay in what Raymond called the "science of population." He believed human reproduction rates depended, first of all, upon economic opportunity, and particularly upon the availability of basic subsistence. Here, at least, were the limits. In a richly favored and largely proprietary America, the natural increase for whites in the free states came close to the geometrical ratios emphasized by Malthus, or a doubling of the population every generation. Not so in the slave states, where the white increase was retarded by up to one-half, either as a direct or an indirect effect of slavery. The opposite applied to blacks. Free blacks in the North increased at only half the white rate, but in the South and under slavery blacks increased at near the rate of northern whites. These demographic patterns, which Raymond derived from a questionable comparison and interpretation of the censuses of 1790 and 1810 (he needed more firm data on both immigration and internal migration), supported both his evaluation of the long-term effects of slavery and his proposed solution to the problem.[55]

It was not hard to determine why slavery retarded white and advanced black fertility. Wealthy landowners generally provided ample subsistence for slaves and also encouraged their reproduction. Every expansion of slavery to the west, such as that contemplated in Missouri, created new demands for slaves, raised their value, encouraged better food and care for such prized possessions, and thus helped insure a greater natural increase. Negroes would eventually outnumber, even drastically outnumber, whites in all slave states. This promised an eventual and terrible reckoning, an exploding volcano of revolt and revenge against whites. Already, slave codes were becoming harsher. Meanwhile, the white yeomen of the South languished without economic opportunity. They had few job opportunities and suffered from the stigma placed on white labor. Either their impoverishment, or rational choice, discouraged marriage and children. In addition, an inefficient slave-labor system insured less overall growth for the South, and less potential population growth for the whole society, or a limit that applied to the whites and not to blacks. Thus, with each passing year the ratio of blacks to whites inevitably increased. But in the North the free Negroes occupied the place of the poor whites in the South. There they made up a degraded and suffering class with few economic opportunities. Raymond believed political discrimination and intense racial antipathy sufficient to explain their fate. He never mentioned any racial inferiority and seemingly did not believe in it.

The policy implications of Raymond's demographic argument were quite clear. Federal and state governments should do everything possible to discourage the further expansion of slavery, for expansion could only lead to an increased number and higher ratios of blacks in America. He wrote his pamphlet to point out all the horrors entailed in the admission of new slave states. At the same time, he urged governments to do everything possible to encourage the gradual and voluntary manumission of slaves. Raymond envisioned public approval and religious sanctions in favor of manumission, wanted the repeal of all laws against it, and opposed all laws that favored slavery, such as fugitive slave codes. He favored colonization in Africa or in the Caribbean, was himself a member of the American Colonization Society, but believed such a humane effort could absorb only a tiny portion of the annual natural increase of blacks in America. Only if manumission slowed the natural increase of blacks could colonization ever absorb the increase even in the distant future. But manumission even without colonization shifted blacks from a favorable to a very unfavorable demographic position. With manumission, the ratio of blacks would begin a downward pattern and thus preclude the horrible accounting in a distant future.

In a sense, Raymond offered a cruel solution tied to the prejudice directed against blacks even in the North. He admitted the social burden of free blacks; many were idle vagabonds, living by theft. But such blacks rarely raised families. Some free blacks imitated the best habits of whites and became provident. These successfully reared children, but they posed no threat. They were good citizens. Raymond thus left an opening for those favored blacks who could still win in an unfair competition, and never doubted that freedom was preferable to slavery despite all the odds against black success in the free world. Yet, in his polemical tract, Raymond never condemned existing white attitudes toward blacks and made his whole demographic solution dependent upon such attitudes. He did insist that blacks were in America because of acts by whites, and argued that they had as much right to remain as whites. Presumably, he felt that those free blacks who survived and assumed white mores would gain full acceptance and full equality.[56]

Slavery illustrated all Raymond's views toward public policy. Southerners, in appealing to the rights of property in defense of slavery, and in trying to expand slavery and thus increase the value of their investment, dramatically illustrated the hypocrisy of bending the moral certainties of natural rights to cover contextual and conventional human institutions. Slave owners clearly held their slaves by leave of the positive laws of a state, laws that deprived blacks of their natural rights. Policy, not nature or God, underwrote slavery, and it was policy that had to change or God would wreak his horrible vengeance on America. Here, as everywhere else, the laws should operate in favor of the enduring interests of the whole community and not so as to favor any individual or group within it. Slave owners would have to suffer losses, at least of short-term profits, but the whole nation would gain by their loss. Typically Raymond once again moved from a broad and even radical principle to moderate proposals. He wanted to end slavery over the centuries, not immediately, and to do it by the gradual withdrawal of legal favors, not by an abrupt implementation of new policies.

PART THREE

—

TECHNICIANS

V

Ricardo Domesticated

IN America, as in Britain, Ricardo's abstract system quickly became an accepted point of departure for economists, both in treatises and in college courses. Not that Ricardo won many slavish American disciples. American conditions suggested needed qualifications or supplements to even his most fervent admirers. Yet Ricardo's influence was so strong (reinforced as it was by John R. McCulloch's diligent explication and the later approval of John Stuart Mill) that no major American political economist until Henry C. Carey followed the original paths explored by Daniel Raymond. The ablest American economist tried either to fit the whole body of Ricardian principles to American realities or to amend and revise those principles in ways that only illustrated how much they remained within the same analytic tradition.

Ricardo published his *Principles* in 1817. A wealthy New York admirer subsidized the publication of an American edition in 1819, just at the time when American colleges and universities began to offer courses in political economy. Ricardo's ill-written *Principles* was not easy fare for laymen nor was it at all suitable as a college text. Most Americans first encountered the Ricardian system through the writings of a glib disciple, McCulloch. In 1823, McCulloch published a long, readable article on political economy in the *Encyclopedia Britannica*. That article turned out to be the first version of a textbook that McCulloch constantly revised and expanded. In New York, John McVickar, who was a part-time minister, a professor of moral philosophy at Columbia University, and man of high social and business standing, republished the article as a small, heavily annotated book, *Outlines of Political Economy* (1825). Even though

McCulloch stereotyped or oversimplified some Ricardian doctrines, his essay was much more than an abstract of Ricardo's *Principles*. He included an excellent history of political economy, which not only dealt with the mercantilists and Physiocrats but also recognized the neglected British forerunners of Adam Smith. And McVickar did more than copy McCulloch. He used introduction and notes to take exception to several Ricardian arguments, or to their use by McCulloch, and proved himself a quite balanced and eclectic student of political economy. He also added a brief section on political economy in America, with deserved compliments for Benjamin Franklin and Alexander Hamilton. He ignored John Taylor and only acknowledged Daniel Raymond in a final note in which he contemptuously dismissed Raymond's pioneering treatise as being diametrically opposed to all the principles of Smith and Ricardo.[1]

Even as his master died and a cult of followers developed in Britain, McCulloch helped establish a Ricardian canon. This included some key doctrines, the law of rent being the most central and most distinctive, but also the one most often challenged by Americans. All Ricardians paid lip service to a second doctrine—a labor theory of exchange value—but McCulloch as well as others usually failed to take into account all Ricardo's careful qualifications. Even McVickar refused to view capital as deposited labor, and on this issue affirmed some of Malthus's views over against those of Ricardo. Ricardians affirmed Say's law, in effect denying any long-term problem of deficient demand. Production creates its own demand. Correlative to this was their insistence that capital accumulation is the mainspring of economic growth. In America, the policy commitments that Ricardo derived from these principles often seemed equally important, particularly his somewhat inconsistent endorsement of private ownership of land, his support for free trade, his belief that taxes almost always threatened capital accumulation, and his horror at any government efforts to control or direct individual economic choices.

McCulloch agreed with the basic assumptions underlying the Ricardian model. These included the old certainties of Adam Smith: that the great body of men possess an inherent desire to acquire goods and rise in the world, and that generally an individual knows better than anyone else what conduces to his own happiness. A free, competitive society is most natural to man, and also most conducive to his happiness. Because of such a firm, allegedly descriptive point of departure, McCulloch argued, with even more pretension than Ricardo, that political economy involved universal principles and thus was in every sense a "science." As such, it could offer reliable guidelines to any government. If any government, anywhere, was to support growing wealth, it had to offer security to individual property, guarantee the enforcement of voluntary contracts, call forth the talent and energy of citizens by allowing them unhampered leeway to engage in any branch of industry they chose, and permit maximum private capital growth by exercising the greatest possible economy in public expenditures.

To McVickar's delight, McCulloch acknowledged the unprecedented prosperity of Americans and attributed this to sound Ricardian policies, to individual economic freedom and low taxes. American institutions fostered the three great stimuli to economic growth: security of property, division of labor, and rapid capital accumulation. But McVickar was morally outraged by one point McCulloch insisted on: that public or national wealth is simply a compound of all individual wealth. Thus, any policy, apart from stealing, that encourages individual accumulation also stimulates the growth of national wealth. The most profitable private use of capital is always in the national interest. Actually, this position is either a trivial truism or a moral absurdity. If wealth is defined quantitatively, as the sum of material objects, then the position is truistic. But as McCulloch used it, he seemed to add a moral certification, to applaud any form and any extent of individual acquisition. McVickar noted that merely speculative trading may enrich one person but only at the expense of another. This not only does not increase the sum of wealth, but may retard the forms of industry that do create additional wealth. More crucial, he believed that some objects of private accumulation are immoral and antisocial, or gained by antisocial means, as for example the individual wealth gained through the slave trade, from gambling, from prostitution, or from the whiskey traffic. Even if such enterprise increases the total of material goods, it still harms a country. McVickar did not offer a final objection—that a simple accumulation theory of national wealth ignores all problems of distribution.[2]

McVickar also demurred at McCulloch's sweeping vindication of factory production. Opponents of a factory system in America could appeal to the great authority of Adam Smith: factories and minute specialization made men into stupid automatons. Not so, said McCulloch. Factory workers were not as dull as farmers. They were informed, enjoyed mutual stimulation from conversation at their work, and developed varied interests outside the shops. Besides, they had no time for dissipation, riot, or excess, and out of physical fatigue, sought their recreation in mental excitements, such as reading newspapers. While McVickar acknowledged the efficiency of heavy manufacturing, he feared its effects and begged for its natural, and not its forced, development in America. He noted the physical and moral evils of factories—workers suffered physical confinement, heat, and impure air; and factory owners employed children for long hours, to the neglect of their intellectual and moral education. Ignorance and vice too often followed. These evils might be correctable through laws or through voluntary association, but he preferred a continuation of morally healthful household manufacturing so long as possible.

On two critical issues—rent and the role of capital accumulation—McVickar fully endorsed McCulloch's views and, by implication, Ricardo's. He ridiculed Malthus's emphasis on demand, and particularly his insane suggestion that governments spend extra money, even wasteful funds, in order to encourage consumption. Production alone creates the power to buy goods, and unlimited human wants assure the will to consume. Then how can gluts be explained? McCulloch denied the possibility of any general glut. A self-correcting imbalance of production (too much of some goods, not enough of others), the result of shifting fashions or disruptive changes in markets brought on by war or the ending of wars, might indeed lead to local gluts or even general gluts within a single country. McVickar denied the possibility of a general glut within America, given our unlimited demand for labor. In any case, both men believed it was absurd to suggest that there could ever be too many goods on the market, although they admitted that there might be the wrong type of goods on the market. The remedy for such imbalances is not legislation, but rational productive shifts by individuals, joined with economy and hard work. Demand, as the correlate of production, suffers from any slowing of capital growth. Thus, the cause of a permanently laggard economy is not overproduction, but underproduction, not a lack of consumption, but too much of the wrong kinds of consumption. That is, wasteful, nonproductive consumption by individuals or greedy governments slows capital accumulation, which inhibits the power of capitalists to put people to work. For example, wasteful indulgence in unneeded servants by the rich diverts funds from potential new factories. Both McVickar and McCulloch assumed that almost all government spending is "unproductive," a rapid using up of wealth, and therefore believed that high taxes are the greatest single threat to capital growth and the greatest single cause of depressions.[4]

McVickar concluded his *Outlines* with a personal sermon, one that was soon typical in American textbooks. Political economy was for the "moral instruction of nations," was to the state what religion was "to the individual," the "preacher of righteousness." What religion condemned as contrary to God's will and subversive of virtue and beauty, political economy proved to be opposed to peace, good order, and permanent prosperity. It showed that moral evils like slavery were also expensive, that tariffs or embargoes were wasteful and extravagant. In political economy, virtue joined self-interest and revealed the harmony of our universe. If the American government could follow the principles of political economy, and McVickar was confident it would, and if the people were religious and virtuous, and he hoped they would be, we would enjoy unending progress.[5]

Only a year after McVickar published his annotated version of McCulloch, Thomas Cooper of South Carolina College published his class lectures on political economy. Although he followed Ricardo in part, and soon gained a reputation as a Ricardian, his book was much too ambivalent and confused to be properly categorized as belonging to any economic school. Although the other great Southern economists—Jacob Cardozo and George Tucker—took Ricardian doctrines as their point of departure, they tried to debunk Ricardo and to refute or revise several of his key doctrines. Both explored very subtle issues; neither wrote usable textbooks. In 1828 Willard Phillips did write a book suitable for use as a textbook, but it was emphatically non-Ricardian and protectionist, almost as heretical to Ricardians as Daniel Raymond's two-volume text. Not until 1835, a decade after McVickar wrote, did an orthodox work suitable for use as a textbook appear; it was written by Samuel P. Newman, a professor at Andover. The *Elements of Political Economy* was eloquent and eclectic, and it deserved a wider audience than it apparently ever gained in its one printing. Newman professed a humble goal—to adapt the principles of political economy, especially the doctrines of the "Father of the Science," Adam Smith, to the "usages and institutions of our own country."[6]

Newman focused on the two issues so critical for both Smith and Ricardo—production and distribution. He wanted to call forth new industry and a greater prosperity in a new nation, and to assure a just distribution of its growing wealth. He deplored class rivalries or sectoral conflict. But unlike McVickar, he doubted that Ricardo, or anyone else, had perfected a *true* system of political economy. So far the new science had no settled doctrines and only a few general principles. Like most other American economists, Newman wanted to mute possible sources of antagonism. He denied the existence of any clear boundaries between sectors. Men never create anything; they simply rearrange or redirect nature in behalf of human needs. They do this in all sectors, with agriculture only first in the line of intentional changes. Although he acknowledged a distinction between productive and unproductive labor, Newman wanted no pejorative meaning to attach to unproductive. He assumed security for private property, but denied that it was within the compass of political economy to justify private rights to property. He granted the special status of unimproved land, which does not result from human labor, but argued that unequal, state-granted titles to such land encouraged care and hard work, even as they catered to selfish principles in man.[7]

On most issues, Newman relied on Smith. Thus, he celebrated the specialization of labor, acknowledged a near-instinct to barter, and usually endorsed economic freedom for individuals and free trade between nations. He decried wage laws, chartered companies, detailed licenses and regulations (except for the regulation of dangerous medications), and tariffs other than temporary ones to protect new and needed industries or those tied to national defense or diplomatic retaliation. For laborers, he hoped for free education and good wages, which he believed were the best remedies for vicious habits and vice. An advocate of more American manufacturing, and of more and better machines, he at least acknowledged the problems of boring work, lowered morals, and temporary unemployment. Education and public safety laws promised to lessen the moral evils, while a gradual introduction of new machines would prevent unemployment. In extreme circumstances, he approved of poor laws and workhouses as humane necessities.[8]

On most technical issues raised by Ricardo, Newman took refuge in generality. He recognized a natural price level based on the cost of production, and believed that supply and demand caused prices to oscillate around this. He also accepted Say's law. But he was unwilling to embrace Ricardo's full rent theory, with its eventual threat of skewed distributive shares. He granted that an active agency in nature often assisted man, as in fermentation or plant growth, and aided him in a quite different sense than did such passive instruments as hoes and plows. Such natural agency allowed a valid distinction between rent and profit. And it was obvious that a rapid increase in population could force man to use parts of nature that offered diminished returns to effort. Yet he was confident that higher costs of production in these industries would be more than offset by better passive machines. Overpopulation was conceivable, but did not seem at all imminent. Where it seemed to exist, the actual evils reflected not too many births but poor institutions. Like so many other American economists, he showed how abstract and contrived Ricardo's law of rent could seem in a young country. Here wages and profits were higher than rents, and workers already collected the fullest share of the national product consistent with continued economic growth. If we could continue to gain more capital and steadily increase our wage fund, then we were assured of economic justice through a "free and natural flow of wealth."[9]

Francis Wayland endorsed most of Newman's views, but circulated them among a much larger audience. Wayland (1796–1865) moved early from the Baptist ministry to a long term as president of Brown University. There he gained some fame as an educational innovator, particularly for endorsing a broader and more flexible curriculum. Like many denominational college presidents, he taught his university's prestigious course in moral philosophy. In 1835 he published his popular text—*Elements of Moral Science*. It went through several editions, eventually selling over 100,000 copies and gaining more adoptions than any of its competitors.

Since political economy constituted a dependent sub-branch of moral philosophy, Wayland typically devoted a section of his textbook to economic issues, and particularly to the foundations of private property. Then, two years later, he expanded this subsection into a separate text with the same title as Newman's: *Elements of Political Economy*. It never equaled its parent in sales or popularity, but probably was as widely circulated in colleges as any rival. No other academic economist had greater personal prestige, and no other comparably placed moral philosopher published an economics text until 1856, when Francis Bowen of Harvard, a Unitarian, issued his *Principles of Political Economy*.[10]

In his moral philosophy, Wayland was a disciple of the great Scottish philosophers, such as Thomas Reid and Dugald Stewart. As a mild Calvinist, he wanted to displace the utilitarian and naturalistic emphasis of William Paley, whose *Moral and Political Philosophy* had long served as a standard text in America. Wayland began with what seemed to him evident from all experience—man has a moral sense or faculty, given him by God. People simply feel certain obligations, find certain experiences good and commendable, totally apart from prudence or self-interest. Man naturally loves harmony, unity, consent. It is his taste for such beauty and for the conduct appropriate to it, and not utility, that provides him standards of moral judgment. Given this innate moral sense and the intellect to understand how things and people relate to each other, a person is a responsible moral agent. This does not assure good behavior, for man's moral sense wars with other impulses and passions, including one's compulsion to indulge in momentary pleasures or to give in to irresponsible self-love. Wayland did not mean that utility is unrelated to moral conduct. But utility is a consequence, not a cause, of moral conduct. A benevolent God has assured that virtuous conduct is coextensive with the greatest possible level of human happiness and communal welfare.

Such a perspective on morality enabled Wayland to define moral philosophy as a legitimate science. All normal people share a common moral sense and have the intelligence needed to understand invariant relationships. The basis of moral growth is esthetic and intellectual improvement. One need only cultivate the moral sense and gain increased knowledge. Such improvement allows an ever fuller apprehension of the laws of God as they pertain to human conduct, since God has informed his creation with invariant standards of beauty and with universal laws. Thus, moral philosophers can stipulate general standards of conduct applicable to mankind as a whole. This does not mean that anyone can stipulate the exact demands of morality in each shifting context, or that moral judgment is automatic or even simple. Some human actions are clearly contrary to our inherent sense of obligation, or clearly based on ignorance or misunderstanding. But others are more ambiguous. The burden of righteous conduct is the ever hazardous application of principles to the complex and shifting realities of the world.[11]

The task of the political economist is the systematic arrangement of those laws of God that pertain to wealth. In his textbook on moral theory Wayland began this arrangement with a careful defense of property rights. Most political economists simply assumed the existence of private property without questioning it, or like Newman, denied that a vindication of such property was within the scope of political economy. But it clearly fell within the province of moral philosophy. Wayland knew he could not simply stipulate private property as one of the built-in conditions of his economic analysis. He therefore argued that a right to property was given by the universal moral faculty. Natural conscience upholds a right of individual ownership, so long as one's possessions do not injure others. The Bible also endorses private property, further proving that it is within the province of God's will. Nothing is more natural, more tied to one's happiness, than the desire to own things, to have a secure use and enjoyment of the products of one's own labor. Nothing is more clear in morality than a universal repugnance to robbery.

Happily, Wayland found, as always, that what is inherently righteous is also supremely utilitarian. The prospects of secure wealth and enjoyable consumption motivate, if not all labor, at least a good share of it, and particularly that most crucial labor directed to agricultural improvements or to the accumulation of new productive tools. Without such a powerful inducement to labor and to save, mankind faces either wretchedness or extinction. Without the beneficial effects of private property, no higher civilization, no arts, no sciences would ever have developed. Wayland followed Locke in his method of determining which forms of possession qualify as morally legitimate property. To the extent only of need and actual use, one has a right to all the free gifts of nature, including the right to use uncultivated and unclaimed land. Beyond that, one has a legitimate claim to all the products of his own labor, or to what he procures by this through exchange. Finally, and more indirectly, one has a right to gifts, inheritances, and even to objects that he claims in the absence of any other identifiable owner (objects found or simply appropriated). Wayland emphasized this final right of appropriation in large part because he so feared any unclaimed or common property. Almost as much as the violation of property rights, common property effectively severs the connection between labor and proportionate rewards and threatens both industry and savings. Any society has a powerful incentive to get all productive resources into private hands. This entails a balancing obligation—to provide everyone an opportunity to gain productive property. Wayland always desired a wide, if not a universal, distribution of property, and often rejoiced that almost everyone in the United States would become a "capitalist."[12]

As a moral philosopher, Wayland also gave more attention to work than did most economists. Since most people have to work to live, a just society must give the fullest opportunity and scope to human labor. It should let everyone work as much as he wants and gain as much wealth as he can. Everyone should be free to enjoy the consumptive returns of labor, except when such enjoyment harms others. Wayland still affirmed an old Calvinist assumption—work, if free and productive, if intelligent and purposeful, is pleasant and fulfilling. Men confined to idleness are miserable. But Wayland rarely distinguished carefully between intrinsic and extrinsic rewards. Often, the appeal of labor seemed mainly to attach to the subsequent consumption it made possible. Only physical need or the hope for luxuries seemed able to spur the most strenuous and unrelenting industry. It was obvious that many people, had they the choice, would not do certain tasks or work as long hours as normally expected of them. Such a reluctance might testify to the demeaning servility that went with types of employment, or show the despair that accompanies abject and hopeless poverty. Then it evidenced evil institutions. But often a propensity for idleness testified only to bad character. In such cases, the highest benevolence involved justice. Those who chose idleness deserved the fullest respect for their choice and the consequences that flow from it. Society should let such people starve. Wayland wanted no poor laws, no redistribution of wealth from the affluent to the poor, for such a welfare system would eventuate in insubordination and class conflict. Those unable to labor deserved charity. Those without work deserved employment. Wayland joined most American economists in backing fully self-supporting work houses.[13]

Given secure property, and thus effective motives for work, the next concern for a society had to be the efficiency of work. Only efficient labor could assure growing wealth. Efficiency depended on a growing supply of raw materials, of fixed improvements and productive tools, of inventories of goods already produced, and of funds to pay for labor. Just as much, it also depends on human inventions, the acquisition of new skills, more specialization of tasks, and an ever more complex network of exchange. Wayland had some of the optimism of Adam Smith. In a normal situation, a society steadily improves in all these areas. It accrues more and more fixed capital, since it has larger and larger surpluses above immediate needs. Wealth steadily increases. Wayland believed himself most original in stressing that the role of intelligence and knowledge and skill is just as important as the accumulation of material capital, and a prelude to it (actually, Say had made the same point). Wayland loved to point out the place of science and invention in agriculture, manufacturing, and commerce. Since such cultural capital does not respond directly to shifts in supply and demand, the early political economists had minimized its role. In a society that encourages invention, Wayland saw no limit to the power of man to labor more and more efficiently. The greatest single clue to American economic growth was continued intellectual improvement, or a position well fitted to a college president. He wanted a subsidized system of elementary schools and government funds for universities and libraries. Only a literate population could be an efficient population (he advocated a literacy test for voting). With needed patent and copyright laws, education would secure continuous innovations in the economy and with this a continuous growth of fixed capital.[14]

Wayland accepted at least a generalized form of Say's law. Any general redundancy of capital was impossible, as was any sustained and general glut of goods. Temporary distortions in the market and periodic business cycles reflected shifts in fashion, production snags, foolish legislation, or sudden inputs of new technology. New machines could create temporary unemployment. They threatened no long-term liabilities. In time, new machines stimulated even more labor and permitted higher levels of consumption. Wayland saw no upper limit to the total human demand for goods and services. Lack of demand could never be a serious economic problem. But unemployed workers suffer in the short run, and for this reason, he recommended that new machines be introduced gradually. Yet he would not countenance laws guiding or slowing technological change. Evidently, suffering victims were to console themselves with the thought that they were sacrificing for the public good; and they could have temporary recourse to public workhouses.[15]

Except for education and patent protection, Wayland wanted no laws directed at increased production. Such laws never worked. They distorted the economy and slowed growth. Capital and labor both had to be free to find their best employment. He granted the need for internal improvement, but preferred government encouragement of private efforts, except in the case of harbor facilities, which would never be built without direct government subsidies. He wanted government-funded experimental farms and factories, but these simply represented an alternative form of education. Americans should reject all monopolies and special privileges, including protective tariffs. Protection only stimulated inefficient industries, transferred capital and labor from efficient industries, cut developed export markets, and penalized consumers by higher prices.[16]

On production, Wayland followed a reasonably clear and precise Ricardian strategy. Not so on distribution. He was too sanguine to embrace the darker Ricardian themes of ultimately exorbitant rents, a bitter conflict between capital and labor, and a final economic stagnation. He accepted a labor theory of value, but found in it a mechanism for continued economic justice. Without careful qualification, Wayland argued that in a free economy labor tends to exchange for an equal amount of labor of the same quality. Long-term, or natural, prices exactly reflect labor costs, including the cost of capital as stored-up labor. Supply and demand, which control momentary prices, also insure that prices will tend to reach their natural level. Given such a labor theory of exchange values, Wayland believed a free market justly and fairly distributed the national product. Labor, the ultimate source of all values, always received its due, however complex the division of labor and the exchange of products. Specialization and much commerce always distinguished a productive, intelligent, and moral people, just as exchange facilitated peace and good will.[17]

In a growing economy, with ever increasing supplies of fixed capital, Wayland believed, wages would grow faster than profits. Efficiency and technology favored workers. In a growth economy, wages would remain far above any natural level in the Ricardian sense. Indeed, a natural minimum wage is that which will sustain the life of a family of four. But a fairer definition of a natural wage is one that will support frugal and industrious parents and all the children that come in the natural course of events. Although shifts in demand determine local and short-term wages, the long-term wage trend is toward equal wages for equal skills. Higher pay for skilled work represents deferred pay for the cost and time involved in learning the skills. In an economy of scarcity or one that is stagnating, with high birth rates, low wages do mean increased mortality. Here Malthus offered only a truism. But in growing economies, such as that of the United States, capital accrues more rapidly than population. Here frugal workers may easily accumulate capital. One possible explanation for our good fortune was our rich, undeveloped resources. Wayland rejected it. Our success largely reflected the literacy and character of Americans, assets that we could retain indefinitely. Our economic opportunities virtually precluded a class system like those in Europe. This deprived us of the luxuries of older societies with great inherited wealth. America offered little encouragement to the fine arts. A very talented painter faced starvation if he emigrated to the United States.[18]

In the American context, profits, as the fair share earned by stored-up labor, could never pose any threat to wages. Profit, as Wayland understood it, sustained the very capital growth that defused the Malthusian threat. Of course, Ricado granted as much if a society could forestall the distorting effects of ever higher rents. To Ricardo, higher rents eventually would reflect food costs so high that wages could not rise above a subsistence level. Then wages would slowly erode profits until saving ceased and growth became impossible. The escape had to be either birth control or a continuous improvement in productivity, particularly in agriculture.

Wayland cleverly evaded the rent issue. He was never vaguer or more general. He noted the factors that determine rent—primarily fertility, location, and relative scarcity, but also beauty and recreational values. Increased scarcity obviously meant higher rents. But Wayland found no great problem with this. He took the typical, almost the universal, American escape: land behaved like any other form of investment capital; the rate of increase in rents usually paralleled the rate of increase in interest on borrowed money. But this did not confront the real Ricardian dilemma. Even if the rate of rent remained low, very high land values would still assure that landowners gained an ever higher proportion of the national income. Presumably, Wayland expected continued capital growth and greater efficiency in agricultural production. These would forestall any natural scarcity.[19]

On monetary and fiscal issues, Wayland remained close to Ricardo. He endorsed a gold and silver currency, for these metals gained their intrinsic values through their cost of production. Given such a reliable and stable standard, he applauded an increased use of credit devices. Sound banks provided needed credit and facilitated private credit transactions. On the controversial issue of bank notes, he offered a balanced evaluation. Forgery and fraud and unwise expansion too often typified American banking practice, but banks of issue created needed credit and helped young men go into business on their own. He preferred many small banks to a few large ones, and believed that special legislative charters supported most of the abuses. He wanted laws that would forbid the issue of small-denomination notes and that would make banks or their stockholders fully liable for all obligations. He did not oppose limited liability corporations, even in banking, provided charters were available to all seekers. Through incorporation, people were able to associate in innocent causes and in behalf of their own greater happiness. Churches and universities demonstrated the value of corporate charters, which in effect created legal persons out of large groups of cooperating people. As much as individuals, they remained subject to all the laws of the land.[20]

For Wayland the one great issue in fiscal policy was taxation. In general he, like Ricardo, feared taxes on the grounds that they usually curtail capital growth. He had the typical American image of exorbitant taxes in European countries, taxes tied to war, imperial adventures, or lavish courts. But when he looked at American realities he lost most of his fears. True, some American taxes went to unproductive areas, for instance, to the military. Soldiers used up ammunition and clothing with no productive returns. But even they remained ready to protect property, and permitted the personal security necessary for confident investment. Other government expenditures, such as for education, directly contributed to capital growth. The critical problem in America was not expropriative taxes, but the less critical one of fairly allocating a still light tax burden. Justice required each person to pay according to services received. Since governments primarily provided protection for property, it was only fair that governments taxed property according to value. But Wayland acknowledged a need for a progressive principle. The poor, including small property owners, deserved tax exemptions. He also deplored taxes on necessities, while he applauded high ones on luxuries. The progressive principle never implied any major assault on wealth. The duty of government was always to encourage large accumulations of capital. The welfare of hundreds often depended upon the wealth of a single millionaire. Leveling taxes represented a war on the poor as much as on the wealthy.[21]

Wayland summarized in an appealing way the economic truisms most generally accepted and approved in America. His was a sanguine, innocuous orthodoxy, with little of the tension and bite of an original Ricardianism. Since he denied any conflict between capital and wages, and made land a form of capital, he tried to remove all the sting from the law of rent. Except for firm opposition to tariffs, he muted his policy recommendations. By transplanting the Ricardian model across the Atlantic, and fitting it to the boundless resources and glorious political institutions of the United States, Wayland converted it into a blueprint for national greatness.

In 1838, a year after Wayland completed his economic text, a more careful and subtle and somber economist—Henry Vethake—published a model textbook. He was consistently Ricardian on all major issues. Vethake immigrated to New York with his parents when only a child. They came from Germany by way of British Guiana, where he was born in 1792. He majored in physical science at Columbia University, studied law, and at twenty-one began a peripatetic academic career. He taught at Columbia, then at Queens College, then at the College of New Jersey, and then at Dickinson College. By this last move in 1821, he had already added political economy to his standard courses in natural science. In 1829 he left Dickinson, studied physics for a year in Germany, and returned to the College of New Jersey, where he again taught a course in political economy. A disappointed supporter of a national university, he helped found New York University in 1832 and taught there. In 1834 he moved to the presidency of Washington College in Maryland, and in 1836 to the University of Pennsylvania, where he eventually served as Vice-President and Provost. By then his interest had shifted almost completely from mathematics and science to moral philosophy and political economy. In 1838 he published the first edition of his text, *The Principles of Political Economy*, which he revised in 1844. Even its title imitated Ricardo. Vethake's book was systematic, balanced, and supremely boring, yet technically sophisticated.[22]

Although moderate in approach, Vethake was personally involved in several controversial public issues and often acted as a reformer. His brother, John, a physician and occasional professor, was a noted founder of the New York Locofocos, and because of his emphatic antimonopolistic position a bit of a political radical by the standards of his day. Vethake generally endorsed Jacksonian policies. But he knew the criterion for an enduring text—celebration of the most conventional beliefs and preferences of his literate audience. What his book lacked in polemical ammunition for extreme Jacksonian partisans on the tariff or on money and banking, it made up in moral fervor. He wrote in order to show the relationship of political economy to morals and religion, as well as to offer politicians objective knowledge. He also wrote in order to show radicals the error of their ways, to restrain the revolutionary or agrarian measures so actively pushed by the ignorant. He hoped the rich would grasp the need for new laws in time to avert violent class conflict. Above all, he hoped the mass of people would realize the cost of violent upheaval, that they would bear existing evils for a time, until reform and greater prosperity forever banished the threat of a horrible revolution. He hoped to reveal the unity of interests in a society, to convince everyone of the vital stake they had in protecting the right of property, to prove that no divergence of interest divided rich and poor. He also wanted to show the irrelevance of partisan politics to most of the evils and blessings of a society, and thus to dissipate illusory hopes of magical economic improvements through new legislation. Likewise, he wanted to prove the interdependence, and the common goals, of all nations. In every way, he insisted that the spirit of political economy, of "our science," was that of "peace and goodwill to all mankind. . . ."[23]

Vethake began with careful and precise definitions, most of which he drew directly from Ricardo. He felt he was most distinct from his master in emphasizing the equivalence of physical and mental labor, and in making skill and types of knowledge a form of capital. This strategy, borrowed from Say, also served his moral concern for lessened class conflict. It allowed him not only to deny that any pejorative connotation attached to the term "unproductive" labor, but also to deny that it had any clear meaning at all. The skill of a poet, a priest, or a physician constituted part of the national wealth, and was as productive of human satisfaction as plows or looms. "Unproductive" was an adjective best applied to consumption, in the sense that we can eat up or use up certain objects with no remnants or returns, even as we use other objects in productive processes. Yet the end of all production is some form of nonproductive consumption, an increase in human satisfaction.[24]

In a much more sophisticated way than had McCulloch, Vethake clarified and extended Ricardo's theory of value. In actual voluntary exchange, as almost everyone conceded, supply and demand determine relative values or, given a stable medium, prices. Vethake properly qualified this by noting that not only changes in supply and demand, but popular expectations about such changes, affect prices. For immaterial goods, such as a physician's skill, price is really wages. This only illustrated in another context the unity of economic phenomena and the similarity between the behavior of prices and wages.[25]

Both prices and wages fluctuate around a fixed point, which is their natural level. Wages vary according to skill and difficulty, but fall into a natural hierarchy. Wages cannot gravitate to their natural level unless supply and demand operate. According to Vethake, these operate only when people reflect self-interest in a continuous and competitive search for employment and for maximum wages. Sacrificial missionaries, willing to work for a pittance, are quite outside the Ricardian game. So are those bureaucrats who work at set and noncompetitive salaries. Vethake was perceptive in noting this point, but was much too restrictive in estimating the extent of noncompetitive returns (English socialists often delighted in demonstrating that almost no salaries or fees among professional or managerial classes ever reflected supply and demand.)

Vethake condemned any violations of market rules other than altruistic ones. He repudiated guild restrictions, union conspiracies, or government wage controls. He conceded that impediments to personal mobility allowed variant regional wage rates. But, given a free market for labor, he urged young men to select the occupation that best fit their talents. Any oversupply had to be either temporary (lower wages would drive some out of that profession) or merely local (cured by people moving to areas of high demand). The same beautiful regulators served to adjust prices to their natural rate. In a free market prices, except those for rare and irreplaceable items, gravitate toward levels dictated by the cost of production. Such a price level assured a supply of products sufficient to meet the existing level of demand and still yield average profits. By cost of production, Vethake meant what Ricardo meant by labor—that is, all returns to direct labor and to the labor stored up in fixed and circulating capital, plus the interest earned by fixed capital for the time it remained in production. Just as much as for wages, Vethake deplored all artificial restraints upon prices, and particularly condemned legal monopolies that created artificial scarcity and thus high prices. He noted and deplored very large producers, who without a legal monopoly often had the power to control a market by temporarily underpricing new competitors.[26]

Vethake fully grasped the subtleties of Ricardian rent theory and, rare for an American, fully affirmed the validity of the doctrine. In America, most rents went to proprietors and thus lay concealed in returns that also included wages and profits. In this case, rent could best be measured by the income advantage of a farmer who owned good land as compared to an equally proficient farmer on poor land. Rent represented a unique type of interest received from a vested title in a natural resource, and a title that gained value through increased scarcity, by a social increment. This meant, as agrarians insisted, that rent was an exception to the rule that wealth represented (or should represent) a return for labor. Vethake refused to deal honestly with the moral problems this posed. He lamely insisted that rent still originated in labor, but in labor performed in a more advantageous context. There would be no wealth of any kind without labor, and thus no rent. But the whole issue was the added returns attributable to a vested title, not the fact of returns. Thus Vethake lent credence to the charge of agrarian economists that no proper, academic economist would ever dare draw the obvious conclusions from Ricardo's rent theory, or even dare explore its fullest moral implications. To them it was so simple—no one had a valid moral right to appropriate land as a market commodity, to exclude others from nature, or to collect any unearned increments.[27]

Like Ricardo, Vethake stressed the inverse relationship between wages and profits. Workers and capitalists compete for the division of all the economic pie left after rents are paid. According to the Ricardian squeeze play, rents would eventually threaten all profits and push wages to a subsistence level. Could Vethake join other American economists and somehow evade this problem? Not really. If productivity per worker remained constant, then population growth even in America would inevitably increase cultivation on inferior soils, raise rents, and depress profits and wages. This would mean less capital accumulation and slowed growth as even the American economy moved toward Ricardo's stagnant and dismal endgame. But as even Ricardo admitted, human invention could indefinitely postpone this decline. If American workers could continue to increase their efficiency in all sectors, then growth could occur with rising population and fixed resources. Vethake believed fewer restrictions on work and on exchange would facilitate such efficiency. The greatest key to growth was in agriculture. Here, Vethake was fearful that technological advances would be slower than in other industries. If so, rents would steadily rise, and because of high food costs, wages would necessarily take a larger and larger share of the national product. Profits would decline, incentives end, and growth stop. But Vethake foresaw no such extreme squeeze in the near future. Higher land values, and higher rents, might slow growth but seemed unlikely to block it. The possibility of major technical improvements in agriculture always remained; these might even allow agricultural production to withdraw from poor soils and actually lower rents. Although he never admitted it, Vethake's analysis suggested a certain animus against landlords.[28]

Vethake usually used the class categories of Ricardo—landlords, capitalists, laborers—even though these did not easily fit American realities. We scarcely had a distinct class of landlords in 1838. Nor did we have a very large class of wage employees. Nonetheless, Vethake stressed that the vast majority of people in a society live on wages, a claim that he somehow had to square with the fact that agricultural proprietors still constituted the largest category of workers in America. He simply argued that, on analysis, the largest share of farm income constituted wages. And it was for such wages that Vethake expressed his greatest concern. The interest of the political economist, he said, was not to promote the interest of the wealthy, but to assure the highest possible remuneration for the labors of the poor man, and to elevate the working man to as high a rank in the scale of society as "the laws of nature," aided by the cooperation of individuals and governments, permitted.[29]

How increase wages? Obviously, by increasing the demand for wages, which means increasing the supply of capital. The ratio of capital to population in a country is the key to wage rates. The national fund available for wages in a free market is always the total amount of net returns left after the deduction of rents and normal (incentive-maintaining) profits. If the population remains stationary, and both capital and productivity continue to grow, then rents should remain stable, the wage fund increase, and profit rates decline. Workers should be better off, although lower rates of profits might eventually imperil savings and thus the continued growth of productive resources. As Malthus and Ricardo had stressed, the great secret of high wages is not distributive shifts as between profits and wages. Over time, the shares remain nearly constant. A temporary shift toward wages either spurs corrective population increases, or leads to such a diminution of saving as to depress the demand for workers. The shift toward profits increases savings, invites a growing demand for labor, and thus the higher wages that once again depress profits. Thus, the only real secret of permanently higher wages is higher productivity by workers. This high output depends not primarily on hard work, but on various forms of fixed capital and on learned skills.[30]

Of course, the Malthusian dilemma remains. Resources are limited. Overly rapid population growth imperils wages and living standards because of the increased difficulty in procuring food and other raw produce. Neither skill nor invention nor hard work can sustain high real wages if population grows at anything near its natural potential. Vethake assumed that birth control was the first necessary condition for any enduring improvement in the condition of the working classes. He took it as a law of human nature that prosperity led to earlier marriages and more children. He thought that even landlords and capitalists, who were in his eyes more refined and so less sexual and more rational than ordinary

workers, would procreate more in times of prosperity. But his observation contained the secret of population control, and one drawn from
Malthus himself. Vethake noted that higher wages, preferably tied to
greater productive efficiency and not to shrinking profits, were self-
defeating if workers used them as an excuse for more babies. But always,
in civilized societies, the economic checks on births already operated at
some point well above subsistence. Workers already enjoyed some luxuries, and were unwilling to give them up. This proved that prudential
considerations, or cultural standards, played a demographic role at all
social levels. One secret of indefinitely growing wages was cultural. The
working classes had to develop more refined tastes, a greater love of
luxuries, higher expectations. Any population would continue to be
checked by the difficulty of procuring the means of support, but a people's
perception of those means could steadily rise. Any threat to customary
living standards, at whatever level, would lead to later marriages and
apparently to a degree of sexual restraint in marriage (typically, Vethake
was not at all specific on this taboo subject).

   This analysis was at the heart of Vethake's moral purpose as a political
economist. It showed the working classes all the horrors implicit in
anarchy or agrarianism. Instead of the disastrous dead end of leveling
legislation, they needed to look out for education, religion, virtue, for
these alone insured them a command over both the necessities and
luxuries of life. He admitted that nothing was more futile than sermons
about sexual restraint, nothing more tyrannical than laws stipulating late
marriages. But surely everyone would respond to arguments that
appealed to his own self-interest. He wanted to enlarge the consumptive
desires of workers, although he did not specifically identify advertising as
a technique. He wanted to make people more rational, or clearer about
their own long-term interests, and thus enthusiastically endorsed public
education. In fact, education was becoming the most prevalent American
panacea for all social ills, and Vethake simply joined the crowd.

   Vethake ended up with a sophisticated, two-tiered scheme of progress
for workers. His first emphasis was necessarily economic, and fully Ricardian. Wages depended on capital growth, so all enlightened workers
should favor improved technology, fight against all restrictions on labor
(such as laws regulating wages, or labor unions that inhibited the free play
of individual energy), and celebrate rather than curse high profits. In a
free society no possible conflict of interest can exist between labor and
capital. But equally important were non-Ricardian cultural and political
strategies that would raise expectations and standards. These strategies
included public education, the moral certification of luxury consumption,
savings banks and benefit societies, and the early achievement of political
power by workers. Enlightened wage earners, who appreciated the har-

mony of interest in a society, the critical role of capital, and the blessings of wealth, would be safe voters. Suffrage would further elevate the character of the people, and direct their thoughts to matters of higher and more enduring importance than sensual gratification.[31]

Like most early American economists, Vethake accepted an orthodox, commodity view of metallic money. Gold and silver rise and fall in quantity and relative value according to their cost of production. Credit instruments often replace gold and silver in circulation, and in effect increase the supply of money, as do higher rates of circulation for either specie or notes. But the value of money that circulates in a free country remains roughly the same, whatever its quantity. Thus, the size of the medium is not important except for matters of convenience, since relative values are unaffected by size. But sudden shifts in the amount of money affect contracts based on money; a rise in quantity rewards debtors and in turn penalizes creditors. Bank notes, the most prevalent form of credit in America, had this distorting and inflating potential. They also drove specie from the country; this created the danger of bank failure and made a nation vulnerable if it needed specie in order to buy foreign goods.

Vethake endorsed the convenience of banknotes, and admitted that credit expansion often stimulated capital growth. Even the export of specie might buy needed machinery instead of quickly consumed luxuries. But the evils of paper far outweighed its advantages. Distortions, speculative binges, political corruption, and market manipulation all too often followed in the wake of bank expansion. Besides, most American banks rested on privileged charters and thereby enjoyed excessive profits. They had a type of market-distorting monopoly, enjoyed the unique privilege of issuing non-interest bearing notes, and in effect had the power of regulating the currency. To this extent, he endorsed the strongest anti-bank arguments of the Jacksonians. But, ever a cautious man, he decried extreme demagoguery. Bank profits were not taken at the expense of the people and did reflect real services rendered. Vethake proposed a tax on excess bank profits as a means of slowing their inordinate increase, and advocated close government control over monetary supplies. He feared the political corruption of a government-owned banking system, yet equally deplored the potential anarchy of completely free banks. Generally, he believed the existing system might work if note issues were restricted to large-denomination bills. Alternatively, the government might issue treasury notes under a subtreasury (he applauded the Van Buren plan), and phase out private bank notes under a gradual retirement schedule, leaving only unregulated but safe banks of deposit. In any case, the federal government needed clear powers over banking through a new constitutional amendment.[32]

Although open to government regulation of banks, Vethake opposed any other government interference with either production or exchange. Such interference always distorted an economy and bestowed privilege on one part of it. He wanted no usury laws to slow the competitive circulation of capital, unless a few private banks already controlled the quantity of money. He deplored any favoritism to a given sector or industry. He deplored special favors to agriculture, but wanted no penalties, such as a single tax. Like Ricardo, he was willing to accept even high rents as an appropriate return on investments in land. Only the free flow of capital in all areas insured the equilibrating adjustments needed in an economy, and alone encouraged maximum investment. He endorsed free trade, both internal and external, and decried any mercantilistic theories of currency accumulation through monetary trade balances. Only on the great issue of protective tariffs did he hedge a tiny bit.[33]

Vethake offered a detailed but yet a moderate critique of protection. A tariff rarely serves two ends—revenue and protection. Only at the small point of equalized prices can it do both. Generally, protection eliminates imports and curtails revenue. Thus, Vethake focused on the purported benefits of protection. Why not protect American workers against low foreign wages? Actually, the price of imports reflected both foreign wages and profits. Low wages in Britain often paralleled high profits, and thus low wages in themselves could not explain British competitive advantages, or prove that the United States could not be competitive in given industries despite higher wages. In any case, low foreign wages on certain products helped to insure a favorable exchange for American producers, since they gained more labor for less. They faced a problem only if, for some reason, they wanted to produce the same items at home. Clearly, no country could get all items more cheaply from abroad; it had to exchange its own low-cost products, and these had to be competitive on world markets. Given an existing, mutually profitable exchange system, which Vethake assumed, tariffs against foreign imports hurt the producers of American exports, hurt domestic consumers, and also hurt foreign workers. To replace imports, consumers had to subsidize more inefficient home producers. Even in a worldwide perpective, the substitution of arbitrarily protected and inefficient production for efficient production necessarily meant a loss of wealth and lowered living standards. So far, this was the traditional free-trade position, and a very persuasive one.[34]

Vethake conceded that temporary protective duties had some good effects. In Britain, protection for home industries helped to break the back of a cruel feudal system. It helped create a middle class, liberty-loving people. He followed Adam Smith in condoning tariffs as diplomatic bargaining tools, or as a temporary means of ameliorating the unemployment occasioned by new foreign duties. He also believed that across-the-board protective duties were well justified as a cushion against the dramatic dislocations that occur during the transition from war to peace. Thus, he defended the tariff laws after 1815, but noted that such cushioning tariffs, to be fair, had to be levied on all imports, not just on a favored few. He even granted a favorite protectionist argument—that protection in America might lead to the employment of redundant labor, and thus, despite inefficiencies and burdens assessed on other producers, still lead to an increased total product. But it came at a dear price—the diversion of existing capital from more efficient enterprise, and eventual threats of unemployment or lower wages in older industries. Thus, any gains promised to be only temporary. In all such arguments, Vethake joined anti tariff economists in conveniently ignoring the possibility of major technological advances in both old and new industries through more intense domestic competition.[35]

Vethake's concessions hardly pleased protectionists. They scarcely concerned themselves with such purely defensive tariffs. Instead, they advocated a positive effort to protect and encourage large manufacturing in America, and through this sought a balanced and self-sufficient domestic economy. Even here, Vethake made a few concessions. Domestic manufacturing offered distinct advantages—more diverse occupations, greater national strength, more incentives for invention, as well as more compact populations, and thus easier access to education and religious instruction. But he saw at least an equal number of disadvantages to heavy manufacturing, not to mention the injustice of special privilege—the possible neglect of agriculture, the boon to speculation, problems of business cycles and unemployment, lowered expectations and living standards in cities, and all the usual moral hazards of factories and cities. Thus, on balance, he affirmed free trade as the "cause of civilization," and lambasted the hypocrisy behind the label "American system." A natural and free and efficient system best fit American ideals.[36]

Vethake used the last section of his text to preach a series of sermons on correct public policy, on the practical lessons of economic science. He urged men of wealth, who enjoyed the favor of providence, to avoid lavish consumption and to set a model of industry, discipline, restraint, and savings. Not that anyone should value parsimony as the only virtue; with Malthus he recognized the dangers of oversaving, of too much capital and too little demand. But generally he saw such an imbalance as unnatural, a result of government restraints on the use of income. He deplored most forms of government inspection or licensing, and castigated wage and hour laws or direct controls on consumption. More indirect controls, such as sumptuary laws or taxes, seemed less dangerous economically and also morally beneficial, but Vethake stressed that his support of the temperance crusade led him beyond the laws of political economy. Alcoholic beverages were objects of desire, a form of consumption, and thus "useful" in a purely economic perspective. In a positive way, government could affect consumption by granting nonmonopolistic charters for internal improvements, and by direct support of public education. Education, even compulsory education, represented a very special type of government investment and one in no way prejudicial to the interests of any class. Although compulsory schooling might have the effect of a child labor law, the manifest benefits of a literate working population benefited even the rich. Except for this one exception, governments should never redistribute incomes. Leveling entailed the horrible immorality of violated property rights, which leads to insecurity and impedes long-term savings. The poor might gain in the short run, but such a policy could only lead to a quick, enormous population increase. Soon all would be poor as a result of such "immoral, irreligious, and degraded" policies.[37]

Private efforts to coerce the free market were just as dangerous as governmental intrusion. Characteristically, Vethake condemned both corporate monopoly and labor organization. As he put it, no one could "deny that unions are an evil." They supported class conflict, inconvenienced both capitalists and laborers during strikes, and raised the price of goods. Besides, all efforts of unions to disrupt the natural course of events were doomed to ultimate futility. Such efforts could not lead to permanently higher wages or else Vethake would have commended their efforts, since this was his announced goal as a political economist. If, through organization and strikes, one group of laborers gained higher wages, they would do it at the expense of other consuming workers, who would now have to pay higher prices for what they consumed. Or, they would gain at the cost of lower profits, which threatened the continued capital accumulation that sustained full employment. In time, even the benefited workers stood to lose all their gains, unless they actually produced more than before. If they did this they could have gained the higher wages through free competition and did not need to seek them through a conspiracy.[38]

Poor laws had the same distorting effect. Political economy, fortunately, taught lessons in line with sound Christian principles, with the concept of personal responsibility. Charity spoils workers. Vethake assumed that people worked because they had to, and that welfare recipients would have little incentive to seek work and that they would have children with abandon. Soon, welfare would so expand as to take all property from the rich and to divert all wealth from productive uses. All would end up poor together, just as Malthus had predicted. Yet, what can a society do about the unemployed? Economic laws might show that unemployment is a temporary phenomena, but people starve in only a few days. Vethake suggested that governments set up temporary work shelters, which would offer below-market wages and be so distasteful that individuals would make every effort to find private employment. Such workhouses would keep people alive, keep up a minimal demand for goods, and help nourish a desire for more luxuries. Such charitable institutions could teach religion and morality, and by careful screening could exclude the lazy or immoral. Surprisingly, Vethake preferred such public relief to private charity. Such evidence of public concern would reconcile the poor to their lot during temporary intervals of unemployment, and help maintain their loyalty to a free economic system that entailed an unequal ownership of property.[39]

Like Ricardo, Vethake ended his *Principles* with an essay on taxation, which he saw as more than a necessary evil. Unlike Ricardo, he half-heartedly endorsed disproportionately high taxes on true rents, which he regarded as a gratuitous form of wealth in large part created by population growth. Yet, he backed away from a single tax scheme, for like Ricardo he noted that honest people had acquired land without any expectation that government would appropriate all its values. A sweeping land tax involved bad faith. Most other taxes fell directly or indirectly on income and profits. Uniform taxes on incomes or profits penalized everyone equally; unequal assessments redistributed wealth, which Vethake of course opposed. He preferred a general and uniform land tax, and beyond that an uniform tax on income. The goal of government should be twofold—fair taxes and minimal taxes. Vethake warned against not only unnecessary welfare but pomp and show or unneeded military expenditures. Yet, more than most Ricardians, he recognized that the crucial issue was not only how much a government takes but what it does with it. Beyond necessary services, certain government expenses, such as for education, were economically desirable because they made possible more production in the future, and thus contributed to the wealth of the state. For extraordinary government needs, such as war, Vethake endorsed government borrowing, though he warned that easy indebtedness often tempted governments into fiscal irresponsibility.[40]

Vethake was not a likable fellow. His moral fervor bordered on insufferable smugness. Yet he was an able technician. For one who worked within a developed tradition and who never really questioned the basic assumptions that underlay it, he was remarkably careful in his definitions, logical in his analysis, and unusually explicit in his shifts from descriptive analysis to normative recommendations. No American wrote a more sophisticated textbook until after the Civil War. He was to Ricardo what Samuelson would later be to Keynes. And within the academic context, few economists moved very far from his orthodoxy. Even his policy preferences were remarkably in line with those of William Graham Sumner, with the certainties of what would later be known as the laissez-faire school in political economy, a school whose assumptions would be refined but not essentially transformed by the neoclassical innovators of the late nineteenth century.

In a sense, Vethake completed the domestication of Ricardian theory. Much more than McVickar or Wayland, he adhered to all its subtleties and even refined some of them. He also carefully fitted them to the American context. Surely no one ever infused Ricardian themes with greater moral idealism. But this was not distinctive to Vethake, and not a unique American contribution. It is all too easy to forget that even a dry and humorless Ricardo was very much a reformer, and that he surely wrote his *Principles* in order to influence public policy. Intense moral concern, even a soaring idealism, was part and parcel of the whole classic tradition. Later images of callousness or resignation, of human impotence or incapacity before the laws of nature, simply do not match the contemporary self-conception of any of the masters of economic theory. Unless one catches the compelling ideals in Vethake's system, one would run the risk of not only misunderstanding his doctrines but of overlooking a large share of the moral and religious certainties of the whole middle period. It may be hard for Americans to accept, but Vethake was completely sincere in dedicating his work to the economic redemption of those who were poor and those who worked.

The keystone of both Vethake's and Wayland's moral views was property, however defined. Various forms of property had an equal importance for millions of Americans, on all sides of the political system, from Whigs to Jacksonians to radical agrarians. And surely they were all correct in their estimate, for the vital moral importance of several forms of property is all but a truism. The agrarians, above all others, accepted the moral preeminence of landed property and tried to guarantee to everyone his own share. Owenites and Associationists agreed and labored to assure everyone a cooperative share of productive resources. If Vethake had a blind side, it was not in his celebration of property but in his refusal to look very carefully at the myriad images, at all the haunting ambiguities, that lay hidden behind the word *property*. He shared this blindness with almost all of his respectable contemporaries.

VI

Three Southerners

SOUTHERNERS dominated the earliest development of political economy in America. John Taylor opened up the enduring issues from his vantage point as a Virginia planter. Daniel Raymond wrote his textbook as a citizen of Baltimore. Already, George Tucker of Virginia had published promising essays on political economy. Then, in 1826, two South Carolinians—Jacob N. Cardozo and Thomas Cooper—completed two of our earliest textbooks in the new field.

Unfortunately, location remained more coincidental than explanatory. From the work of Taylor on, increasing numbers of southerners felt alienated from federal economic policies. But, surprisingly, no one after Taylor translated that alienation into formal economic theory. Even the ablest economic polemics in behalf of Jacksonian policies came from northerners. Neither Cardozo nor Tucker endorsed the doctrines and policies of Taylor. Neither consistently supported the majority views of their state or region. Perhaps because of their very independence, Cardozo and Tucker rivaled Raymond and Henry C. Carey in originality. They achieved this, not by breaking completely with the tradition of Say and Ricardo, but by making major and often prophetic revisions of theory within that tradition. Cooper contributed little that was new to political economy but demonstrated more clearly than anyone else the internal tensions already present in the new discipline.

Cardozo, of Sephardic Jewish extraction, was born in Savannah, but at age ten moved with his newly prominent family to Charleston. He rose from a clerical position to become editor of Charleston's *Southern Patriot* in 1817 and was a newspaper editor and publisher until his death in 1873.

He contributed reviews to several southern literary journals, and wrote critical essays on many subjects. He was an important part of the intellectual and literary revival that briefly characterized Charleston. Politically, he was moderate, an opponent of nullification. He resented extreme Jacksonian attacks on the Bank of the United States and distrusted anarchic private banking, but later supported Van Buren's subtreasury plan. As a critic and journalist, Cardozo's views even on economic issues shifted through time and according to context. But in his 1826 *Notes on Political Economy* he achieved much more than a textbook, for he tried to perfect a coherent theoretical position as original as Raymond's.

Cardozo wrote as an avowed critic of an emerging Ricardian orthodoxy and of Ricardian disciples like McCulloch and McVickar. Like all earlier systems, Ricardo's would perish in time. Moral science was difficult, ever ensnared by the treachery of language. Just as crucial, political economists too easily confused contextual circumstances with universal conditions. Like Ricardo, they unconsciously argued from national circumstances, from relative facts to allegedly universal principles, when what was most needed were comparisons between nations and across cultural boundaries. Ricardo's system was too provincial to be simply transferred to another and different country. If Ricardo's ideas were uncritically adopted in America, his system would retard rather than advance the new science and also encourage disastrous economic policies. Cardozo noted, as had Raymond before him, that the United States was closer to a state of nature than were the nations of Europe. America was the best place to discover universal principles, if Americans could only emancipate themselves from the influence of European intellectual imports.[1]

Like many Americans, Cardozo could not accept the underlying pessimism he found in Ricardo. Neither could he tolerate the class themes in all European political economy, the endless arguments over the contribution or social responsibility of agriculturists on one side and merchants and manufacturers on the other. With Say, he believed that a correct understanding of the principles of political economy would prove the harmony and unity of all productive groups as well as clarify policies that could insure virtually unlimited economic growth. To achieve these goals, Cardozo tried to unearth the fallacies in Ricardo's theory of rent, a theory that seemed most vulnerable in an American perspective.

Cardozo believed that Ricardo, like most earlier economists, erred in giving special status to land and to agricultural production. Ricardo still reflected the bias of Physiocracy, even as he stood the old arguments on their head and make landowners the villains of his piece. Ricardo had adopted a single and, to Cardozo's way of thinking, a simple-minded labor theory of exchange value, which made quantities of direct or indirect labor the sole determinant of natural or long-term prices. Then, totally apart from the determination of such prices, he identified rent as a special surplus tied to the original fertility of the soil. In agriculture alone did nature play a special role and landowners alone reaped the returns of this natural input. Cardozo's counterthesis was that nature is equally active in all forms of production, and that any product reflects the combination of human ingenuity and the uniformities or dynamical laws of the material world. "Nature concurs with man in each of the arts of life." This is obviously true, but Cardozo seemed to ignore the element of growth present only in agriculture. A relatively unaltered land continues to grow crops whereas mined iron itself becomes a plow. Nonetheless, Cardozo believed his theory, if fully understood, would undermine a labor theory of value, defuse all the class connotations attached to agricultural rents, and at least lessen to insignificance the threat of some final rent squeeze against wages and profits.[2]

With this harmonizing theory Cardozo opened up some rich veins of economic analysis but never developed them adequately. He argued that fixed capital (plants and tools) represent more than stored-up labor. They always contain labor plus harnessed natural forces, as easily illustrated by a water-powered flour mill. Presumably, Ricardo would not have denied this, although he did ignore any possible scarcity value in the natural components of capital goods. At times, of course, natural elements are abundant and free, and thus have no "value." But Cardozo argued that, like land under any degree of scarcity, any other sequestered or seized natural entity or force ought to command a rent. He was most prophetic in thus expanding the concept of rent, not only to urban land but to all the scarce components of nature which enter into production. Yet this extension did not necessarily confound the Ricardian labor theory. Just as in the case of land, the Ricardian could argue that capital rents are always price-determined, an argument that faces difficulties but is still consistent with Ricardian theory. Thus, even if capital goods ordinarily earn rent, and are to this extent comparable to land, such rent payments still do not apply at the margin (at the last unattractive watercourse dammed for use, or for the least fruitful iron ore mined). Only the direct or indirect labor costs in such marginal production of capital goods determine exchange values, and the Ricardian price system stands. But Cardozo surely won one point—rent is an all but universal economic phenomenon. If it squeezes profits and wages, it squeezes them in all sectors and not just in agriculture. An economy is an unified whole, not an aggregate of diverse and competing sectors. All truly universal economic principles apply across sectoral lines, making puerile all controversies over the merit of one sector as against another.

In effect, Cardozo concluded that agricultural land is simply one distinctive form of capital and that it behaves in a free market exactly as does any other form of fixed capital. Rent is the payment for those original powers of the soil that yield a surplus above the ordinary profits of capital in a society that has an open, competitive market for land. Whether improved (a labor and a natural component) or unimproved (only a natural component), land sells and rents exactly as any other form of low-risk capital. It sells for a competitive price based on its expected earning capacity. It rents for an amount that always approximates interest rates on well-secured investments. Cardozo thought this insight defused the problem of inequitable rents and redeemed the social standing of American landlords. After all, they only received the normal rate of interest on their land. Who could begrudge them that? But Cardozo too easily confused the rate of rent with the amount of rent. The all-absorbing rent so feared by Ricardo had nothing to do with the rate of rent as a percentage return on the value of land, but only with the total amount of rent returned to land. If a hundred-acre farm, in a populous country of limited expanse, sells for a million dollars, the rent on such a farm would be enormous even if the rate was only a comparatively low 5 percent. The Ricardian problem developed from a scarcity of fertile land, not from any disproportionate returns on investment in land.

Cardozo never realized how completely he had missed the mark with most of his theoretical attacks on Ricardian rent. But he still had another major alternative: he could prove that Ricardian rent theories were specific to England or to European institutions, that they did not apply to America. This provided fruitful alternatives but they were scarcely original ones. Both Malthus and Ricardo granted that the squeeze of rents scarcely made a dent in resource-rich America and would not for decades or even centuries. They also acknowledged the obvious—that the squeeze could be indefinitely postponed by continuous innovation in agricultural methods. Ricardo's point was that such improvements in productivity had finite limits and that sooner or later (the real issue was just how soon) increasing populations would press against those limits, and in so doing transfer all surpluses to rent. Cardozo unfairly condemned Ricardo for ignoring agricultural improvements and reiterated Raymond's confident claim that increased skill, science, and ingenuity would improve agriculture as dramatically as they had improved manufacturing, keeping agricultural production ahead of population growth. But even Cardozo admitted an ultimate limit, for finally the earth could yield no more produce. Then population could grow no more. But he noted that such a time was so remote that those presently living need not trouble themselves about its dilemmas. One senses here the difficulty Americans had in taking this ultimate limit very seriously.[3]

In a final, and telling, strategy Cardozo lambasted English land policy, and with justice argued that Ricardo inappropriately took it as a point of departure for his theory of rent. Cardozo did not challenge private ownership of land or other scarce natural resources. In fact, like Ricardo, he skirted all the subtle problems posed by individual ownership of God-given resources. He simply assumed that good public policy, if not elementary justice, endorsed private and exclusive claims to natural resources. He never specified any narrow qualifications on such ownership, but he did insist that land be open, always on the market at competitive prices. This, after all, was a built-in requirement of a free market. No more than other forms of capital could land be a monopoly and the Ricardian game still proceed according to the rules. Indeed, by assimilating land and fixed capital to each other, by generalizing rent, Cardozo widened the moral implications of "free and open," even as he extended the dilemmas of non-labor-produced property to all capitalized production. If one justifies ownership only by labor expended, then neither unimproved land nor a major component of fixed capital qualifies for individual ownership. Cardozo never ventured along the analytic paths suggested by this, for they led either toward common ownership of land and fixed capital or toward detailed public controls over the private use of such common resources. It seemed sufficient to him that private owners had no special privileges beyond title and that they were always ready to bargain with their land and capital.

Cardozo assumed that English landlords were not ready to bargain. Because they were not, rents in England were truly monopolistic and it was such rents that provided a model for Ricardo. In England, both law and custom served to keep most land in large estates and off the market. Much of it was not even farmed. This raised the price of land far above its productive potential. A contemporary parallel might be the inflated values of land based on recreational use or its status value. In part such monopoly in England rested on legally enforced entails and primogeniture. It went back to the original division of land, to the distribution of large estates to court favorites, and subsequently to the political and social preferences granted to landowners. Such a maldistribution alone lowered competition and raised access cost to prohibitive levels. Finally, agricultural tariffs further protected the English landed aristocracy, although Cardozo certainly could not use this argument against Ricardo. Such monopoly rents had no relevance for America, for here land joined with other capital on a competitive market and yielded the same rate of return. Thus, Ricardo's whole analysis departed from an imperfect form of social organization. Even the fallacy of the Malthusian population theory probably lay here, in land monopoly and in the forced servility of the unpropertied European masses. Cultural standards or expectations, not subsistence, always regulate births. The habits and expectations of free men in America might lead to a prudent control over population, exactly as Malthus in his later writings had hoped.[4]

Cardozo finally hit a target. Surely the image of nonproprietary and even absentee landlords, of a separate social class, appeared in all English economic treatises. This image was culturally specific. But Ricardo was too abstract to be so easily penned in. His theory of rent fully applied to the most free and open forms of tenure. Land prices rose in America even as Cardozo wrote. Rents went up in the populous East, although not fast enough to rescue the declining profits of those South Carolina cotton farmers who owned increasingly depleted soils. The higher cost of access to land or fixed capital helped deter would-be proprietors and eventually insured that most immigrants would become permanent employees without land or capital. In other words, rising rents did play a role, however minimal, in shifting patterns of property ownership and in lessening economic opportunities. Rising rents helped shape an America ever more like England, but as yet rents did not pose any critical threat either to profits or to wages. Technology and productivity continued to grow as fast as the American population.[5]

Despite his effort to defuse Ricardian rent, Cardozo remained closer to a developing orthodoxy than he admitted. Malthus, and even Ricardo in his more hopeful moments, had celebrated the possibility of a growth economy with no losers. So did Cardozo. Given the quantity of natural resources in America, rents did in fact perform exactly as profits did, and land could be considered as one of many investment opportunities. Given a continuous but gradual input of new skills and tools in all sectors, and particularly agriculture, Cardozo believed rents, profits, and real wages could all rise together, as they certainly seemed to be doing in America. An almost magical escalation of growth was possible. As growth occurred, monetary wages would fall because of population growth, but real wages would rise because of an even more drastic drop in the price of goods. Productive efficiency and competition insured lower profits for each unit of production, but higher overall monetary and real profits because of the enlarged volume of production. Farm technology might reduce monetary rents, but real rents would continue to rise because of cheaper goods and lower monetary wages.

Since there seemed an infinite market for goods, Cardozo saw no proximate limits to growth. He accepted the orthodox view of Say and Ricardo on capital—it can never be redundant and is the engine of growth. He did believe international dislocations could cause a general glut, possibly over a whole country, but even this would only temporarily slow the normal pattern of growth in a free country. Machines lower labor costs, but do not in principle displace labor. They only lower prices and increase living standards.[6]

In all possible ways Cardozo applauded a hard money system. He wanted a specie base and complete convertibility for all credit instruments. Unconvertible government paper was a vicious, concealed form of taxation, and it seemed to him the greatest moral evil that ever afflicted mankind. Like Ricardo, he viewed monetized gold and silver as commodities whose values followed the same laws as any other material object. Disproportionate increases or decreases in the supply of specie, related to other market goods, meant abrupt shifts in prices. But in a free society, the supply of specie usually grew at the same rate as the increased need for it to facilitate exchange. The natural value of such specie was tied to the nonmonetary price of gold and silver, and this in turn to the cost of procuring such metals. Unfortunately, in any given country, money often varied widely from its natural value because of taxes or restrictions on the free flow of international exchange. Generally, Cardozo feared the irresponsibility of private banks, particularly small state-chartered banks. Thus he welcomed many of the restraints imposed by the Bank of the United States. Even when backed by adequate specie, bank-note issues or other forms of bank credit (Cardozo came to appreciate the increasing role of checking accounts) easily led to disequilibrium and to exaggerated business cycles. Yet he wanted only limited legal control over private banks. Beyond a requirement of specie convertibility, he backed a special reserve requirement that amounted to a common insurance fund.[7]

Although moderate and open-minded on the increasingly controversial issue of money and banking, Cardozo was rigid in his condemnation of trade restrictions. He viewed tariffs as a form of taxation. Although protective tariffs may stimulate added production and higher profits in favored industries, the stimulus is only temporary. Competitive shifts will soon bring those profits down to the national average, and capital shifts from more efficient and unprotected industries will lower the overall national product, push consumer prices higher, and lower living standards. Cardozo assumed that tariff-favored producers would not use protection to hasten technological innovations or to lower the cost of production. Such assumptions led him to view every form of tax or tariff as a net drain on production—a conventional Ricardian outlook.[8]

Cardozo did not have to ponder weighty economic dilemmas in intellectual isolation. In the same year that he published his *Notes*, Thomas Cooper of South Carolina College at Columbia collected and published his lectures on political economy, lectures that he had prepared in the preceding two years. He then revised and updated those lectures in 1830. Cooper's book, like Cardozo's, reflected its classroom origins and its intended use as a textbook. Cooper tried to draw upon all of the masters—specifically, Smith, Malthus, Say, Ricardo, and McCulloch—and somehow synthesize them or at least glue them together in a convincing whole. He explored no new theoretical paths, made no original contribution to political economy. He revealed an ambivalence on most technical issues, and quite often confessed his own perplexity. In many ways his book was a disaster; it was tortured, confusing, and inconsistent. It revealed the mind of a troubled, disillusioned, volatile old radical who could no longer order his world or confront the future with any confidence. Yet his lectures remain one of the most fascinating documents in all of American history. In his very confusion, Cooper was not only revealing but beguilingly honest.

Cooper wrote near the end of a colorful career. He was born in England in 1759. He studied at Oxford, dabbled in both law and medicine, and associated with an intellectual avant-garde led by the much admired Joseph Priestley. He eagerly joined in several efforts at political and religious reform, became a determined anticlerical Unitarian, abetted the early French Revolution and acclaimed its ideals, and finally joined Priestley in an elaborate but unsuccessful scheme to set up a utopian community in America. Like Priestley, he found political and religious refuge in Pennsylvania, and very soon after his arrival in America he enthusiastically joined the Jeffersonian movement, becoming a close and admired friend of Jefferson's. Eccentric in personality, at times haunted by alcoholism, he was a passionate partisan with polemical gifts rather like Thomas Paine's. Even early in his career his views on cities and on manufacturing and on the tariff were prone to shift and change, and he gained a reputation for unreliability, for all too often accommodating his political views to place and to party. His appointment as a state judge in Pennsylvania was in part a Republican compensation for his imprisonment under the Sedition Act. But his increased disillusionment with mass politics and his flouting of normal judicial behavior disappointed his supporters, and he was removed from the bench in 1811. From then on he mixed writing with college teaching. He held, and then lost, a position at Dickinson College and lost a chance for a desired appointment at the University of Virginia in part because of his anticlerical views. In 1820 he accepted a final position at South Carolina College, where he soon became president and began teaching a course in political economy. He died in 1839.[9]

Cooper came to political economy as a hardheaded and moralistic utilitarian. He viewed political economy as a developing science, but valued it largely for its illumination of public issues. The great end of politics was the greatest good for the greatest number, a formula easy to state but terribly difficult to translate into actual programs. Cooper frequently moved from rather detached if inconclusive analysis to political advocacy. He punctuated his textbook with pungent but often irrelevant statements of personal preference. His youthful radicalism lived on in denunciations of corporations and tariff laws, of a new manufacturing interest, and in class-conscious indictments of great "capitalists" or of government policies intended to make "the rich richer and the poor poorer." He echoed John Taylor with his diatribes against the developing American political system, which did not treat everyone equally and impartially, which enriched capitalists, merchants, bankers, insurance companies, and corporations of every kind by giving them the privilege "to run in debt indefinitely, on a limited liability . . ." In fact, the United States did not even enjoy religious freedom, for chartered and privileged religious corporations abounded, and Americans still tolerated and even paid far too many clergymen. He took a moral stance against all favored orders, all monopolies or special privileges. He celebrated equal rights, equal laws, and equal protection for all honest producers. But like Taylor before him, he believed that individual self-interest was a precursor of righteousness and that a free economy under a frugal and simple and limited government was both a protection against special privilege and a needed stimulus to industry and capital accumulation. In his own terms, he tried to use a Ricardian analysis to speak for the poor and the exploited.[10]

These hints of economic radicalism paralleled other, seemingly discordant elements in Cooper. If not a bundle of contradictions, he was at least a very complex man. He retained the enthusiastic libertarian political motives of his youth. These did not always seem consistent with his class bias and egalitarian economic analysis. Without carefully distinguishing the quite different goals and strategies of moral philosophy and political analysis, Cooper repudiated the natural-rights tradition, falsely assuming it had been a component of descriptive theory rather than a tool for clarifying moral alternatives. Thus, he insisted that phrases like "born free, equal, and independent," or "unalienable, indefeasible rights" were vague and useless abstractions. In their stead, he adopted a radical positive law approach. Power makes right or, in effect, defines it. What is right is only what is "ordained, commanded, directed." Always, the operative law is the law of the strongest. One only hopes the government is the strongest, that its policies reflect the developed loyalties of the community, and that it furthers the greatest good for the greatest number. His observation of popular parties, beginning with the devolution into violence of the French Revolution, taught him the vast difference between an ultimate, constitutional mandate for government, which he applauded, and majoritarian politics, which he deeply feared. Majorities pose the greatest threat to individual rights and to the opportunity for human fulfillment. This distrust of popular majorities, of participatory democracy, did not endear Cooper to many latter-day Jeffersonians or emerging Jacksonians, although most of his views remained consistent with those of Thomas Jefferson.[11]

For Cooper the one obvious end of an organized society was the protection of individual property. This traditional view entailed no cynicism at all, but well expressed Cooper's moral idealism. Property, and particularly land, seemed a prerequisite of personal independence and thus of any concrete form of freedom. A state should grant citizenship only to landowners. Nonowners are properly sojourners and remain in a society only at the sufferance of citizens. This definition of citizenship was not necessarily severely restrictive or cruel, since it might join positive commitments to provide everyone access to land. Then the position had quite radical economic implications, as illustrated by several emerging agrarian schemes well known by Cooper in 1830. Yet Cooper never went so far as universal ownership schemes, although he sympathized with their goals. But he did draw the political implications of the equating of property and freedom. Usually it is in the best interest of a society to prevent unpropertied or illiterate people from voting, a view he confessed he had come to only in old age, and a view that well fitted his South Carolina context. In America, where most men owned real property and were literate, universal suffrage seemed innocuous. But what about the future? Would not factory operatives eventually rule the country? Then men of no property would legislate the property of the rich into the pockets of the idle. Cooper even viewed the tariff as an early instance of such unprincipled plunder. When the unpropertied became the majority, they would subvert the very end of government and legitimize rapine and robbery. He wanted to restrict the franchise to tax-paying householders of a year's residence. Instead of giving factory operatives the vote, he preferred to give them free education and better possibilities of eventual ownership.[12]

Given these preferences, it is hardly surprising that Cooper made property a key concept in his political economy. Here, almost alone, he introduced a great deal more subtlety than Ricardo or McCulloch and rivaled even the emerging agrarians in the cogency of his arguments. Exclusive property is a necessity for developed and civilized societies. Laws have as their primary purpose the security of property. Governments have as their main end the enforcement of such laws. By property, Cooper meant the product of one's labor, or both consumer and capital goods. What about land? Cooper never wove a coherent argument justifying private ownership of land, and in one cryptic comment even suggested that unimproved land and other natural resources did not classify as property. Yet, as he showed in a historical sketch, governments have always vested land in private hands under a variety of tenure arrangements. In the United States we had the most liberal forms of tenure; Cooper joined Jefferson in acclaiming this as an important national achievement. Cooper believed protection for property, in both land and in the products of labor, was a necessary condition for the accumulation of capital and thus for economic growth. Such protection alone provided strong incentives for work and saving, for it alone appealed to the aspect of self-interest present even in the most humane conduct. Even the right of inheritance was necessary as a further spur to industry, even though in principle the world belongs to the living. He wanted laws on tenure to be clear, fair, equal in their application, and limited to the requirements of social good. He particularly deplored all difficult or obscure legal proceedings. Primogeniture led to overly large estates and to a privileged aristocracy. Agrarian laws, or forcible division, could lead to inefficient and overly small farms. He even recognized, with Malthus, some good effects of primogeniture, such as the cultivation of gentlemen of leisure, art, and science. But he rejected all these for America. In an ironic twist, he suggested an anti-agrarian or modified entail law for America, or a law which set a minimum acreage (100) for estates.[13]

On technical economic issues, Cooper usually fell into confusion. He wanted to do justice to all positions, including opposing ones. Thus, he usually pushed in one direction only to draw back and explore others. For example, he generally affirmed a labor theory of value but consistently confused labor as a source of value with labor as a determinant of exchange values or with labor as a useful measure or standard of value. He followed Ricardo and McCulloch in suggesting that the quantity of labor worked up in a product determined its natural or long-term price. Its short-term, monetary price reflected the interaction of supply and demand. But following Malthus, he noted the practical irrelevance of a natural or labor-quantity price, only then to side with Ricardo by judging that in a free market such a natural price agreed with fact 99 times out of a hundred. With Ricardo, he denied the possibility that labor, or anything else, might serve as an invariant standard of value. Yet he noted that an exchange of labor for labor was an equitable moral standard, even though one not usually followed.[14]

Perhaps rent was the best key to Ricardian orthodoxy. Here Cooper was at least a halfhearted disciple of Ricardo's. He noted that rent was as yet unimportant in America, but with his usual foreboding he noted that the age of landlord and tenant was fast approaching. He hoped that money rents would at least prevail over sharecropping, which offered no incentive for land improvement. Given his acceptance of exclusive property in land and his approval of large and efficient farms, he had no prescription for avoiding a growing class of tenants. As he noted, the early inhabitants are destined to monopolize land in all countries. Practically all land was already owned in America, much of it for speculative purposes. This kind of informal land monopoly, with the resulting increase in land costs, was still preferable either to legislated monopolies or to detailed government controls over land use. He saw no infringement of civil rights and no harmful economic effects. The fact of rent was embodied in the laws of nature, in the reality of limited resources, and in the selfish propensities of man. He accepted Ricardo's theories about rising rents but noted the fluid and competitive situation in America. Here, rents still amounted to only reasonable returns to landlords for their claims based in positive law. We had no corn laws to nourish an artificial landed aristocracy. Like Cardozo, he suggested that land in an open and competitive America functioned very much as did any other form of capital. But even here he could not stop with a single consistent view. Falling back on the same error as Malthus, he suggested that agricultural improvements increased rents (in the Ricardian view, they lower actual rents but increase the long-term potential for rent). Or, echoing Cardozo, he suggested that some nonagricultural rents are price-determining, not price-determined, but never provided any illustrations of this claim.[15]

As much as any economist outside agrarian or radical circles, Cooper expressed solicitude for those who labored. He reflected the standard orthodox view—capital is the only engine of growth, the only useful parent of employment. But as soon as he had made the necessary obeisance to capital he quickly turned to the problem of wages. He lamented the plight of people unemployed, without recourse. Starvation comes in a few days; it never awaits the equilibrium purportedly assured by market laws. In most countries wage laborers faced discriminating legislation. In England past laws had prevented worker combinations. All power and most laws favored the owners of capital. He deplored a recent court decision in Philadelphia that defined combinations as illegal. He wanted to realize laissez-faire fully and honestly, with absolutely no laws controlling either the disposition of labor or capital. Let both sides settle their own disputes as equals. He noted the problems of secret combinations among employers and added one of many sermons against the "fraudulent spirit of the manufacturing system," a system which appealed to a mythical public interest even as it sought all the advantages of a monopoly.[16]

Unlike most English economists, Cooper judged the adequacy of wages not by living standards but by distributive justice. But like them, he all but ignored the quality of the work experience, and thus focused upon consumptive returns. The crucial issue to Cooper was how the product was divided, or what proportion of gross returns went to wages, what proportion to profits. Good wages meant workers received a high proportion of the values they created. This led Cooper to favor pay for tasks performed, not a demeaning hourly wage. Like Ricardo, he defined a natural wage as enough to support a man, a wife, and two children at prevailing standards of subsistence. But such low wages reflected a failure to beat the Malthusian equation. He believed that capital growth, improvements in agriculture, and fewer babies were the proper antidote to massed urban populations and growing unemployment, which were already all too evident in Philadelphia. Yet he did not join Malthus in advocating late marriages. Early marriages provided an education in virtue, responsibility, and social feeling. He preferred high infant mortality or positive birth-control techniques to either celibacy or late marriage, and joined Malthus in resting civilization not only on property but on marriage.[17]

Cooper believed free labor was the most efficient kind. Yet he defended slavery in South Carolina as the only alternative; whites simply could not work in the severe heat of the tidewater regions. Otherwise, he believed black slaves a dear form of labor, given their laziness and low work performance, plus the added cost of their rearing, old age maintenance, and continuous supervision. But in endorsing free labor, Cooper did not mean to celebrate the lone proprietor, although here his views were ambivalent. He deplored frontier inefficiency or the bent to make everything at home (a key argument for the tariff). He celebrated even minute specialization and welcomed the cheapness of factory goods. Yet he could not ignore the human cost of specialization. Like Adam Smith, he deplored the numbing effect of repetitive tasks. Like McCulloch, he hoped to overcome this with education and improved use of leisure. Given high returns, factory workers had no cause for complaint on grounds of boredom. But they did deserve regular employment, not the fluctuating demand and frequent unemployment that so often characterized cities. This led him into a detailed analysis of, first, all the evils of British factories and, then, of the shamefully low pay and status of women seamstresses in Philadelphia. Women needed either more job opportunities or their own cooperative shops. Either might help raise female wages. Thus, Cooper both applauded and condemned collectivized and centralized production on the same pages.[18]

No major American economist ever fully endorsed Adam Smith's distinction between productive and unproductive labor, but Cooper came close. He conceded the necessity of personal services; even domestics helped free the time of masters for more efficient attention to production. And surely men of science, men of rigorous thought, were the glory of any society. But he hated clergymen, despised the military, and had disdain for entertainers. The United States carried the burden of far too many nonproductive parasites. Unfortunately, the more sophistic parasites gained the greatest prestige, honor, and pay. Too often even Americans reserved their highest rewards for warriors who murdered and destroyed, or for politicians and priests who cheated everyone, or for singers and actors who merely amused, and that at the expense of good morals.

Meanwhile, faithful teachers and professors who looked out for the welfare of the young received almost no rewards. Thus, he combined class feeling with personal bitterness, and begged Americans to reduce their demand for service workers, beginning with a refusal to pay salaries to clergymen.[19]

Cooper wanted a balanced economy. Everyone should choose his own employment. The government has no superior wisdom here. Beyond these non-guidelines, Cooper could never order his exact priorities. His moral bent led him to favor agriculture and small crafts, to extoll the simple life in rural areas or villages. Yet he often posed as an urbane connoisseur of art and brilliant conversation, which require leisure and rarely develop outside the great cities of the world. He contrasted the healthfulness of agriculture with the mentally and physically debilitating labor of English factory workers. The needs of manufacturing and commerce lead to imperial adventure and war, while farmers stay home and, at worst, fight defensive wars. Agricultural improvements are permanent, for the demand for food remains constant. Manufacturing capital not only wears out but often lies idle because of shifts in fashion. Yet manufacturing gives opportunity to the more intelligent, promotes new technology, and better supports the sciences. Cooper loved new machines and the affluence for all they made possible as soon as the expansion of consumer demand restored and even increased the demand for labor. The long-term benefits justified the possible short-term displacement of workers. After all, we know of no unmixed blessings in human affairs. We have to live with extended misery; ". . . I see not, either how to prevent the evil, or cure it." Thus, the greatest comforts and conveniences of life originated in collectivized manufacturing. Also, concentrated manufacturing created new markets for agriculture and allowed more intensive cultivation. This Cooper desired. He hated lonely frontier conditions and fought against overly rapid westward expansion. Yet for all its benefits, manufacturing led to gluts, unemployment, and unbearable misery. It created a dependent and servile work force even as it concentrated wealth in the hands of a few. On and on Cooper carried this dialectic, with never a clear resolution. In a prophetic sense he celebrated the benefits of collective enterprise and urban concentration for cultivated people such as himself, but could not see a way to achieve these goals without morally unacceptable costs to the lowly operatives who had to do the manufacturing.[20]

On money and banking, Cooper was as always inconclusive. He accepted the usefulness of credit instruments and, like everyone else, wanted sound backing for bank notes. He acknowledged the benefits of banks—safe places of deposit, sources of convenient drafts and checks, and instruments of needed credit expansion. He justified the profits gained by banks even though their interest on outstanding notes often exceeded in value the invested capital by multiples of up to three. According to Cooper's theory, profit rates in risky enterprises were usually up to three times that of normal interest rates, and thus bankers earned their high-risk returns as much as farmers or manufacturers earned their low risk returns. Yet he feared all the abuses of banking—speculation, overly rapid expansion of credit, fleeing specie, and economic cycles, plus the vulnerability of private banks to fraud, political favoritism, or monopolistic power. He offered no remedies for these evils. He suggested no new laws and wanted no government-owned banks, since he believed any government was bound to abuse the privilege of issuing its own paper notes. He acknowledged the restraining influence of the Bank of the United States before the presidency of the hated Biddle, but denied to the federal government any constitutional power to establish a central bank. Perhaps under some political constraints, Cooper in 1830 denounced the monopolistic tendencies of the Bank of the United States and predicted it would soon absorb all private banks or even, monster-like, come to dominate the federal government. Thus, from moderate analysis he easily slipped into an almost reflexive condemnation of selfish moneyed interests, and by such language tried to prove himself a good Jacksonian.[21]

Because of his deep distrust of government, Cooper agreed with all Ricardians on the special dangers of taxation. Taxes impoverish. Like John Taylor, he wanted to restrict governments to essential costs, largely of a police type. Without qualification he argued that the products furnished by taxes "are lost to the nation; they are consumed, destroyed; the nation is poor by reason of this consumption or destruction, however necessary it may be." Cooper also echoed Ricardo in condemning taxes on working capital, for this destroys incentives. He preferred taxes on consumption or, if practical, on incomes. Generally, he hoped governments would pay their own way. Debts were obligations laid on future generations. Echoing Jefferson, he suggested that all necessary debts be paid off in one generation, except those specifically used to purchase future benefits.[22]

Whether from matured conviction or as a sop to the intense feeling of fellow South Carolinians, Cooper vehemently opposed all protective tariffs. He saw these as taxes used to reward some American producers at the expense of all consumers and exporters. He even rejected protection for vital war supplies, or retaliatory tariffs against competing countries.

Just as tariff supporters hid behind a sophistic appeal to a larger public interest, so did the boosters of corporate privilege. Cooper believed bank charters had already made the constitution a dead letter and had replaced the union of states with a despotic, consolidated government. The United States was already glutted by banks, insurance companies, canals, and business corporations, or what Cooper called "public nuisances" ever bent on "exclusive privilege and monopoly." Limited liability had become a "mode of swindling quite common and honorable," a "fraud on the honest . . . public." Like Taylor, he denied to any republican legislature the power to charter corporations, for this was the power of establishing governments and it rightly belonged to a people only in their constitutional capacity. He conceded the need for large accumulations of capital, but thought the only fair mode of collection was legal partnerships with complete liability.[23]

If Cooper made any original contribution to American economic thought, it was in his unusual concern for distribution. The great problem of political economy, as he viewed it, was not growth but how to "*distribute more equally and more beneficially among the whole mass of the community, the wealth in all ways accumulated.*" The goal was to provide to all who labored a reasonable share of the comforts as well as the necessities of life. Ironically, these goals had been best realized in more primitive economies, or on the rough American frontier that the urbane Cooper personally disliked. Civilization seemed to war with justice; progress increased poverty. In every advanced country of Europe laborers barely earned their subsistence, while monopolistic capitalists enjoyed undreamed-of wealth and political power. In America, we had struck at these injustices by abolishing rank, title, primogeniture, and established churches. But we needed to do more. Characteristically, Cooper suggested a progressive income tax and the end of all salaries for clergymen. He wanted not some repressive equality of condition but only to avoid the extremes of Europe, to prevent the establishment of a class of rich men who did not work and a working class starving from a lack of necessities through no fault of their own.[24]

These concerns led Cooper into a detailed consideration of poverty. Already by 1830 poor relief was a growing problem in the cities of Massachusetts, New York, and Pennsylvania. By the poor, Cooper meant a growing class of permanently impoverished people, not the victims of periodic unemployment or misfortune. He saw alcoholism as a primary cause and lotteries as a secondary one. How should Americans deal with such poverty? Cooper believed, with Malthus, that public relief only encouraged dependency and invited irresponsible childbearing. He wanted no poor laws in America, although he saw their justice in an England cursed by oppressive institutions. In America the ill and the disabled and deserted women with children deserved private charity. Victims of natural disasters or disabled war veterans might deserve public aid. Beyond that, Cooper wanted temperance laws, plenty of savings banks, and a major government educational effort. He supported a vast system of schools, reaching from the elementary level, where the state should pay the teacher and the parents provide facilities, to publicly financed secondary schools and universities. He also desired governmental efforts to improve public health and suggested huge governmental efforts in the gathering of needed economic data.[25]

Because of his concern for distributive justice, Cooper acknowledged his temperamental kinship to a developing school of radical economists, a school usually identified by the hated label "agrarian." The agrarians often echoed Cooper's class bias and used his vitriolic language. Cooper also shared their primary concern with the redistributive role of federal policy. Cooper agreed with them that federal policies, so far, had simply redistributed more and more to the rich. He also reflected the working-men's concern for the servility of factory operatives or the futility of sweat-shop laborers. He exclaimed: "God forbid that this country should ever become an exporting, manufacturing country. Let others cherish that dreadful system." But Cooper had no clear answers to the problem of high profits and starvation wages, and he admitted it. He urged everyone to attend carefully to the arguments of the radicals. Specifically, he mentioned two Englishmen, Thomas Hodgkins and William Thompson, reformers who took as a point of departure the rent theories of Ricardo and the factory experiments of Robert Owen. In this country he noted the two pre-eminent agrarians, Langton Byllesby and Thomas Skidmore (see Chapter 9). Insofar as he understood their position, he vehemently repudiated it even as he endorsed their goals.

Cooper believed the agrarians, who wanted to insure everyone access to land, struck at the very source of economic effort and progress—secure private property. The radicals also stressed that laborers should get all returns, seemingly leaving nothing for capital. Thus, their program meant a direct assault on existing owners. Since present owners would not surrender, redistributive schemes really required a revolution. Even Frances Wright, a woman whom Cooper much admired, supported a guardianship education scheme which entailed such large costs as in effect to require an indirect and major redistribution of property. All such schemes threatened to penalize the industrious and reward the lazy because they leveled downward and threatened the leisure and intellect and cultivation Cooper personally esteemed. At times he grew angry at the agrarians, at the new radicals of his day, radicals whose cause he had always acclaimed but whose programs seemed so wild and extreme and uninformed as to be almost blasphemous. He felt a traitor for not joining them; bitter and angry because they posed alternatives that he could not accept. No other respectable economist flattered them with so much attention, but none was more patronizing or bitter toward them. If the agrarians prevailed, Cooper believed, property would no longer be safe and robbery would become the rule. Likewise, he saw no answer in communalism, in the less radical strategies of Robert Owen or the American disciples of Fourier. Such cooperative schemes had succeeded only under a high level of religious fanaticism or under despotic management. They were bound to founder wherever heterogeneous groups of workers gathered, as they did at Owen's colony at New Harmony.[26]

How could Cooper make our society righteous? In resignation, he acknowledged he could not. No one could. Ultimate dilemmas always remained. He wanted free discussion even for Skidmore's extreme redistributive schemes. He wanted more education. But human differences remained; in fact, they seemed to grow ever more conspicuous. These could not be eradicated; perfect justice and harmony remained impossible. All any society could do was try not to throw up artificial obstacles to "honest exertion." In a practical vein, Cooper offered a tentative legislative program to counteract the growing problems of poverty and dependence: end all taxes on necessities, require school attendance until age twelve, erect true workhouses or poorhouses for the temporarily unemployed, set up a progressive income tax, end all bequests to churches, lower government salaries and expenses, set up a national education system, and prohibit marriages for those without the means of childrearing.[27] These partial answers at least offered a more hopeful response than any embraced by the most able and pessimistic southern economist: George Tucker.

More than any other American, Tucker made political economy fit its growing reputation as the "dismal science." His pessimism about the ultimate prospects for mankind at times bordered on fatalism. But his originality also rested on some very subtle technical distinctions. He believed these refuted the distributive theories of Ricardo. In fact, they more nearly extended and refined the Ricardian system toward the marginal utility emphasis of late nineteenth century neoclassicists. Finally, Tucker dissented sharply from almost all American Ricardians on governmental policy. He welcomed a major economic role for government, loved banks of issue, defended the Bank of the United States, and even as a southerner dared take a moderate view on protective tariffs. He loved cities, lauded manufacturing, and defended the role of an affluent upper class. Atypically for an American economist, he never assumed the role of a reformer except on the limited issue of banking.

Tucker spoke with the authority of prominence and position. His biography resembles that of John Taylor as much as his economic thought contrasted with Taylor's. Although born in Bermuda (1775), he came to Virginia at age twelve for his education at William and Mary, and there grew to maturity among eminent relatives (among them, St. George Tucker). As an adult he practiced law, procured a large estate, served several terms in Congress, and wrote polished historical and philosophical essays. He had literary ambitions and wrote passable biographies and novels. As a nominal Virginia Republican, Tucker relished the more extreme nationalist policies of Madison, but in the United States Congress at least bent his convictions to fit his district's hostility toward the tariff and internal improvements. Nonetheless, his futile support in 1824 of William Crawford and the caucus system helped insure his defeat. After he left Congress in 1825, he won, with the support of Jefferson and Madison, a prestigious appointment as first professor of moral philosophy at the new University of Virginia, a position that Thomas Cooper had also sought. Since moral philosophy embraces political economy, it is not surprising that Tucker soon offered a separate course in political economy and eventually published his own textbook. Tucker, like Cardozo and Cooper, lived a long life (he was 81 when he died in 1861) and devoted his intellectual energies in his last three decades almost exclusively to political economy. In 1845, at the age of seventy, he retired from teaching and moved to Philadelphia, where he wrote two additional books on political economy plus a detailed statistical analysis of the 1850 census.[28]

In his later years Tucker was more Malthusian than the later Malthus. He had been less pessimistic during his earlier career as a politician. In an essay written just before 1822, he joined most Americans in denying the Malthusian formula. He then welcomed population increases in America, and like Henry C. Carey later, argued that population density was conducive to virtue, a view he never completely abandoned. Without mistaken governmental responses, population concentration did not need to be dangerous or trigger such checks as depravity and vice. He trusted other checks might stabilize population, as they had already in some developed countries. Somehow, an advanced, urban-centered civilization retarded births. Disease and vice had a role, as possibly did city diets or air pollution, but new habits and manners seemed most critical. Late marriages, extended periods of childhood dependency, and high living standards meant sexual restraint, at least for the upper and middle classes. His analysis, many years later, of American demographic patterns tended to bear out his early wisdom, for indeed birth rates by 1850 seemed to be dropping in our cities, suggesting an eventual levelling off of population. But even in his early optimism Tucker already doubted that the lower classes would ever learn prudence and restraint. History certainly offered no evidence of this. In crowded cities, these classes already faced Malthusian checks, and Tucker almost fatalistically accepted these as the inevitable cost of the higher civilization gained by those at the top. The lower classes would have to pay a high price for progress; this theme was woven into all his later economic analysis.[29]

When he took up the serious study of political economy, Tucker made the man-land ratio the crucial departure point of all his analysis. In this he anticipated William Graham Sumner, but unlike Sumner he never believed capital accumulation could indefinitely postpone a coming food crisis. Tucker's thinking and analysis thus led him, during the same years, in a path just the opposite of that taken by Henry C. Carey. Carey assumed that nature was infinitely fecund; Tucker, that it was finite and limited. The idea of natural scarcity underlay all his technical doctrines, beginning with his theory of value.

Tucker rejected a cost-of-production theory of exchange value. In a primitive economy, with all natural factors plentiful and free, the actual or market price of articles always tend toward an exchange of labor for equal labor of the same difficulty, or what Tucker called a "natural price." Momentary prices, in all cases, reflect the interaction of supply and demand. Tucker was perspicacious in noting the psychological nuances affecting demand and in recognizing the varied elasticities of demand for different products. The intensity of desire was all-important. When no natural scarcities are involved, increased demand for articles (either more demanders or more intense desire by the same population) raises prices and thereby encourages increased production. In a short time, these temporarily higher prices have to fall back toward their natural level, for if labor is the only factor involved in the supply of a product, one would be inclined either to make it for himself or to hire someone else to make it for him so long as its market cost remained above its labor equivalent. In this conventional analysis, Tucker agreed with Adam Smith.[30]

In all production, man and nature cooperate. Even a diamond has to be unearthed, picked up, or transported. But when natural components are plentiful they have no exchange value. Only when they are scarce and appropriated as property do they command a price or lease for a rent. Tucker stressed this natural scarcity. It meant that many products, if not most, have a combined labor-scarcity value. The diamond is a good example. So is wheat. So was the price of southern slaves. This seemed to suggest a significant revision of Ricardo's denial that rent ever "determined" prices. The critical word was "determined." Tucker made clear that it is always the interaction of supply and demand that "determines" the price of any article or service, including the price of land, capital, or labor. Many prices have rent as a component but not as a direct determinant. Ricardo was therefore correct in one sense—production at the extensive or intensive natural margin always duplicates the general situation in a state of nature. In a developed economy it is only at this margin that prices exactly match the total direct and indirect labor cost, or labor-capital cost. But it makes no sense even here to say with Ricardo that the cost at the margin determines the price of goods even though they do have a one-to-one relationship. The total demand for goods that have a scarce natural component determines the price, and this demand in turn reflects the relationship of population to natural resources. For example, given population increases, fixed resources, and thus higher food prices, people will devote labor and tools to marginal land, for the demand-induced prices now make such investment as profitable as other competing investment opportunities. Marginal prices do not determine food costs, but rather prior food prices determine the location of the productive margin. This meant, to Tucker, that Ricardo's treatment of rent needed extensive revision.[31]

From his labor-scarcity theory of value Tucker turned to the problem of distribution, where he made his major technical contributions to political economy. He began with some basic assumptions: Nature is limited, and where most scarce from a human perspective, it is already privately owned, usually by a small proportion of the population. Tucker neither defended nor carefully analyzed such private ownership. As scarcity first became apparent, those with power or influence simply grabbed the best resources, thereby reflecting in their zealous pursuit of self-interest what the uncensorious Tucker called the "great law of all animated nature." To this natural source of wealth man brought his labor. He produced consumable goods, services, or labor-saving tools useful in his future production. Through the equilibrating effect of supply and demand, the value in exchange of consumables and tools did gravitate toward the quantity and quality of labor that produced them as long as they involved no scarce natural factors. As soon as they did involve scarce resources, then both consumables and tools exchanged for more than a labor equivalent, or in other words commanded more labor than went into them. The extra value represented the "rent" cost, although Tucker usually restricted the term *rent* to farmland and to mineral resources. But he noted that labor-saving tools earned returns on their scarcity, no matter whether that scarcity was tied to their material components or to the skills and knowledge they embodied. Thus, in effect, he reduced the problem of distribution to two factors—wages and rent. What people generally called profits always reflected varied combinations of those two—that is, returns to appropriated scarcity or to stored-up or managerial labor.[32]

From these assumptions, Tucker deduced his theory of normal economic evolution. In the long run, as population increases, the prices of all raw produce, and most critically food, continuously rise. Since food is a large component of real wages, the long-term trend in wages has to be downward. The trend can be temporarily arrested or even reversed through important agriculture or mining improvements, but sooner or later a larger population will nullify all possible gains. This dismal trend is

in part relieved by possibilities of an enlarged consumption of manufactured products in which labor rather than raw produce or depletable
minerals is the major component. Increased population, lower wages,
and vast improvements in manufacturing techniques all promised continual price reductions. But Tucker scarcely conceived of an ill-fed but
otherwise consumptively blessed population, for he still saw food and
other basic necessities as the only normal outlet for working-class wages.
Thus, with Malthus and Ricardo, he saw limited births as the only hope
for the mass of mankind, and he hoped for such results much more than
he realistically expected them. Given this dismal evolutionary perspective, the remaining issue was how economic "progress" would affect
various classes. Who would lose and who gain along the way?[33]

Ricardo's answer had been straightforward. Landlords would be the
only gainers. Workers would lose up to a point, but then their wages
would stabilize, not only at a population-maintaining level but also at a
level that took account of their existing habits of consumption. Capitalists
faced the worst long-run prospect, since they would eventually lose
almost all profits as higher wages cut into their returns. Tucker considerably revised this prospect. He granted future gains for landlords but
believed that Ricardo overestimated them. Equal gains also lay ahead for
major capitalists, if by that label one meant those with accumulated
wealth invested in other than land. Those who only had their labor to sell
would bear all the losses. With no hint of any concealed political purpose,
Tucker went far along the path Marx would later take in describing a
widening gap between two economic classes. Those with accumulated
wealth could gain from growth in population and productivity; those
without were doomed to lose. Of course, Tucker admitted that mitigating
factors might postpone the harsh reality for workers or allow exceptions
for a favored few. These factors included exceptional talent or luck for
individuals; rich resources or beneficent political institutions for a nation.
A few individuals would move up and down the social scale, and favored
countries like the United States might enjoy extended intervals of general
economic growth. But nothing except an unlikely stabilizing of population could reverse long-term trends.

Unlike Ricardo, Tucker denied any possible conflict between rents and
profits. Whatever the cost of ever higher rents, the capitalists would not
have to bear them. People with accumulated wealth, in whatever field of
investment and so long as they received political protection, had a
cushion against the dire effect of unchecked population growth. Tucker
emphasized the mobility of most forms of capital, a theme that he could
have borrowed from Lord Lauderdale. It made no sense in a free economy to talk of rents squeezing out profits. Land, if bought and sold freely
on the market, represented one of many competing avenues of invest-

ment. The rate of return to land could not soar above other returns or above normal interest rates, for if rents rose investors would shift money to land purchases and thus bring rent rates back down to the competitive average. Since rent is earned by all scarce means of production, not just land, the very distinction between rents and profits merges and blurs at a hundred points. But the mobility of capital offered no consolation to workers. Population pressure still drove up the value of land, raised the proportion of national income accruing to rents, raised the cost of raw produce, and necessarily depressed wages.[34]

Unlike other American economists who viewed land as a form of capital, Tucker realized such a merger in no sense lessened the pessimistic implications of Ricardian rent theories. In fact, it worsened the implications for most of the population, for Tucker assumed that in a developed economy the vast majority of people would be wage earners who would be forced to spend the largest share of their wages to buy ever more costly food. Rising land values and rising rents were possible only if owners of land and capital could force workers to absorb all the effects of diminishing returns. Tucker had no doubt at all about their ability to do this, all the way to almost unimaginable depths of misery for workers. If wages absorbed all the cost of scarcity, then economic evolution, which normally involved a rising population and dramatically increased productivity outside of agriculture, could continue to bestow ever higher rewards on a favored few. With the steady expansion of the total per capita product in manufacturing and services, the affluent would obviously enjoy rising living standards, for they consumed most manufactured luxuries and most services. The competition of capital, plus a high level of political security, might gradually lower the rate of rents, interest, and profits, but the increasing value of land and fixed capital, the growth of savings, and greater efficiency in manufacturing still insured increased consumption at the top. For the wealthy an increase in the cost of raw produce, a minor portion of their consumption, would scarcely affect their overall wellbeing. Only one possible dilemma faced the owning class—natural scarcity might prevent any growth in their numbers, or eventually force some of their children into the working class. Implicit in Tucker's model was an eventual decline in the total product. Such diminishing returns suggested great insecurity for those at the top, in part because of their political vulnerability. Unlike Marx, Tucker examined none of these issues.[35]

Tucker assumed no fixed minimum wage. The burden of scarcity could be indefinitely passed down to workers in the form of reduced wages. Since supply and demand controlled wages in a free market, workers had no alternative but to suffer all the costs of rapid population growth. If wages had a fixed natural floor, then Ricardo was correct in seeing an eventual squeeze on profits. He then only erred in supposing a class of rent-collecting landowners could insulate themselves against the squeeze. If workers, however numerous, could successfully demand wages adequate to sustain their population, then the inherent limits of nature would more quickly penalize all owners of wealth, including landowners as fully as those with wealth invested elsewhere. Ultimately, the possibility of rent rested upon a surplus product. If no land could produce more than the ordinary and competitive cost of labor and capital needed to farm it, then rents ceased. If, as population increased, the fixed minimal cost of labor steadily narrowed the surplus, then obviously no class could avoid a gradual impoverishment. Parallel to the decline of rent would be the fall of profits for every other form of investment. Here Ricardo was correct. The higher, fixed cost of labor would steadily diminish profits in manufacturing and commerce.

Tucker saw a two-stage fall of wages. In the first, workers would have to accept a coarser diet as they progressively gave up meat and grain and vegetables finally to live on potatoes, the one food crop that yielded the most calories per acre. When a growing population made even potatoes dear, then shrinking wages would kill off wives and children, for the nearest approximation to a minimum wage would be just enough potatoes to keep a single worker alive, at least for a limited period of time. Such attrition, of course, served as the most effective form of birth control and in time promised to reduce the supply of labor and even competitively improve wages as the land-man ratio improved. But meantime the owning class had protected all its income, and by that very fact probably continued to procreate at a high rate. If so, many of their children were destined to fall into the working class, for at the extremes of natural scarcity only a limited elite could expect to live in insulated and civilized comfort. Thus, in a final equilibrium economy, wages would stabilize just below a population replacement level and pay for only the coarsest food. Meantime, less talented or less fortunate upper-class children would steadily replenish the working classes.[36]

Tucker seemed to view this outcome with equanimity. The cruel costs at the bottom were part of life, compensated for by the enhanced, urbane pleasures and creative accomplishments possible at the top of a fully developed economy. He accepted something close to the cultural pattern already visible in Western Europe. He showed no anger over, suggested no injustice in, the price paid by the imprudent at the bottom of the scale. He wanted no egalitarian schemes. If all families were on one level, then all would move toward poverty in tandem, albeit at a slightly slower pace than that followed by the existing working class. In such an egalitarian society everyone would be vulnerable to temporary crop failures or natural disasters. The savings of the wealthy at least provided a buffer against short-term scarcity even for the poor, for philanthropy rescued the unfortunate. Tucker also approved of minimal welfare institutions, such as public workhouses.[37]

Not only did Tucker assimilate land and capital, but he used a more sophisticated theory of demand to challenge the details of Ricardian theory. He often misread Ricardo. For example, he falsely accused Ricardo of basing rent solely on differences in soil fertility and thus overlooked his theory of declining returns to new increments of capital, which applied even to soils of equal fertility or to those equally well located to markets. But on one issue he correctly identified a major doctrinal conflict. Ricardo assumed a near-fixed demand for raw produce, with food or even corn (wheat) the type for all agricultural production. Thus, he believed that the short-term effect of new agricultural techniques, or of some miraculous increase in soil fertility, was always lowered rents. This implied that "rational" landowners would oppose progress. They profited only from economic adversity, since lowered productivity caused short-term increases in rent. Tucker mistakenly believed Ricardo saw agricultural improvements as a permanent limit on rent. Actually, in the Ricardian model agricultural improvements increase the potential for surpluses above productive costs. As soon as population increased, they made possible a higher level of rent. Thus the only issue was short-term effects, and here Tucker was by far the more sophisticated in his analysis.

If the demand for food is completely fixed, then Tucker conceded that improvements in agricultural production would lower rents according to the Ricardian formula. Increased productivity would then mean lower food prices, at least until population increased. Lowered food costs, by lowering the competitive cost of an existing labor supply, would raise profits outside agriculture. Thus, capital would shift from marginal land, or from the final incremental addition of capital to existing land, into other industries, decreasing the demand for access to land by capitalists and leading to lower rents. Tucker was not alone in smelling a rat in this Ricardian analysis, for landowners historically had sought improved productivity. Tucker had already shown that profits and rents are linked to each other. If such divergent trends in rents and profits developed, as Ricardo had predicted, then the corrective was almost immediate, for the capital withdrawn from land would soon reduce returns outside agriculture to the same level as rents and thus at least check and minimize any rent declines. Losses for landowners meant losses for all owners of scarce productive resources, and historically such owners had not suffered such losses.

Ricardo's most critical error, Tucker felt, was to misjudge the market effect of increased productivity in agriculture. The demand even for food, in quantity or quality, is not fixed, and food is only a part of agricultural production. Always, in any population, large numbers of people would like to buy more meats or higher-quality vegetables if they could afford them. Thus, increased productivity in agriculture meant lowered prices, but also increased demand for agricultural goods. Tucker argued, in effect, that a ten percent increase in agricultural productivity did not mean a ten percent reduction in acres farmed or in the capital and labor devoted to agriculture. The exact impact on prices is beyond exact prediction, unless one knows the exact degree of variability in demand for each agricultural product. Ricardo falsely assumed that changes in productivity led to proportionate shifts in the relative scarcity of land. Although the proportion of the total product going to rents inevitably declines with increased productivity, Tucker argued that this decline would very often not match the gains a landowner realized from the larger output. That meant he would gain from the increased product. For example, a miraculous 10 percent increase in soil fertility might lead to an 8 percent increase in food consumption, primarily in the form of higher quality foods. This might mean only a 3 percent fall in food prices, and no more than a 5 percent drop in the rate of rents. A farmer who formerly collected as rent 40 percent of the wheat growing on his land, or an equivalent money rent, might be able to lease his land in the next year for 38 percent of the wheat. But if production on 10 acres grew from 200 to 220 bushels, he would still collect almost 84 bushels rather than 80, and even at the 3 percent reduced price this much wheat would still command more labor than the 80 bushels the year before. In effect, increased productivity had the same beneficial effect as a good crop year.

Of course, the long-term benefits to landlords were much greater. Population increases would eventually raise farm prices even higher than before the miraculous fertility increase, and when this happened landowners and other capitalists could collect all the added returns at the expense of lowered wages. This, Tucker believed, reflected the historical pattern and made landowners "rational" in seeking improvements and higher productivity along with capitalists in all other investment areas. He believed varied elasticities of demand meant that all parties might be able to share in the immediate benefits of increased agricultural productivity— landowners, capitalists, and laborers—but only landowners and capitalists benefit in the long run. The exact new patterns of distribution depended on various levels of demand, not only in the demand for food but also in the demand for various tools and forms of labor that affected supplies. This was a much more complex picture than the one presented by Ricardo. Tucker even talked graphically about demand and supply curves, anticipating later marginal utility formulas.[38]

Tucker in effect perfected a neo-Ricardian and very complex model of economic growth. If a mass of people could so limit births as to keep population growth lower than rises in per capita productivity, Tucker envisioned a bright and harmonious future. The interests of all analytically distinct classes then converged, for in a free economy the market fairly distributed the immediate benefits of growth. Laborers could steadily gain larger incomes, but risked losing all such gains by an excessive rate of procreation that Tucker believed almost inevitable. Such population increases assured a downward trend in wages. He even used long-term wage trends to predict the eventual emancipation of slaves. He never approved of slavery, not even on purely economic grounds. But he did think most estimates of slave inefficiency were highly exaggerated, and he identified sophisticated incentives and forms of emulation among fortunately situated slaves. Even after he moved to Philadelphia and escaped the pressures of southern opinion, he still argued that slaves were as happy and well-cared-for as northern wage laborers. But, overall, slavery lessened the motives for industry on the part of blacks and, much more damaging, degraded manual labor for southern whites. Fortunately for southern whites, slavery could not exist in a more developed and populous economy or one with greater natural scarcity. Inevitably, the same falling wages already observable in Europe would make the cost of rearing and boarding slaves, plus maintaining older slaves, much costlier than hiring "free" labor. Obviously this would happen long before the wages paid for more productive "free" labor became insufficient to maintain a stable population. Surely no one ever offered a gloomier reason for eventual emancipation.[39]

At a policy level, Tucker seemed much less pessimistic than in his distributive analysis. After all, the United States was not very far along the path of economic development. It seemed at least a century short of any severe wage-depressing natural scarcity. Tucker predicted a population of 240,000,000 in 1937, and only then a possible scarcity of resources. He did not give much credit to illusory hopes, but recurrently speculated that the United States might beat the population squeeze, that our high living standards might somehow retard births and allow a continuous rise in wages. In any case, the immediate imperative for a growing America was an increase in manufacturing, for we had almost exhausted the world market for our agricultural produce. He welcomed more clustered population, more intensive development, urbane civilities as well as vices, and the growing ability of the United States to match the cultural achievements and the military power of Britain and France. This desire for national power led him to support government-funded schools, government charters and other incentives for internal improvements, and even temporary protective tariffs to nourish infant but needed manufacturing industries, even though such tariffs meant productive inefficiencies and higher costs to consumers. The larger goal was to get people to work, to reduce a developing redundancy in our labor force. When he focused on such immediate priorities, he seemed to forget what he characterized as the fundamental law of political economy—in the progress of society, food prices go up and wages go down.[40]

In almost all his discussion of public policy, Tucker probed new avenues of government action. He deferred to southern opinion only in limiting certain economic roles to state governments and in refusing to argue purely constitutional issues, which were outside the province of political economy. Tucker wanted government economic policy to support and coordinate privately owned enterprise, not displace it. He lauded the security of persons, property, and contracts, and often lamented too much detailed government intermeddling. His views often anticipated or followed those of Daniel Raymond (whose text he briefly used at Virginia) and those of Lauderdale and Malthus. As early as 1812, in some unsigned essays that were obviously influenced by the views of Hamilton, he defended government fiscal policies oriented toward economic growth. For example, public borrowing might attract domestic wealth wasted in luxurious consumption and be spent in ways calculated to draw idle men into useful employment. The deferred taxes made possible by borrowing might allow more rapid private capital accumulation and thus allow growth to lessen the effective cost of a debt. Like Raymond, he emphasized that the crucial issue was not indebtedness, not the size of a debt, but how governments spent the money. If the economy grew, a government might borrow the total increase each year and without paying back a cent still not penalize any American. Not that Tucker recommended such a growing government debt. But he at least suggested it as a possibility. The limit on government debt seemed always to move ahead of the debt itself, and a borrowing country might continually realize the possible stimulus of larger government expenditures. A growing debt encouraged higher prices. These depreciated the value of older debt paper, and thus served as a tax on the debt holders, lowering the effective cost of funding. Negotiable debt paper also served monetary needs and in that way often stimulated economic activity. But Tucker noted that a debt might not be invested in improvements, but be wasted. And by certain tax policies, debts might further enrich the few and impoverish workers. As always, Tucker believed actual policy could not be deduced from any abstract principles but had to be judged according to variant empirical realities. [41]

In *The Theory of Money and Banks*, which he published in 1839, Tucker offered the most sophisticated treatise yet written by an American on money and banking. In it he tried to refute the "heresies" so widely disseminated by pro-Jacksonian publicists and economists, and he may have had William Gouge specifically in mind. Tucker celebrated money almost as enthusiastically as would Henry C. Carey. Like Carey, he defined it as a lubricant of an economy and compared its instrumentality to roads and canals. By money, he meant gold and silver, which had intrinsic qualities that made them the ideal media of exchange, although their monetary role ultimately rested on convention and on law. Money, by facilitating minute divisions of value and thus continuous exchange, made many products more valuable than they would have been under a barter economy. It aided specialization, served as a barometer of market shifts, by ease of storage invited more savings, and served as a standard for various forms of credit. But, however useful it was, he did not see any need for an excess of money, which he believed was like an unused road. It took capital away from other beneficial uses. The needed amount was not easily specified, for it depended on the potential number of profitable exchanges, on the rapidity of circulation, and above all, on the degree to which credit instruments replaced money in transactions. More developed countries, with concentrated populations and greater specializations in labor, required more money than the United States, where so many people lived on farms that were nearly self-sufficient, where barter still survived, and where government taxes were low. But in a highly sophisticated economy the need for money once again decreased as credit instruments replaced it. Most transactions there involved paper transactions, mere shifts of balances on accounts.[42]

Like the Ricardians, Tucker relied on specie movements to match money supplies to local need. Nations short of specie imported it rather than consumer goods, for in such a case foreign gold was cheap compared with domestic prices. But Tucker would not follow John Taylor and the Jacksonians all the way on the equilibrating effect of a world market. Once again he stressed psychological factors. Large imports of specie do not necessarily lower its value or raise prices of other products, for people may hoard gold and thus curtail its circulation. Likewise, exports of specie do not necessarily trigger lower commodity prices, for the deficiency of money may stimulate either more rapid circulation or a substitution of more credit instruments, such as bank notes. Only gross shifts of supply need affect prices, and then the effects attach largely to prices determined in the domestic market. Even a dramatic increase of money in the United States would have limited impact on total world money supplies and thus on international prices. Because only certain domestic articles reflect a gross shift in money supplies, the effect there is often magnified, as is illustrated by speculative booms in real estate, the one article not at all related to stabilizing world prices. Shifts in money can occasion undesirable and unjust cycles of boom and bust, but Tucker recognized that, in fact, such monetary shifts are usually exaggerated by the parallel effects of bank credit. Thus, he accepted the great importance of a stable circulation, but unlike Jacksonians, he did not want to give up all the benefits of bank notes. Instead, he wanted a detailed regulation of such notes and thus a much more complete governmental control over the circulation.[43]

Since negotiable credit instruments replace money, they share all its virtues. In addition, they are often more convenient; and by extending or maximizing the utility of an often limited supply of money, they help nourish saving, stimulate industry, and thereby promote national wealth. Expanded credit particularly aids would-be entrepreneurs. Such credit, if limited to loans of specie, would either be prohibitively costly or else the United States would have to accumulate such specie at the cost of badly needed foreign imports, including machines and other capital goods. The type of desirable economic growth envisioned by Tucker, particularly in new heavy manufacturing, was all but inconceivable without a vast reliance on credit. Of course, credit carried its own perils, such as periodic orgies of speculation, a resulting loss of confidence, rapid retrenchment, and economic depression. Most of these dangers related not to private, noncirculating debt paper, which always constituted the largest component of national credit, but to negotiable instruments, which in the United States occasionally included government debt paper but largely involved bank notes. Here was the greatest opportunity for abuse. In a detailed essay that is quite instructive even yet, Tucker minutely described the state-based American banking system and its many and obvious flaws. So far, he concluded, state laws had been limited in scope and ineffective in implementation. Thus, he offered his own prescription for a sound American banking system.[44]

Almost all state-chartered American banks had the same general problem. Because of charter provisions accepted by irresponsible or corrupt legislatures, most banks were drastically undercapitalized. A bank typically began operations with twenty-five percent or less of its legal capital paid up in specie by subscribers. This meant they met subsequent installments by borrowing from the same bank. The total interest charged on such stockholder loans usually amounted to less than the total of dividends paid on what was essentially fictitious stock. To remedy this evil, Tucker urged that States enact stringent capitalization laws and allow no banks to begin business until the capital in the form of specie was in hand. He also wanted minimal capitalization laws, but with the minimums varying according to the size of cities.[45]

The most obvious evil of American banking originated in bankers' active complicity in speculative booms. They typically followed this up with a devastating credit contraction often accompanied by a suspension of specie payments. Private bankers sought the highest earnings possible, and in doing so often opposed the public interest. Banking policies, so far from moderating business cycles, almost always exaggerated them. Bankers often loaned their notes too freely, at too low a rate of interest, and to the wrong people, including family members or political favorites. At the peak of a boom created by their own reckless expansion, they often began calling in loans too quickly or subsequently enforced new and overly stringent credit standards. During speculative booms, bank notes largely replaced specie, much of which flowed abroad to cover trade deficits, leaving inadequate bank backing for notes and the likelihood of suspension or bank failure. So far, legislatures had condoned or legitimized suspension, thereby avoiding numerous bank failures but not panic and depression. But such abuses could be controlled. Nothing was more foolish than to throw the baby out with the bath water, to give up the benefits of banking because of the failure of governments to regulate it properly. Tucker believed antibanking agitation was as foolish as attempts to ban steamboats from the Mississippi because a few poorly constructed ones had exploded.

Although he welcomed the effects of bank competition, Tucker did not want to take the risk of completely unregulated banking. He accepted the often reckless atmosphere of America, which made it very unlikely that we could match the example of Scotland, with its numerous free or unchartered banks. Yet banks were too vital to a country, too closely tied to the government responsibility to provide a sound currency, for government to shrink from the task of controlling them. This meant carefully drafted charters and detailed regulatory laws. Tucker preferred such regulation to state ownership. Government banking might provide large public profits and reduced taxes, and banking was certainly so tied to the public interest as to fit within the accepted role of a sovereign. But Tucker knew too much about governmental ineptitude in America. He suspected that government bankers, with their enormous power, would lack banking skills, be lax in enforcing stringent criteria for loans, and above all, be prone to factional favoritism. Instead of government ownership, he recommended federally chartered but privately owned central banks, like the late and admirable Bank of the United States. It had insured an uniform currency, checked several abuses by state banks, and offered needed services to the government. But to meet political objections to its potential power (which Tucker personally discounted), he proposed three national banks, regionally located for convenience and blessed by the effects of orderly competition.[46]

The federal government could control national banks but had no direct control over state banks. Tucker recommended a series of state regulations, knowing that very few states would have the will to implement them. He wanted limited-term charters, which would set legal limits on bank note issues, limits tied either to actual paid-up capital or, better yet, to a stipulated specie reserve in bank vaults. He desired severe penalties for excessive issues. He also suggested penalties on all failures to redeem notes in specie, stringent disclosure and public audit laws, and limited terms for bank directors. He believed each state should own a minimum share of stock in each of its banks and should appoint public stockholders. Given rigid capital requirements, and evidence of public need, he wanted legislatures to charter new banks freely, thus assuring all the checks of competition. Banks owed the public taxes on their earnings and particularly on excessive profits. To be fair to the public, he felt banks should be required to pay low interest on demand deposits. He wanted to help protect minimal specie reserves by means of laws prohibiting small-denomination bank notes. He rejected other reform strategies, such as the required safety or insurance fund then being tried in New York State (an early version of FDIC), which he believed had not worked effectively. Since the United States maintained no appreciable debt, he saw no reason to stipulate that banks have a certain percentage of their loans in government paper. Above all, he opposed any modification or relaxation of limited liability provisions in charters. Without this accepted corporate device, he doubted that prudent men of wealth would dare invest in banks at all. In these recommendations, Tucker was not particularly original. All of them, except possibly his trinity of federal banks, had other advocates. But no American economist better understood banking or joined such a fervent enthusiasm for American banks with such an honest and harsh analysis of their inadequacies.[47]

Tucker ranks among the three or four most honest and creative economists of the mid-nineteenth century, European or American. More than any other American he confronted without flinching the implications of his up-dated and perfected Ricardian model. In this he moved beyond his southern contemporaries, although Cardozo anticipated most of Tucker's rent theory. Cooper saw all the distributive dilemmas posed by private ownership of unlimited quantities of land, but could find no personally or economically acceptable solution. His ambivalence went beyond personal considerations, beyond a defense of his social class. He believed that continued economic growth as well as the survival of a genteel culture depended on an unlimited right of accumulation by individual landlords. Thus, he embraced agrarian distributive goals without daring to embrace agrarian means—land redistribution and limits on the amount owned by any individual. Instead, he recommended a series of then unachievable legislative palliatives, or early intimations of a regulatory or welfare state. Cardozo expanded the concept of rent to include a component of capital goods. But instead of exploring the monopolistic implications of unlimited individual ownership, he stressed unending economic growth as a magical solution to most distributive problems.

Both Cooper and Cardozo celebrated a proprietary society, but in ways that always secured the well-being of those who already owned land or scarce capital goods. They never explored the plight of those who suffered less and less opportunity to own land and capital. In these respects, Tucker was more honest.

Even as Karl Marx struggled to clarify his critique of Ricardo, Tucker traveled much the same analytic path. But he offered no moral critique of social institutions. He not only held to the widely recognized distinction between political economy, the descriptive science, and policy advocacy, a separate moral endeavor; but he also deliberately refused to draw policy implications from his analysis or even suggest any such implications. As if he were a completely detached observer, he simply read out the long-term economic prospects. Short of rigid controls on the birthrate or a continuous expansion into new land, every society faced the prospect of a narrowed owning elite and a steady drainage of the least competitive members of this class into a growing nonowning class usually existing or expiring at or just below a subsistence level. Unlike Marx, Tucker suggested no political alternative, no institutional way out. No eventual economic heaven awaited the masses of mankind. He never seemed to feel that such a dire outlook was either fatalistic or tragic. He accepted the horrendous cost of progress. He claimed only to be realistic. Yet, more than any other economist, he reinforced the anxieties and fears, the profound doubts about America's future, that so characterized the middle period.

PART FOUR

—

ADVOCATES

VII

Protectionists

EARLY American political economists generally sought to identify universal principles or laws. This goal justified their frequent claim to scientific standing. But they insisted that such principles or laws, because of their very objectivity, were supremely useful, a direct benefit to policy makers. This made the study of political economy vital for American politicians. It also insured that the line between scientific description or analysis and overt policy advocacy was a very thin one. Economists of an academic bent, like Henry Vethake, or those concerned to market a textbook on many campuses, like Francis Wayland, often scrupulously refrained from commenting on controversial government policy, leaving to politicians the task of drawing what often seemed obvious policy deductions. But few economists managed even this much restraint. And on one issue in particular—protective tariffs—policy concerns often seemed to determine principles and laws.

No American economist completely avoided the "great tariff debate." Most were actively either for or against protection, or found their writings being used by one faction or the other. Those American economists in the tradition of Ricardo always supported free trade, and their views clearly predominated in college and university courses. That fact lent credence to the dissenters' frequently expressed contention that a monistic Ricardian orthodoxy dominated American economic thought. Those dissenters who laid claim to the greatest originality were apt to voice this contention all too often. In fact the two most brilliant and original early American economists—Raymond and Carey—were or became extreme protectionists; and a numerical weighing of publications by American economists shows a near standoff on the tariff issue. But for a Raymond or a Carey, the tariff issue always took its place within a much larger analytical context. At a less sophisticated and less academic or "scientific" level, the tariff debate led to many single-issue economic polemics by committed laymen. In a few cases the advocates on each side went beyond mere popularization. On the protectionist side, Willard Phillips and Calvin Colton were exceptionally sophisticated advocates of Clay's American System. They made some limited contributions to economic analysis and also helped give intellectual respectability to a raging public debate. They carried on a policy tradition that had begun with Alexander Hamilton, the first great protectionist.

Hamilton never claimed to be an expert economist, although he deserved that title more than any other American of his generation. He did conceive of himself as an economically informed statesman, committed to quite clear economic goals appropriate to what he conceived as a new *nation*. The term *nation* was more appropriate for Hamilton than for any other architect of early American governments. He always wanted a strong, unified United States, with a capable central government and a self-sufficient and prosperous national economy. He hoped the United States would soon rival the leading European countries, particularly Britain, in wealth and power. He was concerned with the sum of total wealth, with the strength and power of the whole union, and not so much with issues of distributive justice within the economy. He believed the individual stood to gain more, in the long run, from a thriving national economy, and even from the satisfaction of being part of a prosperous and powerful nation, than from any leveling legislation or from divisive, class-oriented attacks on wealth and privilege. If the rich grew richer, so much the better, if their wealth helped stimulate the growth needed to help the poor become less poor.

Hamilton worked to gain a fully consolidationist constitution, but with only limited success. He achieved only a partial charter for a centralized nation. But he did gain a charter that enabled the new federal government to overcome the fiscal ineptitude of the old Congress. He then tried to complete his nationalist program by introducing precedent-setting economic legislation under the paternal authority of President Washington. His most grandiose plan, which called for a whole spectrum of aids to heavy manufacturing, represented the greatest intellectual achievement of his life, but it won only very limited congressional approval.

As Secretary of the Treasury, Hamilton formulated a broad but controversial fiscal program. He worked out a detailed and ingenious plan for funding both the domestic and foreign debts of both the federal and state governments, and for establishing a federally chartered national bank. Funding, in itself, was not controversial. In order to retire its own due bonds, the federal government had no alternative but to issue new debt paper. But Hamilton's proposal to assume the state debts raised the divisive issue of state rights, and because of its unequal impact on different states, it also raised questions of equity. Payment at full value of the domestic debt, which by now was largely held by speculators, also involved equity, and therefore controversy. James Madison and a coalescing group of incipient Republicans used this issue to suggest that Hamilton favored the "moneyed classes" as against the yeomanry. Yet, in part because opponents could suggest no practical alternatives, Hamilton won his way. He felt he had established the good faith of the United States and in upholding public contracts had also established a vital moral principle. He made further emergency borrowing possible at low interest rates and by ingenious new debt obligations even helped relieve the shortage of money and credit in America. In fact, he saw his fiscal measures as the first, but in themselves still inadequate, government aid to manufacturing.[1]

Hamilton's famous 1791 "Report on Manufactures" took two years of careful preparation, and was by far the most impressive public document yet issued by the new federal government. In it, Hamilton announced an economic goal that seemed almost beyond controversy: to make the United States independent of all other countries for military and other essential supplies. No one disputed the need or the goal, but the means Hamilton proposed started a long controversy. Few people opposed either manufacturing or a self-sufficient economy. In fact, every president up to Abraham Lincoln praised manufacturing along with agriculture and commerce. Celebrating these three sectors, our economic trinity, early became a national ritual, and one not ignored by either Jefferson or Jackson. But it is clear that the image intended by the word *manufacturing* varied immensely from one person to another. Hamilton clearly wanted to encourage, not just the processing incidental to agriculture or more household manufactures, but fully specialized urban shops and, where appropriate, integrated factories. The crucial problem for him was how to achieve such goals and yet honor the conventional wisdom. He had to tread lightly and with great cleverness. As he recognized, he had to refute several near-truisms of his day, (all of them endorsed by Adam Smith): that agriculture is superior to other industries, that private choice alone should determine paths of investment, and that aid for one economic sector creates one especially favored economic class at the expense of all other sectors.

In a general way, Hamilton agreed with those conventional beliefs. He admitted the foundational importance of agriculture, applauded the freedom and independence it bestowed on farmers, and accepted its favored position in America. Since over 80 percent of Americans were in agriculture, Hamilton dared not slight their "calling." Instead, he pointed out the benefits to them of expanded manufacturing, and denied the often repeated but vulnerable Physiocratic argument that labor in agriculture alone leads to a real surplus. Instead he argued, anticipating Say, that nature cooperates with man in all forms of production. But Hamilton's main response to the Physiocratic doctrine was even more astute; he said, in effect, so what? The issue of productivity was meaningless; closely analyzed, it was a metaphysical abstraction of no utility. Whether manufacturing added to the total volume of national production or only changed the form of such production was a bogus issue. That manufacturing did change the form of products, rendering them more useful and desirable, was the important issue. If such labor were not expended, much consumption would cease, living standards would plummet, and the profitable employment of labor in such processing would give way to massive idleness. Farmers would then have no reason to grow raw produce that required processing for human consumption, and so even agricultural workers would be plunged into idleness as the economy moved back to a primitive and barbaric level. Whether manufacturing added to the value of raw produce or not, it tremendously increased the demand for such produce and thereby effectively raised the total production of a society, just as farming did. In fact, if expert farmers could not exchange products with specialized manufacturers, they would have to spend part of their time in home manufactures to sustain even the lowest level of subsistence, and so they would lose all the potential benefits of specialization. This argument was fully consistent with the views of Adam Smith. Thus, the Physiocrats offered Hamilton a nice, easily demolished target.

Hamilton also echoed some of Smith's positive arguments in behalf of manufacturing. Here labor is subject to greater improvement than in agriculture, both by more minute specialization and by the easier adaptation of machines. This meant, to Hamilton, that manufacturing was the real growth sector of any modern economy, the final clue to national strength. In agriculture, labor tended to be intermittent and poorly disciplined; in manufacturing, it could be constant and well disciplined, and such manufacturing labor in its possible variety provided scope for ingenuity and enterprise. To Smith's argument that agriculture alone provided returns to rent (a payment for nature's added productivity), Hamilton offered a persuasive counter-argument, which was soon to become virtually the standard American response. Land, he contended, functioned in America as a form of capital and rent was only a kind of interest or profit. Whether a given sum invested in agriculture returned higher profits than a similar sum invested in manufacturing was simply an empirical issue, tied to context and circumstances. In America we had no firm evidence on relative returns, but Hamilton believed some manufacturing already yielded profits higher than those in agriculture. Furthermore, wherever farmers had access to land at almost no cost, the cases were not comparable. Such a natural windfall gave a temporary advantage to agriculture; for this reason Hamilton never promoted heavy manufacturing in less-developed frontier areas.

For the coastal states, Hamilton saw enormous benefits in increased manufacturing. Specialization and new machines would increase worker productivity, as they had in our earliest cotton spinning mills (Hamilton himself was involved in a vast promotional scheme for textiles at Paterson, New Jersey). Large-scale manufacturing would use redundant labor, particularly women and children. He applauded the English cotton firms, in which as much as half of the labor force was composed of children, some of very tender age. We had heretofore lost the returns of such labor. Also, a developed manufacturing industry would entice more European immigrants, particularly those unfitted for, or disinclined to enter, agriculture and also those with needed mechanical skills. Manufacturing offered skilled workers outlets for their inventive energies and talents, while it provided a wider array of challenging investment possibilities for men of wealth. Such manufacturing would also create new demands for raw materials and thus serve to animate extractive industries. Hamilton shared none of Adam Smith's concern over the lowered quality of the work experience in factories or Jefferson's concern for the servility that went with wage employment.

These clever arguments suggested that the United States could have vast new manufacturing without challenging the role and status of existing agricultural proprietors. No farmer need suffer displacement or loss of status. Women, children, and immigrants could staff the mills and thereby contribute a net addition to national wealth. To all this Hamilton added what became the classic argument: manufacturing provides a home market for surplus agricultural products. He pointed out the vulnerability of American farmers, who had to depend on export markets and international prices. In trade, the United States remained a virtual colony of Europe and was always subject to ruinous trade restrictions and unfair terms of exchange. Increases in our export-oriented agricultural production would eventually run up against the problem of lowered market demand. The world market for tobacco and foodstuffs was not unlimited. Even though a diversion of our limited capital into manufacturing might slow the settlement and development of our public lands (Hamilton doubted this), that might serve the national interest by averting agricultural surpluses and resultant low prices. Hamilton preferred the improvement of existing farms and an ordered agricultural development to the prevailing mad scramble for new lands to the west.

His opponents could agree with some or all of Hamilton's contentions about the virtues of manufacturing. Some might even concede that manufacturing was as productive as agriculture, that it could grow on our agricultural base without displacing farmers, and that we needed a secure market for our increased farm product. But they insisted that manufacturing ought to develop naturally, without artificial and privilege-engendering subsidies. If conditions were ripe, it would develop without special aid. If conditions did not favor it, then it should not develop and indeed would not develop successfully without severe distortions and direct government favoritism. Adam Smith was the authority for all such arguments. To counter them effectively, Hamilton had to walk a fine line. On the one hand, he had to prove that America was ripe for manufacturing growth, that we had the basic requirements. Yet he had to prove that his special incentives or subsidies were necessary to launch such a development. He admitted that labor was both scarce and costly in America because of the ever present lure of cheap land and entrepreneurial status. But it was only males who demanded high wages; women and children would work for less. Immigrants were ready to flock to America. Hamilton, like almost every other propertied American, welcomed rapid population growth, which seemed likely to lead to increased land values and lower labor costs. When native-born American males entered manufacturing, it would be as investors or managers. Most native males would remain in agriculture and commerce and there benefit indirectly from manufacturing. As compensation for wages well above those in Europe (who could do other than rejoice in such wages?), we would have clear savings in transport costs and we could also use machines more extensively to reduce the need for labor.

What about capital, particularly if we developed more capital-intensive or mechanized industries? Hamilton professed ignorance of the amount of wealth available for manufacturing, particularly since much of the funding would originate in Europe if we offered promising prospects for profits. His own fiscal program—the bank and the funded debt—had dramatically extended the domestic sources of credit. This was one advantage of a national debt, and one appreciated in Britain. Throughout his report, Hamilton displayed his admiration of the British economy and the supportive functions of the British government. This gave ammunition to those of his critics who saw clearly the darker aspects of English manufacturing—its human costs—and deplored Hamilton's efforts to transplant the ugly and class-divisive mills of England to free and independent America.

Hamilton believed that unless the government fostered the growth of manufacturing through subsidies, manufacturing would grow only very slowly. He stressed the role of experience and habit, which induce people to remain in their present occupations. The high early risks in new manufacturing, the developed advantage of European countries with mature firms, and above all, the bounties and aids already offered manufacturing in Europe placed us at a particular disadvantage. Given the great benefits of domestic manufacturing, we had no alternative but to use subsidies to some extent. This meant robbing Peter to pay Paul, for no doubt protected manufacturing goods would at first be more expensive than former imports. But, said Hamilton, using another classic argument that came up constantly in the great tariff debate, competition would subsequently lower domestic prices to international levels, making the effective subsidy to manufacturing short-lived. But the crux of Hamilton's argument was the need for national economic independence and self-sufficiency. He could not deny that some private interests would gain short-term benefits from his proposals and others would suffer short-term losses, but he believed the nation as a whole would gain important benefits and that, in the long run, all sectors and interests would benefit. The arguments of free-trade exponents, who favored competitive national specialization, depended on the existence of world peace and international comity, assumptions contrary to international realities in the midst of the French Revolution and a developing European war. Hamilton used the tensions of his day to buttress his plea for a range of manufacturing subsidies: protective tariffs, selective trade prohibitions on both imports and raw material exports, direct bounties to favored industries, premiums on favorite articles, exemption of needed raw material imports from reverse duties, awards for invention, quality control regulations, better banking services, and internal improvements to enhance domestic transportation. Except for some mildly protective tariff rates, Congress turned a deaf ear to all of Hamilton's proposals.[2]

Many proponents of large-scale American manufacturing kept up Hamilton's crusade after his death. They organized such associations as the Philadelphia Society for the Protection of National Industry and with some success appealed for tariff protection in the economic crisis that followed 1815, and again in the late twenties. Eventually, on the tariff issue and on support for a balanced economy, Henry Clay became Hamilton's political successor, while his American System became almost the only distinguishable early platform of a Whig coalition that formed in opposition to Andrew Jackson. In the early national period, the ablest and best-known spokesman for protection was Mathew Carey, a wealthy Philadelphia publisher. Generally, Carey expanded on Hamilton's arguments, but he felt a need to attack British economists.[3] The growing currency of the "new" system of Ricardo and McCulloch, added to the lingering authority of Smith and Say, seemed to give enormous intellectual authority to the free-trade position. Carey cultivated Daniel

Raymond as a promising exception, but the independent and eccentric Raymond embraced too many heresies in other areas to head a school of protectionist economists. Foreign proponents of protection like Lord Lauderdale and the Americanized German, Frederick List, were men of much lesser stature than the great British economists. But the problem of intellectual leadership was not acute until well after 1833. Politically, the tariff issue did not solidify firmly along party lines until after the nullification controversy, and firm Democratic support for free trade was hardly an infallible test of party loyalty before the Whig tariff bill of 1842. It was then that Willard Phillips and Calvin Colton published the most partisan economic arguments in behalf of protection.

Both Phillips and Colton were born and reared in Massachusetts. Both came from old Puritan families. They had in common a moral seriousness, a great sense of communal solidarity, and a repugnance to undisciplined individualism. But their careers were very different. Phillips, a precocious youngster, graduated from Harvard with a brilliant record. He stayed on for a few years as a tutor (this position would later be his only claim to academic status). From teaching he went into law and practiced in Boston. He had journalistic skills, published articles in most leading magazines, and briefly published a journal of his own. He served one term in the Massachusetts Assembly, and in later years was the president of a large mutual life insurance firm. He wrote highly regarded books on insurance and patent law. His political views paralleled very closely those of a Massachusetts neighbor—John Quincy Adams. Phillips early developed an interest in economic theory and in later years recounted, with some bitterness, his early ensnarement by the groundless postulates and sheer sophistry of the Ricardians. But he quickly extricated himself from such logical traps, and in 1828 he published one of the two or three earliest American textbooks on political economy, *A Manual of Political Economy.*[4]

By 1828 Phillips was already defending protectionist policies. But this issue had not yet moved to the center of political debate and did not yet involve any passionate commitment on his part. Thus, his little manual was eclectic and amazingly balanced; it deserved more respect and more readers than it ever won. Its very virtues—among them were brevity, the absence of exaggerated claims, and a willingness to consider differing points of view—probably helped reduce college adoptions. Phillips shared certain viewpoints with Raymond and, like Raymond, took the demand theories of Malthus and Lord Lauderdale very seriously. Yet he blunted these with doctrines from Smith and Ricardo, economists he would later denounce with great vehemence.

Phillips viewed political economy as a new, uncompleted science. Confusion still reigned on all major issues. Systems came and went. He claimed no finality to any of his views. He could not even fully embrace some eclectic combination of existing systems, and throughout his text he revealed a great deal of skepticism about the most widely accepted doctrines. If he displayed any distinctive outlook, it was in his Puritan sense of the importance of communal solidarity, a general outlook which he shared with Raymond, Colton, and Carey. Phillips did not yearn for a return to a primitive nature or to the independence this allowed. He celebrated interdependence and cooperation; for they, and only they, made possible a highly productive labor force and general prosperity. By cooperation, by organization, by belonging to a great market, American workers could consume more goods than a savage monarch. Like John Quincy Adams, Phillips sought a developed and complex economy, which meant more organization, more tools, more exchange, more specialization, more education, more self-discipline, more art. It meant both more work and more efficient work, but work was "the great business of the world."[5]

Because he was writing a textbook, Phillips had to address all the issues that were by then traditional in political economy, beginning with value. He could identify no convenient standard or measure of value, for even different forms of labor defied exact comparison. At any time a product will obviously exchange for a certain amount of labor, but this may not be the same amount of labor that produced it. The intensity of desire for products shifts over time. He agreed with the Ricardians that the cost of production usually has more to do with exchange values than any other single factor, and that prices do tend toward a natural level tied to the cost of production. But the relation of price to cost is not a stable one. Phillips noted lags and inelasticities in prices. Higher production costs are more quickly passed on in higher prices than are lowered costs in price cuts. But it is also true that customary prices may long resist even the pressure of higher cost, presumably at the cost of lower wages or lower profits or both. These insights into the real behavior of people, into lag factors and the complexity of market adjustments, reinforced Phillips's skepticism over the proclaimed usefulness of very abstract theory. It also made him sensitive to the complex, chain-reaction effects of price reductions. With Lauderdale and Malthus, he feared what had clearly threatened man in the past—periodic gluts or stagnant periods of little economic growth. These reverses showed the complexity of demand and also suggested the benefits of mild inflation. Generally, rising prices sustained industry and insured more stable growth.[6]

Phillips applauded the legal foundations of private property in America. He believed that arguments derived from the principles of both natural justice and utility vindicated secure private ownership of labor-derived products and of land. He mentioned several different kinds of tenure but clearly favored the fee-simple titles granted landowners in America. Given secure private titles to land, and any degree of scarcity, then lands obviously and rightly earned rent. And if one could legitimately charge rent for land, clearly one could also command interest for money, which is exchangeable for land. Thus, Phillips followed almost all American economists in correlating land with productive capital and in tying together the rates of rent and interest, given equal risk. Because he wanted market demand to determine both, he joined his voice to the American chorus of condemnation for usury laws.

The economic advantages of fee-simple land ownership lay in the effect it had on owners, particularly on single owners of small farms. America was prosperous, not just because of rich natural resources or low rents but because of individual habits of industry deeply ingrained and passed on from generation to generation. Phillips did not celebrate frontier conditions, although he never showed the kind of extreme distaste for the frontier that Carey would. Actually, frontier land was all but worthless; settlers gained little but an opportunity to make wealth through arduous work. That was enough. Ownership energized people as no other incentive could. Individual proprietors embraced self-denial and hard work and developed an unrivaled drive and ambition. The typical American wanted to own his means of production, tried steadily to improve his land or to gain other forms of capital, and was usually quite willing to consider better techniques of production. People under other conditions of labor—slaves on southern plantation or operatives in British factories—understandably worked less hard, developed less ambition, and were rarely able to accumulate savings. In America those who had not achieved proprietary status knew bitter frustration and discontent, for they had failed to attain what amounted to a national norm. But even their discontent was energizing. It led to increased effort, not to the benumbed acceptance or despair visible in the unpropertied masses of Europe. Our proprietary economy had its own problems. Phillips particularly deplored land speculation, which diverted money from more productive investment, sometimes for years. It also contributed to periodic business distress. But even depression had little adverse effect on American economic growth. Since most American producers were independent proprietors, with assured access to basic subsistence, hard times only spurred them to work even harder and to practice greater thrift. We suffered little unemployment and little dependence. American workers continued to improve their farms or household shops even in the midst of financial panic.[7]

Although he glorified the character traits of independent proprietors, Phillips foresaw the growth of integrated manufacturing in America and believed it to be desirable. So far, abundant and cheap resources, low taxes, and the hard work of individual entrepreneurs had assured high levels of production and steady growth, which made possible the much-acclaimed high wages and profits earned in America. Here money was always scarce, interest high. Americans who had savings usually invested them in new land and kept very little money for lending. These high factor costs meant that the United States would rarely be able to compete in foreign markets with low-wage, low-profit European manufacturers. For these reasons, Phillips believed, the main avenue of growth lay in a balanced national economy, which required increased domestic manufacturing. This meant more city dwellers, more people working for wages, but a payoff in greater efficiency and higher living standards. But to maximize economies of scale, he wanted our factories dispersed in every town and village. This promised local markets for agriculturists and lower transport costs and would retain for all Americans the considerable benefits of low rents. More importantly, Phillips wanted to preserve the frugality and industry that characterized individual entrepreneurs. He asked employers in cities to foster these habits, to encourage or reward savings and home ownership. Our wage workers should all be aspiring capitalists, with an ardent desire to gain property and with enough hope to work unremittingly to achieve such desires. Thus, in a sense, Phillips envisioned collective enterprise in America without any of the servility associated with European factories. His was the perennial dream of American protectionists, that we could realize all the economic advantages of specialization and association and yet suffer none of the human costs.[8]

On problems of distribution, Phillips usually followed common sense. He cavalierly dismissed Ricardo's rent theory as "somewhat metaphysical" and "now almost exploded," but never bothered to refute it in any detail. He granted the obvious—when privately owned resources became scarce, their value necessarily rose and they commanded more rent. In the absence of new tools and greater efficiency in production, such higher rents necessarily depressed wages. High land values and rents in America had usually reflected economic growth, and therefore were innocuous. The new tools and techniques sustaining the growth had provided the means for higher wages. But Phillips granted the practical difficulty of keeping wages, profits, and rents all high at the same time. Of the three, high rents were least advantageous to a country, and he believed that rising rents at some unspecifiable point represented a clear detriment to any national economy. Given American resources and the ingenuity of American workers, he foresaw no such early danger for the United States. In fact, unlike almost every other American economist, he defended the higher rents created by the English corn laws. They raised food prices, of course, but they also stabilized agricultural prices and made England less dependent on foreign producers. Typically, Phillips wanted national self-sufficiency in as many areas as possible, but especially in foodstuffs. He pointed out that high food prices fed a form of continuous price inflation in England, which supported gradual growth and in effect reduced the burden of Britain's large national debt. He doubted Britain could meet payments on its debt in an era of deflation.[9]

Phillips denied any inherent conflict between wages and profits. High returns to investors usually reflected a growing demand for labor, and thus higher wages. He understood the difference between the total amount of profit, which he wanted to be high, and the rate of profit, which most benefited a nation when low. This meant that the ideal condition for growth was low interest rates accompanied by so much accumulated capital per capita that even those low rates still meant very attractive returns to individual investors. Since America was still accruing capital, these enviably low interest rates lay ahead, at a more mature stage of development.[10]

Since economic growth in America meant more wage laborers, Phillips attended carefully to their prospects. The lowest category of workers, unskilled day laborers, constituted a very vulnerable, and thus a very dangerous, class. They were first to lose their jobs in an economic decline, had limited self-respect, and were very susceptible to mob action or insurrection. Phillips accepted a public responsibility for the unemployed. He saw no humane alternative to some carefully devised form of work relief on farms and gardens. Private charity always leaves some to perish from want. But minimal subsistence was not an appropriate goal in America. Every laborer should have a job and should earn enough to save a bit. Those who would not save when they had the means earned no solicitude from Phillips; they deserved only subsistence wages. But men of good character, of typical American character, had to have a "way up," a realistic possibility of rising out of a dependent laboring class. If they had no real chance to become entrepreneurs, workers would fall into sullen and angry defiance or even into the passive stupor of slaves, and thus become mere "machines of production." Hope was essential, for with hope workers would endure bosses and dependence for a time. In addition to good wages for workers, Phillips wanted public education for all children, continued high public respect for all types of work, and an active political role for all workers. Literate, franchised voters could channel their discontent into constructive reform, not destructive violence. Unlike many of his contemporaries and unlike Colton, Phillips did not see western land as a practical alternative for day laborers. They had neither the capital nor the skills to homestead. But the lure of western land had helped insure the very small number of such laborers in America and also the comparatively high wages they usually received. It was farmers, not wage workers, who moved west. Typically, a New England farmer with small acreage, or one of his sons, moved to larger farms in the West. Without this opportunity, many farmers in the East would long since have been forced into wage employment.[11]

Even as early as 1828, Phillips reserved his greatest zeal for recommendations on commercial policy. He applauded exchange, including even our limited foreign exchange (seven percent of our national product) so long as it profited our country, but not necessarily foreign trade that profited the producers or merchants directly engaged in it. He emphatically denied that private interest always paralleled the public interest. Inherent in the very purposes of government was control over private will and interest in behalf of the larger community. This responsibility of government did not stop short of the economic sphere. A government benefited all by providing free education for a few. In the same spirit and for the same reasons, it needed to regulate and coordinate the whole economy. If, for instance, some new agricultural technique promised a dramatic rise in productivity, the government was justified in setting up experiment stations or using other means to encourage the early adoption of such techniques. He delighted in this analogy of experiment stations, and used it for several different purposes. If a new but risky industry promised long-term benefits, then the government clearly had a responsibility to support such an experiment by tariffs or other modes of subsidy or protection. If the government could get more people working or get them working more efficiently, then it had a clear duty to do so. Phillips had only contempt for free-trade arguments or sophistic arguments in favor of domestic laissez-faire. In 1828, as later, he delighted in listing fifteen or twenty accepted areas of governmental economic coordination or regulation. He wanted more rules, more guarantees of fair play, more licenses or safety rules or standards to protect consumers.

This general outlook underlay Phillips's views on the tariff. Like Daniel Raymond, he desired protection for potentially efficient and productive manufacturers. Temporary protection might be necessary to cushion high early risks, and permanent protection to stabilize prices or prevent foreign dumping, even when our domestic prices were normally lower than import prices. Phillips's two main goals were domestic self-sufficiency and an increase in the total amount of work. He believed that the free traders were being unrealistic when they posited a world permanently at peace, in which national selfishness played no significant role, a state of affairs possible only through a single world government. If tariffs temporarily or even permanently raised consumer prices, they were still in the public interest as long as they inspired industry on the part of those heretofore underemployed or unemployed. He saw the limits, and the risks, of export markets for raw produce, and he hoped that security could be found in the virtually unlimited expansion of domestic markets.[12]

After he wrote his text, Phillips became passionately involved in partisan tariff debates. In an 1850 polemic in behalf of Clay's American system, he dipped his pen in vitriol. He ridiculed and berated the "theories, sophisms, and policies," as well as the "dogmatism," of the dominant free-trade economists. He said that they advocated policies more dangerous than those of Saint Simon, Fourier, or the 1848 Communists; that their theoretical abstractions threatened the very survival of Christendom. He despaired when he reflected that such absurd notions had long prevailed in most American colleges, that they had found endless support among southern slave owners, and that their influence was apparent in the "demagoguery" exhibited by the Polk Administration.[13]

Phillips directed his most devastating attack against the "let alone" policies of free-trade economists. Not even Henry Carey had a more organic view of society than Phillips, who talked of the United States as a spider web, as "one immense network" in which all individuals were reciprocally dependent, with action by one inevitably affecting all the others. If mankind was to have government at all, and to enjoy its benefits, it had to accept the obvious—laws do affect the industry of a people. Only cheats, pickpockets, and impostors sincerely cried out for *laissez-nous faire.* Any economic system was indissolubly tied to the economic policy of a state. Since legislation, and often even the potential of legislation, inevitably conditioned economic activity, the real political issue was whether national economic policy was to be planned or unplanned, carefully calculated to accomplish defensible moral goals or effected blindly by an aimless "shoot at random" approach.

The proper end of economic policy should be more, and more useful, voluntary industry, and with that a realized happiness for a greater number of people. Phillips doubted that anyone rejected this goal. The real issue was what policies best served it. Free traders, behind their patently false claims of laissez-faire or even neutrality, had in effect chosen to favor agriculture and commerce as against heavy forms of manufacturing. But Phillips believed that the mass of common people in America were largely immune to the abstractions of "metaphysical" economists and wanted their government to succor and protect all forms of useful industry, not in behalf of any one class, not to protect existing wealth, but to increase the sum of national wealth. The criminal law, as well as guarantees for property, were all predicated on the need for more useful industry. So were laws that provided for taxes, military protection, education, patents, inspections, licenses, coinage, poor relief, wills and inheritance, internal improvements, franchises, and charters. Such laws not only promoted industry but often specifically favored home industry as against foreign. Any government that refused special protection to home industry, that opened our markets to cheap foreign goods, in effect legislated in favor of foreign producers and penalized our own. To call free trade "neutral" was absurd, for it so penalized American laborers as to be "wicked, calamitous, and ruinous."[14]

Phillips carefully listed and defined eleven fallacies of a somewhat caricatured free-trade school, and then offered slashing, clever, often angry refutations of each. Their first and greatest fallacy was that a laissez-faire policy was possible without anarchy. Amost as crucial was the absurd theory that what individuals supposed to be in their own best interest was also advantageous to the total community. From these two the other fallacies followed: that one import is as good as another so long as a free market operates; that the interest of one country dovetails with the interests of all, or that boundaries and nationalities have no economic role; that men are primarily buyers and sellers, not producers; that there is an unlimited market for all goods produced, and in particular that world markets will absorb any imaginable increase in American agricultural output; that regardless of the role of legislation or of circumstances, a given amount of capital invested in any industry will create a given number of jobs; that policy makers can assume full employment in an unregulated economy, and that all men, women, and children work at fair wages; that the welfare of a country can be recorded at the end of each year by a profit and loss mode of accounting; that the millennium has begun, since war will never again occur; and, finally, that any production for which a country is economically suited will spring up spontaneously, at the proper time, and in spite of any form or volume of foreign competition.[15]

In his most perceptive critique of free-trade theorists, and particularly of Ricardo, Phillips concentrated on what he understood as Say's law. This, he believed, was a key to the Ricardian model, the one issue upon whose accuracy it depended. In this, he agreed with many later economic historians. Yet, so many ambiguities surround Say's law, and the law takes so many forms, that it is impossible to know if Phillips was really on target. What he denied was that the overall sum of effective demand in a market, by definition, grew as fast as supply. Of course, no economist ever denied the existence of temporary or local but always self-correcting maladjustments between the supply and demand for any given product, based on shifting tastes and market misjudgments by certain producers. In fact, such local or temporary maladjustments helped guide the magical equilibrating shifts in the allocation of capital and labor that best enabled a free market to fulfill human wants. Usually, arguments over Say's law, over the possibilities of a general glut, foundered on the scope of "general" or on the length of "temporary."

Phillips believed his rejection of Say's law involved critical issues. By his standards, a country suffered a general glut if, over extended periods of time, any of its people remained without employment, suffered under-employment, or even were unable to use many of their developed skills. Thus, he made a "superfluity of labor" and not panic or famine or even widespread distress and suffering the key factor in identifying a glut, although famine was always a prominent manifestation of a glut in coun-tries whose populations already lived near a subsistence level, as in Ireland. The problem with Phillips's definition, of course, is that he so relativized the meaning of glut as to make it fit any country whose economy lagged to any extent behind its fullest productive potential. To Phillips, even the prosperous United States suffered such a glut, for here, despite our vast resources, our high demand for labor and our realized personal freedoms, large numbers of people were unemployed (most women and children) or underemployed (most farmers during part of the year). Look how many farmers rushed off to California in 1849 with no loss of agricultural production back home. Meanwhile, we had a super-fluity of farm products and a scarcity of many manufactured goods. He saw absolutely no possibility that a free market (the sum of various choices made by private individuals or interest groups) would soon, or indeed ever, correct our underutilization of resources. A few individuals and groups always gain short-range benefits from a sluggish economy. Selfish individuals would always calculate their behavior according to short-term consequences, for a person may only expect to live a short time. But a wise community calculates policies for all generations. Only positive, calculated growth policies by government, only numerous gov-ernment incentives and protections, could bring full employment and a level of prosperity even close to our national potential.[16]

Of course, existing federal policies were not really neutral, despite their laissez-faire camouflage. Some reflexive increase in tariff rates was not the rational alternative. Phillips recognized the inherently competi-tive interests of different producers. A high tariff on raw wool penalized woolen mills. Tariffs on iron at least temporarily raised the cost of most capital, beginning with the crucial rails needed for our booming railroad system. Thus, Phillips asked for carefully-thought-out, flexible tariff rates, with widely varying rates for different items. This passed on to politicians the divisive task of forming tariff legislation, of trying to determine in each case what served the public interest. But unless Con-gress accepted this responsibility, it would continue to further the in-terests of Great Britain. The United States, as an exporter of raw pro-duce, remained an economic colony of Europe. Protection of key manu-facturers could terminate that dependency; free trade promised to take us back toward a fuller colonial relationship.[17]

The most persuasive Democratic arguments against tariffs skirted purely economic issues. Some people ranked other national priorities above maximized output. Above all, Americans had committed themselves to freedom, to an economic environment in which each man could attain property and an entrepreneurial role. Thus, Democrats in Congress stressed not only the redistributive injustices of tariffs but the factory system they would nourish. To them factories meant increasing riches for a few owners and managers, servile dependency for workers, and the beginnings of a hated class system. Protectionists had to respond to such arguments or lose the debate in the public forum, where proprietors, and proprietary values, still dominated. Phillips only partially confronted the challenge by emphasizing increased small-scale home manufacturing along with highly collectivized factory production. He frequently praised free artisans, and applauded proprietary manufacturing in all areas where it remained efficient. But in many industries, such as textiles, household manufacturing was clearly no longer competitive, and Phillips wanted the United States to thrive in all profitable areas. He desired economies of scale, although he noted that these did not always accrue to large firms. He always argued for decentralized even if large factories, or for a local mix of agriculture, manufacturing, and commerce.[18]

Like most protectionists, Phillips emphasized the benefits for the consumer of large-scale enterprise. Mass production and low unit prices meant economic benefits for all, even if some reaped more benefits than others. Only an irrational jealousy could nourish opposition. Such jealousy, and plenty of politically motivated demagoguery, had to lie behind the Democratic crusade against "capitalists," the rich, and all corporations, as if it were a crime to establish a great system of industry. The Democrats stigmatized men of competence for investing in such enterprise, for using their wealth productively. These same Jacksonians were often wealthy themselves or hypocritically trying to become rich. Their continuous condemnation of factory owners, but not of affluent merchants and planters, proved malignant motives and sordid minds. The Jacksonians had borrowed too many of their ideas from Ricardo, ideas based on the assumption of fixed social classes, which amounted to a libel on American institutions. Here sons of the rich frequently became poor, just as sons of poor men frequently rose to great riches. Again, Phillips foresaw a quite different institutional development for American factories, since American wage workers, unlike European ones, were in no sense oppressed or under any dire economic compulsion. They bargained freely. Industrious men, even when employees, knew their employer was as dependent on their work as they were on the wages they received. Here egalitarian mutuality prevailed, and even if all manufacturing capitalists became rich (they certainly would not), no one would have any reason for resentment. All profited from their success and they certainly deserved the same protection of the laws as anyone else.[19]

Despite such an idealized portrait of industrial harmony, Phillips rarely explored the nuances of employer-employee relationships. Like practically everyone who wrote on political economy, he professed the most solicitude for the masses of working people. But their welfare, as he described it, typically rested on high wages and not on individual autonomy or fulfilling work. High wages, based on efficiency and high per capita productivity, meant leisure, education, and certain comforts heretofore reserved for the wealthy. This meant an eventual chance to escape wage employment. "We all believe," he said, "that the well being of the masses should be cared for, and that the rate of wages has a predominating influence upon it." Protection thus entailed high returns and greater economic security for existing farm owners and self-employed craftsmen. Admittedly, large-scale enterprise meant more wage workers, but the voluntary status of laborers and the harmony of interest between capitalists and workers eliminated most aspects of servility, and along with that any threat of mobs, strikes, or conspiracies.[20]

Phillips clinched his protectionist arguments by stressing purely economic benefits. Besides benefiting all classes, a balanced and growing national economy would even expand international trade and raise tariff revenues, an argument that could only seem foolishly contradictory to free-trade exponents. Already, as Phillips had demonstrated, we had a developed export market for many of our manufacturers, not usually in Europe but in nearby areas of Latin America. Overall, we had to pay for imports with exports (a typical free-trade argument). Lowered tariffs threatened the survival of our export manufacturers, and thus promised to reduce our total exports, since markets for our raw produce were already saturated. Exports maintained the existing level of imports, and the duties from imports largely underwrote the expense of our federal government. Such manufacturing exports also proved how competitive were ingenious American producers, even with our high wages. Surely such competitive products required no tariff protection at home. Not so, said Phillips. Foreign dumping was always a threat. Tariffs on such items provided needed security to investors, and thus protected lower domestic prices for consumers. Let large European firms regain our markets, even by selling at a loss, and they would quickly raise prices back to their original level. With such arguments, Phillips pictured protection as a device to aid all classes: it would secure profits for investors, permanently raise wages for workers, in many cases significantly lower prices for consumers, and even increase tariff revenues.[21]

Calvin Colton (1789-1857) lacked the breadth of Phillips. But he was infinitely cleverer and more original as a critic of reigning fashions in political economy. Of Puritan descent, he graduated from Yale and then from Andover Theological Seminary. He was a Presbyterian pastor until his voice began to fail, effectively ending his career as a preacher, although he continued to publish popular works on religion. He also converted to the Episcopal Church. In the mid-thirties he served in London as a correspondent for the *New York Observer*, where he wrote flattering tour guides on America. After his return to the United States in 1835 he became the ablest pamphleteer of the emerging Whig party, and was for a time editor of the *True Whig* in Washington. In 1844 he became the official biographer of Henry Clay and also edited Clay's papers. He wrote from an intensely partisan position. His 1848 book on "public" economy amounted to a ringing defense of the American system. He dropped the label "political economy" because of the complete degradation of politics by the Jacksonians. This book, the only one he ever wrote on economic theory, helped gain him a chair in "public economy" at Trinity College in Hartford, a post he held until his death. Colton came to know the western expanses of America better than Phillips ever did. Whereas Phillips always displayed the great sense of social responsibility and the genteel moral elitism of a John Quincy Adams, Colton learned from Henry Clay a more egalitarian outlook. He expressed a soaring, at times blindly optimistic, idealism. This idealism, despite or perhaps because of its holistic emphasis, had implications for American institutional development fully as radical as the more atomistic and class-based criticism of the so-called Jacksonian intellectuals.[22]

At the very least, Colton was brash. He attempted nothing less than a complete refutation of the free-trade position and of the vast structure of economic theory undergirding it. He began with the most sophisticated analysis of the scientific status of political economy offered by an American before the Civil War. He did not deny in principle that some aspects of political economy might yet become scientific, in the sense of embodying truly universal principles or laws. But the discipline certainly had not attained such a status as yet. Colton could find no uniform propositions that applied to all places and all times. Contextuality so far had dominated economic speculation. Drawing on the work of Comte and Mill, on their identification of social subjects that as yet encompassed too great complexity for rigorous scientific status, he described the purported principles of the Ricardian system as mere summaries of empirical experience, with no proven or provable generality beyond that of the repeated observations that originally suggested them. Political economists had moved indiscriminately from specific circumstances to rules or laws, but had never been able to deduce from general laws the occurrence of specific events. Unlike physical scientists, economists could not subsume events under uniform causal relationships. This did not mean that the limited generality of political economy made it useless, but only that its principles had utility within a particular and defined empirical context, and this usually meant within a given nation. Even the most general concepts and relationships in political economy, those that clearly explained phenomena in many different contexts, always coexisted with so many local particularities as to have variant policy implications from one country to another. Any empirically valid and reliably useful political economy still had to be a national political economy.[23]

This understanding of the discipline led Colton to two major strategies. He was forever exposing the provincial biases and the deceitful political goals he found in British free-trade theory, and balanced this by a glowing description of the many unique characteristics of the United States that necessitated our own distinctive political economy. In effect, Colton viewed the economic analyses of Malthus, Ricardo, and McCulloch as parts of a vast British conspiracy to dominate the rest of the world. Orthodox theory was the leading intellectual weapon of British colonialism, a weapon first honed by Adam Smith, although Colton found some redeeming qualifications and some moral sensibility in Smith. Viewed from the perspective of the dominant economic interests in Britain, the free-trade orthodoxy was rational, for it was perfectly congruent with the competitive international position of British merchants and manufacturers. And as an offensive weapon in the jungle of international commercial rivalry, it had so far worked to perfection. Because of its internal coherence, its logical simplicity, its sophistic claim to scientific objectivity, and its widespread dissemination by British spokesmen, by prestigious academics the world over, and even by calculating imitators in America, it had won for Britain one strategic advantage after another and usually without even a fight. In fact, all too often, as in Jacksonian America, the victims of British exploitation acted the part of willing slaves; they embraced the very sophistries of their masters.

Colton ridiculed the idea of a family of nations. Countries all differed and inevitably had conflicting interests. Open and free competition inevitably favored older, stronger, and more developed countries. It enabled rich nations to accrue more wealth, while it retarded the growth and increased the dependence of young, less capitalized countries. It was obvious why Great Britain favored free trade—it had a competitive advantage over all other countries because of its superior arts and developed productive capabilities. But Britain had practiced protection earlier in order to build up its capital. Now, as the big bully of the commercial world, it naturally cried out for free competition, knowing it could always win if it could persuade its enemies to remain unarmed and unprotected. Behind the camouflage of idealistic-sounding free-trade slogans, Britain continued to practice a form of robbery on the rest of the world, exchanging small amounts of its labor for large amounts from abroad.[24]

Although Colton admitted and even admired the industrial strength of Britain, he had only sympathy for the oppressed workers of England and of all Europe. No American chauvinist ever drew a sharper contrast between European and American social conditions. European workers still lived under an oppressive class system, the lingering heritage of an earlier feudalism. A few owned; most served. English free-trade economists always assumed the existence of three classes of people: landowners, capitalists, and unpropertied workers. Their talk of rents, tithes, and poor rates made no sense in America. Their analysis did not apply to a classless society. Malthus and Ricardo assumed that workers would live at a near-subsistence level and that few of them would ever aspire to property and a managerial role, even in the unlikely event that such opportunities existed. To the free-trade economists, the masses in society were "mere working machines." They also assumed as normal a narrow and essentially idle landowning "rent" class. Colton painted an awful picture of oppressed, slavelike, illiterate, unfranchised European tenants and factory workers who were doomed to live all their lives near a subsistence level. Yet the great names in political economy had all justified and explained their plight, excused oppression, and in a sense made God responsible for it. The owning and exploiting classes in Europe stole two-thirds of the value created by labor. This meant that the masses of Europe had a great battle to fight against their masters (Colton wrote before the possibly liberating results of the 1848 revolutions were known). They had to right all the "wrongs done to labor" by oppressive and expensive governments, by men of rank, by owners of great estates, and by commercial millionaires. By a gradual and peaceful economic revolution, the American masses had attained their present status and freedom. Colton feared only a violent revolution could bring the same emancipation to Europe, although he still hoped that the eventual commercial success of a free and protected American economy would force European ruling classes voluntarily to adopt our own free institutions rather than lose all their markets.[25]

The glories of American freedom highlighted the gloom of Europe. In America the masses had gained the fullest freedom in all human history. From a Hegelian perspective, Colton pronounced our vulnerable but remarkable achievement as a new stage in the universal progress of freedom. By *freedom* Colton did not mean an ethereal abstraction, or slant it at all toward expressive rights, such as freedom of religion, speech, or press. He gave it an almost exclusively economic meaning. To be free is to enjoy a commercial right, or the right to acquire wealth and to control it, which in turn requires that one have control over one's labor and a secure claim to all its products. Only these rights make one independent, and at the personal level they were the rights for which we fought the

American Revolution. Protection against cheap goods produced by the oppressed classes of Europe was now necessary to preserve this economic liberty. Increased American manufacturing, more home markets, and economic balance were indispensable for the continued economic opportunity that allowed Americans to be free. Thus, in a virtual tour de force, Colton eulogized the proprietary man so beloved of Jacksonian spokesmen, yet argued that only positive governmental intervention and more associated enterprise could protect and preserve such freedom.

Colton assumed every American man wanted to be free, and that except for slaves every single one of them had excellent prospects for gaining a free status. Every self-respecting American wanted to be a proprietor of a freehold estate and to be exempt from arbitrary taxes and tithes. Colton believed that the United States had almost no permanent tenants or wage employees and also no idle elites. Here all worked and all made up one economic class. As he put it, in reference to Europe: "Ours is a different world from theirs. Things here started different, have grown up different, and are different." Even rare and exceptional deviations from the American pattern, such as the widespread tenancy system in the Hudson Valley, so ran against the American grain that they provoked intense opposition (he referred to recent rent strikes in New York). Thus, at one point Colton argued that "rent does not exist here. God grant it never may!" Americans would suffer no masters; "ages, all time may roll away, before it is likely that one American will be able to force another into his service, from the necessity of the latter, and dictate his wages."[26]

Colton celebrated new and ever larger factories. In their American context they offered no threat to the proprietary norm. Even when employed, Americans still worked for themselves and had an equal voice in determining their wages. The vast majority worked on their own farms or owned their own shops. Those who hired out did it only to acquire capital and set up for themselves. At least for men, Colton foresaw no permanent wage employment, for such men would insist on being "lords of their own position and destiny," or "lords of their own domain." In America property remained open to all. By effort, anyone could rise in the economic scale. Everyone could gain capital. Such ownership was the great principle of freedom, and without such property freedom could not long endure. Independent to begin with, American workers typically aspired to an improved condition, to ever more property. They all wanted to "get rich, to become wealthy, to rise in the world." All seemed possible to the young man, however low his starting point. No one here was born like cattle, to be fed and worked. Of course, Colton never argued that everyone could be rich. Entailed by rapid individual mobility were dramatic failures as well as dramatic successes. But he still insisted upon the energizing possibility. Anyone might get rich.[27]

The universal entrepreneurial opportunity which Colton celebrated rested on several foundations, including free education, the franchise, and high wages. Colton, like most American economists, eulogized our free schools and rejoiced that our workers had always been literate. But underlying all these American advantages was plentiful, cheap land. Colton embraced the most extreme frontier thesis. Wage workers bargained as equals in America only because they always had options. Anyone could reject job offers, and "turn away, and live and prosper." Never yet had American laborers been so driven by necessity that they had to accept unsatisfactory wage offers. Not that they dictated their own terms. But as a "last resort the American laborer can at anytime go to the back woods," which offered a security for the independence of American labor "for ages to come, if not forever. . . ." This critical alternative insured American workers their high wages and even undergirded their right to vote. Colton admitted that most urban workers did not want to go "to the back woods," but all could, and many of the best had. He applauded the ongoing westward trek, which progressed like the undulating waves of the sea, men ever "moving on, and extending [the nation's] limits, by the impulses of freedom, and the natural desire for independence." Those who trod westward into the wilderness never had to meet landlords demanding rent. One step farther, and one could always be free of the world. There "has never been, and never will be" a time, he said, "when a laboring man cannot turn away from the wages offered him, . . . and go live an independent life in the unoccupied lands of the country." This opening to proprietorship, "for ever existing," made American laborers independent. This was the most important truth about America. So much depended on it.[28]

Given this ever present option, American laborers were all able competitively to demand all the values that they produced. Their wages were up to three times higher than those in Europe. No exploitative idle class could arise in America. No inherent conflict of interest divided labor and capital, although Jacksonian demagogues had long tried to create an artificial conflict. The lack of any separate owning class, of any privileged political elite, guaranteed a harmony of interests. Some people naturally came to own more capital or tools of production than others. This stored-up labor was a national asset. In America, the owners of capital had no possible means of becoming the class oppressors they were in Europe, where a few monopolized land, controlled politics, foreclosed entrepreneurial opportunity, and collected all surplus production. Hypocritical Jacksonian charges of "monopoly" made no sense. Many of our wealthiest manufacturers had begun as poor men. Every American worker could become at least a small capitalist, and since in America land and its improvements functioned as a form of capital, a majority of American workers were already capitalists.[29]

According to Colton, American wages allowed the average worker to save 50 percent of his income. He never specified how large a family the average worker was presumed to have, nor did he make other needed qualifications. With no captive or docile labor force, those who hired such dear but proficient American laborers could only serve to expand economic opportunity, not foreclose it. Profits could not long remain higher than wages, since even windfall profits, whether from new industries or as a result of new technology, would be quickly forced down by competition. Whatever the distribution of ownership, American capital had to function as a tool of labor, not the reverse. The capitalist was only a proxy for his employees and fully as dependent on their voluntary cooperation as they were on wages. Should capitalists, by luck or brilliance, gain high profits, workers were sure to share them, for high profits would entice new investment and create ever more demand for workers. Every time a capitalist hired a poor man, one more person was on his way toward proprietary independence. Only a lack of jobs would insure a growing mass of dependent and servile men in America, and thus completely foreclose the existing road to a managerial status.[30]

Like most other protectionists, Colton painted a rosy picture of the new textile factories of New England, particularly the concentrated mills of Lowell. There thirty thousand people had moved from agriculture or other industries, leaving behind their lower wages. They helped create a great market for southern cotton as well as for a more specialized and more profitable agriculture in the immediately surrounding areas. Like Phillips, Colton wanted decentralized workshops clustered beside our gardens and pastures. He simply would could not hear of, let alone respond to, charges of factory paternalism, arbitrary wage cuts, or cruel working conditions. His image of America simply excluded such possibilities, by definition. Such oppression could occur only where people had no alternatives, where they were bound to particular jobs by the lack of any other way to make a living. The typical American laborer, at Lowell as well as on a farm, was industrious and thrifty; worked essentially for himself; reaped all the rewards of his own labor; was literate, informed, and even acquainted with books and the fine arts; and had the opportunity to build up an estate and, through high moral standards, to earn a good name and command respect. He was a free and equal participant in a political commonwealth. What more could one want?[31]

Colton believed high tariffs were necessary to preserve the independence and high living standard of American workers. Such positive protection was a prerequisite of continued freedom. A flood of low-priced European goods threatened the continued growth of American manufacturing. Established factories might survive without protection, but investors were unlikely to launch new enterprises. We had all but exhausted the foreign market for our agricultural products. Unhappily, our exports were products for which there was a relatively fixed demand. Our acknowledged productive advantages in agriculture would count for naught and might even hurt the United States, if they led to flooded international markets and low prices. The continued expansion of American agriculture, and the crucial role of westward expansion in keeping open options and opportunities, depended on home markets; and this in turn meant increased domestic manufacturing. Only a balanced economy, one with complementary and continuous growth in domestic agriculture, manufacturing, and exchange, could prevent unemployment, labor surpluses, and low wages. In a sluggish economy, with unemployment or underemployment, our workers would lose options, become as vulnerable as European laborers, and in effect become an American proletariat. In these arguments, Colton tied protection almost entirely to the interest of those who labored, and particularly to those day laborers who were at the lowest and most vulnerable position in the economy, or the ones who above all others needed the frontier option provided by an expanding agricultural market. The only other alternative, and a dismal one, was a return to subsistence agriculture and therefore to give up most of the benefits of civilization.[32]

Colton used one very clever argument in his effort to gain the support of farmers for high import duties. He argued that manufacturing was really a form of agricultural labor and that imported manufactured goods from England really represented a camouflaged competition between American and British farmers. Tariffs against manufactured goods were really a mode of protecting our farmers against unfair competition. His point was that a large component of the manufactured goods imported from England reflected agricultural production. Manufacturing is always a processing or refinement of raw produce. The value of the end product reflects the values added at each stage. Instead of exporting lumber, a country may choose to export furniture; instead of wheat, flour or even packaged cereals. Not only do the originating farmers receive their share of the final value of such refined products, but part of the added-on value in manufacturing ends up in the hands of farmers who sell food to provision manufacturing workers. As Colton calculated it, Britain exported eight times more camouflaged or worked-up agricultural produce to America than she imported from us, and this threatened a continued drop in our agricultural prices. It was foolish for American farmers to continue to provide Britain cheap raw produce for such "working up," for in the case of grain or of mineral products they had to compete with nearby European sources. These European competitors enjoyed cheap farm labor. Home processing not only promised higher prices for the raw product (at least to the extent of saved transport costs), but the new employment would simultaneously create an expanded market for foodstuffs. Finally, if we were to expand our agricultural exports, we had everything to gain from exporting as many of them as possible not in their raw but in a worked-up form. Such refined products had a high value in relation to weight and the cost of transportation, and much more than in farming the processing allowed numerous economies of scale. Admittedly, this analysis did not apply to cotton, which European farmers could not grow. But even cotton faced other foreign competition and some inherent limits on the continued expansion of demand, which again indicated the necessities of a growing home market.[33]

A more technical argument for protection involved what Colton claimed was an original theory about money—in fact, it duplicated theories developed at about the same time by Henry Carey. Colton emphasized the instrumentality of money, which he defined as specie. It was an indispensable tool for facilitating exchange and thus, indirectly, for expanding production. A nation without money was helpless, headed back toward barbarism, for barter permits none of the finer divisions of value or widely distributed demand so essential in a complex economy (only money is universally acceptable in exchange). This indispensable role of money meant that the free-trade economists made an error of critical importance when they undervalued the importance of money and favorable trade balances. Colton re-embraced the wisdom of mercantilism. A nation inevitably suffered from trade deficits and usually gained from trade surpluses, from the net import of specie or at least the accumulation of foreign credits payable in gold and silver. Given the critical instrumentality of money, any country must protect its supplies, and this often entailed tariffs or other restrictions on the free flow of goods in international commerce. One should never sell his tools until he is ready to leave a business. Yet Colton granted with Adam Smith that specie was not part of the consumable wealth of a nation but a special form of fixed capital (special for its unrivaled durability). This seemed to mean that a country needed only so much money as exchange transactions required. But Colton was reluctant to set any limits on the supply of money. The need for it grows, or should grow, through time. Growth-inducing policies in America, such as protection for new industries, promised a very rapid growth in the need for money. Thus, his bent was toward more and more money. He always wanted enough not only for present needs but for future expansion. He thus argued that it was almost impossible to accumulate too much.[34]

In what appeared an inconsistency, Colton celebrated the role of credit instruments in increasing the total circulation. Insofar as credit could replace money, why insist upon increasing supplies of specie? Seemingly, he assumed some necessary ratio of specie to credit instruments. He talked vaguely of two to three times as much credit as specie. He thus wanted more of both money and credit, almost without limit. It was impossible, he said, to have too much commercial credit. Accessible and cheap credit was as important for capital accumulation and growth as were increasing monetary supplies. Colton praised both the first and second United States Banks, condemned Jackson's attack on the second bank as a concealed war on credit and growth, and endorsed a steady growth in fully convertible bank notes. He did concede the possibility of too many bank notes, and because he distrusted many of the existing state banks, he wanted federal checks on private banking policies, preferably through a federally chartered but privately controlled central bank. He feared any politically motivated and dictatorial executive controls. He did not want another Andrew Jackson.[35]

Colton denied that protective tariffs were in any sense taxes on American consumers. This claim involved more than the usual protectionist argument that a stable and secure economic environment would quickly induce enough domestic competition to lower prices below those that preceded a tariff. Almost everyone agreed that import duties amounted to a sales tax. The controversy was over who paid the tax. Free-trade advocates not only suggested what seemed obvious—consumers immediately pay it—but often insisted that an added burden fell on those who produced export commodities. Fewer imports meant less foreign credits bidding for American products. Typically, Colton would not analyze the tariff issue from the perspective of any class of consumers, producers, or export-import merchants. Like Phillips, he insisted that the immediate interest of individuals often ran completely counter to the public interest. In particular, he acknowledged that import merchants could suffer from increased tariffs. Consumers of protected products (or those that would soon be produced in large quantities in this country) could suffer temporarily higher prices, but this was a small sacrifice compared to the revenue duties they already paid on tea or coffee or bananas. Often the high profits already earned by foreign capitalists meant that exporters would absorb most of the cost of tariffs through reduced prices and lower earnings. In this case, the elites of Europe paid an appropriate tax in order to keep their privilege of selling us goods produced under an oppressive labor system. Colton, with a typical play on definitions, liked to argue that free trade entailed a form of foreign taxation from which only protection could rescue American workers. By this, he meant that free entry for European goods exempted rich capitalists in Europe from paying any taxes to America, and thus left them with the high earnings needed to pay for their own elaborate and costly governments. By letting them profiteer so freely, we helped underwrite an iniquitous and oppressive economic and political system. Conversely, the free importation of the products of cheap foreign labor meant a concealed income tax on

American workers which far outweighed any slight and usually temporary increase in the cost of consumer goods. Either through reduced
wages or unemployment, workers paid the high price exacted by destructive foreign competition. And the slack in one sector affected the demand
in all others, meaning that all American workers came to share in this
camouflaged income tax.[36]

Viewed as a composite whole, Colton's clever arguments for protection
developed the full implication of American exceptionalism. Colton estimated that American workers earned three times as much as the oppressed workers of Europe. He attributed this high productive advantage
to American resources, to low rents and widespread property ownership,
to the superior workmanship and high motivation of free workers, to the
industry and skills engendered by education and mass literacy, and to our
own inexpensive nonimperial governments. In addition, the fair, labor-
proportioned distribution of income in America prevented the emer-
gence of a large, nonproductive, and idle leisure class. These economic
achievements decisively set us off from the rest of the world and at the
same time marked us out for intense economic competition. The owning
and ruling classes in Europe wanted to grab as many of our economic
assets as they could. In part because of the false lessons learned from the
reigning school of British economists, the Democrats had helped pave the
way for such foreign exploitation. Free-trade policies had made us a
peculiarly rich colony of Europe. But the developing imbalances in our
economy, the increased vulnerability to foreign prices, the prospects of
gluts and underdevelopment and economic stagnation, meant that our
unique advantages might disappear all too soon. This added a sense of
urgency to the whole protectionist cause.

Such a perspective invited an emphatically nationalist bias, as strong in
Whigs like Colton as in any of the Democrats. But for those with the
perspective of Colton, a vigorous, defensive nationalism required intensive and balanced economic development. Here was the path of continued opportunity and with it economic independence, both national
and individual. For many free-trade advocates, these same goals suggested an entirely different program. Since they saw no possibility of
personal independence within large collective enterprises, they had to
hope for a continuing foreign market for our highly efficient agriculture,
for continued economic opportunity through the expansion of agriculture
and small-scale manufacturing, and for enough living space to accommodate a growing nation of proprietors. The hopes that Colton invested in
decentralized but still large-scale manufacturing, they pinned on continued territorial expansion. Both factions agreed, at the very least, on
the necessity of continued economic growth. The real crux of their
arguments, as in fact it proved to be in so many of the congressional

debates on the tariff, was their divergent views on the nature and the possibilities of large-scale manufacturing. Were factories and corporate forms of ownership compatible with free men? American economists could no more agree on the correct answer to this momentous question than could politicians.

VIII

Jacksonians

THE very word *Jacksonian* plunges one into a semantic jungle. Conventional histories of the United States that cover the period from 1824 or 1828 to at least 1850 are cluttered with Jacksonian movements, Jacksonian parties, Jacksonian ideologies, and all manner of Jacksonian myths and symbols. The label reflects laudable, often desperate efforts to identify some significant and widely shared beliefs or policy commitments in the middle period of our history. But, so far at least, the labeling game has gone awry, leading more often to confusion than to clarity. Quite simply, historians have not agreed on what *Jacksonian* means.

Andrew Jackson was a very complex man, but was in no sense a theoretician. People of diverse commitments loved him and found expression for their deepest yearnings in him or in an emerging Democratic Party. In response to circumstances, in behalf of strategic political advantage, as an expression of traditional loyalties, or in response to the persuasive advice of disciples, Jackson often tenaciously supported policies or fell in love with those most threatened by his numerous enemies. He then made support for such policies a test of loyalty or even moral acceptability. His war against the second Bank of the United States is the best illustration of these traits. But the bank war, in particular, involved policy ambiguities. Those who detested all forms of special privilege, all monopolies, all corporations, and all banks, found themselves allied with the managers and stockholders of state banks that lusted after federal deposits or greater leeway for reckless expansion.

Unfortunately, most people now use the label *Jacksonian* for much more than the policies of Jackson or his administration. At the very least, it identifies the policies most often advocated by the emerging Democratic Party, and possibly even a political style or rhetoric. These policies or styles only began to coalesce, to become a verbal ritual, after the Whig success of 1840. If one does not look too closely, if one ignores the varied nuances of possible meaning behind a common verbal stance, then those who considered themselves faithful Democrats remained very close to the political and economic commitments of John Taylor. They feared a consolidation of economic power in the Federal government, largely because they believed that power would inevitably eventuate in privilege, in legislation favoring those already wealthy and powerful. Thus, they embraced a limited view of Federal economic powers under the Constitution, even as the economic role of state governments often increased at a dramatic pace, and even as Federal and state judges so interpreted or transformed the law as to favor rapid economic development.

On Federal economic issues, the Democrats eventually achieved something close to a consensus, one best expressed in negative terms. They were against protective tariffs, liberal corporate charters, banks of issue, and certain types of federally funded internal improvements. They were for a cheap and limited government and an early and generous sale of public lands. Democrats tried to exploit existing class feelings. They generally linked freedom and independence to property and to an entrepreneurial role. Perhaps above all, they wanted to preserve an America made up of independent proprietors. They professed a special solicitude for American workers, meaning farmers, small merchants, shopkeepers, mechanics or craftsmen, and even a small but growing number of wage employees. They were suspicious of large-scale merchants and financiers, and particularly critical of the new and ever larger factories of New England. They loved to talk of equal opportunity and to lambaste monopoly and privilege, great riches and luxuries, pretension, affectation, and artificiality. Other issues divided the Democrats. The Mexican War and the territorial expansion that followed gained no support or only begrudging support from many northern Democrats. The politicizing of the slavery issue sounded the death knell for any coherent Democratic cause. Defensively, and in the end unsuccessfully, Democrats struggled to keep slavery off the agenda of federal politics, and to maintain a workable national alliance whose southern component was absolutely critical.

Much of the Democratic appeal was not uniquely Democratic. Obviously, no one applauded privilege and monopoly. And the followers of Adams and Clay made as full, and often as effective, an appeal to the working people (almost everyone in America) as did Democrats. The most fervent Whigs equaled the Democrats in celebrating the entrepreneurial or proprietary individual. They outdid the Democrats in applauding American exceptionalism. But still they differed. Above all else, the leading Whigs repudiated laissez-faire policies and denied any valid basis for class conflict in America, except as a contrived result of hypocritical Democratic demagoguery.

This left as a core of conflict the proper economic role of the federal government. Adams and Clay, and their academic apologists, believed that a positive and even a paternal federal government could guide the whole economy toward increased productivity and higher returns for all. They rejected the "capture" thesis of Taylor—that an enlarged economic role for government inevitably entailed added privileges for the powerful. Wise policies, supported by the electorate, could serve the public interest, the interest of both rich and poor. Whigs typically celebrated the benefits of growth, of increased production and consumption, and minimized problems of distribution. Joined with this was their ready, even eager, acceptance of economic interdependence, of forms of cooperation or association. The Democrats looked to Europe to find what corporate ownership and factory production promised for America—concentrated ownership, narrowed entrepreneurial opportunity, and servile forms of wage employment. It meant a vicious class system, a new form of feudalism. The Whigs disagreed. Given the distinctive American context, the independence of workers, the results of the franchise and public education, Americans could achieve all the efficiencies of collective enterprise without suffering the class divisions of Europe. Free Americans could join together as equals even in factories. Mutuality and cooperation already attended the needed and inevitable industrial development that was well under way in America.

Given the broadness of the Jacksonian label, a wide variety of political economists might be labeled Jacksonians, and in fact many have been. Our most sophisticated Ricardian, Henry Vethake, supplied highly technical support to Jacksonian opposition to charter privileges and protective tariffs. At the other extreme, the most radical agrarian economists supported Jackson on the bank issue and approved of his views on the public lands. But few Ricardian academics or agrarian radicals were direct advocates for the Jackson Administration or supported all the planks in Democratic platforms. Not so the two most loyal Jacksonian political economists—Theodore Sedgwick and William Gouge, both from the North. They served as effective counterparts to such Whig polemicists as Phillips and Colton. Less partisan was Condy Raguet, who supported free trade and laissez-faire without reference to election priorities. None of the three—Sedgwick, Gouge, and Raquet—made any important technical contributions to political economy, although Raguet's sophisticated insights into American banking practices compare favorably with those of all other contemporary experts except George Tucker. Gouge and Sedgwick were largely advocates and popularizers, but only Gouge had much influence on lay opinion.

Theodore Sedgwick (1780-1839) was an unexpected and early convert to the Jacksonian party in Massachusetts. Sedgwick's more vigorous and successful father and namesake gained an enduring reputation as a revolutionary patriot, an early antislavery lawyer, an ultra-aristocratic Federalist congressman and senator, and a judge on the Massachusetts Supreme Court. The father moved the Sedgwick family to its permanent site at Stockbridge, where for the next four generations it remained the most successful and prominent in western Massachusetts, producing several able lawyers, politicians, businessmen, and writers. The second Theodore attended Yale, read law and then practiced for a period in Albany, but because of various illnesses he returned to Stockbridge to live the life of a country gentleman and politician. He ran unsuccessfully for Lieutenant Governor on the Democratic ticket, and served in the Massachusetts General Court. He gained some local fame for his antislavery stance, for temperance advocacy, and for early and enthusiastic support of a public school system. In the last years of his life he wrote a rambling three-volume treatise and travel report entitled *Public and Private Economy.* He intended these volumes as a guide for laymen, but in the first two volumes included a simplified and vaguely Ricardian survey of the developed doctrines of political economy. More than any other contemporary, he explored the causes and the effects of poverty, and by this alone gained a small niche in the history of economic thought.[1]

No one ever more enthusiastically applauded the proprietary ideal than Sedgwick. No one better reflected the preponderant American beliefs about a good society. He began and ended with property, by which he meant both land and productive tools but not consumer goods. He was certain that only secure ownership could support a civilized and humane society. With John Taylor, he believed all men had a passionate love for property. Given the possibility of consummation, such love supported order, diligence, temperance, and hard work. Property secured independence of mind and political leverage and eroded all currying for favor and all servility. Propertied men did not have to beg wages from heartless businessmen, nor did they have to bow to political masters or join in political factions. Americans were free and happy because of their sacred property, upon whose security rested all their welfare.[2]

From his extensive European travels, Sedgwick knew how unique were Americans in their open opportunity to own property, and thus in their degree of realized freedom. In most of the world a few owned while the wretched masses lived in hovels. The great goal of political economy was to reveal how property might be generally distributed among farmers, mechanics, and laborers. When widely distributed, it encouraged the industry and savings necessary for continued economic progress, or for what Sedgwick foresaw as a future of undreamed-of riches. Of all productive property, land was most crucial. Owners of land governed the world.

God gave the earth, or what Sedgwick called the "people's farm," to mankind, not to a privileged class. Only patient, hardworking, orderly, and virtuous people deserved it, whereas in most of the world such people remained hirelings while a privileged and indulged few monopolized the earth. Sedgwick surveyed the Western history of property and land, and traced the evolution of tenure laws from slavery to money rents to fee simple. Only in an America blessed by an almost limitless wilderness, and in a society blessed by English law, did a whole people finally claim their natural birthright. Here we had a race of men nourished in freedom. Here every city mechanic could at least own a city lot. Land was everywhere prized as a possession "to be improved, augmented, beautified. . . ." He wanted to educate every American child to look forward to, expect, and later demand ownership.[3]

Like John Taylor, Sedgwick stressed the vulnerability of freedom. He was not as pessimistic as Taylor about the threats already at work, but he clearly feared them in the future. His task as a political economist was to teach not just legislators but the common people of America how to protect and extend freedom or, to put it another way, how to maintain and even broaden the opportunity to own and improve property. Our great national and "Christian" commitment was to provide equal opportunity for all. This meant a constant vigilance against unequal laws and monopoly, against the institutional subversion of our system. But it also required the continuing cultivation of a particular type of character in individuals, of an array of beliefs and preferences and habits appropriate to free men. Too many economists concerned themselves only with institutional maladies and ignored private economy. By stressing both, by issuing warnings to statesmen and by offering detailed instruction to individuals, Sedgwick hoped he could help the United States fully realize the advantages of her bountiful resources and her free government. He could then look forward to an America enriched by the glories of science, enlightened by universal and equal education, improved by better husbandry, ennobled by charity to the poor and the handicapped, and dignified by increased leisure for workers and by generous and hospitable social pleasures.[4]

Sedgwick was sure that if Americans wisely used the resources provided them by God, no one had to be poor. Efficient work combined with fair exchange could provide all with reasonable comfort. He envisioned no Malthusian squeeze. Yet, as a sensitive and conscience-stricken Sedgwick found in his foreign travels, nine-tenths of the people of the world were already mired in the deepest poverty. The peculiar hardship and tragedy visited on the poor was not that they had to labor—work was a blessing, for "skillful, productive labour, makes a great portion of the happiness of every man"—but that they had to labor disadvantageously and for other people. Their employers took most of their wages and gained high social standing. Working people in Europe were a degraded class, mere "hewers of wood, and drawers of water," not even able to marry into the higher classes. In this context, their labor could not be fulfilling, for it barely provided even a subsistence. They were destined never to know any of the joys and the fulfillment of work. In language reminiscent of that of his Puritan ancestors, Sedgwick argued that God gave everyone a vocation and decreed that pursuit of it would make one useful and happy. Free men also labored for the future, with foresight, frugality, and hope. From his work, he rightfully expected not only more consumption but intellectual and esthetic rewards.[5]

Speaking for affluent Americans like himself, Sedgwick lamented: "We know so little of the poor." He tried to show his readers the world of abject poverty, the fate suffered by the other nine-tenths of mankind. He hoped such knowledge would help heighten the American love of, and respect for, property. Sedgwick offered a detailed description of the life of the poor—their excessive, life-shortening labor (often all members of a family, children included, worked fourteen hours a day in ugly factories, under unhealthy working conditions); a complete lack of leisure, education, and books; insufficient, monotonous, coarse, adulterated, and unnutritious food, with little or no meat; terrible, crowded habitations, whether rural cottages or urban tenements; fuel of poor quality, such as chips, splinters, or dung, or nothing more than the warmth of cattle; no cash, and thus unending credit purchases at artificially high prices; frequent illnesses, epidemics, and a rate of infant mortality twice as high as that among the rich; and finally the prevalence of vice and crime, for the despairing poor often ended their lives in jails or poorhouses.[6]

Only a few Americans suffered such abject poverty. Our primary goal was to avoid it. But we already had our own poor or near poor, even though they at least usually had the vote and were literate. Sedgwick described the lot of unskilled day laborers in America, who had no regular employment, owned no productive property, and had no security against illness or unemployment. Not one in a hundred owned a lot or home. Many lived in unheated hovels. Too many became wards of the public. Rural hired hands rarely owned a cow or grew a garden or lived in anything better than a hut. He noted that both our urban and rural poor knew no intellectual pleasures, had no grace and beauty in their meager lives. Many had to work their children and deny them a free education. Even backcountry farmers who owned their land too often lived on the fringes of poverty—in debt, with old or inadequate houses, no pride in their estate, and little or no education for their children. Few farmers built adequate barns, raised good gardens, bred pure grades of cattle, or even saved manure. Factory workers in New England fared little better.

Even at such showplaces as Lowell, whole families lived in rude and rented houses, and most children passed up an education to work in the mills. City journeymen often rented their houses and few seemed to save much money.[7]

In Europe the primary cause of poverty was clearly institutional and thus primarily political. The poor there made up an oppressed class. Not so in America. We had our institutional problems, caused by irresponsible banking, inflated currency, business cycles, corporate privilege, and land speculation. As a Jacksonian Democrat, Sedgwick fought against all of these. But as yet these incipient forms of oppression did not account for most American poverty. Instead, it resulted from ignorance or deficiencies of character in individuals and thus would yield only to instruction and self-help. The poor in America could rise out of poverty by hard work and frugality. Sedgwick analyzed the culture of poverty (to use modern terms). Poor people, including many recent immigrants, lacked wisdom and habits of thrift. They aped the latest fashions, indulged in luxuries, drank alcoholic beverages, and fell into other forms of vice. Too many seemed to lack ambition and an intense love of property. Too few saved money for buying land, a home, or tools. Many seemed content to work for others, or to remain in what Sedgwick considered antisocial or vicious occupations (most forms of domestic service; jobs tied to mere ostentation, to the latest styles or fashions, or to sports or amusements; and work connected with lotteries, horse racing, and gaming). Like so many other commentators, Sedgwick assumed that the average, frugal, unskilled worker in America could live on one-half of his wages, and that the other half offered a road to emancipation, to a proprietary role and at least moderate comfort. Of course, not everyone could reach the top and someone had to do the lowly tasks. Sedgwick applauded even factories. But one could move up. Factory jobs could be temporary, a way-station in one's career. Thus, in the mode of Poor Richard, Sedgwick filled his three volumes with self-improvement suggestions for the poor, with sermons against fashions and styles and fads, with eloquent arguments for temperance, and with pleas that workers struggle to save and invest and thus better themselves.[8]

The lessons were not all for those at the bottom. Particularly in Europe, but to an increasing extent in America, the worst indulgences and habits of the poor reflected an emulation of the rich. The English upper classes set a horrible example of moral license and economic indulgence. Poor men tried to ape the conspicuous consumption, the immoral fashions and customs, even the hope of living on luck and without work, visible in so many of the upper classes. Americans were not always practicing democrats, not always entirely weaned from the aristocratic past, for they still borrowed their snobbish manners and much of their finery from Europe.

The point was obvious: if the poor were to learn the needed lessons of simplicity, frugality, temperance, and independence, they needed to see such virtues practiced by the affluent. Almost as damaging as aristocratic manners and consumptive indulgence were the overly selfish and grasping habits of too many speculators or businessmen. "It is not the good things of the earth that hurt a man, but it is having all the good things to one's self that corrupts the soul. At present, the horrible evil is the want among our 'brother men' of many of these common, simple good things that are necessary for all, and that God designed for all. . . ." A single-minded pursuit of wealth by the able insured a class system in America, a top and a bottom to society, an owning elite, and servile workers.[9]

Sedgwick recognized that his prescriptions for self-improvement meant nothing to southern slaves. He denounced slavery as inconsistent with democracy, in part because it degraded free labor. God would not let such a taint, such a poison survive in America. This expectation entailed no belief in racial equality. Just as Sedgwick accepted God-ordained differences of ability, and thus different levels of achievement and degrees of wealth, so he also believed God had separated mankind into five races. God chose to place the whites at the top. Through a long course of degradation, the blacks had fallen to the bottom. The white race had to go forward as head of the human family. Sedgwick feared any corruption of their pure blood, and thus wanted no intermarriage or even political rights for blacks. The gradual and voluntary emancipation he expected in the South had to accompany Negro resettlement. Only with prospects of removal could blacks be safely educated. He well expressed the hopes of so many northern Democrats: that the slavery issue would solve itself, that southerners would move to emancipation as certainly as "men's minds will expand and become nobler." Sectional strife frightened him as did nothing else. Northerners should leave the South alone to solve its own problems when the time was right. Northerners could console themselves in the meantime with the knowledge that the cause of liberty was always advancing. In the interim, notherners even had the duty to put down slave insurrections, for freedom could not be gained by revolt, by the murder of men, women, and children of "our white blood and family."[10]

William M. Gouge supported the Jacksonian administration even more explicitly than did Sedgwick. No other American economic writer ever became more closely identified with a single issue and a single presidential administration. Gouge (1796-1863) was from Philadelphia, by trade a journalist and publisher. While editor of the *Philadelphia Gazette* he became a local authority on American money and banking. In 1831, scarcely a year before Jackson decided to veto a bill extending the charter of the Bank of the United States, Gouge left his newspaper in order to write a book on banking. His *A Short History of Paper Money and Banking in the United States* appeared in 1833, right in the middle of a growing national debate on banking policy. Gouge completed a second edition in 1835, and published five editions by 1840. The book was a best seller for the times, undoubtedly the most widely read American book on a serious economic issue before Henry George's *Progress and Poverty*. It proved very useful to the Jackson administration, won commendations from practically everyone in the Administration, and was constantly quoted in Democratic newspapers and roundly condemned by Whig journals. Gouge's sharp, pungent, and fervent advocacy appealed to the new workingmen's movement in the cities and gained favorable notices in most labor newspapers. Several translations were published abroad, and William Cobbett, the English radical and Chartist, wrote the introduction of a separate and retitled English version. The book helped win Gouge a clerk's desk in the Treasury Department, where he boosted the subtreasury plan later adopted by Van Buren. After 1841, Gouge left the Treasury to edit a *Journal on Banking*, and slowly modified his harsh views on banking. He became a technical expert on banks and a well-known bank auditor. He wrote reports for the Treasury Department and a book on Texas finances, and served as an auditor for the State Bank of Arkansas.[11]

Gouge did not condemn all forms of banking. He endorsed banks of deposit, those that discounted commercial paper, and even those that loaned specie. He condemned only the lending of bank credit in the form of bank notes. Although he never pushed his analysis so far, he might have agreed with Raguet that even bank notes were quite proper so long as they served only as a convenient, one-to-one substitute for specie held in bank vaults. Besides the economically distorting effects of bank notes, or problems endemic to banks of issue, Gouge also identified a number of specific evils of American banks, from their special charter privileges to all manner of chicanery and corruption. Surprisingly, the most astute defenders of banks of issue, including George Tucker, generally agreed with Gouge's list of shortcomings. But, unlike Gouge, they believed that the evils were correctable either by regulatory laws or improved business practices.

Both critics and defenders of banks of issue recognized that private bank policies almost always reinforced, if they did not actually cause, business cycles. Gouge believed the easy expansion of bank credit, made possible by bank note issues, not only encouraged new economic activity but all too soon led to a rapid inflation of prices and even to speculative booms. The effective increase in the total circulation not only raised domestic prices but freed specie for export. Momentarily, Americans indulged themselves on imported goods. But the loss of specie only hastened the day of reckoning. Lowered reserves threatened the ability of banks to redeem their own notes. Often, in fact, the scarcity led to a general suspension, which Gouge saw as a normal banking strategy in times of extremity. When pressed for specie, banks had to retrench, which meant a refusal to lend or, more often, a refusal to renew their short-term loans. The calling in of loans launched a deflationary cycle, with disastrous effects on many debtors. The rapid slashing of overall demand in the economy increased unemployment, causing a panic or depression. Bank policies were, in a sense, always in phase with the cyclical trends in the economy, but therefore completely out of phase with the public interest. For, as Gouge saw it, the ever more sharply defined business cycles profited bankers and other large capitalists, in other words, those people in a position to predict or manipulate the market, and also reckless speculators who had no capital to lose and thus might win in a gamblers' paradise. Everyone else lost.[12]

Even the least critical friends of banks condemned the imprudent and reckless excesses that marked early American banking. But in their view these excesses, which were after all correctable, did not cancel out the vital good banks did in opening up new sources of credit, enouraging new enterprise, and enabling private individuals or groups to accumulate badly needed capital goods. Since we had vast unexploited resources and entrepreneurs eager to exploit them, we needed ample credit to make up for the perennial scarcity of specie, and banks alone could offer a flexible, expandable supply of credit. Gouge agreed that we needed ample credit. But he believed with John Taylor that banks of issue did not adequately meet that need. Young men anxious to buy a farm or to improve one or to launch some commercial enterprise needed long-term credit, not the sixty- or ninety-day notes offered by banks. Or, if they did borrow from banks in the confident expectation of continued renewal, they were the first people to be destroyed in a credit crunch. During an economic downturn they had no other source of credit and no possible means of paying off a note. Easy bank credit, under these circumstances, was an illusory help at best. What the country needed was a stable currency, secure long-term credit for honest entrepreneurs, and steady economic growth, not the wasteful booms and busts that accompanied our credit system. As Gouge saw it, bankers too often loaned to friends and to poor credit risks. They had little reason to be responsible, for as credit brokers they loaned other people's money. Thus, bank credit tended to flow to speculators, to sharp operators, to those who put on a show of wealth and respectability, but generally those with poor morals who really tried to live on the work of others. The most crucial and responsible forms of credit originated not in banks but in privately negotiated loans.[13]

For Gouge, bank notes seemed a particularly pernicious form of credit.

When borrowers accepted bank notes in the form of a loan, they in effect entered into a two-way credit contract. They exchanged their own debt paper for bank debt paper. But not as equals. They paid the bank for the risk involved in their paper. The bank paid them nothing for the risk they assumed. At a set date, private individuals had to redeem their paper or contract to extend it. Banks never really faced such an accounting, leaving their negotiable notes to circulate indefinitely. Hidden from public view was the real financial situation of an issuing bank, and thus the likely long-term value of the notes. Such notes took the place of specie but lacked its intrinsic value and guaranteed stability. Indeed, notes were legally redeemable in specie, but this did not mean that it was always practical or even prudent to demand specie. Gouge noted the strategies used by banks to prevent redemption, including even the threat of a bad credit rating to would-be redeemers. Some banks had notes outstanding that amounted to eight times the specie on hand. In a crunch they had to suspend. Notes might then depreciate, to the detriment of bank creditors who held them. To avoid such a catastrophe, bankers often caused a worse one by unexpected pressure on their debtors, with extreme deflationary consequences.[14]

Gouge rarely focused exclusively upon the economic effects of banking. His forte was moral criticism. He was constantly on the lookout for injustice, unfairness, or special privileges. He found plenty in American banking. Bank charters themselves were the original and most basic injustice. State-granted charters of incorporation bestowed privileges on bank stockholders and managers that were denied to ordinary citizens. Thus, Gouge condemned all chartered corporations, as did many other Jacksonians. By the time he wrote, some of the older antimonopoly arguments no longer applied. Until 1800, or even later in many states, legislators had granted few corporate charters or franchises, but often expressly or by implication used them to vest an exclusive right over a particular market. Tied to the monopoly right were high expectations of communal benefit, as in bridge, turnpike or canal companies. American courts, well into the nineteenth century, recognized corporate exclusivity and upheld damage suits against new competitors. But both legislative intent and court interpretations had clearly shifted by 1830. Legislators turned out corporate charters almost as rapidly as they collected bribes or responded to enormous political pressures from would-be entrepreneurs. When Gouge wrote, the United States had over 500 chartered banks and an increasing number of business corporations. Instead of an exclusive market, most banks as well as other business corporations freely competed with each other. Except in transportation, few had control over even a restricted market. These changed realities helped split the early antimonopoly groups into two competing factions. One faction, dominant and soon to be successful in New York, decided to join the devil they could not beat. They fought for a general incorporation law, both to end all the legislative corruption and to democratize a privilege. But the other faction, which also supported Jackson and included the most radical workingmen's organizations, continued to condemn all corporate charters. Gouge took their side.[15]

In his hostility to all corporations Gouge was John Taylor's loyal disciple. Since a business corporation had special privileges granted to it by government, it defied the ideal of an equality of rights. For example, individual farmers, merchants, and manufacturers remained fully liable for all their debts. Not so bank stockholders. Like Taylor, Gouge argued that corporations were miniature governments with the prerogatives of a sovereign. Yet, unlike American governments, they did not rest upon any popular consent. Corporations epitomized antirepublicanism or aristocracy. People with wealth were not satisfied with the advantages they already had. They pooled their wealth, gained artificial immunities, and then tried to gain greater wealth through the profits insured by privilege rather than through hard work. Americans had already rightly rejected the old props of aristocracy, such as entail laws. But the abundance of land in America made entails superfluous anyway. We had unlimited land but a continuous scarcity of mobile capital. Yet by bank charters, which amounted to a form of capital entail, we granted control of this capital to a few wealthy stockholders and thus created our own money lords. Their control over floating capital would soon enable them to control most fixed capital. Large corporations would eventually be able to control markets, eliminate new competition, and gain an effective monopoly. In extreme cases, such as that of the Bank of the United States, such powerful collectives would be strong enough to defy even governments.[16]

Despite the questions of inequity and special privilege, most American economists already conceded the potentially greater efficiency of corporate enterprise. Seemingly, only large accumulations of capital allowed the greatest economies of scale. Gouge disagreed. He ignored the issue of scale and, like Taylor, emphasized the problem of motivation. Private interest was the primary source of efficiency. Since corporations entrusted their business to hired agents, clerks, and laborers, corporate enterprise had to be more careless, expensive, and inefficient than individual. The paid functionaries of corporations would surely be less trustworthy than the immediately supervised employees of ambitious farmers or merchants. In fact, Gouge judged corporations to be so inherently inefficient that they could never survive in America without monopoly privileges. Without limited liability, corporations would never compete successfully with individual entrepreneurs. Critical for society was the impersonality and insensitivity of such legal abstractions. Corporations had no sensitivity, no sense of responsibility, for, although legally immortal, they had "neither bodies to be kicked, nor souls to be damned."[17]

Gouge believed that banks, besides exemplifying the evils of all corporations, particularly corrupted our political process. He cited the widespread bribery used to gain liberal charters, since legislators normally received bank shares. Favored constitutents had the edge. Logrolling allowed local delegates to trade off favors, to the extent that observers might assume state legislatures existed primarily to serve stock jobbers. Once chartered, banks faced a small prospect of future charter reduction or amendment. Limited-term charters were routinely renewed so long as a bank avoided bankruptcy. Once established, a bank carefully cultivated patrons within the state and used paid agents to influence both legislators and voters. As Gouge knew from personal experience, banks had great power over newspapers, particularly through loans to editors and through advertising patronage. They had been able to prevent a full public discussion of the evils of banking. Bankers purchased friends, bought off enemies, corrupted politics, and, until Jackson, had all but captured the federal government. Because of banks and other corporate influences, we had moved away from our original national commitment—to have only laws or institutions "absolutely necessary," and "perfectly just in principle and equal in operation."[18]

Notably lacking in Gouge's book was any concentrated attack on the Bank of the United States, although he frequently included it in his criticism of banks of issue. He surely must have realized that the Bank of the United States exercised some discipline over small, inadequately funded, and reckless state banks, but he never acknowledged this. This lack of a focus on the Bank of the United States, joined with his detailed indictment of the specific abuses of state banks, made Gouge a less than perfect ally of the Jackson administration. Of course, Jackson made clear his aversion to all banks of issue, but his cabinet included men closely connected with or even involved with state banks. Jackson's famous 1832 veto message focused specifically on the Bank of the United States, on its unconstitutionality, its monopolistic privileges and sheltered profits, its ties to rank and wealth, its susceptibility to foreign stockholders, and even its special favoritism towards state banks. Because of its charter privileges it exemplified artificial distinctions and thus violated the equal protection of law. Perhaps because he had no constitutional authority to do so, but surely also for strategic political reasons, Jackson avoided any generalized attack on state banks or on state charters. He cited the natural rights of individuals to engage in banking as much as in farming, and noted that state charters circumscribed this right. But the states, even as they bestowed such privileges on a few, could make state banks subject to taxes or in other ways render them accountable to the public interest. They could not tax or control the Bank of the United States. Thus, in an indirect and subtle way, Jackson appealed to state banking interests long jealous of the power of the Bank of the United States, or to westerners anxious to have more liberal credit through new state banks. This was a much more accommodating political strategy than any one might deduce from Gouge's purist theories.[19]

Gouge had no doubt that the special privilege of note issue involved excessive profits for banks. He ignored the effects of competition among banks, or the competition of banks with other avenues of investment. He defined excessive profits as a tax on the public, and illustrated his point by the record of the banks of Pennsylvania. They had a lendable capital of just over $6,000,000. In private hands, loaned at a legal 6 percent, this would earn just over $350,000 a year. But the same Pennsylvania banks had over $17,000,000 in loans and discounts at an effective 6.4 percent, which earned them about $1,100,000 a year, or an excess of $750,000 tied to the privilege of issue. This revealed the high cost of legislated privilege and supported swollen salaries for bank officials or fat dividends for stockholders. Gouge estimated this total annual tax at nearly $8,000,000 nationally. This unfairness was multiplied in most banks by shabby and deceitful means of raising legal capital. In all its horrible detail, Gouge revealed how speculators only paid the first small installment of their subscription in specie, immediately began banking operations, and paid later subscriptions by loans from their own bank, paying interest lower than the dividends earned by such stock. For such stockholders, the realized profits on real capital advanced could be astronomical. By a later buying and selling of their shares, aided by their privileged knowledge of changing bank prospects, they added huge capital gains.[20]

Beyond the specific evils of banks, Gouge saw in them the most prominent example of a generalized political corruption. He blamed nearly every political and economic evil in America on banks of issue. Their unequal privileges insured a growing class separation, as the rich grew richer and the poor poorer (surely the most repeated cliché of the whole middle period). Bank charters created an unequal status for the portion of the nation's capital owned by the rich and the idle, and discriminated against all other capital. This violated property rights and caused increased unemployment or dependence among the working people. For individuals, wealth and poverty might reflect luck, varied levels of skill, or greater or less work. But for whole classes of people, wide differences of wealth proved political privilege. If bankers, as a class, were rich and farmers as a class were poor, then only corporate privilege could explain the disparity, for bankers worked no harder than farmers and reflected no higher level of skills. With greater riches gravitating to the few, America would suffer the inevitable consequences—more demand for luxuries, all manner of new and wasteful indulgences in fashions and finery, and a growing demand for domestic servants. The rich would employ intellectuals to rationalize their ill-gotten gains, while artisans and farmers would sink deeper into poverty and barely survive. To prove that this terrible decay was well under way in America, Gouge analyzed the problems faced by farmers and cited the extremely low wages earned by women in cities.[21]

Banks also demoralized the whole society. The low ethics of bankers—their chicanery, legislative bribery, gross favoritism, and callous contempt for note holders at times of suspension—might soon infect everyone. The desire for unearned wealth might lead men into increased debt they had no means of repaying or lead bankrupt men to seek new wealth before they paid old debts. Even as the rich gambled at race tracks or fell into the boredom of idleness, the disadvantaged might fight back through violence in order to even the odds "in the struggle for riches." Working people, who could not even afford to educate their children, had to live near a subsistence level. Disease and shortened lives would result. Those who survived would learn that in America only wealth bestowed status and permitted happiness. Thus, the common people faced grievous economic insecurity, or themselves fell into an ethic tied only to greed and acquisition. For everyone, the love of wealth threatened to become a blind passion.[22]

What was the solution? Should we abolish all banks? Gouge's arguments pointed in that direction. He denied any public benefit from banks of issue. They raised interest rates, were far too unsound for safe deposits, usually loaned to the wrong people, and interfered with natural exchange rates. Bank notes were indeed more convenient than specie, but credit transfers usually sufficed. He also rejected popular reform strategies. Clever bankers would easily circumvent stringent standards for loans or avoid any strict public accounting. But Gouge realized the devastating effect of an immediate outlawing of bank notes. Thus, he proposed a remarkably mild expedient—an early prohibition on all notes under five dollars, and then gradually up to those under one hundred dollars, and only in ten years a complete prohibition. Such a gradual transition would allow the steady importation of needed gold and allow an adequate circulation at the end of the transition period. He assumed that private credit would replace bank loans and even extend the total circulation.[23]

Since each state chartered and controlled its own banks, Gouge knew such a proposal was unrealistic without Federal support. Thus, he wanted the Federal government to refuse to accept bank notes for all its collections, and to balance this with its own subtreasury system to handle its own local accounts. This alone might assure the demise of bank notes, although Gouge considered other legal initiatives. Private, unchartered money dealers could continue to provide needed banking services. Without limited liability, they would be prudent. Numerous, they would compete effectively and even pay interest on demand deposits. If such private money shops did not meet local needs, and as a last resort, Gouge approved government-owned savings banks for deposits and transfers.[24]

Condy Raguet (1784–1842) offered a more sophisticated and less polemical critique of American banking than had Gouge. He also remained much more detached from partisan politics or from immediate political controversies. Raguet, also a Philadelphian, was a veteran of the War of 1812. He worked as a merchant and journalist, and in 1815 wrote his earliest book on money and banking. This helped establish him as a recognized banking expert during the single term he served in the Pennsylvania Senate. In 1825 he assumed a diplomatic post in Brazil, only to resign it under controversial circumstances in 1827. He then returned to the United States to become a leading national spokesman for free trade, or as he conceived of himself, a lone northern voice crying in the wilderness of protection. In these years he was an influential friend of Henry C. Carey's and possibly helped persuade Carey to endorse free trade in his earliest economic treatises. Raguet published a series of variously titled journals in support of free trade, and then in 1839, three years before his death, completed the most perceptive critique of American banking written up to that time.[25]

Raguet first embraced political economy as a popularizer. He defined his journalistic support of free trade as simply an effort to disseminate the lessons of the great political economists, the masters of a new science. In his articles the names of Smith, Say, Ricardo, and McCulloch appear frequently. He specifically applauded America's own leading Ricardians, including McVickar, Cooper, and Vethake. Free trade was only the most conspicuous policy implication of Raguet's one unifying economic belief: *laissez-nous faire*, a motto he even printed on the frontispiece of his books. Over and over again, on every controversial issue, he recommended the same solution—leave alone and let natural processes proceed without hindrance. Thus, he opposed not only protective tariffs but subsidies for internal improvements, corporate charters, and all state support for banks. In all economic endeavor, he wanted private and usually individual entrepreneurs to take all the risks and reap all the benefits. It was never the business of government to assure lesser risk or to compensate losers. He applied this formula evenhandedly, castigating organized workingmen for their attack on capital as enthusiastically as he condemned manufacturers who sought special charters or tariff protection. All interest groups were too ready to seek special advantages for themselves, and thus they dared violate the evenhanded justice meted out by natural markets and free competition.[26]

Raguet was not as bitter or as clearly self-serving in his antitariff posture as many southerners. He even justified the temporary protection offered cotton and woolen mills in 1816. Like the protectionists, he hoped for a balanced and self-sufficient American economy and rejoiced in the fact that by 1835 we already produced nine-tenths of our own manufactures. Reasoning like Adam Smith, he argued that new American manufacturing would originate and grow naturally when American conditions made it profitable. He condemned only subsidies, which he saw as a sort of force feeding, a deliberately inefficient and artificial form of economic development. He expected that a thriving American textile industry would develop in due course and recognized that many of our manufacturers were dependent on imported raw materials and thus already profited from free trade. Although an advocate of manufacturing, Raguet clearly feared the social effects of large factories and offered the usual dismal portrait of the English mills. Such factories employed children, helped create awful slums, paid only subsistence wages or worse for unremitting toil, precluded any independent political role for ignorant and poor workers, and thus created a wicked class-ridden society that was the very antithesis of republicanism. He celebrated the free craftsmen and the small shop owners of America, by implication praising the dominance of small manufacturers in his own Philadelphia.[27]

Like all free-trade advocates, Raguet emphasized the economic advantages of national specialization and ignored the vulnerabilities this created in time of war. Given a necessary, overall balance of exports and imports, then the American consumption of foreign goods offered as much employment to Americans as domestic consumption and permitted the most productive use of our industry. This argument was logical, but ran smack into the protectionist argument that America already faced limited markets and ever lower prices for what had hitherto been our most efficient products—food and fibers. This meant, said the protectionists, that we faced gluts and underemployment, and that the situation would worsen until we built our own manufacturing to absorb surplus labor and to create home markets for farmers. Raguet denied the assumptions on which this protectionist argument was based and saw it as a ruse by large manufacturers to help slow our agricultural expansion and the migration to western lands, all in order to create a pool of surplus laborers ripe for exploitation.

Raguet denied that we had a glut in agriculture, and believed we never would so long as free, or at least cheap, land provided an opportunity for our youth. The very fact that so many free men still chose to invest their labor and capital in agriculture proved its continued profitability and documented the fact of great economic opportunity and high wages in America. But Raguet did not fully answer the protectionist's arguments, for he idealized a near-subsistence form of agriculture along with small manufacturing. Obviously, this could offer refuge for an almost limitless number of families, given the extent of our unused land. Protectionists desired commercial farmers able to engage in profitable exchanges with manufacturers and to enjoy ever higher living standards, or preferences shared by most southern free-trade advocates. Raguet stressed the romantic, noneconomic benefit of agriculture and home manufacturing—the independence, health, literacy, and happiness of proprietors who need never know an "earthly superior." Like everyone else, he left the tariff debate stranded somewhere between divergent images of a good society.[28]

The crisis of 1837 inspired Raguet's one major book, *A Treatise On Currency and Banking.* Once again he hoped to translate political economy into laymen's language, but this time he failed (the *Treatise* was often quite technical). He ended where he might have begun—with a general theory of money. After his years of experience and study, Raguet concluded that the total money supply of a country included circulating specie, circulating government notes, bank notes, and demand deposits. He included demand deposits because depositors had the same power in the market as owners of specie or note holders, and he noted how bank checks had largely displaced other modes of payment. He also recognized that an augmentation of deposits through bank loans and increased use of checks had the same effect on money and credit as bank note issues. This sophisticated understanding of money led to a major and prophetic policy recommendation—that the United States government issue periodic statements on the money supply, and by this be able to see and predict and possibly prevent credit crises. Being an advocate of extreme laissez-faire, Raguet certainly did not want detailed regulation of banks by the federal government but he did hope it could assure a full disclosure of information. Such information might make it possible to avoid a repeat of what happened in 1837. But he knew the difficulty of such an accounting. The United States had more than 900 banks, chartered by 26 states and territories; and they had no common mode of accounts or public statements. State governments were remiss in demanding reports or accepted clearly fraudulent ones. The Secretary of the Treasury used them to compile an almost useless annual report, filled with inaccurate tables. Given the federal system, Raguet could only plead for federal and state agreement on a common mode of reporting and the submission of quarterly statements. Even with such agreement, he acknowledged that it would be very difficult to aggregate all the data.[29]

Raguet lauded the role of specie. He noted the convenience of both gold and silver and argued against any legally fixed ratio of values between them. He wanted supply and demand to establish their relative values. Then, in the absence of trade barriers, specie would flow to countries according to need and in response to trade balances. When gold was plentiful and cheap at home, American importers sent it abroad until its value so rose and domestic prices so fell as to nearly match those abroad. The match would never be exact. Most foreign transactions involved credit, or the buying and selling of bills of exchange. Merchants in New York normally did not pay for English imports by shipments of gold but by buying up local bills of exchange drawn on English firms or banks. Only when such credit instruments were so scarce as to sell at a premium that matched the shipping cost of gold did specie begin to travel the oceans. Thus, both trade and bills of exchange fluctuated within the margin set by the cost of shipping specie, and the shifting cost of bills of exchange provided a constant barometer of relative trade balances. Shifts in the prices of bills usually sufficed to bring trade back toward a balance. Such bills cushioned the effects of temporary imbalances and helped stabilize exchange rates between different national currencies. Barring war or disaster, countries whose money supplies were tagged to specie could trade indefinitely without major convulsions or shifts in prices.[30]

Such a firm specie base did not mean any limit on credit, but in fact offered the kind of equilibrium conducive to stable credit arrangements. To Raguet, the use of secure credit indicated an advanced economic system. Raguet saw plentiful money supplies and easy credit as indispensable tools of new capital accumulation. Credit, the "great creative power," released new energy; it opened up new land and enabled young men to get a start in life. He welcomed foreign loans and deplored the distorting effect of usury laws, although naturally low interest rates spurred growth. Raguet, like Henry Carey later, celebrated the instrumental role of money, and drew analogies between money as a very durable instrument of exchange and the less durable tools used by mechanics. This outlook would seem to predispose Raguet in favor of banks, as it did Carey. It did lead him to applaud most banking functions, but at the same time to the conclusion that the evils specific to American banks overbalanced their benefits.[31]

Of the three traditional types of banks—banks of deposit, banks of discount, and banks of issue—only banks of issue were profitable in America. Only unwanted government subsidies could sustain profitable banks of deposit and discount, although Raguet fully endorsed these two functions. Banks of issue often performed these two needed functions, but gained their profits primarily by lending their credit. Here was the critical issue. Raguet had no quarrel with banks that lent their own capital in the form of notes, holding most of that capital in uncirculating specie. But such restricted issues threatened bank profits, and few small American banks could afford to be so judicious. Few could resist making large loans of their own credit in the form of notes. Even this expansion of credit had positive benefits. Bank notes, if not suddenly issued in large amounts, temporarily increased monetary supplies and raised prices. Then exports of specie slowly stabilized prices at an only slightly inflated, new international level. The economy then functioned as before, but with a mixed base of specie and credit. The benefit to a country rested upon its export of specie. Almost for nothing, a country gained a windfall of imports. Although a one-shot addition to national wealth, these imports might be endlessly productive if they took the form of capital goods. Thus, Raguet granted as a continuing national gain the normal interest returns on all paper used to displace specie. If $100,000,000 in notes freed that much specie for export, and continued to circulate in its place, then a country benefited by about $6,000,000 a year.[32]

Unfortunately, American banks overdid a good thing. They issued excess notes, often in a desperate but ultimately self-defeating competition for profits. Like Gouge and other critics, Raguet traced the devastating effects of such excess, in the temptation of easy but reckless use of credit, in speculative binges, in the illusion of new riches. The early energy released by credit soon led to credit-based consumption, to artificial and economically unsound capital formation (as for unneeded canals). Eventually, people stopped work to gamble. Timid and fearful people would then begin a run on banks, causing a debacle as the bubble collapsed. Beleaguered banks called in loans and often suspended payments. And finally the nation suffered a depression, in large part because of bank policies.[33]

Raguet acknowledged that prudent banks of issue might serve, rather than threaten, the public interest. He wanted bankers to loan their capital, but urged them to keep their capital in such secure assets as government bonds or real estate. Beyond this, they could safely loan a moderate amount (he could not say how much was safe) of their credit in the form of short-term (sixty-day) business paper. If so restricted, bank credit would parallel and encourage business expansion. Circulation could match monetary needs. By business paper, Raguet meant notes that represented property held or sold, such as the discounted notes of a wholesaler who had consigned goods at credit to a retailer. Raguet considered unsound all bank credit for speculative purposes, or what he called "accommodation paper." This included loans guaranteed only by signatures, not property, and normally used to launch new entrepreneurial endeavors. Not that he opposed personally negotiated credit of this type, but only that it was too risky for banks and unsuited to the short-term safety required of banks. If banks violated the criteria of only short-term, business-secured credit, they would all but make inevitable runs by timid depositors and then catastrophes so harmful as to outweigh all the public benefits of banks.[34]

Given the legal foundations of American banks, Raguet saw no reason to expect that banks would exercise such prudence on their own. Experience proved its absence. Our chartered banks had not dealt honestly with their creditors. They were often unable to meet their obligations, used various schemes to put off creditors, and often delayed the export of gold demanded by depositors or exporters. Like Gouge, Raguet expected no moral sensibility in corporations. They would serve no other goal but maximum profits. He particularly lamented the behavior of American banks in times of legal suspension, when they used a shield of government protection to default on the contractual conditions by which people accepted their notes. Many banks continued to make loans, or even to issue additional notes, during suspension, thereby gaining profits on money owed to their own creditors. They did not consult creditors or even consider paying interest on the notes they refused to redeem in specie. Some banks even paid dividends to stockholders during suspension, when clearly any profit should have gone to their own creditors. Banks also renewed loans rather than calling them in as quickly as possible, when they should have borrowed money to redeem outstanding notes. Confounding such flagrant irresponsibility was the steady, devious evasion of capital requirement set by charters. Raguet laid bare the "fraud and illegal extortion" involved in the credit arrangements used by stockholders to create their mythical capital. Finally, Raguet criticized what many considered a virtue of our banks: their dealing in bills of exchange. With very detailed and technical arguments, he tried to prove that profitable open-market operations by banks, because of banks' ability to manipulate credit and thus to control local prices, distorted the adjusting or equilibrating effects of a free market in bills.[35]

Going beyond the specific abuses in American banks, Raguet joined Gouge in lamenting their larger moral cost. Our banks encouraged the worst possible ambitions and goals: those of speculators and gamblers. They tempted men to undertake grandiose schemes, only to fall into forgery, evasion, and deceit. Because of the unusual privilege of limited liability, they preached an eloquent lesson on injustice. Banking was often synonomous with moral callousness.[36]

What was the solution to so many banking evils? Despite his belief in laissez-faire, Raguet advocated stringent legislative remedies. But, characteristically, he preferred what he saw as a practical impossibility—laws providing for the forfeiture of charters as a penalty for suspension, and laws making the owners and managers of banks fully liable for corporate debts. Such laws would, in effect, reduce privileges already granted and make banking again subject to the regulation of laissez-faire. Individual self-interest would prevent most abuses if the owners knew they would have to forfeit their own property if their bank failed. But, unfortunately, the principle of limited liability was so well established in the states as to prevent any such simple but radical solution. So Raguet, normally the advocate of laissez-faire, had to advocate detailed state regulation, the same strategy George Tucker had suggested, except that Raguet wanted even more stringent controls. He endorsed a much publicized New York banking law, taking exception to only a few minor points.[37]

The New York law, much like the later Federal Reserve Act, limited note issues to those engraved by the state but signed and issued by local banks. Banks could secure notes equal to the amount of federal or state debt owned by the bank and deposited with the state Comptroller. In addition, a bank could have one-half of its notes backed by deposited mortgages on improved and productive New York land, provided the land was worth twice the face value of the mortgages. Ten days after an appeal to the Comptroller by an aggrieved creditor, and with clear evidence of default, the Comptroller could publicly auction off the bank's bonds and mortgages in order to pay creditors. In addition, the bank was liable to a 14 percent annual penalty paid to the holders of notes refused redemption. Raguet disapproved of only one New York provision, that which allowed the banks to increase their capital on request. This enabled them to buy off pressing creditors by making them stockholders.[38]

Raguet's final prescription on banking revealed the dilemma that so often confronted Jacksonians. Once Adam tasted of the forbidden fruit he could not return to an earlier innocence, however much he might have yearned for it. Once American state governments had chartered numerous and often powerful business corporations, they closed most pathways back to a simple proprietary society. A realistic Raguet paid his obeisance to that impossible and beautiful ideal, but ended up recommending an array of new state regulations to control such ungainly creations as chartered banks. But given our federal system, and the immunities provided by the equal protection and interstate commerce clauses of the federal constitution, even proposed state regulation could succeed nationally only if universally accepted, a most unlikely eventuality. In fact, no other state enacted a law as stringent as the one in New York. The only other alternative was a major federal role, either by a Constitutional amendment granting to the federal government the exclusive power to charter corporations, by a revived national banking system, or by strict federal regulations over state banks. But these were the very options that most violated the let-alone thesis embraced so fervently by Raguet and by other avowed Jacksonians.

IX

Agrarians

AFTER 1828 a number of agrarian theorists offered a thoroughgoing challenge to existing economic arrangements in America. Such agrarians dissented even more radically from the major schools of economic analysis than did the socialist disciples of Robert Owen or the American Associationists, who largely echoed the eccentric doctrines of Charles Fourier. More critical in the context of this book, only the agrarians among American radicals developed any coherent and distinctive body of economic theory. The Owenites had enormous impact in America and influenced much agrarian thought, but Owen's American disciples wrote no significant essays on political economy. Arthur Brisbane, the leading American disciple of Fourier, applied a slightly watered-down Fourierian critique to the American economy, but his books and articles never moved beyond a quite literal echo of his French master, complete with detailed advice on managing vineyards. Thus, beginning with the work of Thomas Skidmore, and climaxing in the efforts of George Henry Evans, agrarianism became the one truly dangerous and sinister position in political economy. Even the later threatening and ominous meanings attached to such other vague labels as *anarchism* and *communism* scarcely matched those attributed to *agrarianism* by respectable and established Americans in the early Jacksonian era.

Agrarian theorists did not originate among the people at the bottom of our economic ladder. Most were articulate city mechanics. They perceived themselves as direly threatened by contemporary economic developments, and offered their critiques from that defensive perspective. They suspected that the early promise of America had already been betrayed, and foresaw a most dismal future unless Americans made major changes in land and tenure policies. This perspective gave a distinct flavor to their ideals. Whig economists often lamented the indefinitely postponed realization of the American promise, but through supportive governmental programs they hoped to move ahead to richer forms of association and much more generous living standards. Jacksonian economists often echoed John Taylor. America *was* a great moral achievement, but an achievement already threatened, on the verge even of major internal subversion and inevitable decline because of special privileges supported by overly intrusive governments. Both Whigs and Jacksonians assumed fee simple ownership of land. The Jacksonians often also assumed continued geographical expansion and thus a continued equality of economic opportunity so long as governments secured freedom but otherwise left people alone. The Whigs stressed internal economic development and growth and, with it, greatly expanded consumption. The agrarians mistrusted both visions, for they focused upon the vulnerability of the one assumption underlying both—the legitimacy of existing property arrangements. They drew their own special deductions from Ricardian rent theory, deductions quite at odds with those already drawn by American economists or those soon to be drawn by Karl Marx.

Marx welcomed collective enterprise, both for its productive efficiency and its historical necessity. He also made his economic analysis in Europe, where the prelude to collective enterprise had not been free proprietorship but, for most workers, either serfdom or exploited wage labor in fields or cottage industries. As he subjected the policies usually associated with Ricardian theory to an intense moral critique, he identified the central issue as private ownership. Here he agreed with the agrarians. But he looked to remedies that retained accumulated capital and associated modes of production, both of which already existed in the industrial centers of Britain. So long as scarce natural resources, as expressed in land and in capital goods, remained in the hands of a few, he believed that workers would never receive any of the benefits of new technology. All the surplus product—that steadily enhanced final product that remained after payments for capital goods and for near-subsistence wages to laborers—would normally accrue to owners. Even periodic labor scarcity, and competition for workers, would lead, not to permanently higher wages, but to consolidation of firms and lessened competition. Like George Tucker, he believed owners could pass all the burdens of growth to workers. Thus, Marx proposed the socialization of land and capital, not the atavistic return of property to inefficient individual proprietors. Such a socialization promised to restore the full benefits of economic growth to workers, whose labor alone made it possible.

Despite the evident appeal of the proprietary ideal in America, cooperative and communal schemes always attracted fervent minority support. In fact, on close inspection, proprietary and cooperative ideals rarely reflected contrasting social ideals, but rather the outer extremes of carefully nuanced differences of emphasis, as illustrated by the appeal of both to American transcendentalists. Proprietary advocates assumed specialization and interdependence plus a wide range of cooperation and sociability. Collectivists argued that true communalism did not mean centralized control but the fullest and most authentic individualism. Owen and Fourier found plenty of American disciples. Also, many fervent advocates of proprietary autonomy continued the strong Puritan emphasis upon social solidarity, as did Henry C. Carey. But on the whole, our mechanics as much as our freehold farmers rejected any full-blown collectivism, and instead sought economic salvation through some form of continued individual ownership. The agrarians simply explored some of the most consistent implications of the proprietary ideal.

Unfortunately, the word *agrarian* has suffered a common fate—it has become so generalized in meaning as to lose all discriminating content. Sloppy writers make it virtually synonymous with "agricultural." Since the word *agrarian*, by its Latin roots, pertains to land, it does bear a relationship to rural life and to agriculture, since both involve access to and use of land. But so do all city pursuits. If one wants to identify an economic sector, or an occupation, the correct label is "agricultural." "Agrarian" properly identifies beliefs or policies related to land, to rules of access or tenure, to the size of estates, or to modes of inheritance, but not to beliefs about the superiority of farming or the glories of rural life. Not surprisingly, therefore, early American agrarians were city artisans, not farmers. The primary target of agrarian schemes throughout history has been large landowners.

The meaning of *agrarian* was much clearer to newly independent Americans than it is today. Our founding fathers knew its origin—in various Greek and Roman efforts at land reform, and particularly in a scheme first advanced in the Roman Republic by the controversial tribune Tiberius Gracchus, and later also supported by one of his brothers. In 133 B.C., Gracchus forced through the most famous agrarian law of all history. It came in response to problems both rural and urban. Increasingly, large rural estates on conquered, publicly owned lands squeezed out small farmers, creating a mass of unemployed citizens who drifted into the cities. The Gracchan Law, although never completely implemented and soon modified, set limits of approximately 300 acres on the amount of public lands that could be enclosed by any one family, and it established a board to allocate surplus or reclaimed lands to the poor in the form of small, nonalienable plots. The law established the two original and enduring agrarian goals—laws to limit the size of estates and programs to insure broader access to land. Because of a paucity of primary sources, historians have been able to infer many different goals that might have motivated the Gracchans. But the more overt and straightforward interpretation—that they sought to increase the number of independent proprietors—made them virtual heroes in America, however much Americans might object to their dictatorial political tactics or the redistributive implications of their acreage limitations.

For eighteenth-century Americans, the most recent meaning for the word *agrarian* came from James Harrington's influential seventeenth-century utopia, *Oceana*. Harrington had two strategies for maintaining freedom in his idealized and imaginary society: mixed government and a near-universal, although far from equal, ownership of land. Harrington, who lived in a country whose natural resources were already fully owned by a few, believed that widespread land ownership required an agrarian law, or else aristocrats would force the common people of *Oceana* into the English pattern of tenancy and political dependence. Thus, the agrarian law of *Oceana* required equal descent and set limits on the size of estates. Under the influence of Harrington, Americans often referred to an "Agrarian," meaning a law limiting acreage.

By 1776 *agrarian* clearly suggested redistributive or leveling legislation. Ordinarily, such laws would seem dangerous or threatening. In Europe, even to broach agrarian schemes was to recall the land grabs of the Peasant's Revolt or the scandalous redistributive proposals of the English Diggers. But such schemes seemed threatening only in a context of special privilege or unfair land monopoly, and surely these were irrelevant in revolutionary America, with its abundance of inexpensive land. Few early Americans foresaw eventual land monopoly as an American problem; they felt that the repeal of all entail and primogeniture laws and the acquisition of the Louisiana Territory precluded such an eventuality. Our repudiation of all legal props of rural aristocracy long seemed, both to chauvinistic Americans and to such articulate foreign visitors as Tocqueville, the most significant and radical domestic achievement of the revolutionary period.

In 1829 Thomas Skidmore turned an irrelevant label into a political challenge and converted *agrarianism* into a radical crusade. Not until the twentieth century would the label again convey an innocent or innocuous image. But Skidmore did not launch an agrarian movement out of a vacuum. In moral theory, he drew upon the ancient natural-law tradition. He or his disciples also exploited the rent theories of Ricardo. Together these sources provided the theoretical tools needed for a devastating attack on large estates and on high rents or high land costs. Skidmore had important "agrarian" predecessors, but it is not clear how much he knew about them or to what extent he borrowed their ideas.

In Western moral theory, land always posed dilemmas. By the seventeenth century, the right to property had begun to gain the same sacred position as the two inseparably related concepts of life and liberty. But property, above all else, meant the products of human labor. If not secure in the possession of such products, one had no security of life and no prospect of personal autonomy or independence. If a government aspired to any moral status at all, its first and clearest obligation was to protect life, liberty, and property. But how did such moral theories relate, not to what man has produced by his own labor, but to natural gifts, to air, water, sunlight, fertile soils, and all manner of minerals? These are not produced by man, but are the necessary raw material of all his artistry and all his consumption. To Western man they always seemed the gift of God, provided in common for all mankind. Can one rightfully "own," can one buy and sell, these natural resources? And if so, under what circumstances and with what qualifications? These moral issues were as complex and as vital as any ever faced by Western man. To their credit, American agrarians confronted them as directly and honestly as anyone could.

Nature is involved in all production, beginning with the picking of berries or the hunting of game. One cannot completely disentangle the products of labor from their natural preconditions. Thus, the primary moral issue relating to property has always involved access to nature. In a primitive society, the right to join the hunt, to fish in streams or lakes, or to join in the harvest of nuts and berries, is prior to the subsequent privilege of retaining and disposing of one's game or fruit. In an agricultural society, the most critical right is one of access to and secure use of cultivatable land. As man develops more elaborate tools, and carries out more complex manufactures, this right expands to include access to all manner of minerals and natural energy sources. If one wants to explore the ambiguities that have long surrounded the word *property*, then one could talk of access rights (admission to the hunt or to the fishery, freedom to fence and improve an uncultivated field, or permission to dig and consume coal or oil) as a primary form of property and control over the products of labor so expended as a secondary form.

These two types of property intertwine at many points, but they suggest very different problems in distributive justice. One's labor-produced possessions may tempt but do not threaten anyone else. The more I produce by my hands or by my tools, the more I have to consume or to exchange with others, and my production need not threaten anyone else. In fact, my increased product may indirectly help others, because it means a greater quantity and diversity of products available for exchange. But nature is finite. Only so many hunters have a chance for a kill in a given forest. Berries are limited and also perishable. Above all, cultivatable land or exploitable minerals are limited. Maybe, because of the potential of improved tools and skills, nature can provide an almost unlimited amount of subsistence. Yet, even if this were so, a relative scarcity remains. An increase in one person's property in nature may be at the expense of others. What if one person had the will and the power to "own" all hunting parks, all land, all fisheries, all mines? Then everyone else would be his slave. Yet secure and exclusive access to portions of nature, either for individuals or for cooperating groups, seems necessary for the most productive use of nature. The problem for public policy is thorny: How gain the benefits of exclusive use and yet not steal from others what, from almost any consideration of justice, is their natural inheritance?

These dilemmas challenged moral philosophers, but rarely provoked extensive or honest debate among American and English political economists. For early Americans, the dilemmas seemed almost as remote as natural scarcity. Expansion onto new lands, or the exploitation of unconquered frontiers, has always provided an easy escape from the more subtle problems of property distribution. But the moral heritage of colonial Americans contained plenty of precautionary warnings. Too briefly characterized, this heritage was Christian with a distinctly Protestant tinge. Nature was a common possession, but a possession given to mankind on the condition of its responsible and efficient use. This entailed exclusively private use of land, a position endorsed by Thomas Aquinas but most enthusiastically developed by Protestant reformers, by Christians who placed great emphasis on stewardship, on the doctrine of vocation or calling, and on a democracy of work. The English Puritans, like the French Huguenots, carefully worked out a natural-law vindication of individual land ownership. Labor and need alone justified property claims, either to portions of nature or to consumer goods. Waste— gathering more berries than one could eat or fencing land one could not cultivate—was sinful, for it threatened the welfare of others. In a sense, John Locke codified developed Christian views on private property; he added nothing very distinctive. For example, the Puritans in New England anticipated every qualification he made in his famous chapter on property in the *Second Treatise*.

If labor alone justifies property, then how can one "own" land? Of course, the question turns on the meaning of "own." It is hard to find any justification but that of expedience for any type of land ownership that entails all the rights attached to consumable commodities. To Locke, for example, the basis of land ownership was labor-produced improvements. He, like the Puritans, saw property as an extension of self, as certain natural objects fully assimilated to one's personality through artistry. Raw nature remained alien, apart from man, and thus scarcely a proper subject for ownership, except in the sense that all mankind "possesses" it in common as an esthetic asset. But improved nature, that portion transformed by labor, takes on a peculiar status. Technically, the primitive component, the undeveloped potency of the soil, remains part of the common store. But this is inextricably bound up with man's improvements. If labor justifies ownership of these, then it also justifies some form of secure tenure over the land to which they are attached. This moral claim justified enclosure and exclusion. In a context of plenty, of ever-expanding frontiers, the economic value of land derived largely from improvements, not from original access rights. With scarcity, or so it seemed to everyone before Henry C. Carey, the exchange value of land more and more reflected the value of access rights; then the moral dilemma of monopolistic land ownership, of ever increasing rent, became urgent, as it did for Ricardo.

The moral vindication of labor-related land ownership, and even the elevation of such ownership to the status of a natural right, implied all manner of qualifications. The right to land, or to any productive property involving a primitive natural component, has a double entailment. Morally, one could argue that the most crucial entailment is the positive right of everyone to acquire land, at least up to their fair share of the whole, a proposition that became the primary platform for American agrarians. Secondly, it entails security of tenure, or the protected right to retain and use one's improved land or, possibly, even the right to sell or bequeath it to others. But how determine a fair share? And how keep land ownership in balance with a growing population without violating the retentive rights of existing owners? Surely, "ownership" of nature implied something closer to an indefinite lease or special tenancy than commodity-like control. For example, does not the use of land imply a responsibility to preserve rather than deplete its fertility? As Locke stipulated, and as early Puritan land policies revealed, the labor-related justification of land ownership has inherent limits. Beyond what one needs for cultivation, beyond what one actually uses, land is not an object for ownership but a public asset. Thus, the Puritan towns saved back all unused lands for future generations and tried to prevent absentee ownership or purely speculative uses of land. In fact, Locke made the unanalyzed suggestion that land enclosure was an inherent right only so long as other land of equal quality remained available somewhere for people without land. He seemed to avoid the radical implications of this by frequent references to America. But here was the opening for later arguments that land rightfully reverted to common ownership and cooperative shares precisely when that individual ownership became to any extent monopolistic, or as soon as it led to exclusive scarcity and to exploited people.

Although land monopoly or fears of future land monopoly was rarely a major dilemma or issue in colonial America, it did surface on occasion.

As early as 1698, Charles Davenant, an English visitor in the colonies, deplored the large accumulations of waste land by southerners, who desired a hedge against depleted soils on their home plantations. Not only did they use bribery and fraud to acquire land, but they had already acquired a monopoly of good lands. He wanted the Crown to vacate questionable claims, and to grant title only to those who lived on and actually farmed land. In the period just before the Revolution, Governor Cadwallader Colden deplored huge holdings in New York and wanted to break them up through high land taxes. In the New England towns, frequent and often bitter conflict over the disposition of town lands kept the subtle dilemmas of tenure alive throughout the colonial period. In 1722 Joseph Morgan, a friend of Cotton Mather's, applied familiar natural-law arguments to the land question, in effect making himself the first identifiable American agrarian. He wanted to apply Locke's test of need and use to Massachusetts land. Any ownership beyond that seemed to him unjust and contrary to the scriptures. The earth was not a proper subject for speculative buying and selling. Extensive unused holdings drove up land prices, excluded the poor from land, and in effect reduced them to slavery. He wanted the Commonwealth to vacate all titles to unused land, and thus bring it into the market, so that everyone could regain his birthright from God. In 1746 an anonymous New Jersey pamphleteer asked for taxes to make large estates so unprofitable that owners would have to sell them. Even Thomas Jefferson, by seeking a fifty-acre birthright for each Virginian, qualified as an inspirational hero of most later American agrarians.[1]

Modern Anglo-American agrarianism, at least as a coherent theoretical position and an organized new movement, began in 1775. Thomas Spence, an English schoolteacher and advocate of a phonetic alphabet, launched it in a lecture entitled "The Real Rights of Man," which he delivered before the Philosophical Society of Newcastle. His reward was being expelled from the society at its next meeting. The lecture began his career as a notorious radical, since he continued to publish polemical and inflammatory pamphlets. For his publishing and his agitation he served at least three jail terms. No longer welcome as a teacher, he lived on his earnings from a small bookstore or later from peddling books. Shortly before his death in 1814, a group of his disciples, led by one Thomas Evans, formed a Society of Spencean Philanthropists, and until banned by Parliament, they worked openly in behalf of his agrarian scheme. Spence, who was of low birth, frequently gathered his followers in urban taverns. In his radicalism and his polemical skills, he resembled Thomas Paine, although he carried on a running controversy with Paine over agrarian issues.[2]

Spence, in his famous speech, tried to draw the correct implications of natural law, as he had learned it from John Locke. He soon aired a whole spectrum of agrarian principles. Few successors added anything except various implementing strategies. Spence asserted an universal and natural right to liberty and to land. Before government, in a state of nature, each person had by logical implication as equal a right to the land as to air and sunlight, for all had to live by the returns of the soil. If excluded from nature, no one could live. This proved to Spence that by right this common land could not be sold or given away, for to so alienate it was to deprive posterity of access to it. Yet, most organized societies, instead of infringing natural rights no further than absolutely necessary, had invested land in a few owners, as if the owners had made it by their own hands and therefore had a right to call it their property and do with it as they wished. In England, most people had access to nature only by permission of those lords of the soil who had power over life and death. In fact, Spence chose to call them "Gods," for poor wretches were so completely dependent upon owners that they literally lived and moved and had their being in landlords. Nonowners had no political power, no place at all except in heaven. They paid dearly for their access, while economists rationalized the existing land system as the best possible.

Spence had a plan. He asked the people of England to gather in their parishes and form themselves into corporations. These corporations were to take over control of all parish land, and hold permanent title to it. A corporation could not sell land or give it away, any more than it could sell children into slavery. The parish corporation was to lease small, family-sized farms to all citizens at low rents proportionate to the value of land. The rents would serve as a single tax to pay for all government services and improvements, or for what the people thought proper. Beyond this public rent or single tax, Spence wanted a free economic market and endorsed a cheap and economical government. Politically, he wanted each parish to adopt a secret ballot for town meetings, and for all parishes on the same day to elect delegates to a limited central government. He envisioned a citizen militia and a generous system of welfare for those in need. Free from the cost of an idle class of owners, and from expensive governments, Spence believed his free parish plan, when universally adopted, would insure that everyone in the whole "earth should at last be happy and live like brethren."[3]

Spence launched a larger movement than he probably anticipated. His scheme proved irresistible to a growing number of disciples. It was also frightening. He campaigned for it tirelessly. In one pamphlet he composed a utopian account of later events on Robinson Crusoe's island that illustrated the idealized results of his scheme. Crusonia used its single-tax fund to develop free schools, public libraries, and a national university. Lease holders were bound to a rigid land ethic but could bequeath their improvements to their children so long as no one had more than one farm. The laws were few; lawyers, unneeded. Beyond that, Crusonia was a free market, in ideas and in goods. The Crusonian creed illustrated this:

> All men, to Land, may lay an equal Claim;
> But Goods, and Gold, unequal portions frame:
> The first, because, all Men on Land, must live;
> The second's the Rewards Industry ought to give.[4]

Jailed and persecuted, Spence became ever more bitter. He acknowledged the revolutionary impact of his scheme. He wanted the people to organize and, if necessary, use military means to recover control over their land. Spence promised to leave landlords in possession of all movable goods only if they peacefully surrendered their land. He condemned as foolish tenderness the qualms over dispossession expressed by many, including even Thomas Paine. Some farmers had indeed purchased their land, but they knew they bought stolen goods. In any case, most of the value of land rested on the labor of the landless, not on the labor of purchasers. Every infant was born with a full right to his share of the earth, a principle honored even by the animals of the forest. Spence berated landlord oppressors in the strongest language: he called them "villains," with "ill-gotten gains," who "warred on infants." He condemned the "bloody landed interest" as a "band of robbers," really only "beasts of prey," "barbarians," "oppressors," "usurpers." Finally, as he matured his single-tax scheme, Spence added an appealing annual dividend. The rents, he expected, would more than pay the cost of a limited government. Thus, up to two-thirds would remain as a surplus, which he proposed to divide up as an equal annual dividend for all, with added sums payable at each birth and at each death.[5]

Spence's disciples continued their Society until at least 1820. Yet, the enduring influence of Spence is hard to unravel. William Cobbett, one of the leaders of the later Chartist Movement, knew Spence and attended his 1801 trial for sedition. Robert Owen and his disciples echoed many of Spence's concerns, but for obvious reasons did not claim any direct descent from such a notorious radical. It is even more difficult to trace Spence's influence in America. Thomas Skidmore never acknowledged him, and possibly never knew about his single-tax scheme. In any case, Skidmore's agrarian scheme had little similarity to that of Spence's. George Henry Evans almost certainly knew of Spence, but he never gave him any credit for his own agrarian sympathies. As far as I can tell, he was neither a kinsman nor an acquaintance of Spence's leading disciple, Thomas Evans, but he was a frequent correspondent of Cobbett. The leaders of the workingmen's movements kept close contacts with English radicals, particularly Owenites and Chartists. Quite often, as in the case of George Henry Evans, leading American radicals had emigrated from (or fled) Britain, but then retained close ties to their birthplace. Only in the sense of a shared radical tradition can one directly relate Spence to agrarianism in America. But Spence did influence Thomas Paine, and both Skidmore and Evans considered Paine one of their cultural heroes.

Even as Spence gathered his disciples, Paine tangled with the agrarian issue. He ended up with a proposal so much milder than Spence's as to seem innocuous. Paine wrote his little essay, "Agrarian Justice" in 1795–96, in the context of the French Revolution. He hoped he could shape land policy in a new France. He wrote to ridicule the complacent acceptance of inequalities of wealth, and specifically to refute an orthodox clergyman who praised God's wisdom in making men both rich and poor. Paine, with typical cleverness, noted that God made only male and female, and that he gave the earth to all as an inheritance. But something had certainly gone wrong. Misery and poverty had accompanied progress and civilization. The most affluent countries had the greatest polarities, the greatest wealth and the most poverty. The American Indian tribes knew no such extremes, but the world's population did not allow a return to such a primitive economy. Thus, Paine asserted a thesis: the lot of people should never be worse because they were born in a civilized society. They should at least realize the living standards of a savage, or what one might call a minimum wage. Paine sought ways to avoid the violent dispossession and redistribution Spence recommended, yet to fulfill the principle of natural justice.[6]

Paine accepted the basic premises of Locke and Spence. The earth was, originally, a common property. All were born in nature as joint proprietors. But cultivation required labor-produced improvements that were inseparable from the land itself. That fact justified enclosure, but in justice the cultivator "owned" only the improvements, not the portion of the earth to which they were joined. This meant that only the society as a whole could rightfully collect true rents and that every cultivator in justice owed his rent to the state. This position would seem to point toward a single-tax scheme, either like Spence's or the related one later developed by Henry George. But not so. By elaborate estimates, really little more than guesses, Paine sought to discover the original value of unimproved land. At the early stages of cultivation he estimated this at 10 percent of total value, since rents were at first very low in ratio to the value of improvements. This meant that existing owners of land had an unjustified claim on at least one-tenth of the market value of their assets. Because these original owners had enclosed all of nature, in time the value of their land had multiplied, until up to one-half of the world's inhabitants lost their natural inheritance. This assured the extremes of wealth and poverty. The requirement of justice was to return to the dispossessed the value of their natural inheritance. To do this, Paine proposed a 10 percent inheritance tax on all land and even on personal property. This tax was to maintain a fund which would pay every person, at age twenty-one, the sum of fifteen pounds sterling, and after age fifty, an annual retirement stipend of ten pounds. This, he believed, would fully compensate owners and nonowners alike for their original claim to an equal share in an unimproved nature, and possibly even leave an additional sum for the lame and the blind.

This early social security scheme not only involved highly dubious financial estimates, but totally ignored many of the nonconsumptive benefits usually claimed for land, such as personal independence and control over one's own labor. Paine emphasized the diverse benefits of his scheme, particularly for France. It would assure the young a good start in life, enough to buy a cow and agricultural tools or enough to operate a small farm. It would break up a hereditary poor class and stop others from falling into it. As for men of property, they could now enjoy riches with a good conscience, knowing that they profited from no special privilege and that their inheritance would help eliminate misery. Such a scheme would also cement a political consensus among all economic levels and help ensure a stable republic. Although Paine opened with agrarian principles, he ended up not with land reform but with an easy and appealing argument for a mild and almost painless form of redistributive welfare.[7]

From Spence and Paine on, the land issue remained on the agenda of English social reformers. Percolating among English artisans, it became one ingredient in the Chartist Movement, and lingered on in the rustic commitments of John Ruskin and William Morris. The agrarian view gained its first academic adherent in 1781, when William Ogilvie of Aberdeen University anonymously published a monograph on *The Right of Property in Land*. In a much more speculative and restrained fashion than Spence, he offered a detailed analysis of land tenure, both historically and in the context of moral theory. From a Lockean and a Calvinist perspective, he tried to prove that "owners" had a rightful claim only to the value of improvements, not to the rent value of land. Ogilvie proposed several tenure changes in Britain, or in his terms a "progressive agrarian."[8] But his cerebral essay had little if any contemporary impact. Instead, it was the rent theories of Ricardo that forced both political economists and practical reformers to consider the problems posed by land monopoly and growing rents. Ricardo, without intending it, provided a logically incisive foundation for both agrarian and socialist schemes for social betterment.

Of the first two major American economists—John Taylor and Daniel Raymond—only Raymond flirted with agrarianism. Ironically, later historians would often call Taylor an agrarian, but only by a grievous misuse of the word. As a large landlord, he was emphatically opposed to agrarian laws and believed that the American tenure system was open and fair, for it involved no special privileges and allowed no monopoly. It was Raymond, the advocate of positive government regulations and incentives, who accepted the principle of ultimate public ownership of all land and who flirted with the idea of state recovery of titles on the death of owners. He even advocated the mildest of agrarian legislation—equal descent laws.

Langton Byllesby published the first angry American economic treatise in 1826. This began a tradition of class-conscious economic advocacy by those who identified themselves with an American working class. Byllesby was born in Philadelphia, of English ancestry. A printer by trade, as were so many of his successors in the radical tradition, he owned land in eastern Pennsylvania, dabbled in new inventions, and tried his hand at newspaper publishing. It was during an extended residence in New York City, where he worked as a proofreader, that he published his one book, *Observations On The Sources And Effects of Unequal Wealth*. The book grew out of an intellectual environment that spawned the Working Men's Movement in both Philadelphia and New York. Central to it were the reforms of Robert Owen and books published by him or by his disciples, such as William Thompson. In fact, Byllesby's title closely paralleled a recent book by Thompson. Byllesby moved much closer to English agrarian analysis than had Raymond, but he never supported a coherent agrarian program.

Byllesby, like all his successors, swore by Jefferson and drew his moral principles from the opening arguments of the Declaration of Independence. Yet things had gone amiss. The promise of the Revolution, although not yet in complete ruins, had somehow been betrayed, a theme soon echoed by all agrarians. Since vast evils had survived from former ages, inequalities of wealth continued to grow. Many Americans could not pursue happiness, at least not with any hope of success. In his more pessimistic moments, Byllesby lamented that a noble effort had been so quickly subverted by "selfish, dishonest, and ambitious" men, and that our deviation from first principles had led to a tyranny by a few and near-servility for most. Although his tone was reminiscent of Taylor's, he lamented different evils. The four sources of our difficulties paralleled those identified by the Owenities: war and defense efforts, fixed property in land, the distorting role of money, and trafficking instead of simple and equal exchange. From heroic warriors we had fashioned our own tyrannical privileged classes. By vesting in them full ownership of the soil, we gave too much to the first dividers, who took more than their fair share, excluded others, and claimed their excessive land absolutely, without limit. Now young men who reached twenty-one found their share of the earth already occupied. As population increased, more and more would be excluded, since no amount of hard work and thrift would enable them to purchase land. Such a lack of opportunity meant more crime. This analysis led Byllesby to affirm the critical agrarian principles—the government should restrict ownership by need and use, and forbid all speculative or indulgent uses of land. Or, as he said, any one person should have a right to occupy only so much soil as his physical labor could turn into a fair share of the comforts of life. More was unjustly held, and held as an injustice to all the propertyless.[9]

Despite his dutiful assertion of agrarian principles, Byllesby had little personal interest in agrarian reform. He borrowed his agrarian themes from English sources, from men who chafed under a landed aristocracy and who nourished Ricardian images of an ultimate rent squeeze. These images never matched his own judgements about economic injustice in America. He was a skilled mechanic largely concerned with the special problems of his fellow urban tradesmen. From the land issue he turned, with greater zest, to the evils of finance and commerce. Like John Taylor, he lambasted a paper aristocracy, the class of bankers and moneylenders who manipulated monetary supplies for their own benefit. Likewise, and so typical of traditional artisans, he castigated the new class of acquisitive and unscrupulous merchants, who conspired to gain illegitimate profits through unequal exchange. Both financiers and merchants monopolized credit or cornered markets in order to cheat the working class and in order to live in idleness and luxury. Byllesby hated interest more than rent. The machinations of sinister middlemen, not American landlords, lay behind the vast and growing inequities in America. Byllesby typified the perspective of mechanics in his demand that producers regain control over their production, that they use their newly gained political power to crush the horde of parasites who now took up to one-half of the product and left workers with barely enough to live on. He had no trouble identifying the monopolistic devils—they were merchants, clerks, bankers, officers of insurance companies, lawyers, and bureaucrats. Byllesby did not yet confront the problems posed by American factories, but he noted how often large investors and merchants flooded the market with British cloth or controlled new labor-saving machinery, collecting high profits even as massive unemployment afflicted the displaced American workers. Competition forced down wages, and surplus urban workers remained helpless.[10]

Like so many of his urban successors, Byllesby addressed hmself to the problems of beleaguered journeymen—low wages, lowered social status, and less effective political power. He saw only temporary relief in public works, in new roads and canals, although he desired such improvements.

He doubted there would be any significant growth of demand, for most consumer desires had already been fulfilled. Since capitalists, not workers, owned the new and expensive machines, greater productivity failed to help the producing classes. England, where the great mass of men and women were denied their birthright in the soil, and where workers never owned capital, seemed to prophesy the dismal future of Americans. Already, Philadelphia and New York were alarmingly like London in their crime rates, prisons, paupers, and welfare costs. Such arguments seemed to be a perfect preparation for an agrarian solution—help the surplus workers move onto the soil and allow competition to raise the wages and status of artisans. But Byllesby did not take this option. He was too much influenced by Owen, yet too loyal to an existing, fluid, and individualistic mode of urban life to endorse communalism as more than a partial answer. Thus, drawing on the ideas of William Thompson, he proposed cooperative associations of city tradesmen. They were to pool their shops and tools, offer equal pay for equal labor, end all competition, and, by thus nullifying all advantages of a prime location, escape high city rents.[11]

Byllesby seems to have expressed well the frustration and resentments of independent artisans. In 1827 several Philadelphia trade societies banded together in a city-wide alliance—the Mechanics Union of Trade Associations. For unclear reasons, some later historians would identify this as the beginnings of an American labor movement, whatever one means by "labor" or by "movement." The united Philadelphia societies backed standouts by individual trades, particularly supported a strike by Philadelphia carpenters, and fought for a ten-hour day, or strategies endorsed by later labor unions. But the leaders of the Philadelphia societies, and the vast body of members, were still independent journeymen, not operatives or even wage employees in the later sense of that label. Some still owned shops and most owned their own tools. They were not only artisans but often small merchants, since they still retailed their products from their own shops. Others, such as the independent carpenters, still negotiated their own job contracts. But members of some organized trades, the dock workers for instance, already suffered the lowly status of wage laborers. It was in part to prevent a similar loss of status that the artisans joined in united political action.

The Philadelphia Mechanics Union developed a very class-conscious analysis and supported a range of reforms. The leaders were part of a radical intelligentsia led, more often than not, by printers or aspiring journalists who had direct contacts with English reformers like Owen and Thompson. Owen even visited Philadelphia and gave his open support to the workers. The Mechanics Union sponsored a library and an educational institute, tried to develop cooperative stores, and addressed the country through a sympathetic and pioneering newspaper, *The Mechanics' Free Press*. In 1828 members of the fledgling union sponsored Working Men's candidates in local elections, and soon had a reasonably well-organized Working Men's Party. They only supported candidates who backed a public school system, who opposed lotteries, and who were willing to challenge the powers of chartered banks and other monopolies. Free schools and the evils of monopoly usually took precedence in their proclamations and platforms, but they espoused other causes—they were against imprisonment for debt, all forms of speculation, and the use of prison labor, and they hoped to establish a new exchange system based on quantities of labor.[12]

Agrarian issues remained secondary in Philadelphia. But in an 1828 legislative petition, the Philadelphia workingmen asked for free access to twenty to forty acres of public land for each family. They did not want titles to the land, but rather a legalized right of pre-emption, a form of tenure that they hoped would end the speculative buying and selling of land. By their scheme, if any public tenant failed to occupy and cultivate land it was to revert to the government. If leased land developed into towns, then the lease holders were to receive only a reasonable compensation and their share of the lots. They justified this petition by the now stereotyped arguments of natural law. Everyone has to occupy a portion of the earth, and each person has a "birthright in the soil." If others control this, then they deprive people of "life, liberty, and the pursuit of happiness." Without access opportunities, the "great body of the people" could not enjoy "a true spirit of independence," nor "exercise the freedom secured to them. . . ." They saw little relief in public land sales, which priced lands beyond the means of city workers and led to an unnatural exclusion. They asked the federal government to reserve all public lands for the use of working people, as the only effective way of preventing future land monopoly.[13]

When the workingmen of New York, inspired by the successes in Philadelphia, erupted in a flurry of organization and political action in 1829, they temporarily made these agrarian issues their central platform. They did this under the compelling influence of a heretofore obscure young printer, Thomas Skidmore. Even today we know very little about him. He wrote a notorious book and helped organize a Working Men's Party in 1829, and then spent the last three years of his short life in bitter controversy. But it was he who, almost single-handedly, pushed the issues of property and land reform into American politics. As a result he gave the word "agrarianism" a sinister meaning to most Americans.

Skidmore's book had the alluring title: *The Rights Of Man To Property*. His text was the opening sections of the Declaration of Independence; his avowed mentors Jefferson and Thomas Paine. Skidmore took property seriously, as did all agrarians. The right to property was the most basic human right. Freedom depended on access to nature. Everyone deserved this. Exclusive ownership of land by any one class placed all others at its mercy. Even if in 1829 New York State owners were restricted to five hundred acres, there would still not be enough land for everyone. New Yorkers already faced the scarcity Ricardo had predicted. Since New York had no restrictions at all on acreage, large estates abounded; tenancy was common. Since the tenure system allowed a monopoly by some, it already warred against man's right to property.[14]

According to Skidmore, in a state of nature all had equal access. At the beginnings of a society the only fair division seemed equal shares. Subsequently, everyone still deserved their proportionate share, and by right should have it. Why should anyone be artificially excluded from their enjoyment of the fruits and productions of the earth? Ordinarily, labor gives one a claim to property, but this was clearly not so in the case of land, which comes from God. Here ownership claims rested only on political choice, either by the consent of a people or by tyrannical imposition. Unless they voluntarily relinquished their right, everyone remained a joint heir of a common nature. Skidmore stressed that even the territorial claims of nations rested on the consent of other nations. This proved to him that holders of large estates had no right to them. Unfortunately, in the American Revolution the founding fathers had failed to heed the hard logic of property rights. Skidmore rebuked Jefferson for replacing in the Declaration of Independence the substantial and sacred right to property by the mild and vague euphemism "pursuit of happiness." By not guaranteeing access rights to everyone, our new governments denied rather than upheld the ideal of human equality, and insured an early class division between the rich who owned the land and a dispossessed poor.[15]

Skidmore seemed most dangerous not because of these moral principles, but because he moved from them to some concrete proposals. He wanted to remedy past mistakes of policy by a very thorough agrarian reform. He began with life tenures. He condemned all existing inheritance laws, which gave fathers discretionary control over an inalienable right, over what God intended for all his children. Skidmore urged the people of New York, who were sovereign, to use their power to restore property rights. By constitutional amendment, they could divest all private owners at death, and allow the state government to redistribute property in equal shares to children. But this would leave existing inequities. Skidmore wanted to take New York back to a state of nature and make a totally new start, this time without error or injustice. He proposed a new constitutional convention for New York, and hoped the people would use it to vacate all existing titles and to cancel all debts. After a state inventory of all real and productive property, each person over twenty-one would receive a claim to his proportional share of the whole in the form of a credit instrument or dividend. With these, individuals would bid for their share of property in a great state auction and receive a lifetime claim to what they purchased. If shareholders wished they could combine their share in a corporate pool. The state was to withhold a portion of the common wealth in order to assure the equal education of all children, either by parents or by state boarding schools. All property reverted to the state at death and funded new shares for those reaching maturity. A share was fully one's own, to do with as one wanted, except that it was a crime to give it away. One could take it abroad if in mobile form, or use it in exchange. Improvident people might lose all or most of their share in a lifetime; able people might accumulate considerable wealth. But note that any claim to a share remained valid only so long as the original shareholder lived, not for the lifetime of a purchaser.[16]

Skidmore had other goals. He stressed women's equality, wanted suffrage for blacks and Indians, was strongly opposed to banks and corporate charters, wanted to prohibit all usury, sought a unicameral legislature for New York, and favored boarding schools to neutralize the ill effects of bad parents. Apart from his agrarian leveling he often expressed conventional social attitudes. Given an equal start in life with equal education and equal property, everyone should be completely on their own, to work or to starve. He hated charity or public welfare except for the disabled, and wanted to dispossess anyone, including ministers, who refused to aid the common defense. He wanted no rules or restrictions on labor and exchange, no limits on an open and fully competitive economy, although he did favor protective tariffs. As much as had John Taylor, he loved a frugal and simple government and hated foreign luxuries.[17]

The first workingmen's movement produced only one other treatise on economic theory: Stephen Simpson's uneven and confusing *The Working Man's Manual: A Theory Of Political Economy, Etc.*, published in 1831. Simpson, a political maverick from Pennsylvania, claimed both Jefferson and Hamilton as heroes, and in his book celebrated the antimonopoly position of John Taylor even as he gave his own support to the Bank of the United States. He followed Taylor in emphasizing America's exceptionalism, and repeatedly warned against a return to the European class system, or capitulation to a new feudalism tied to a paper aristocracy, to corporate privileges and banking chicanery. He enumerated all the grievances of workers, and in his jeremiads expressed with passion the class bitterness of urban mechanics who felt themselves slowly falling into abject slavery. But Simpson's positive recommendations for practical action proved elusive and contradictory. Much of this book was sheer rhetorical bombast, long harangues against privilege or wealth or even college degrees, or repetitious reiterations of the rights of workers. He argued that a deepening inequality in America arose from corporate monopoly and a monopoly of the land, but illustrated land monopoly only by an outdated attack on the Penn family in Pennsylvania. Other diatribes against landlords and the unequal distribution of land seemed directed at Europe, not America. He saw only temporary answers in agrarian laws, but endlessly asked for the right of laborers to control their own lives.[18]

In a sense, Simpson tried to combine Taylor and Raymond, a difficult task at best. His perspective was that of urban mechanics, not farmers. He loved the small shops of his day, and naturally feared the coming of large factories. Like Byllesby, he resented and feared large merchants and financiers, and usually quoted Taylor in support of this antipathy. Like most Jacksonians, he believed that a hard money policy and rigid laws against usury and monopoly might help preserve a proprietary economy. In this vein, he wanted diminished government intervention, fewer grants of privilege, and more freedom. But even as he condemned corporations or any form of capitalist privilege, he defended protective tariffs, a vast public education system, internal improvements, and detailed sumptuary laws, or the very form of positive government that made him an avowed ally of Henry Clay's American System. His defense of the Bank of the United States, perhaps as a repayment for personal favors from the Bank, was a defense of one monopoly to check other less responsible monopolies. Simpson well illustrated how a fervent, class-conscious friend of free mechanics could opt for a positive government, simply because he believed with John Quincy Adams and Henry Clay that through the franchise working people could mold such policies to serve their own interests.[19]

The early workingmen of New York City embraced Skidmore's principles, not Simpson's. Under the general slogan of equal education for all children, equal property for all adults, and equal privileges for all mankind, a gathering of craftsmen in New York City met as early as April, 1829, and by the fall appointed a Committee of Fifty to draft a list of grievances and political proposals. They also nominated candidates for the state Assembly and Senate. Skidmore, a member of the original committee, and surely the most influential member, won its full endorsement for his agrarian scheme. To achieve an equal division of property, the committee recommended a revolution by workers, but a revolution carried by the vote rather than the sword. The committee certainly contained other able men, including as one of its three secretaries Robert Dale Owen, the son of Robert Owen. Owen had just moved to New York from his father's colony in New Harmony. He and the brilliant but erratic Frances Wright brought with them a former colony newspaper, *The Free Enquirer*, which they used to support a range of workingmen's causes, above all their own distinctive educational theories. Thus, next to land reform, the founding committee most emphasized education. A second committee dubbed An Association For Protection Of Industry and For The Promotion Of Rational Education, endorsed a complete system of free, nonsectarian, republican education, since an enlightened and virtuous working class was as indispensable to free institutions as universal manhood suffrage. Never before had urban workers encountered such a brilliant and varied spectrum of intellectuals or such a challenging and radical array of proposed programs.[20]

Besides the transcendent goals of equal property and equal education, the Committee, and the workers themselves as they gathered in frequent meetings at both city and ward levels, embraced many less crucial causes. During the first few heady weeks they condemned the spirit of party faction, the degeneration of politics into intrigue and self-interested power seeking, and the proliferation of lawyers and other nonproductive classes; they demanded a unicameral assembly, shorter terms of office, fair pay for all elected officers, and in all cases direct election by the people on a general ticket. Like the Philadelphia artisans, they condemned charters and monopolies of all types and stressed above all else the evils of banking in New York City. They fought against imprisonment for debt and prison labor, asked for a worker's lien law (to secure to actual workers a claim against completed buildings up to the value of their unpaid wages), condemned the militia system, asked for less expensive legal processes and more equal taxes on property, and insisted upon a complete separation of church and state, which entailed the continued delivery of mail on Sunday. While the new party fought for such political goals, the workers continued to seek more direct economic goals, such as a ten-hour day, within their own trade societies. The Working Men's Party and friendly newspapers applauded these goals, publicized local standouts, and even supported from a distance early labor organizations among shop girls in New England cotton mills.[21]

Who were these workingmen, so ready to respond to people like Skidmore, Owen, and Fannie Wright? According to their own early proclamations, they were "mechanics, manufacturers, artisans, operatives," or all who lived "by their industry." A subsequent and related "New England Association Of Farmers, Mechanics, and Other Working Men" actually tried to recruit both farmers and operatives. Excluded by these avowed standards were all those "not living by some useful occupation;" that is, bankers, large merchants, brokers, and all rich men. Despite the broad membership rules, and evidence of masters, clerks, and even physicians involved in the ward organizations of the New York Working Men's Party, almost all of the identified leaders were mechanics, and the strongest leadership came from the more highly skilled and better-organized trades. New York thus far contained few factory operatives, although Party leaders professed great concern for the plight of factory workers and certainly recruited support among dock workers and other wage employees.[22]

Judged by its early platform, the New York Working Men's Party was primarily an agrarian party, and surely the most determined one in Anglo-American History. The original committee explored all the principles of Spence and Skidmore, and often in subtle detail. It traced the evils of land monopoly from the Norman Conquest of 1066, and saw exclusion from the land as the source of all the other injustices of society. But alas, the enthusiasm and verve and soaring hopes of October, 1829, lasted only a few weeks. Skidmore's redistributive scheme provided the perfect opening for a devastating attack on the fledgling party by established politicians and all the older newspapers. It seemed that no "respectable" people in New York favored the right to property, at least after Skidmore had clarified the positive and quite radical implications of such a right. In any event, here was an issue, and soon an effective label, to put down a new and potentially powerful political organization. As later events proved, the artisans could control elections in many wards and mobilize a critical minority citywide or even at the state level. But what is not clear is the degree to which the mechanics of New York really grasped and endorsed Skidmore's redistributive scheme. Even if one conceded his principles, those allowed other modes of implementation. And, in fact, from the very beginning the Party distinguished abstract principles and ultimate goals from political tactics. The agrarian impulse scarcely remained dominant until the November elections of 1829, but had it remained central this would not have meant that endorsed candidates would have used the agrarian issue in local elections.

Within a month of the Committee of Fifty reports, a majority in the Party had repudiated Skidmore's agrarian schemes and also the agrarian label. Skidmore withdrew his disciples, founded his own party, and edited his own newspaper, but even before his death in 1832 his faction was little more than a personal cult. The winning majority moved education from its secondary to a primary position, and briefly went along with the ideological views of Owen and Wright. But before the end of 1829, workingmen's politics had become hopelessly schismatic and confusing, and eventually even the Owenite wing split, since many workers could not accept the guardianship scheme of Owen and Wright (they wanted all children to be reared in special boarding schools, funded in part by a tax on wealth and in part by payments from parents). Although moderates compared to Skidmore, Owen and Wright, who were free thinkers and advocates of racial and sexual equality, seemed wild and threatening to conventional New Yorkers and, presumably, to many artisans. Thus, in 1830 the Working Men's movement continued to grow, but the less radical groups came to prevail as the fascinating ideological phase of the early days gave way to practical politics. The workingmen's movement slowly became a mere wing of the emerging Jacksonian Party, particularly after Jackson's bank veto. The self-conscious workingmen maintained their separate party identity only until the depression of 1837. But out of the workingmen's ranks came many of the Equal Rights Democrats, or Locofocos, a pro-Jackson but anti-Tammany faction in New York. Meanwhile, agrarianism seemed fully disgraced, a hated label without a single serious and effective advocate.

But it was not dead. Agrarian ideals continued to simmer in the mind of one destined to become by far the most notable and successful American agrarian—George Henry Evans. He was born in 1805 to a middle-class English family. His mother died when he was very young, and at the age of fourteen he joined his father, a former soldier, in emigrating to New York. According to his brother's later account, George received a classical education in England. The family settled in Binghamton, New York, near relatives, among whom were several printers; and George completed an apprenticeship in printing at nearby Ithaca. He there published a small reform periodical before moving in 1829 to New York City where he was active in the new and exciting Working Men's Party. He possibly also saw in the new ferment a professional opportunity, for he owned a press and launched what quickly became the official voice of New York workers, *The Working Man's Advocate*. By then, the twenty-four-year-old artisan had some enduring political and philosophical commitments, commitments which he more fully developed in the hothouse intellectual atmosphere of New York City, where he eagerly joined in frequent intellectual discussions at the Hall of Science, discussions often led by Owen or Wright. Evans now swore by Jefferson and Thomas Paine, and echoed the free-thinking and anticlerical views of Frances Wright. His brother Frederick became part of this same intellectual circle, but subsequently converted to the Shakers and by the middle of the century was the most articulate Shaker leader. From Frederick's biased perspective, George and his circle of intellectuals were simply infidels. But Frederick absorbed and continued to affirm many of the ideals of agrarianism, which he believed could be best fulfilled in the Shaker colonies. For his part, George always had a tender sympathy for communalism, although he never believed it an acceptable reform for most Americans.[23]

As he later admitted, Evans at first fell completely under the sway of Skidmore's ideas. He chaired the original committee on education, and stayed with the pro-education faction when the Working Men's Party first split late in 1829. In fact, his *Advocate* followed the pure Skidmore line in only the two original numbers. The third weekly edition dropped the equal property part of its masthead. In the fourth issue, Evans repudiated any redistributive device, noting that only a minority of workingmen had ever subscribed to Skidmore's scheme. In December he tried to clarify the label *agrarian* and to establish that it had to do with the Gracchan effort to keep the rich from grabbing all public lands, and not with Skidmore's radical proposal to divest existing owners. Evans and his faction came under vicious attacks from Skidmore, and by mid-1830 Evans dismissed Skidmore as overly radical and refused to carry on a continued controversy in competing newspapers. Soon, Evans made few references to agrarianism, except to counter critics who used the label to discredit the Working Men's Party. Just before Skidmore's death in 1832, Evans insisted that Skidmore's goal of vacating existing land titles meant revolution and bloodshed, or something close to anarchistic chaos. He believed threatened owners would leave the country if they had to give up their farms. The idea of state confiscation, and a great public auction, seemed visionary in the extreme, as if everyone was able enough to make a wise choice at the auction. The pity of it all was that Skidmore, or the futile efforts of his small and impotent party, had continued to embarrass a legitimate and politically astute workingmen's movement.[24]

After Skidmore's death, Evans re-embraced a mild form of agrarianism and supported it in the pages of the *Advocate*. By then, he had made his newspaper the principal organ of New York's artisans. In part it reflected some of the varying and shifting concerns of working men, in part the personal commitments of Evans. The sharp, pungent class partisanship and the continuous digs at corporate privilege, Wall Street, and capitalist bankers echoed the rhetorical style of all the workingmen's press. But he was personally involved in attacks on organized religion, the opposition to sabbatarian laws, and the support of temperance and abolitionist movements. Evans became a fervent but not uncritical supporter of Jackson after his bank veto, and would later try to claim him for the agrarian cause. His own experience led Evans to doubt the possibility of successful economic efforts by organized workers apart from parallel political agitation. Nonetheless, he helped organize the first National Trades' Union Convention in 1834. Actually, delegates came from only six nearby cities. But this first American effort at solidarity allowed Evans to designate his *Advocate* as the sanctioned publication of a national movement. More important, he won the convention's endorsement of a strong agrarian platform.[25]

At the end of 1835, Evans was nearly bankrupt and had to retreat to Rathway, New Jersey. He moved to a small farm, kept his press, and for a few months continued to publish his beloved *Advocate*. He combined a new emphasis on subsistence agriculture (he featured front-page articles on agricultural improvements) with continued support of Jacksonian candidates. The *Advocate* continued to claim the sanction of the National Trades' Union, which assembled for its second Convention in 1835 without giving added emphasis to the land issue. But to Evans's delight, a close friend, John Commerford, now headed the National Union, and in his presidential address made free public land a key issue, the great "outlet of relief" for urban workers. No strategies could save the *Advocate*, which expired late in 1835. From his farmstead, Evans had to watch the agonizing depression of 1837, and the expiration of the last remnants of the Working Men's Party and the National Trades' Union. In seven years of public silence, as he undoubtedly brooded over past failures, Evans matured a final agrarian strategy, one keyed not only to all the traditional principles of agrarianism but to American political realities. The next time around, Evans was determined to win.[26]

His spirits revived by contact with the soil, his fortunes improved by economic recovery, Evans resumed his reform and publishing career in 1844. He first announced his new crusade through an intermittent periodical, *The Radical*, which he published in New Jersey, but launched it in earnest back in New York City in the spring of 1844. There he revived his *Working Man's Advocate* (the name was later changed to *Young America*) and used all the successful organizing techniques of 1829, including committee reports, vast street rallies and outdoor meetings, ward-level clubs, a barrage of petitions, appealing pamphlets, a network of colporteurs modeled after those of evangelical societies, and successful efforts to penetrate trade unions and other reform movements. By the summer, Evans had a growing organization with capable leaders, growing newspaper support, easily exploitable enemies, and what already promised to be a national movement. At first Evans referred to his embryonic organization as the Agrarian League, and hoped it would eventuate in a People's Rights Party. But his organizing committee borrowed an old label from Robert Dale Owen—national reform—and adopted a constitution for a National Reform Association (NRA), which proved an enduring title. The NRA would become the largest agrarian and land reform organization in American history.

Evans now had a fully coherent diagnosis of American ills and a quite specific solution for most of them. He continuously reiterated the surplus labor thesis. Because of restricted access to land, too many mechanics competed for employment in the cities. This resulted in depressed wages and frequent unemployment. The only permanent solution was to assure each American family a "natural right to the use of a portion of the soil sufficient for his subsistence," and for the Federal Government to reserve all existing public lands for such homesteaders. In most countries, such goals would have meant a Skidmore-like program of dispossession and redistribution. Not so in America. Except for state laws limiting the amount of land owned by any one family, Evans wanted to avoid a confrontation with existing owners, even though on principle he continued to deny any abstract right to hold property in nature. The public lands permitted a milder remedy. Evans urged the Federal Government to offer a free, exempt, nonalienable homestead of 160 acres to every landless family that desired to go onto the land. By exempt, he meant land that could not be mortgaged or in any way made liable for debt. By nonalienable, he meant land that could not be sold; even improvements could be sold only to purchasers who owned no land. In addition, Evans emphasized a formal township plan of settlement, with parks, public buildings, and clustered lots for mechanics, all surrounded by 160-acre farms. This scheme, calculated to appeal to various communal groups, never became very important to the NRA.[27]

Evans hoped to rally a second workingmen's movement around the controlling issue of land reform. He launched his movement in New York City and tried to recruit many of the veterans of 1829. The new movement began with a meeting of mechanics at Croton Hall. William Lyon Mackenzie of Canada gave one of the key addresses. This meeting established a Committee of Thirteen to draft an address to the "working classes." John Commerford, of the old National Trades' Union and the best symbol of trade union federation, enthusiastically endorsed the work of the Committee. He would soon chair another committee to draft a constitution for the NRA. The surplus labor theory and land reform made up the orthodoxy of the new movement; all the early effort centered on the clear political goal—to achieve a new, agrarian land policy at the federal level. But this was not Evans's only concern. He always combined national reform with other, less critical political goals dating from 1829, goals such as free public education, restrictions on monopoly, sound money, and debtor relief. He also paired it with the limited and direct economic goals of the trade societies, most particularly their struggle for a ten-hour day. In fact, in his appeal to city workers, Evans practically married land reform to the ten-hour day movement.[28]

The lament of urban mechanics underlay all the early petitions of the NRA. As Mackenzie emphasized, so much of the American promise of 1776 had been realized—a plethora of natural resources, prosperous farmers, unexcelled manufacturers, universal suffrage, the end of entail and primogeniture, the disestablishment of churches. Yet the working classes of the cities seemed to sink ever deeper into misery, with thousands recently unemployed. Throughout the national reform crusade, leaders cited studies of urban distress or referred to city crime and woeful living conditions. The Committee of Thirteen emphasized the role of machines in replacing labor, with a resulting decline of handicrafts, but saw no way to reverse the trend. More and more artisans would be forced into factories as servile laborers, or else they would continue to face lower wages and periodic unemployment. Thus, free, independent, and self-respecting workers were trapped without a path of escape, since few could accumulate enough money to buy public land. Indeed, as national reformers often admitted, real wages for skilled workers in some trades had risen, but not, they believed, at the rate of overall national growth. Their share of the pie declined, and this accompanied growing insecurity and the threat of mere employee status.

From a later perspective, free public land seemed a very inadequate answer for these quite real problems. After all, how many urban mechanics had the skills for success in agriculture or wanted to leave their urban homes and workshops? And the original price of public land, then $1.25 an acre, was only a very small part of the total required to develop a productive farm. Evans responded to these issues with some ambivalence. His own experience in New Jersey did not sour him on rural life. Quite the contrary. He eulogized the freedom and independence of farm life and believed many urban workers would want to homestead if they had the opportunity. After all, what better answer for surplus workers? But land reform was not addressed primarily to the potential back-to-the-lander, but to those who chose to remain urban mechanics. If only the surplus left, then the people who remained would regain the bargaining position and the social status of an earlier period. Also, Evans did not celebrate frontier conditions or the life of pioneers. He deplored them. His township plan attested to his concern for compact village settlement, with household manufacturers accommodated as well as farmers. With free land, all rents would fall, more workers and more immigrants would then choose independence on the land, household manufacturing might increase at the expense of factories, and the national economy could become less dependent on foreign markets. With such self-sufficiency, ordinary government costs would decline. Workers, already benefiting from more free schools, would regain economic opportunity.

Evans believed, as would Henry George later, that universal access to land would bankrupt land speculators and significantly lower the price of all improved land. As Eastern states faced population losses, they would have an increased incentive to adopt the main national reform proposal for state governments—restrictions on the amount of land owned by any one family. This meant that the best homestead opportunities might eventually be on unused private lands now brought onto the market, or in areas relatively close to urban workers. He foresaw vast technological improvements in agriculture, and thus a steady lessening of the rigors of farm life. What he seemed to ignore was the problem of skills and markets. He argued, perhaps on the basis of his own experience, that anyone could live on the land, but frequently suggested state subsidies to help establish workers on their homesteads. Such subsidies would be cheap compared to extended welfare grants in the cities. Presumably, Evans expected continued increases in manufacturing but believed machines, not more labor, would absorb most of the increases. Only agriculture could accommodate a growing population. But who would buy the increased farm output? Evans never really explored this issue. Instead, he and other national reformers stressed subsistence agriculture and local autonomy. Mechanics could supply their own needs by part-time farming, and continue their trades on a part-time but fully indepen-dent basis, presumably selling to full-time commercial farmers. Thus, he envisioned less crowded cities and a merger of rural and urban life styles.[29]

The organized Working Men's Movement had expired in the panic of 1837. Evans proposed to rebuild it around land reform. To an extent, he succeeded. He carefully involved only professed workingmen in the founding of the NRA. Five members of the founding committee listed themselves as printers: Evans himself; Mackenzie; John Windt, who was a partner in the *Advocate*; Mike Walsh, a wild Irishman who would later become a Congressman; and Thomas A. Devyr, a key leader in the early movement. The other members of the founding committee all listed their trade by their names; and as in 1829 they represented the more skilled or better-organized crafts (a smith, a machinist, a bookbinder, a picture frame maker, a clothier, a carpenter, a chairmaker, and two cordwain-ers). Evans used the *Advocate* to publicize strikes and to point out the evils of New England factories, or what Orestes A. Brownson, in an address reprinted in the *Advocate*, called the new "industrial feudalism." By the fall of 1844, agents of the NRA were assiduously cultivating embryonic labor organizations in the New England textile towns. Mike Walsh, an out-spoken labor agitator and leader of a turbulent group of Irish firefighters called the Spartan Band, briefly joined his vituperative periodical, the *Subterranean*, to Evans' *Advocate* (Walsh proved too reckless and too libelous for Evans), and worked effectively within the labor movement. Walsh hated the factories, and tried with little success to radicalize the exploited shop girls.[30]

Evans and his friends both supported and penetrated other labor organizations. In October, 1844, Evans and Walsh attended, and won a strong land reform commitment from, a Working Men's Convention in Boston. Then, in March, 1845, the national reform leaders joined the New England Convention in calling for a national meeting of trade societies and reformers of all varieties. Only twenty-four official dele-gates attended, a disappointing turnout reminiscent of the Trades' Union Convention of 1834. But the small group was particularly amenable to national reform, and this and ten subsequent "Industrial Congresses" became, in effect, the national conventions of the NRA. The first Con-gress stressed the right to education and to the soil, and reflected other than national reform priorities (notably the goals of labor unions and of the supporters of Fourier). Subsequent congresses frequently joined the ten-hour day to land reform, but Evans made sure that land reform was always the central motif. It is a mistake to conceive of the congresses as national labor conventions, but in these years they were the closest approximation of a national federation of workers. The congresses, besides endorsing political candidates who favored free land, supported a wide variety of popular reforms, from the peace movement to cooperative shops, from public education to women's suffrage, from abolition to free trade. The congresses met in Boston, Philadelphia, Cincinnati, Chicago, Albany, Washington, Wilmington, Trenton, and Cleveland, as well as New York City, where they met twice; most delegates represented local national reform clubs scattered throughout the country. In the later congresses, the claim of catholicity, of an ecumenical blending of all labor and reform elements, seemed more and more illusory.[31]

National reform blossomed in the heyday of Association, or "social reform." To a large extent, Arthur Brisbane, the ideological prophet of American Association, offered the same critique as Evans of the new factory system, and even of land monopoly, and tried to appeal to the same grievances of urban workers. But his critique led, not to free land, but to the complicated Phalanxes advocated by Fourier. Brisbane had a wide and often very respectable following, including Horace Greeley of the New York *Tribune*. Evans found Fourier's writings tedious, mysterous, and impractical, but acknowledged that his American disciples were sincere and praiseworthy. The colony idea would not appeal to the rich and, because it required stock subscription, would not be available to the poor. Thus, the several Fourierite colonies would remain a bit of a sideshow to American society. To Evans, the schemes of both Owen and Fourier seemed to represent grafts on an old and rotten system since they left untouched the basic cause of distress—land monopoly. The Associationists also seemed too accommodationist, too anxious to find middle-class support, and thus equivocal on such issues as Negro rights or even on the natural rights of mankind.

Evans's past ties to Skidmore and to the Working Men's Party gave him a less respectable image than Brisbane, and separated him further from middle-class intellectual support. But Evans sought the broadest possible appeal, and thus tried to establish areas of agreement with the Associationists rather than emphasizing differences. The early response to the NRA in Fourierite journals was hostile. But Evans eventually won Brisbane's endorsement of land reform. Evans published many Associationist articles in the *Advocate*. He also admitted that, in the distant future, when land was scarce even in America and none left for free homesteads, new tenure arrangements would become necessary and these would undoubtedly involve some form of communalism or association. But for the present, Evans knew his constituency too well to embrace communalism as the sole answer for workers' distress. He knew that most workers, if at all interested in the land, wanted secure access to their own farm.[32]

The growing abolitionist movement represented an even larger target for national reform penetration. Evans worked hard to build bridges. Long a bitter critic of slavery, Evans in effect wrote off the deep South as a constituency for land reform. Yet he fully embraced some key southern arguments—that factory employment constituted a form of slavery, very often more cruel and vicious than black slavery in the South. Land reform, as he saw it, was a great crusade to prevent an American factory system, a centralized and collectivized form of production owned and managed by a corporate elite. From this perspective, Evans publicly accused the best-known New York abolitionist, Gerret Smith, of being one of the "largest slave holders" in America because his vast land holdings denied access to the land for innumerable fellow men. They had no alternative to wage slavery. This opened a fascinating correspondence between the two men. Smith eventually converted to agrarianism. He gave away part of his land to homesteaders, contributed funds for the first and most popular NRA pamphlet ("Vote Yourself A Farm"), and later supported agrarian homesteads in his abbreviated career as a Congressman.[33]

Evans believed, correctly, that the issue of free land would have broad appeal, and insisted that his organization keep this issue uppermost. At the very beginning, he announced an agrarian pledge as a test of Association membership, and adhered to it against much early opposition. The pledge was straightforward: "We, whose names are annexed, desirous of restoring to man his Natural Right to Land, do solemnly agree, that we will not vote for any man, for any legislative office; who will not pledge himself, in writing, to use all the influence of his station, if elected, to prevent all futher traffic in the Public Lands of the States and of the United States, and to cause them to be laid out in Farms and Lots for the free and exclusive use of actual settlers." Soon, national reform leaders in local clubs forced politicians to affirm or reject this pledge. As early as the 1844 elections, the NRA began endorsing friendly candidates, and even ran unsuccessful candidates of its own in New York City.[34]

As always with a single-interest campaign, an important goal was public understanding and endorsement. Evans proved himself a promotional genius. Within months he had built up a network of support from sympathetic newspapers; the newspapers supporting the NRA campaign eventually numbered in the hundreds. His most influential convert was Horace Greeley, who affirmed national reform goals as early as 1845, and soon made national reform his prime commitment, at the expense of Associationism. Because of the national circulation of the *Tribune*, Greeley did more than anyone else to nationalize the movement. Such was his preeminence that many people associated land reform more with him than with Evans. With national exposure, local clubs formed in almost all areas except the deep South; in time the movement gained many effective local spokesmen and some diversity of perspective. Evans spoke for urban mechanics, but free land appealed to would-be home-steaders in the West, and particularly to groups already bitter against land speculators or even the United States Public Land Office. Thus, outside New York and Pennsylvania, land reform gained its ablest leaders and largest followings in such states as Ohio, Illinois, and Wisconsin. At one time a Wisconsin representative and both its senators pushed national reform legislation in Congress. Beginning in 1844, the NRA kept a steady stream of petitions flowing into Washington; and wherever it was power-ful enough, it besieged state legislatures with homestead and acreage limitation bills. New York considered several. One acreage limitation bill won on the first two readings in Wisconsin, and finally failed only because of strong opposition from Milwaukee (the bill not only limited farm acreage to 300, but limited city owners to two 1-acre lots).[35]

In order to win converts, Evans muted some of his older concerns. For example, he concealed his views on religion and welcomed Biblical and Christian defenses of free land. He also borrowed strategies from Bible and Tract societies. Hired agents distributed the publications of the Association, while paid lecturers went on broad regional circuits. Local agents maintained correspondence with the headquarters in New York, and carefully cultivated support among local agricultural societies, labor unions, or even church groups. Active members not only signed the agrarian pledge, but in the beginning paid a small dues ($.25 on joining, $.02 a month thereafter), but one feels that members were never as critical to the organization as sympathetic fellow travelers. Although never secret or fraternal, the NRA soon had its repertoire of poems and hymns for use in monthly meetings. The first of these, the "Agrarian Song," dates all the way back to the beginnings in 1844:

1   We are all true Reformers,
               And fearlessly we stand.
           We labor in a righteous cause—
               The Freedom of the Land.

Chorus: Oh, Oh, poor sons of toil,
               If ye would happy be,
           Go, plant yourself upon the soil,
               And be forever free!

2   The landlords all oppose us,
               And turn their noses up;
           But we will soon bring down their rents,
               And that will use them up.

And so on, in a very sentimental vein, for nine verses.[36]

Diversity of support and a degree of respectability never softened the moral fervor of Evans or lessened the radical implications of his version of land reform. Acreage limitation and a nonalienable, permanent lease system for public lands struck at the very heart of traditional land policy. Evans frequentiy contemplated other agrarian reforms in the future, such as a high land tax on all large holdings. Yet his use of traditional natural-law arguments disarmed critics. Many denounced land reform as impractical or fanciful or dangerous, but almost no one offered a reasoned refutation of its principles, a fact successfully exploited in NRA publications. Tirelessly, Evans kept on denouncing the vast inequities that allowed the rich to get richer and the poor poorer. He continually tried to incite laborers to fight back, to refuse to submit to wage slavery and demeaning public welfare. And when he appealed to workers, he could not forbear personal confession. This showed how deeply he was affected by his near-bankruptcy in 1835. When he came back to New York City he could only note the vast increase of mansions and luxury, and at the same time the worsening status, if not wages, of laborers. Then he could protest how America had failed Jefferson and the Declaration of Independence, since in New York City a child was often born in another's home, or even in the streets, "without the right, should it survive to maturity, of gathering the wild fruits of the earth, or planting a grain of corn, while another comes into existence and possession, or with the legalized right and means to purchase, land enough to support thousands, and perhaps hundreds of thousands!" Yet hypocritical Americans still proclaimed life and liberty as unalienable rights.[37]

As was typical of many Jacksonians and most organized workingmen, Evans was not scrupulous in his economic analysis. He preferred the battle over high principle to the comparison of economic models or the gathering of hard economic data. He was often grievously in error in his estimates of the percentage of national income that went to the wealthy. His was the bent of a publicist, a journalist, a propagandist. Yet he was not prone to nurse grudges, and he was extremely tolerant of differences and ready to hear and respect the position of opponents. He could not understand the near-paranoid anger of a Skidmore, and found himself uncomfortable with the verbal assaults of a Mike Walsh. He thus won converts, such as Gerret Smith, while men of lesser good will would only have antagonized them. Evans also had vital political gifts—the ability to sacrifice small goals for large ones and the patience to await a fuller public understanding.

Others had to take up the burden of careful economic analysis. The aggressively agrarian themes of the NRA demanded a new theory of political economy. The theories of Taylor, Byllesby, and Simpson were inadequate, for none of them gave enough emphasis to the land issue; Skidmore was much too radical, and therefore an embarrassment. Thus, two national reformers, Joseph Campbell and John Pickering, wrote long essays on political economy. Both embraced land reform after having espoused a panacea usually identified with Josiah Warren of Ohio. Warren expanded upon a theme of the Owenites—the inherent evils of pecuniary commerce. He wanted to replace money-based exchange with a labor-based system, and he established a much publicized co-operative store in Cincinnati, in which workers received credits for the amount of labor embodied in any product they deposited at the store. The principle of equal exchange, which drew upon the moral content of a labor theory of value, had wide appeal. But Warren moved far beyond this principle. He concluded that the abolition of greedy commerce would also remove the need for any government or for any other collectivity that swallowed up the free individual. Because of his logical development of this position, he is often identified as the first American anarchist. But it was his ideas on exchange, his animus against money, that most influenced his leading disciples, and that were most closely related to land reform.[38]

John Campbell was an Irish-born weaver, a former Chartist, and a virtual political refugee in America. In 1848 he published a short book on equality. He borrowed distinctively Marxist terms, applauded Rousseau and Paine, but ended up close to Warren. He desired few laws, no political parties, no banks, and above all an end to the existing commercial system. He also recommended labor-based exchange. But unlike Warren, he saw monopoly in land underlying all other forms of exploitation. He cited numerous historical examples of such exploitation and then argued for a standard agrarian platform, a position that he could have borrowed from Evans or from related Chartist land policies. He saw land as a common inheritance, wanted homestead exemptions, and proposed to limit access to need and use. The solution for all ills was both free soil and equal exchange.[39] But Campbell only grafted land reform onto his developed system. The NRA still needed one of its own members who could place agrarianism in the context of academic political economy. John Pickering of Cincinnati, another disciple of Warren's, accepted this challenge, but he gave much greater attention to problems of equitable exchange than did most land reformers.

Pickering argued that all respected political economists, beginning with Adam Smith, had sold out to "capitalists." They had viewed people who had to sell their labor for wages, not as humans but as timber or ore to be used as employers desired, and had consistently supported the established privileges of a moneyed aristocracy. By "capitalist," Pickering meant those governed by only one motive—to make money—and those who lived on the labor of others at whatever competitive price they had to pay. In America, a capitalist with five thousand dollars realized enough annual profits to hire one worker, and thus could live on that labor without working himself. A millionaire could hire two hundred such slaves, which only illustrated the end effect of concentrated wealth. Such large accumulations meant that others had no wealth at all and had no alternative but to sell themselves. Given these inequities in wealth, the rich easily gained larger and larger shares while hired workers realized less and less, as was so clearly illustrated by industrial progress in England. Those with wealth always controlled governments and obtained special privileges and protections from legislatures. Like Veblen later, Pickering bitterly noted that those who did not work but rather managed the labor of others enjoyed greater status and respect than the millions whose labor actually created all wealth. And given this distortion of values, the working classes of America could anticipate no benevolence from above, but had to assert their own prerogatives and use their own political clout to remedy the deep institutional evils that threatened to make them wage slaves in the emerging American factory system.[40]

To Pickering, the source of all economic evils was an unjust distribution of property that concentrated it in the hands of a few lords of land and capital. A political society should secure to everyone their just rights, including personal security, the right to retain the product of one's labor, and a right to an equal use of all natural elements. Since no person would ever voluntarily surrender these rights, loss of either signalled tyranny. Pickering, like Evans, believed that Western governments had violated these rights, while those who rationalized such governments often justified such violations by hypocritical appeals to the right of property or to law and order. The violations had led to a vicious class system, with most people stripped of their natural inheritance and reduced to cringing servility. The mass of people had been robbed, usually with the connivance of government. But at least they had no moral obligation to obey such unjust governments. He thus adopted a coherent natural law position and argued it well.[41]

Land lay at the root of all evils. Too often, said Pickering, political economists had refused to distinguish between legitimate property, a product of human labor, and the elements of nature. Early governments illegitimately vested nature in a few, with no moral test or accountability. Now, people bought and sold these natural elements, a fact that horrified Pickering as much as the buying and selling of slaves. In fact, it amounted to the same thing, for anyone cut off from nature was a slave. Granted these qualifications on property, Pickering was basically Ricardian in his conception of value, in his emphasis on the benefits of capital accumulation, and in his emphatic endorsement of free exchange and open competition. He wanted, not equal wealth, but equal access to wealth. This entailed not only access to land but to tools and skills. Implicit in his analysis was the ancient belief that no one should exploit natural advantages, such as superior intelligence or newly discovered techniques or inventions. In a truly just society each would enjoy his share of nature, and each would share all his talents or new knowledge with others, so that all could enjoy a steadily improving living standard. Pickering wanted absolutely no monopolistic exclusion, no special favors of any sort, no penalties on anyone, and no special honor or unequal rewards for any honest occupation or profession.[42]

Pickering, unlike Warren, defended money as a medium of exchange and saw gold and silver as the finest form of money because of their intrinsic, labor-produced value. Like his fellow workingmen, he feared government-endorsed forms of paper money, for such fictitious money offered abundant opportunities for people to be dishonest by law, to manipulate and exploit others. When any exchange system moved away from barter or the use of gold and silver, when it involved various credit instruments, it jeopardized stability of value and thus fairness. Manipulated credit, or debased currencies, almost as much as vested title to land, allowed a few to gain control over most productive wealth. The dispossessed then had only property in themselves, which they had to hire out as if they were machines. Pickering agreed with Evans that the legal emancipation of southern slaves would effect little if such freedmen had no access to land or capital. But Pickering, with his greater sympathies for the nearby South, pushed his argument much further than Evans. As he saw it, white workers had no interest in freeing the slaves. Freedmen would simply increase the labor surplus in the North and increase the power of the money lords over workers. The developing conflict over slavery was between northern money lords and southern landlords, and boiled down to an empty argument—who exploited the most?[43]

In offering solutions to economic injustice Pickering cut a broad swath. He indicted all identifiable forms of privilege, all modes of distorting a fair distribution of the products of labor, from tariffs to banking charters. But in keeping with his basic philosophy and purpose, he always came back to land. The power to produce wealth grew by leaps and bounds in the nineteenth century. Human wants knew no limits. Thus, the seeming prospect was an unending growth of wealth and population. But the existing distribution gave all the rewards to a few and left the rest in increasing misery. Capital took too much; labor received too little. The exploitation of labor by capitalists remained possible only because of land monopoly, which created massed and vulnerable laborers ripe for exploitation. The first answer was simple—open up nature and let free competition do the rest. Beyond this, governments needed to abolish funded debts, bank charters, and protective tariffs. These reforms promised higher wages and lower rents. Combined with equitable but voluntary systems of exchange, and temperance, they could lead to a regenerated America.[44]

Pickering wrote in the heyday of National Reform. He was its last economic spokesman. Even he seemed to sense that the movement would not gain its stated goals. No state ever actually set acreage limits. The Federal government never granted free public lands with agrarian qualifications. Land remained a market commodity, and both rents and the price of access rights continued to increase.

It is not even clear whether most members of the National Reform Association grasped the finer points of agrarian arguments. If Skidmore erred in tying moral principles too closely to an optional scheme of implementation, Evans erred in the opposite direction. His continued emphasis on free public lands for actual settlers was so broadly appealing that program often obscured principles. By reaching out for the broadest possible support for limited legislative goals, Evans unintentionally helped mute and conceal the radical content of his philosophy. For example, the popular NRA pamphlet, "Vote Yourself A Farm," appealed to acquisitive desires. In it Evans stressed citizens' joint ownership of the public domain and everyone's right to have his own home and to till the earth for a profit. He lambasted land monopolists, argued for acreage limitation, and promised a right to the sale of improvements only, but he never clearly and straightforwardly explained nonalienability or emphasized that in his view rights in an agrarian homestead should amount to a sort of permanent lease and not to the type of ownership that allowed one to collect unearned increments.[45] And even Evans had no evidence that actual homesteaders were willing to give up speculative values in the soil, while the best evidence we have today indicates that they were not.

Equally unclear is the impact of national reform upon federal land policy and, in particular, upon the eventual passage of a homestead act. The class rhetoric of national reformers only echoed the same language used by innumerable Jacksonians. Many of Evans's arguments for free land were not distinctive. From the earliest debates on pre-emption, westerners claimed a special right to the soil, deplored land monopoly, berated speculators, and joined southerners in charting the evils of eastern factories. But they always assumed a right to full, commodity-like ownership. On a few rare occasions, Congressmen framed arguments a long agrarian lines. In 1838, Representative Caleb Cushing of Massachusetts, then a Whig but later a Democrat, fell back on Puritan moral theory to defend pre-emption, and this in opposition to the dominant opinion of New England. He went back to Locke and admitted a right of enclosure only to those who subdued, tilled, and sowed the land, and thus annexed it to themselves by labor. Only the sweat of one's brow could justify withdrawing land from the common stock. Moral philosophy, he argued, favored the rights of actual settlers over purely positive law claims.[46] A few years later, Representative William W. Payne, a Jacksonian Democrat from Alabama, unknowingly joined Evans in a defense not only of pre-emption but of what seemed almost forgotten in their day, man's natural right to "an equitable part of the soil." Payne acknowledged this right, at least in the abstract. Even governments had no right "to monopolize the domain, and deny to a creature of God—placed upon the earth by Him, and doomed by Him to draw his subsistence from it—so much thereof as may be required to supply his necessities."[47]

Of course, these were exceptions. Payne never intended his abstract claim to do more than justify the rights of squatters. But even such rare examples revealed how well Evans could appeal to conventional ideals. Supporters of reduction, pre-emption, graduation, and eventually free homesteads generally and consistently argued that it was the duty of government to provide maximum opportunities for ownership and independence. Only a few defenders of eastern manufacturing ever dared deny such an obligation. After Andrew Jackson endorsed a non-revenue disposition of public lands to actual settlers, to cultivators who made up the "true friends of liberty," an abstract commitment to ease of access became a part of Democratic orthodoxy. Thus, Evans later claimed both Jackson and Thomas H. Benton as early, but not yet fully enlightened, prophets of national reform. In any case, the national reformers did more than any other group to make free homesteads a compelling issue by the early 1850s.

Not only did the NRA mobilize public support, but it soon had a handful of members or active supporters in Congress. Throughout the fifties, national reform homestead bills, or amendments to homestead bills, or cession bills mandating state homesteads on national reform principles, competed (unsuccessfully) with other homestead bills that lacked the key qualifications—exemption and nonalienability. In Congress, agrarian qualifications gained support from congressmen in key reform districts, such as those in Wisconsin, but offered a convenient weapon to homestead opponents, who consistently lambasted "agrarian" and alien sources of homestead agitation. Even Buchanan, in his veto of a homestead act in 1860, referred to it as an agrarian measure. Unable to get a whole loaf, increasingly unable to win even the most modest agrarian amendments, national reformers usually accepted small gains and applauded increased support for any homestead bill at all. Perhaps most critically, Horace Greeley endorsed the Homestead Act of 1862. Whether the NRA role in Congress hastened or delayed homestead legislation, its larger propaganda effort was one necessary condition for the early success of such legislation.[48]

Evans died in 1856. His movement was then at its peak if gauged by the number of local clubs or supportive newspapers. But it already suffered from respectability and from partial success. The slavery controversy, the regional concentration of national reform sentiment, the close ties to abolitionists, had helped shift the political base of national reform. Himself a former Locofoco, and a longtime Jacksonian, Evans naturally expected more support from Democrats, and at first probably gained it. But by the mid-fifties he found political support for his legislative goals more often among Free Soilers, Whigs, and a few Northern Democrats, or from a developing political coalition committed, for quite varied reasons, to free homesteads. Except for Andrew Johnson, who led the homestead forces in the House, southerners united in opposition to even limited land reform and used the label *agrarian* to indict the homestead movement. Largely through the Free Soil movement, several Midwestern land reformers participated in the formation of a new Republican Party and helped secure its endorsement of a homestead act. National reform ideals also lived on in radical Republican efforts to secure land for freedmen.

The death of Evans, the narrowly focused priorities of war, the Homestead Act of 1862, and the slowly lessening number and influence of urban craftsmen all helped insure the demise of organized agrarianism. A few land reform clubs lasted into the seventies, but the Civil War effectively marked the end of the NRA (the last Industrial Congress met in 1856). But its principles, and much of its critical analysis, revived in the economic theories of Evans's reverse namesake, Henry George. Precluded access, unearned increments, and high rents absorbed George as much as they had Evans, but George no longer confronted the tempting prospect of a large public domain. Thus, he tried to open up nature and renew individual opportunity by socializing rent. This strategy, although quite distinct from that of the NRA, served traditional agrarian goals—to reclaim man's natural inheritance by restoring his inalienable right to a share of the earth.

PART FIVE
———
HENRY C. CAREY

The Abolition of Rent

HENRY C. Carey was easily the most perverse and the most original American political economist before Veblen. In so many ways he left himself open to legitimate criticism—in his logical lapses, in his frequent abuse of historical data, in his simplistic and illegitimate appeal to the purported identity of physical and social laws, in his cavalier caricatures of opponents, in his extremely polemical and even arrogant argumentative style, and in his elevation of private or provincial interests into absolute and universal truths. But he played well the role of intellectual gadfly. No one in Europe or America so gleefully and, at times, so effectively punctured all the intellectual pretenses of Ricardian orthodoxy. No other early American economist was half as stimulating and provocative or as suggestive and prophetic.

Reminiscent of Benjamin Franklin, his most famous fellow Philadelphian, Carey moved from youthful success in the publishing business to a mature career as an author and intellectual. His father, Mathew Carey, a political refugee from Ireland, founded a profitable Philadelphia publishing business and, as a disciple of Alexander Hamilton, worked and wrote extensively in support of protected American manufacturing. Matthew even qualified as one of the founders of American political economy through the 1822 publication of many of his lectures and speeches, although he never moved far from the tariff issue or wrote anything that came close to a systematic treatise. But the father's concerns found their eventual fruition in his son, for Henry became not only the most famous and fervent American advocate of protection, but also, as a self-conscious son of Ireland, one of the bitterest enemies of the British Empire.

Young Henry gained his education largely in the publishing trade. He read numerous reference books on geography and natural science. He also learned from a wide range of intellectual and business associates attracted by his wealth, social standing, and famous hospitality. Born in 1793, Henry started work as a salesman for the family firm as a mere teenager, and in 1825 took over its direction. After a decade he retired from any active role, lived on his income from a wide array of investments, and devoted all his time to political economy, or to what he later called social science. By his death in 1879 he had written a dozen major books and countless pamphlets, articles, and published letters, making him by far the most prolific and also the most repetitious economist in nineteenth-century America.[1]

Carey matured his economic system over twenty years. He retained a few central doctrines from his earliest books, slowly added new ones, and eventually completed a reasonably coherent and quite original system. His approach was distinctive. More than any of his contemporaries, he tried to be fully comparative and historical, at times at the risk of overlong and boring surveys of conditions and policies in India, China, Ireland, and the major European countries. He used all the statistics he could dig up from his reading, and stressed (much more than he exemplified) both conceptual precision and the use of mathematics. Unlike many American economists, he did not challenge the universalist pretentions of Ricardo. Instead, he affirmed and even exaggerated the universal and lawful status of the discipline. This meant that Ricardo was simply wrong in his system, not in seeking a universal model. Carey, who usually showed not the least hint of self-doubt, proposed to do it right, and believed he had achieved a fully verified science. Unlike his opponents, who in Carey's view all suffered from the blinders of class or national allegiance, he believed himself able to move from the contextual to the universal. Yet, as his opponents so often charged, Carey was in the happy position, always, of discovering that universal principles were the very ones that buttressed personal and local interests, whether his publishing business, Pennsylvania coal mines, or the youthful iron industry.

Carey launched his new career as a political economist in 1835 with a rare personal achievement, a short book. His *Essay on the Rate of Wages* revealed a Ricardian point of departure, yet suggested the basic themes developed in his later work. In 1835 he was unusually sanguine about American economic policies, fervently proclaimed American uniqueness, and was extremely optimistic about the economic future. Although close to Ricardo on many technical issues, and in several respects a loyal disciple of Say's, Carey already followed most American economists in rejecting all overt or implied themes of class conflict. Since Carey had earlier imbibed the protectionist theories of his father and of several business associates in Philadelphia, and since he later became such a vehement and extreme protectionist himself, his firm support of free trade in 1835 shows how completely he was under the sway of his earliest teachers. He had guided his own economic education by reading Smith, Say, Malthus, Ricardo, McCulloch, Mill, and Senior. He knew Henry Vethake, corresponded with Thomas Cooper, and for a time reflected the influence of his friend Condy Raguet. It is not surprising that such imposing, often academic, intellectuals could have a great influence on the developing theories of an almost middle-aged businessman who now dared plunge into a new and intricate discipline. Carey began his serious writing in a period of prosperity and economic optimism, a time when the results of the compromise Tariff Bill of 1833 still seemed unthreatening, and before the terrible debacle of 1837 forced almost everyone to reevaluate American economic policies.

Carey used his *Essay* to demonstrate the unparalleled economic achievement of the youthful United States, and then to explain that achievement. After surveying a virtual avalanche of economic data drawn from a remarkably diverse range of sources, Carey concluded that American workers were easily the most efficient and best rewarded in the world. He estimated (an educated guess) that the provisions secured by eleven days of work by an American required sixteen days in England, eighteen in Holland, twenty-eight in France, thirty-eight in China, and seventy-four in India. In an even more elaborate estimate of national economic achievement, Carey awarded up to a hundred points to a country for maximum achievement in five areas—security of person and property, freedom of action, freedom of commerce, habits of industry, and quality of productive capital (including land). On this scale, the United States achieved a total of 460 points (out of a possible 500, its largest debit being for restraints on commerce), Britain 400, Holland 315, France 225, China 135, and India only 75. But this alone slighted the American achievement. After deducting taxes from the totals, the United States led with 440 points, the other countries having, respectively, 300, 265, 175, 129, and 65. This survey embraced all industries, and our high score to a large extent reflected the high productivity of American agriculture.[2]

Even in this first book, Carey declared his personal independence as a scholar. The masters of political economy had all revealed subjective biases and had used facts selectively. Above all, they had unconsciously extrapolated universal assumptions from national peculiarities. Had they attended more carefully to the unique situation in America, where the people were sovereign, where no elites had yet bolstered their privileges by corn laws, monopolies, restrictions, high taxes, and imperial wars, they would not have ended up with such pessimism or with the vindication of so many discords. The United States illustrated the advantages of republican political institutions, of governments that secured persons and property, advanced free trade and free industry, valued peace, and taxed moderately. It was this institutional context, not free land or low population density or plentiful natural resources, that accounted for the superior economic achievement of Americans. Unlike Malthus and Ricardo, Carey saw no early or even any ultimate natural limits to such growth, either by population increases or resource scarcities, and no basis for internal tensions between sectors or classes. Given prudent policies, mankind already lived in the best possible economic universe.[3]

What was the principal secret of growth? In 1835 Carey agreed with the Ricardians; increased capital alone supported growing productivity and ever higher wages and profits. But even this early he began to be aware of ambiguities in the word *capital*. Without yet finding the correct words, he already anticipated his later definition—capital is any artifact or skill or knowledge that increases man's power to direct natural events. Thus, in 1835 he argued that knowledge and skill qualify as capital. Anyone skilled in any form of production is a capitalist, as much so as those who own land, plant facilities, material tools of production, extensive inventories of goods, or money for lending or investment. Such a broadened definition of capital threatened the conventional distinction, or purported opposition, between wages and profits. Returns to work and skill are practically undistinguishable. The acquisition of a new skill by a worker meant either higher wages or the realization of profits according to arbitrary semantic conventions. Carey found wages and profits so interactive and interdependent that he often reduced both to a complex but single entity. This merging of analytical concepts, this refusal to accept dualities of any sort, became a dominant strategy (or a perverse trick) in all Carey's political economy. Eventually, as the John Dewey of nineteenth-century political economy, he tried to reduce to unity all possible dualities.[4]

Since wages and profits are complementary, owners and workers, even when separate people, have no divergent interests. They often did not understand this. Carey's duty as a political economist was to re-educate them, to promote harmony. Immutable laws controlled the allocation of wages and profits over the long term in any completely free market. Thus, Carey dutifully denounced all government interference with distributive returns, condemned unions or combinations of any type, and particularly condemned all trade restrictions including protective tariffs. He believed competitively determined wages and profits correctly rewarded ability and effort. Even a lowly, unskilled wage worker in America could rise by industry and economy, given our environment of freedom. He had no reason to resent men with more skills and tools, for the more of these in an economy, the greater the opportunities and the higher the wages.

But even this early, and without clearly realizing what he was doing, Carey undercut Ricardian theories about distribution. In a Ricardian model, a magical thermostat controls long-term distributive shares. Temporarily high profits lead to corrective wage increases. But temporarily higher wages, based on a high demand for workers, leads to the corrective of increased population growth. Thus, over the long term, workers receive as wages all that the economy allows, for they receive the whole fund available to pay workers. Should they receive more, profits drop, capital accumulation slows, and an economy stagnates. This led both Malthus and Ricardo to advocate population control by workers, and allowed Ricardo to define natural wages as the bare subsistence toward which wages always tend unless people practice sexual restraint. Thus, the wage-fund theory not only seemed to vindicate any existing pattern of distributive shares in a free market economy, but reflected a hauntingly pessimistic mood. Finite resources combined with the normal inclinations of mankind—to reproduce freely—sooner or later would assure for the mass of mankind the lowest possible wages consistent with a stable population. To avert this fate, the mass of workers seemingly had only one option—to frustrate normal instincts, either by celibacy, which was unnatural, or by birth control, which was immoral, or by late marriages.

Such conclusions horrified Carey. As he later insisted, they even seemed to challenge the wisdom of God and the harmony of his creation. Fortunately, these theories also contradicted history, for Carey found in his data evidence even in backward countries of rising real wages accompanying increasing population. Of course, such evidence could be accommodated within the numerous qualifications and exceptions offered by Malthus and Ricardo (Carey was rarely fair to either man), but Carey thought that a model in which the exceptions always ruled was useless even if not contradictory. Thus, he affirmed an alternative model, one that assured, given correct polices, an unending growth of population, even higher rates of growth in productivity, and a perfect harmony of interests. He tried to demonstrate that, historically, the faster the rate of population growth in the United States, whether through natural increase or immigration, the more rapid had been the growth in per capita income. He refused to attribute this happy result to distinctive and temporary natural advantages in America (as had Ricardo), but as yet could not identify the universal laws that explained it.[5]

Carey's emerging growth model seemed to imply an unlimited fecundity in nature, plus ever increasing returns to scale through an ever finer division of labor. This is at least where he ended up. By 1835 he calculated that the earth could eventually support with rising living standards a population of thirty billion, and he seemed not at all appalled by the population density this entailed. The earth could become an intensely utilized but artful and beautiful garden. Since the Ricardian law of rent best illustrated a doctrine of diminishing returns, and rested on an assumption of natural scarcity, rent theory seemed the proper point of attack to such an inveterate optimist. In his *Essay*, Carey deferred any detailed assault. Like so many American economists, beginning with Alexander Hamilton, he evaded the problem of rent by assimilating land to capital, rent to profit. In an open society land represented one form of productive wealth and competed equally with other forms of capital according to its earnings. This strategy was intellectually inadequate, as Carey soon realized, for it avoided the critical issue—unearned returns to those who controlled access to nature. Even if land were fully open to investors, even if it sold according to its earnings, extremely high land prices could still squeeze out all wages and profits. Thus, the thorny issue of rent became first on the agenda for Carey's next book.

With all natural impediments and dilemmas discounted, Carey saw only political and institutional impediments to unending economic growth in any country. The United States offered an all but perfect institutional model. Other countries had enjoyed economic growth, despite restrictive institutions, but none at the American rate. Here, governments assured security of persons, contracts, and property, offered educational opportunities, and encouraged internal improvements. Beyond that, they properly left people alone. Although he still supported free trade and envisioned a degree of international specialization, Carey already showed what was to be a lifelong commitment to economic balance and thus to increased American manufacturing. He celebrated the moral as well as the economic achievements at Lowell (he compared them as moral phenomena to Niagara in the physical world), and decried factory laws as much as apprenticeship or poor laws. He believed America was already an investors' paradise; he welcomed foreign investments (the profits did not create direct demand in America, but created a demand for our exports); and he rejoiced in unregulated banks, canals, and railroads. The greatest single threat to growth was high taxes, usually tied to war or imperial adventure. Fortunately, taxes in America had been low and fairly allocated. Never again would Carey be quite so sanguine, even about America.[6]

Carey's *Essay* whetted his appetite for more intricate theory. He wrote, but never published, a single volume on the harmony of nature, which he quickly expanded into a verbose, rambling three-volume treatise, *Principles of Political Economy* (1837). Although only a resting point on his way to a fully new system, the *Principles* contained his most original technical work as a political economist.

Carey opened with a purportedly new theory of value. Although in some sense labor is always the source of value, he believed the relative value of objects in exchange rarely reflects any exact quantity and quality of direct and indirect labor inputs (Carey defined capital as stored-up labor). Carey thus rejected a simple, cost-of-production explanation of long-term or natural prices. Instead, he borrowed a persuasive and almost obvious insight from a contemporary Canadian economist, John Rae, but one first suggested by Adam Smith and then made reasonably explicit by Say. In exchange the value of an object reflects, not the past labor that went into it, but the estimated future labor needed to reproduce it. Carey made this "reproductive labor theory" one of his trademarks and used it effectively to further several of his theoretical arguments. It embodied the dynamic elements that so typified his whole approach. Given a steady output of new skills and new tools, older plants and tools, even without wear, still command less and less returns through time, for less and less labor is needed to reproduce them. This fall in capital values meant a steadily increasing share of the total product went into wages. Laborers gained most from new productive techniques. Equality steadily increased in any progressive and free economy. Since Carey meant by wages the returns both to effort and acquired skills, by implication he included access to education as a prerequisite of this egalitarian outcome. In any case, he looked forward eventually to an economy in which every person owned shares of capital and enjoyed almost equally high wage-profits. Carey believed that with this argument he had laid to rest in one full swoop all contemporary concerns about distributive injustices in a growth economy.[7]

Next, Carey challenged Ricardian rent theory, with some startling results. He devoted one large book to allaying fears of ever higher rents. Never was Carey more elusive in argument, more treacherous in his concepts. Behind all his tortuous arguments lay one central and startling doctrine—rents do not exist in a free economy. Carey was the first and possibly the last economist to banish rent entirely from his economic analysis, although McCulloch and others had minimized the extent of true rents. To accomplish this feat, Carey had to deny the existence of any natural scarcity. Nature is an inexhaustible, infinitely expandable source of human satisfactions, provided man can gain the needed power to guide its processes. Until man transforms or transports a part of nature by labor, it has no exchange value in an open and free market. Like air or water, the soil is immediately open to human use, free for the taking until transformed by labor. An acre of land as much as a gallon of water gains exchange value only through human labor, and at any one time it has only as much value as the labor required to reproduce it in its present form or place.[8]

This denial of any true rent seemed to achieve the goal of earlier American economists who had tried to assimilate land and capital. As Carey put it, ". . . value in land, . . . cannot exceed the amount of labor bestowed upon it, and must generally fall short of it. . . ." By definition, rent is a payment for a scarce natural object. But to Carey there were no such objects, only scarce products of labor. And since capital is only funded labor, Carey had completed another reduction. Every economic return, even when called rent or profit, is a form of wages. Yet, without careful qualification, this clever reduction seems absurdly mistaken, completely contrary to experience. Unfortunately, Carey was not always careful in fortifying his position.

Carey never meant to argue that the actual value of a farm or a mine only reflected the labor an owner had invested in its improvement. In fact, he usually discovered the sale value of a farm in a free market to be much below what the hard work in improving it seemed to justify, for here again a rapid improvement in agricultural technology tended to subvert the value of land as a species of fixed capital. With each passing year, the cost of bringing a farm into production went down. But at times land values were clearly above reproductive costs. This was the case with American public lands, which sold for a minimum of $1.25 an acre even though the federal government had not improved them. Why did they have so much value? Because, said Carey, of the public expenses involved in making them accessible, or the combined public and private expenditures that helped to bring roads and markets close enough to make farming possible. Thus, quite often, the value of land reflected social capital, and at times private owners seemingly reaped unfair returns by gaining an undue share of this value. But this rescue of a tantalizing doctrine by recourse to social capital was ultimately sophistic and circular. All that Carey ended up proving was what Ricardo assumed—land so inaccessible as to be unusable earns no rent. To attribute all so-called "rent" values to labor, to the private and social costs of making land usable, does not, in itself, alter the Ricardian dilemma. It only reformulates the problem. What Ricardo meant by rent might be expressed, without changed practical implications, as those returns to legal owners based not on their own labor, or on what they paid others for labor, but on a legal right to collect most of the rewards from communal work.[9]

Carey never pursued the problem of unearned increments. He was no early Henry George. Presumably, he expected land taxes to allocate the cost of public improvements fairly, and so saw no inequities in what existing owners gained from leases or sale. Purchasers simply paid for improvements and for exemption from early social costs. Because of his reproductive principle, Carey knew early pioneers would never regain more than a token of their early and inefficient work in "manufacturing a farm." But the crucial issue posed by Ricardo was not only that of allocating the cost of social capital, but the apparent inequities that inevitably accompanied growing natural scarcities. Since Carey denied any inherent scarcity, he seemed to make scarcity, in so far as it existed at all, a purely political issue. He acknowledged the role of sovereign states in determining tenure arrangements. A government might hold all lands itself, or grant full control of all land to a favored few. This would constitute a monopoly by taking land off the market and exempting it from the operation of economic laws. Thus, Carey designated the resulting access charges as special taxes rather than rents. He saw such appropriation as political dispossession, a form of tyranny. Carey also acknowledged the role of luck in all economic endeavors. Unexpected windfalls (the discovery of oil on a farm) could raise land values dramatically for a few, even as unexpected natural disasters might lower values for others. But such shifts in value only reflected the accidentally unequal distribution of a total sum of values still fully derived from past human labor (Carey would even calculate the labor that went into the invention and development of automobiles as part of the determinants of the value of a new oil field).

It is tempting to attribute Carey's views on rent to the unique tenure system of America—to widespread ownership, frequent land sales, and the absence of entails or primogeniture. He took great pains to deny any such institutional bias. He argued, and cited endless statistics to prove, that even in England the price of land was sufficiently market-responsive to be well below the original labor cost of improvement. In fact, it closely matched the labor cost of producing similar farms under English conditions. Thus, what purported to be "rents" in England simply reflected the normal interest on capital expended in producing farms. He did admit some small, added income for English landlords based on corn laws, but this income constituted a special tax for their benefit and not properly rent.

What if through time a minority of honest people came to own all accessible, improved, and fertile land in a country, and refused to sell it to anyone else? Could they not collect true rents in addition to collecting deserved payments for the lease of improvements? Carey assumed land to be on the market, competing with other investment options. Unless they conspired with each other, landowners could not afford to refuse profitable sales. Successful collusion meant a form of politically supported monopoly or conspiracy. High rents then represented returns to political privilege, a form of taxes, and not payment for scarce resources.

Although legal claims to unimproved and inaccessible land had no real economic value, Carey admitted they might have speculative value. One might expect real values to accrue to such land in the future as a result of new roads and markets. He later condemned speculation and wanted to tax away its advantages. Thus, he continued to argue that all land values, apart from special government privileges, derived from human labor, including even a share of the vast effort over centuries that lay behind the building of populous communities. The sale value of any land reflected the contemporary cost of reproducing such land with all its communal assets.[10]

At the heart of Ricardian rent theory was the idea of necessarily diminishing returns to labor and capital in agriculture. Given land of varied fertility, inferior soils can yield returns similar to rich soils only by the application of more labor or more capital or both. As a growing population has to utilize poorer soils, then more and more human effort has to go into agriculture because of the small returns at the price-setting margin of cultivation. In a free market economy, one with private ownership of land, landowners on good land can collect as rent all the surplus product attributable to the superior fertility of their soil over that at the barely profitable margin. Even were all land in a state equally fertile, Ricardo assumed the original application of capital and labor would yield more than later increments, and that landowners would still collect non-labor-produced rents as soon as returns to later increments of capital or labor began to decline. With population pressure and rising food prices, agricultural capitalists would be able to earn competitive profits by more and more intensive and yet labor- and capital-inefficient cultivation. To gain access to portions of the equally fertile land, they would be willing to pay higher and higher although uniform rents. The landlords, in effect, collected all the increasing advantages that accrued to the first increments of capital. Thus, all surpluses above the returns at the extrinsic (last soils taken into production) or intensive (last capital committed) margin went to landowners. Their rent returns inevitably increased with rising population unless a nation gained access to new soils or improved its methods of cultivation. Ricardians always acknowledged new frontiers and new agricultural technology as defenses against rising rents, but both defenses surely had natural limits. This was obvious if, as they assumed, nature was itself limited.

In a sense, by denying any rent at all Carey overthrew the Ricardian formula. But he hardly altered the pessimistic implications of Ricardo. If a landlord class gained ever larger shares of the national income as a result of increased population and manufacturing, it scarcely mattered whether they collected rents or disproportionate shares of the accumulating returns on public improvements. Ultimate impoverishment still faced all non-landowners. Thus, to overturn Ricardo, Carey had to fashion additional weapons. In the *Principles* he could only note a historic fact—the proportion of total wealth (not the amount) going to landlords had steadily declined. Carey confusingly used the term *rent* for what landowners charged for use of their labor-produced farms. *Rent* was to him only a distinguishable species of profit, or only wages earned by stored-up labor.

Thus, his reproductive formula easily accounted for ever lower "rents," which in Ricardian terms were not rents at all. As it became easier to manufacture farms, the value of older farms, manufactured back when technology was less sophisticated, steadily dropped in comparison with the labor invested in their improvement. With population growth and economic development, landlords received, not a larger share of the national income, but a lesser share, although Carey was confident new levels of productivity could still assure rising land values and higher total rents. History and theory beautifully joined, but not in a way that challenged Ricardian theory. Ricardo might well have accepted Carey's reproductive formula, and have granted that it accounted for lower, but in no sense dangerously lower, rates of profit in agriculture as well as in manufacturing.[11]

What about the eventual, much deadlier threat of diminishing agricultural returns? What about the inevitable transfer of more and more wealth to those who gained early access to and control over nature? Carey had only one alternative. He had to deny that diminishing returns to land were a logically necessary, or even a logically appropriate, effect of economic growth. He had to develop an economic model that assured, not diminishing returns to labor and capital, but ever increasing returns even in agriculture. This was where he ended, but he did not quite get this far in the *Principles*. The nagging problem of inferior soils constrained him. If people first appropriated and cultivated the best soils, how could a country avoid the spectre of diminishing returns when a rising population required the cultivation of inferior land? And how could Carey deny that the original grabbers could subsequently cash in on that fertility, and actually charge Ricardian or non-labor-produced rents? Obviously, with improved technology, infertile soils might be turned into farms as productive as earlier ones on more fertile land, and all at less cost. Carey emphasized this. But at a new stage of agricultural technology, fertile soils could be improved at still less cost, and with such new technology older farms on good land would not lose as much of their relative value as those on poor land. The gap remained, and a valuable natural component still seemed to be working for some farmers more than for others. Carey had no recourse to social capital here. This would explain the convergence of land values only when "inferior" entailed inaccessibility. Often, "inferior" meant infertile, and such land often existed side by side with the best soil; its owners enjoyed the same benefits from roads and canals, nearby markets, and churches and schools.

Instead of agonizing over these seemingly disproportionate returns to better land, Carey celebrated the magical and harmonizing effects of growth. Given an unending increase of human powers over nature (only inequitable policies could slow the progress of human intelligence and mastery), then nature became ever more generous. Eventually, an acre could grow what a thousand grew at an earlier stage of development, and the real frontiers were always in one's backyard. This meant that, even as farmers utilized inferior soils, all land yielded a dramatically increased output. The escalating productivity reduced to insignificance any differences of return based on fertility. At best, diminishing returns meant only slightly slower growth on less fertile land. And who could begrudge the farmer who grew slightly larger crops than a nearby neighbor? Most likely, he was an older farmer, who had manufactured his land in the past and had paid dearly for his later advantage by enormous expenditures of inefficient labor. He had grubbed by hand the new ground now cleared by horses.

Carey most lamented the divisive implications of Ricardian rent analysis. It seemed to indict landlords for receiving huge, unearned rewards, and made radical agrarian schemes seem just and logical. Carey hoped to prove that farmers always earn their profits and that the landowners' share of total national income declines with technological progress, but that the value of land and total rents can still increase with growth, although always at a slower rate than for wages. This meant that every person in a free society, every class if one admitted separate classes, had an equal stake in growth, in gaining new powers over nature. In time, all could be nearly equal in wealth and income.[12]

So far, Carey had used brilliant, or at least clever tactical maneuvers to outflank Ricardo. He had to postpone the final rout. But even these maneuvers reinforced some already mature commitments. Carey was among the first American economists (Tucker was closest) to support a model of intensive economic development. He wanted more people, clustered in more compact settlements, and involved in more subtle divisions of labor and more complex cooperative efforts. He hated wars, expansion, frontiers, colonies. He deplored sparse populations, scattered settlements, the rigors of pioneer life, and the meanness, jealousy, and lack of cultivation such conditions produced in people. He was not in the least attracted to wilderness or an unimproved nature. All this might suggest an urban bias. Not so. Carey never approved of large cities, and eventually he made a type of intensive agriculture the major key to a sophisticated economy. But he saw in Ricardian theory, as in Jacksonian policies, a theoretical vindication of expansion, and a bias in favor of space, sparse populations, and high land-man ratios. This, to him, entailed a return to barbarism if not to savagery. The great opportunity for human progress was in concert, in intensive communal effort, in the fullest possible diversity of conjoined occupations and roles, or in what Carey came to eulogize above all else—association.

Carey's technical emphasis on social capital furthered these goals. He believed that in a developed community the quality of one's life, even the economic values one realized, always involved a mix of individual and collective achievement. In developed communities rates of profit tend to be low, but this is more than balanced by the tempo of economic activity, by a high level of productivity, by social order, by the discipline and morality of people, and by many social amenities. The total amount of profits can be very high despite the low rates. In thriving and growing communities real wages also tend to be very high, but even these fail to express all the benefits for workers, for wages join with forms of public consumption and with an enlarged possibility for vocational fulfillment and eventual proprietary status.

Given these benefits, Carey saw in British colonization schemes evidence of deep institutional maladies. Later he would indict the westward movement in America. Surely the people who rushed to Oregon or California, as much as those who travelled to Australia, turned against normal human instincts. They had to be driven by deep, politically caused inequities at home. A migrating population always attested to social pathology, to policies founded on the erroneous principles of Malthus and Ricardo. Carey's analysis had made clear that undeveloped land had no economic value, except possibly in a speculative context. Yet, by the 1840s New Englanders rushed to the west, a sure indication of foreclosed economic opportunities at home. Those who ventured onto frontiers gained, at best, near worthless lands and high rates of profit on their meager but desperately needed capital; they lost so much—the social capital of settled communities (roads, schools, churches, markets) and the economies of scale made possible by cooperation and a division of labor. They would have to expend many hours of arduous and inefficient labor to bring land into production under often primitive conditions, and would suffer all the loneliness, all the intellectual and spiritual hunger, of frontier isolation. Only desperate men, without property or opportunity, with nothing to lose, would dare such a venture or profit from it.[13]

In *Principles*, Carey continued his battle against dualisms and against all inherent sources of conflict. He now denied any valid distinction between consumptive and productive goods. The food on a holiday table helps nourish health, and thus makes possible future production. Even a diamond ring is part of the inventory of a jewelry store, or a needed morale builder for a young lady. Likewise, any distinction between necessities and luxuries proved too arbitrary to be useful. A work of art, which may seem only a luxury, may help entice new levels of taste among productive workers.[14] Nothing ever stood alone in Carey's system. Isolated entities simply did not exist or played no logical role. Only in two cases would Carey concede any pure returns to capital, or to past rather than present labor. This was "rent" for improved land or for other productive resources, and completely riskless interest on loaned money. All other alleged "profits" of capital, such as from the tools owned by a worker or from his acquired skills, or from the risk value of a loan, or from the concern or managerial attention given to investments, were as much wages as profits.

Consistent with this perspective, Carey believed that in a free society all returns were earned. They reflected the proper reward for effort, skill, concern, or even the anxiety of a creditor. Finally, just as he denied any land rents, so he minimized returns to natural gifts, to talent or innate intelligence. Even if such gifts commanded a price, he clearly disapproved of any "rents" collected on God's gifts, and later fought against any secreted techniques or selfish profiteering on any new knowledge that could, through sharing, improve the lot of everyone. Thus, he appealed to high principle in his long battle (one book and many articles and letters) against international copyright agreements, a battle that he waged in the name of more and cheaper books for American readers, particularly school children, but which his critics connected with his own compelling economic goals as a publisher who frequently pirated English titles. He accepted limited patent and copyright protection, but considered these legal means of securing earned wages for creative people, not a form of monopoly.[15]

Carey's bent was always toward social solidarity and cooperation. To further these goals, he turned, in the last two volumes of the *Principles*, from technical to policy issues. He had demonstrated, to his own satisfaction, that nature itself represents unlimited possibility. Without elaborate rationalizing, he had also assumed that American political institutions were almost perfect. He applauded not only the sovereignty of the people as expressed in the role of constitutional law, or the representative and democratic nature of our legislatures, but also the federal system, a subtle and effective division of responsibility between local, state, and national governments. Thus, the only weak link in his grand scheme of progress had to be human ignorance or malice, largely expressed in grievously mistaken or deliberately tyrannical governmental policies. These alone led to "disturbing causes" in the normal and progressive evolution of a people from primitive, scattered, inefficient farms to developed, richly associated, and prosperous communities, which he usually found best exemplified in the towns of New England. There, so far at least, American governments had performed with all but perfect economic wisdom— by securing persons and property, giving complete sway to private effort, minimizing taxes and maximizing private consumption and capital accumulation, or by generally encouraging voluntary association on behalf of mutual benefit and greater individual autonomy. His surveys of other countries, even including China and India, proved to him that to the very degree that other countries failed to foster voluntary association, they had failed to achieve the economic prosperity of New England.[16]

When he wrote the *Principles*, Carey still found little to fault in federal policies and focused his criticism of America on the backward South. He continuously counted the blessings of Americans, or at least those who lived in the vanguard Northeast. He celebrated his countrymen's widespread respect for labor, engrained habits of industry and thrift, and exemplary morals. He celebrated what he saw as the keys to American prosperity—electoral politics, widespread property ownership, international peace, social harmony, high wages and full employment, short working hours, absence of special privileges, low taxes, generally low tariffs, limited licenses and regulations (although still too many for his taste), agricultural improvements, full and absolute land tenure, the growth of domestic manufacturing, free public education, low credit cost, a general trust that sustained credit, and even the developing system of free banks. He particularly appreciated new factories, with their short hours, high wages, and wonderful opportunities for young, unmarried women. As the American economy grew, capitalists became richer, but not at the rate that workers gained new levels of affluence. Americans thus achieved ever greater economic equality. Most American taxes were local, assessed directly and in fair proportions on land and incomes. They reflected ability to pay and social benefits realized, unlike taxes on consumption or capital, which usually penalized those least able to pay. The one exception was the federal reliance on tariff revenue, for this constituted an indirect tax that penalized consumers without regard to their ability to pay. Although Carey still opposed both revenue and protective tariffs, he now noted the disruptive effects of rapid cuts in protective duties, particularly for the local iron industry.[17]

Carey believed free political institutions in America were as much the consequence of economic prosperity as the cause. In a society with steadily increasing power over nature, and more realized cooperative association, anyone could gain the autonomy that undergirds political liberty. Whereas wealth abets liberty, poverty supports tyranny. He used this view of freedom to offer a hopeful and conciliatory analysis of Southern slavery. In the primitive and meager beginnings of society, a physically strong elite normally grabs all the land and reduces everyone else to slavery. Land held by the sword has no value except that created by the labor of those who improve it, but appropriators steal most of those values through a form of political tyranny. As people cluster, as they divide up tasks, as nonagricultural industries grow, as workers are able to unite in collective action, the power of those original and usurping landlords declines. But their security and economic welfare improve. They gain better police protection. The larger total product supports their rising living standards, even as the rate of rent declines and they have to accept a smaller share of the national income. As both land and fixed capital claim smaller shares of the total products, real wages climb and the whole society moves toward equality and universal freedom.

The same evolution should take place in the South. By 1837, Carey predicted the early demise of black slavery, at least if the North did not agitate the slavery issue, thereby precipitating retaliatory measures by southerners. Already comparatively well-treated and valued, as evidenced by their natural increase, southern Negroes were destined to gain ever larger proportions of production as the southern economy expanded. In the form of goods, they would reap the higher wages that come with economic growth, and this in turn would improve their physical and moral condition. Already, able blacks received wages and enjoyed other contract-like incentives. As slave values rose, they would steadily gain even more control over their own lives. A share-cropping system would eventually evolve, simply because it would increase the productivity of slaves and improve landlord profits. The next step would be complete emancipation, and a free and more profitable labor system. But this normal evolution depended not only on outside forbearance but on continued economic growth in the South. If England really favored emancipation, she could best help by repealing the corn laws and increasing the demand for southern food crops.[18]

Carey gave very little attention to problems of banking and credit in *Principles*. In 1838, in the midst of a financial crisis, he published *The Credit System In France, Great Britain and The United States*. He used it to advance a very prophetic thesis—that a complex and interdependent economy rests upon a system of trust and cooperation, or on various lines of credit given and received. Honesty, reliability, responsibility, adherence to contracts or even to implied commitments, undergirded a sophisticated and developed economy. From a certain perspective, and under well-defined and lawful rules, a form of allocative and not eliminative competition does characterize such an economy. But to Carey, economic development moved always toward increased trust and away from brutal, lawless, selfish, or even very acquisitive forms of conflict. This insight served him well, and he certainly had a valid, proprietary claim to it. Such a view allowed Carey to paint developing associative institutions, such as banks and limited liability corporations, as morally innocent and fully constructive examples of increased trust and as the necessary agents of continued economic progress. No one else in pre–Civil War America enveloped early forms of economic collectivism in such a moral glow.

In a new play on economic reductionism, Carey now reduced profit, rent, and interest to forms of credit. All involved payments for the use of productive assets. The cotton mill owner loaned his facilities to workers and took a share of their product as payment for the loan. Or, if the workers did not function as a collective, each worker turned over or loaned all his product to the owner, and in return received his proportionate share back in the form of wages. Trust informed all such exchanges, and the more credit offered and used, the more cooperative division of roles and obligations based on such trust, the more productive and more expansive the society. Later, Carey would call such a system of voluntary exchanges "commerce."

Credit relationships made money very important to Carey. It grew more so as he perfected his final theoretical system, for it was money that most clearly facilitated trust or credit or commerce. It was the tool of ownership transfer, and ease in such transfers was necessary for any complex division of labor. Consistently throughout his economic writing, Carey defined money as specie. Because of inherent qualities, almost as if by divine intent, gold and silver were the ideal commodities to serve as money. But, of necessity, gold and silver cannot make up more than a small component of the total circulation, which includes all negotiable credit instruments. Given safeguards, such as an adequate specie backing, Carey always applauded credit devices. They represent increased levels of trust, offer cheap and convenient tools of exchange, and often dramatically expand the effective quantity of money in a country. This Carey wanted. Ample money and credit meant more economic transactions, a faster tempo for economic life, more industry, and more rapid growth.[19]

As credit transactions increase in a developing economy, clearinghouses become necessary. These banks, or "money shops" as Carey liked to refer to them, offer several needed and specialized services. In effect, banks buy and sell money and serve as credit clearinghouses. They hold deposits, shift private balances to facilitate credit transactions, and, with the backing of either assets or liabilities, issue their own convenient notes. Solid, responsible banking was at the heart of a workable credit system, an indispensable link in a highly associated and interdependent growth economy. Carey rejoiced in the stability and security of northeastern banks. They had the lowest failure rate in the world. Not so southern and western banks, and so much the worse for economic progress in these sections. Although Carey had supported the late Bank of the United States, he preferred the small, local banks of New England, with their broadly based ownership. Trade in money should be as free as trade in any other product. He thus defended completely private banking, with no

government regulations beyond minimal capital and reserve requirement. To facilitate free banking and normal competition among money
shops, Carey wanted states to issue bank charters to all applicants.[20]

To Carey, complete freedom of association entailed limited liability
corporations. For people with savings (Carey was particularly solicitous
of small tradesmen, farmers, widows, and orphans), the ability to join in
voluntary but associated economic effort was a precondition of freedom.
Unlimited liability practically precluded such joint enterprise. Carey
always opposed any arrangement in which an individual was responsible
for the whole group. Such joint responsibility or solidarity threatened
individual autonomy and invited centralized and nondemocratic management. Limited liability, a system of mutual trust or credit, was a mark of
economic sophistication. So long as the privilege remained open to all
groups, Carey could not understand why so many economists, and so
many Jacksonians, viewed limited liability as a monopolistic privilege, as
a form of unfair competition based on an illegitimate pooling of wealth.
He noted, correctly, that governments were limited liability associations,
with individual citizens not liable for any more than their fair share (their
taxable liability) of its obligations. He found the same principle in university and church charters and in mutual insurance companies. In his
enthusiasm, he defended incorporation as a vested right of citizens and
argued that any government that refused to grant charters freely, or even
qualified such charters by detailed regulations, infringed human liberty,
as did courts that challenged limited liability. In the type of verbal tour de
force he so loved, Carey argued that government interference with the
right of corporate association, or any attempt to dictate the terms of
association beyond setting clear and simple legal conditions for gaining a
charter, amounted to monopoly, to a damaging restraint on commerce, a
direct interference with the security of persons and property. The refusal
of the federal government to extend the charter of the Bank of the United
States was an infringement on the freedom of action of its stockholders,
an assault on liberty only in part rectified by the new charter obtained
from Pennsylvania.

What about possible corporate abuse? In principle, a corporation was a
legal person and subject to the same criminal laws as any other person.
Carey stipulated that corporate charters be public, known to the world.
Both investors and those who dealt with the corporation would know the
rules and assume the risk accordingly. Implicit in Carey's glorification of
corporations was his belief that an association of cooperating people
would be more socially responsible than most isolated individuals. And,
to be fair to him, one has to note that his image of a corporation
bears little resemblance to General Motors or International Telephone
and Telegraph. Essential to his definition was the active involvement of

shareholders in the management of an enterprise, as in the small-town banks or local ironworks that helped create his image of a typical corporation. Even as he lauded limited liability, he condemned the large and impersonal companies of England, and later he fought against large centralized corporations in the United States.[21]

With his theories about money and banking, Carey completed the first phase of his work as a political economist. He had developed a reasonably coherent system, and one technically significant for its reproductive labor theory of value and its unprecedented and revolutionary approach to rent. Had Carey been content to rest here, or merely patch up the internal weaknesses of this early system, he would today have a much more distinct niche in the history of American economic thought. But these earlier labors were only the groundwork for the much more daring and controversial theories of his later life. Between 1838 and 1847, years of depression, Whig triumph, and Democratic resurgence, he rethought his whole economic system. He repudiated little of his earlier work, but placed it in a much broader context and drew from it very different policy guidelines.

XI

Down from the Hills

BY 1847, Henry C. Carey aspired to a new role. From publishing he had turned to the technical problems of political economy. Even that proved too narrow and confining for his almost cosmic interests. Now he wanted not only to extend and complete his economic theories, but to relate them to the totality of human behavior and even to universal physical laws. He first announced his revised economic system to the world in his most influential book, *The Past, the Present, and the Future* (1847). He then expanded on his ideas, somewhat repetitiously, in two topical books, *The Harmony Of Interests, Agricultural, Manufacturing, And Commercial* (1852), and *The Slave Trade, Domestic And Foreign* (1853). Taken together, the three books amounted to a second three-volume economic treatise that replaced his earlier and now outgrown *Principles*.

Historical developments and personal concerns lay behind Carey's revised system. By his own testimony, the extended economic malaise after 1837, during a time of free trade, led him to examine the whole history of protective tariffs in America. What he found—a close correlation between high tariffs and general prosperity, and between free trade and economic stagnation—made clear that his earlier system was mistaken and incomplete. It retained too much of the virus of Ricardianism. Other personal changes he did not note, but they surely conditioned his new policy commitments. He became much more solicitous of personal and local economic interests, particularly the erratic and vulnerable coal and iron industries of Pennsylvania. He increasingly shared the typical Philadelphia jealousy and resentment of a commercially ascendant New York City. Irish sympathies reinforced old Anglophobic views. Religious and moral concerns deepened, and he felt an increasing distaste for any vulgar, selfish, purely acquisitive approach to economic issues.

A close friend, Stephen Colwell, exerted an increasing influence on Carey. Colwell combined a generally profitable entrepreneurial role in the iron and steel industry with notable religious and philanthropic services, particularly to the Presbyterian Church and Princeton Theological Seminary. He was also an economist, who published highly technical works on banking and who castigated selfish, non-Christian individualism and competition under a socially irresponsible form of "capitalism." Carey adopted few of Colwell's theoretical doctrines, but absorbed from him what could be called an early social-gospel orientation. As a result of such moral concerns, Carey's later books became more idiosyncratic and more deliberately polemical. Although he continued to stress a logical harmony of interests, he actually identified more and more devils, more evil and selfish men who refused to play by the economic rules or who joined in a selfish conspiracy to exploit most of mankind. With age he lost most of his earlier optimism, particularly about the American economy. Well before his death in 1879 he often seemed bitter, disillusioned, and spiteful.

In *Past, Present, and Future,* Carey announced a great natural law of human progress, which in its fullest grandeur had theretofore remained undiscovered. Since his law was an evolutionary one, it remained a bit elusive. In general, he clarified the necessary preconditions of economic progress, which were no other than increased human association and with it more power to control nature, or a slightly amended version of Adam Smith's pre-Malthusian law of progress. Notably, from this point on, Carey claimed Adam Smith as a progenitor, even as his denunciation of a much caricatured Malthus and Ricardo became ever more shrill. In this reformulated evolutionary pattern, Carey believed he had found the one great insight that Smith had completely overlooked and also the final weapon to overturn the whole Ricardian system. Contrary to what everyone had assumed before, mankind in its advance toward civilization first moved onto and cultivated the poorest soils, the thin and barren hilltops of the world. At this primitive stage of development, a few scattered, isolated, under-capitalized farmers enjoyed almost no benefits of association and could wring only the barest subsistence from nature. But with every new baby, every new tool, and every new skill, these original human families were able to move closer together, to divide more tasks, to develop extensive social capital, to diversify their agriculture and to add various forms of manufacturing. Finally, they were able to move down from the hills onto the rich bottomlands of the world. With more population in each limited area, with a richer sharing of talents and tasks, they cleared the lush forest, turned under the deep prairie grasses, or drained the fecund swamps in order to utilize the richest, deepest, and most productive loams.[1]

This evolutionary pattern purportedly refuted all Ricardian theories of diminishing returns, and was the logical anchor for a theory of ever increasing returns. It proved Ricardo's system to be a "manual of the demagogue, who seeks power by means of agrarianism, war, and plunder." Instead of Ricardo's dismal perspective, based on man's need to utilize increasingly inferior soils as population increased, Carey "proved" a glorious outlook for man. He gained increased power over nature as a consequence of population increase and a greater clustering of people together in limited spaces. Since the margin of cultivation moved always toward more productive land, demographic and economic growth insured ever higher wage-profits. Since such growth always undercut and diminished the relative value of older land, it precluded any increased and immoral returns to early settlers, and thus finally confirmed Carey's earlier denial of any true rent.[2]

If anything, Carey found Ricardo's theory of diminishing returns to agricultural capital even more ridiculous than his theories about resort to inferior soils. Carey always stressed that early development costs were the most dear, whether in agriculture or in manufacturing. In fact, he had little tolerance for such sectoral distinctions. All is ultimately agriculture, since all products derive from the cultivation of nature. A farmer often had to do more than grow crops; to make them available for human consumption, he has to refine them through subsequent stages of production. Alternatively, Carey's celebrated ironmasters in Pennsylvania were simply farming a part of nature and then further refining the immediate product. Whether one arbitrarily classified an enterprise as agricultural or manufacturing, the original application of capital and labor tended always to be very inefficient, as proved by a pioneer homestead. Every subsequent step was easier and more efficient, or what amounted to a "takeoff" theory of capital growth. Each step revealed more options, more perfectly liberated man's intellect, and lowered social overhead. Carey saw no reason, in any area, to set limits to such increasing returns. Even if economic growth did not lead to the use of more fertile land, new skills and tools would still assure a steadily growing output from already cultivated land. As he put it, the earth, unlike all other machines, improves with use. The more taken the more that is left. It is "the great labor savings' bank, and the value to man of all other machines is in the direct ratio of their tendency to aid him in increasing his deposits in the only bank where dividends are perpetually increasing, while its capital is perpetually doubling." Thus Carey inverted Malthus, with a vengeance. Nature, not population, increases its yield geometrically, and the only ultimate or inescapable check to this rate of increase is too limited a population.[3]

It is easy to ridicule Carey's magical system. His non-Malthusian model, taken to its ultimate and logical extreme, seems as ambiguous and wrongheaded as even the most simple-minded version of Malthusianism. Carey saw his "down-from-the-hillside" discovery as his greatest contribution to social science. In reality, it was little more than a useful heuristic device to support his underlying assumption of natural fecundity and unlimited economies of scale. Despite his pretense of historical verification, the theory was neither clear nor even close to being fully persuasive, Even in his *Principles*, Carey explored the ambiguities in such concepts as "best" or "most fertile" land. In his final theory he still assumed that men always utilized the land that yielded most for their existing tools and skills. It was "best" because of location, inherent fertility, or receptivity to developed technology. Thus, in a functional sense of the word, men always chose the "best" land. Indeed, with better tools and new skills, or with the advantages of concert, they might eventually find previously unusable land to be the "best." But, again, they might not, and any fair historical survey would show contextually variant patterns of land development, with inherently more fertile soils (in a purely chemical sense) often cultivated first, not last. It is little more than perverse cleverness to argue, as an universal law, that all civilization began on barren hilltops. Carey's use of such an empirically vulnerable hypothesis invited undeserved contempt for his now remarkably coherent economic model, a model that shared all the formal merits of the Ricardian system, perhaps largely because it was a consistent inversion of Ricardo.

Two implications of his new model governed most of Carey's subsequent policy commitments. One seems remarkably prescient in the late twentieth century. Nature's bounty, of course, is only conditionally available to man. Man must adapt to nature's uniformities and learn to guide its lawful processes. And he must respect this great machine. He must care for it and improve it. This led to another Carey trademark, what might be called his "manure theory." At least today, no one should laugh at it. The one critical, inescapable secret of continued and accelerated growth, Carey believed, was man's dedicated solicitude for the great earth machine. England had neglected this machine. Southern cotton growers had abused it. Both sowed the seeds of ultimate economic decline, for just as nature is infinitely giving to those with proper piety, so it becomes niggardly and even vengeful toward the impious. Thus, in a sense, Carey substituted a voluntaristic version of natural scarcity for the deterministic one first proposed by Malthus. As he tried to clarify a proper land ethic, Carey idealized agriculture more and more. Broadly and properly conceived, agriculture encompassed not only the use of nature but the careful replenishing and building up of nature. Anything short of this, any form of farming that decreased the capacity of the earth, or even failed to increase that capacity, did not deserve the label agriculture, for the most crucial part, "culture," was missing. Thus, in the history of the world, Carey found almost no true or "scientific" agriculture. He finally concluded that it was by far the most demanding and complex occupation, tied to the most sophisticated forms of scientific knowledge. It always was the last to develop in human evolution. In fact, agriculture scarcely became possible until human association came close to perfection, and until various forms of manufacturing had already matured.[4]

What about manure? Carey used the word generically, to mean all the by-products of human production and consumption. It encompassed industrial waste (the fertile dust of granite mines), crop residues, ground-up animal bones, city garbage, even ground limestone and potash, as well as human and animal excreta. Thus, Carey argued that of all the "raw material required for the purposes of man, manure is the most important, and the least susceptible of transportation to a distance. . . ." It was the "lifeblood of a nation." Man's duty to improve nature had two aspects. One duty was to make it more amenable to human needs. But even more critical was the need for various types of recycling.

Carey became a lay expert on agronomy, and expounded all the latest theories about soil improvement. Simply stated, what came out of the land had to go back again. So much farming in America involved only the taking. Americans shipped not only cotton to Britain but, unwittingly, a shocking percentage of their soil nutrients. Nothing came back. In one sense, man alters but never diminishes nature. Yet his rearrangements can jeopardize his survival; minerals washed into an ocean can grow no corn, at least not for untold centuries. The more he thought about these issues, the more Carey denounced commodity agriculture, or the type that entailed the shipment of bulk products to distant markets. He also saw a fatal flaw in large commercial cities. They are not only far from sources of agricultural supplies but collect and lose large quantities of waste products. The best solution seemed to be a close integration of farming and processing in decentralized but diversified communities, with all the residues of production and consumption recycled into the local soil. In his "manure theory" lay one of the secrets of his new defense of tariff protection—to keep all our American manures at home.[5]

The second implication of Carey's completed system was that waste accompanies most forms of long-distance transport. Not only does manure end up at the wrong places, but such transport usually wastes energy. This did not mean that Carey opposed all distant exchange. Environmental conditions or ancient skills made the growing or processing of some very desirable products regionally specific; and in those cases and those alone, international commerce was justified, particularly in refined and finished products. He never proposed to give up the consumption of French wines and silk or Swiss lace. But insofar as possible, he wanted to bring producers and consumers close to each other, and particularly wanted to merge farms and factories. Once again, the New England village or small mill town served as his model. There nonsubordinating exchange, or what he called "commerce," took place easily, without middlemen, and with little energy wasted in moving products from one place to another. The next level of association or interdependence should link neighboring towns according to economically justified forms of specialization, and so on up to federated nations and even a profitable but limited international exchange between quite independent and economically sufficient nations.

In every case, Carey believed the local community should take care of as many of its own needs as possible. More distant exchange easily degenerated into "trade," an increasingly evil word in Carey's vocabulary. It entailed not only necessary middlemen and often high transport costs, but also the likelihood of dependent and exploitative relationships. Trade usually involved not the voluntary association of equals, but bargaining between great, centralized, market-controlling wealth on one hand and dependent, vulnerable, exploited workers on the other. These workers, by the design of the great capitalists who at great expense and with elaborate military efforts maintained such unequal markets, usually lived on the frontiers of the world, grew basic commodities, and bore all the burden of transport and of layers of profit paid to various middlemen. Trade meant economic imperialism. British capitalists had perfected the system and, with the cooperation of Jacksonian policy makers and southern planters, were now about to universalize it and make it permanent.[6]

Much more than technical economic doctrines supported Carey's new war on "trade." Deep emotional and moral commitments added fervor and force to his arguments. Critics could easily point to a recent and rapid reduction in transport cost, which seemed to make regional and national specialization ever more rational. No matter. Transport costs were not essential to Carey's argument. He rejoiced as much as anyone over transportation improvements. These, used in a local context, facilitated "commerce." No one valued the railroads more than did Carey.

In part, Carey's defense of regional self-sufficiency fed on his philosophical doctrine of association, on a complex, almost metaphysical conception of the ideal human community. Such a community, made up of autonomous individuals, of people who control their own economic options, required diversity or else it risked centralization. This was a subtle point. Most people are not, by talent or inclination, bankers. If diverse individuals are to find vocational fulfillment, then any community needs to offer a diversity of tasks. By fitting themselves to the very interdependence of a voluntary community, individuals at the same time are able to develop their own uniqueness. Otherwise, purely acquisitive or consumptive goals dominate economic life, and soon individuals function as objects or commodities in impersonal and centralized forms of collective life. A few people at the center make the critical decisions. Individuals become servile. Or, to avoid this, they have to move to the frontier, the favorite American escape from centralized dependence. But on the frontier only a few occupational options are available, however diverse personal talents and preferences. There the individual has to fall back toward barbarism, as he leaves behind the rich intellectual and spiritual returns and the high living standards that are possible only in compact communal life. Carey had equal distaste for centralization, the perversion of healthy collectivism, and for isolated frontier existence, the perversion of individualism.

Other less explicit concerns reinforced Carey's growing antipathy for "trade," or what so many of his contemporaries called "commercialism." Surely Emerson, who visited at Carey's home, helped nourish such a distaste. Like so many affluent second-generation businessmen in our history, Carey took seriously the possible transmutation of values that threatened Americans, and that so easily infected businessmen and political economists. The gaining of wealth could become a single-minded pursuit, an end in itself, whereas correctly conceived wealth was a necessary means to other humane goals. In the local and still almost personal and manageable world of Philadelphia, the proprietors that Carey knew, from wealthy ironmasters and bankers to local mechanics and nearby farmers, had not surrendered to vulgar and compulsive acquisitive goals. Altruism and spiritual values still pervaded and nourished communal concern. Colwell represented the model entrepreneur. Surely the idealized towns of New England even better exemplified Carey's idea of a proprietary but "non-capitalist" society.

Carey attributed no such generous qualities to distant, impersonal financiers and merchants. They were the exploitative "capitalists," the evil men, the dangerous conspirators of Carey's later books. Like so many reformers in the middle period, and particularly the Owenites, Carey distrusted anyone whose only business was buying cheap and selling dear. Unlike producers who also bought and sold locally as part of a desirable and necessary commerce, full-time traders or brokers assumed a social role that so easily reinforced the most antisocial and immoral character. Either rootless wanderers or urban manipulators, many never married or had children, but were always on the road, in taverns, with prostitutes. They never developed the values Carey so admired—"home values." They escaped responsibility, accountability, and too often had the ethics of a gambler. They missed the integrative effects of association, even as they often missed the moral influence of the most basic associative unit, the settled family. So easily they fell into one ethic—get rich. Because of their enormous political leverage, they easily pushed these acquisitive goals upon a whole society. In his later treatment of merchants and financiers, Carey used language remarkably reminiscent of old John Taylor, and at one point borrowed Taylor's definition of a "capitalist." Even the personal frustration of his own business dealings supported these attitudes—detestation of the wealth and power of a British elite, jealousy of the centralizing power of Wall Street, fear and resentment of middlemen, even on rare occasion a tinge of anti-Semitic resentment toward Jewish merchants or bankers like the Rothschilds.[7]

Carey's completed economic model was, by intent, an almost cosmic defense of protective tariffs. At a political level, he became an eloquent if belated spokesman for the pro-tariff cause, an admirer of Henry Clay, and a fervent Whig and later Republican. He rehearsed all the pro-tariff arguments but of course most emphasized a home market. He believed that protected manufacturing was a prerequisite of close association, of continuous economic growth, and of the eventual attainment of real agriculture in America. He hoped to end the prevalent, non-agricultural soil mining typified by single-crop commodity production for distant markets, as in cotton, wheat, and tobacco. Unending natural population increases, and continued high levels of immigration, were precluded by any continued reliance on commodity farming, which Carey saw as a distinctively frontier and colonial type of pseudo-agriculture. Commodity markets were already saturated. Surpluses in export crops had already made too many commodity farmers fully dependent on international prices, prices usually manipulated from Britain. Given a continued economic commitment to primary raw material production, and the import of most finished products, even America would soon exemplify the Ricardian model—too many people pressing against limited and rapidly depleting resources.

The Ricardian system now stood revealed for what it really was—a concealed rationalization of a world economy controlled from an imperial center. The architects of such an economy manipulated and exploited the masses of mankind in colonial areas, or all the people who exchanged large quantities of their labor, and large chunks of their share of nature, for small quantities of labor embodied in finished products. Ricardo had defined man as a mere object, as a commodity, and thus had supported a system of greed and callousness. Great Britain, by monopolizing techniques and machines, by its head start, by its slave-like wages, by the market power over competitors it exercised through large centralized firms, and by its direct political and military domination of much of the world, had perfected an imperial system. It paid the price of almost continual war. The United States had gained its political independence from Britain, but unfortunately had not yet secured its freedom from this imperial system. Periodically, the United States tried a so-called "free trade" policy that only anchored economic colonialism. Such policies promised eventual economic disaster, a disaster so far averted in part by our superior political institutions, by the sheer magnitude of our resources, and by one counterbalancing and often overlooked import—human beings. After all, man remained by far the most intricate and useful productive machine, and so long as people streamed westward across the Atlantic the United States gained some recompense for the bad bargains it made in European markets and for its continual loss of manure. But, obviously, as the Ricardian knew, under such unfair terms nature would soon begin to exact its revenge and American living standards would decline, probably as politicians desperately sought a temporary reprieve through territorial expansion at the expense of Indian tribes or Mexicans or other helpless people. But not only did such expansion have limits; it also meant less association as desperate families fled back toward barren hilltops or desert wastes.[8]

Carey, like Calvin Colton and other protectionists, continued to advocate free and *equal* commerce among nations. But "free trade," given the dominance of Britain in the world economy, really meant continued exploitation from abroad and arrested economic development at home. Carey believed truly associative, that is, nonmanipulative and nonsubordinating, intercourse was impossible between technologically advanced countries and less developed ones. In particular, he believed free and equal trade was impossible between primarily manufacturing countries and those committed to the export of raw materials or agriculture commodities. Such trade was inherently unequal. Power and control flowed to the manufacturing centers as surely as did all the manure. Thus, Carey believed the slogan "free trade," as used by the British and by American allies, was a hypocritical defense of a very exploitative imperial system, and one that enriched only a relatively few manipulators even in Britain.

Ironically, Carey did not predict an ultimate reduction in world trade because of protection. He expected an increase of nonexploitative trade between commercial equals stimulated by tremendous leaps of productivity in balanced national economies. Nations are like individuals, who compete fairly only when they are economic equals, when they enjoy a liberating degree of economic self-sufficiency. Servants do not trade freely with masters. A master's insistence upon free trade is only a clever ruse to try to get servants to acquiesce in their lot. Thus, the United States should favor free trade with Britain as soon as it gained a mature, developed, independent economy of its own. Then it could sell finished goods. Implied, but not emphasized by Carey, was the further suggestion that the United States might advance its own interests by pushing "free trade" in less developed areas of the world. Carey believed such a policy completely immoral, although he once lamented that if an economically powerful United States was unfortunate enough or foolish enough in the future to acquire colonies, and did not exploit them, this would be the most remarkable fact in all human history.[9]

Carey emphasized the noneconomic benefits of a protected and balanced American economy. He stressed the importance of a rich communal life and the need to keep young men at home rather than pushing them off to distant homesteads. Local economic development would encourage desperate farmers to diversify rather than try to grow more cotton or wheat even as world prices kept falling. Association, alone, would break up the centralized, subordinating cotton plantations of the South. But he knew the economic returns would be bounteous. Like Daniel Raymond and others, he argued that the conjoined development of manufacturing and of intensive forms of mixed agriculture could double and triple the productivity of American workers. Commodity farming was terribly inefficient, with its seasonal bursts of work followed by long periods of idleness. Frontier farming and household manufactures were not only capital-deficient but permitted little specialization. More critical, increasing numbers of Americans would have no place in an already glutted agriculture. Abundant quantities of labor already went unused, and this included the self-rewarding labor of young women. Increased production would alone take care of all the problems of distributive justice, as more and more of the national product accrued to labor. Business cycles were simply inconceivable in such a self-sufficient context. Thus, Carey used the magical potential of rapid growth to overcome the two major arguments against protection—the fear of diminished productivity from a less effficient allocation of labor and resources, and the fear of redistributive penalties necessarily assessed to some existing producers. Even at the level of taste, his emphasis on getting people closer to each other, on voluntary and nonsubordinating but tight association, set him apart from most free-trade advocates, who usually welcomed more space, more expansion, and who associated individualism with some degree of isolation.[10]

The usual complaint that protective tariffs inevitably raised domestic prices, and thus penalized consumers, seemed perversely irrelevant to Carey. Of course, protection immediately increased certain prices, at least above the frequent price-cutting levels Britain had resorted to in order to maintain a world monopoly. But higher prices, in themselves, might benefit a country, for they might help stimulate new capital accumulation and more work. The crucial economic goal was to increase our power to direct natural events. Surely Americans, given the needed incentives to launch new manufacturing enterprise, could soon attain skills and tools to match any in the world, and with these attain the greatest possible efficiency in production. Surely, given their political institutions, their attained freedom and independence, they could best realize all the economic benefits of association. All else was pure gain. Local manufacturing eliminated transport costs for both agricultural goods and finished products. Protection allowed more local specialization, and thus ever increasing local economies of scale and a broader range of career options for individuals. Above all, and in part as a consequence of high prices and wages, such a largely self-contained local economy could escape international price fluctuations and always hum along at full speed. Or, to use the physical analogies Carey was so fond of, a balanced economy could maintain "rapid motion," eliminate "internal friction," and achieve "full circulation."

By 1847 Carey had revised his earlier scale of national achievement. Instead of measuring attained productivity, he now looked more carefully at developing trends. England, second from the top in his early hierarchy, now dropped to the very bottom level among developed countries. Extrapolation from its existing policies revealed a future more dismal than that of any other country except for its exploited colonies. France rose in Carey's estimate, while Germany, loosely federated, and under the protectionist policies insured by its new Customs Union, drew his fullest praise. The coming nations were all protectionists—Germany, France, Russia, and the Scandinavian countries. The position of the United States was now equivocal. Still at the top, still blessed by the greatest potential, it could lose all by a continuation of the free-trade policies of 1846, or gain the very summit of human achievement would it but return to the tariff policies of 1842.[11]

Why so harsh an evaluation of Britain? As imperial master of most of the world, it surely would prosper at home. Not so. As the "workshop of the world," Britain accrued benefits only for a few privileged large manufacturers and merchants, for the centralized bosses of a conspiratorial and narrowly selfish system. Because of its centralized manufacturing, England had neglected the highest science: agriculture. Indeed, its people clustered, but they did not enjoy voluntary association. Instead, with increasingly meager returns and more servility, they functioned as mere economic automatons in centralized collectivities, or really in a type of communism. A few privileged landlords controlled a backward agriculture, even as a few lords of capital ran the ugly and dehumanizing factories. Large entrepreneurs squeezed out smaller ones, who had to become wage employees. In fact, employment in England never reflected a free choice among options or served as a way station on the road to proprietary freedom. Not only did the British system sustain the depletive commodity agriculture that supported southern slavery, which was yet another conspicuous manifestation of British imperial policy, but it enslaved its own citizens. Carey's portrait of English workers—excluded from land; reduced to subsistence wages; without hope; functioning as owned commodities; in effect, manufactured generation after generation in sufficient numbers to run the cotton mills—was as harsh as in any Jacksonian or even any Marxist critique. He thus portrayed effective resistance to the imperial system, particularly by the United States, as a means of emancipating masses of Englishmen, including mere children, who functioned as adjuncts to machines. The development of balanced and self-sufficient economies in the outlying, commodity-producing areas would cut off the unequal flow of trade and force England to revitalize its own agriculture. As England moved back toward economic balance, toward its own needed forms of free association, the great law of progress would emancipate its citizens as surely as it would emancipate blacks in America.[12]

Carey's bitter hatred of Britain increased as he grew older. In his last book (1872), as he neared his eightieth year, he offered one of the most scathing indictments of an economic system ever written. He drew upon extensive Parliamentary reports on factory conditions and on such recent critics as John Ruskin, and even borrowed the class rhetoric of Marxists. Compared to what he read about English workers, the plight of former southern slaves had been "an enviable one." The "toiling millions" in Britain, "whether in the field or the workshop, whether male or female, young or old," all moved in "the direction of that 'proletariat' at which they are now admitted to have arrived." The great capitalists of Britain not only subjected British workers to their power, but controlled an army of five hundred million slaves around the world, in a "war of capital on the labor of mankind at large. . . ." Reforms in England scarcely touched the roots of this evil. The only end to such a system had to be internal disturbances and foreign wars. To think that Malthus and Ricardo had supported such evils. How easily they, who had never really worked, justified the plight of the people who did. Not content merely to rationalize the subjection of English workers, they used an insidious doctrine of "survival of the fittest" to justify the conquest and subjugation of all purportedly "inferior races." Carey surveyed the wreckage. Not only Britain but other European powers had plundered and murdered in half the world, leaving scenes of horror without parallel in the world's history. They even pretended that such exploitation was Christian, as if Jesus had prophesied that the "strongest will inherit the earth."[13]

Not even the Physiocrats placed as much emphasis on agriculture as Carey did in his later years. But his vision for American agriculture was, to say the least, eccentric. Here he was also a very poor prophet. In human evolution, he saw a steady progression from the commons of nomadic herdsmen to a full and complete division of land into individually owned and managed farms. Any remnant of common pastures or fields, any qualification on full individual ownership, seemed to him retrogressive and economically disastrous, for they all lessened individual freedom and responsibility and invited less effort and even less cooperation (again, such commons invited subordinated roles, as under feudalism). Only a self-interested owner, in contrast with a serf, tenant, or employee, would be sufficiently motivated to take the extra effort to cycle manures, to work toward a truly scientific agriculture.

Although the first secret of economic growth in America was diversified manufacturing, Carey did not envision any reduction in agricultural employment. Just the opposite. He foresaw a steady growth in the number of farmers as population continued to grow. Such growth required not further territorial expansion, not even a rapid development of the West, but a much more intensive and complete utilization of land in the populous East. He always described the Eastern soils as most fertile, either because of soil characteristics or locational advantage. Such intensive agriculture entailed not ever larger farms but ever smaller ones. His ideal seemed to be ten-acre farms, each with enormously efficient tools and a wide range of crops, from vineyards to orchards to truck crops and dairying, with very little grain or livestock. Carey preferred vegetarian diets to meats, and hoped for the elimination of animal fats in food and animal fibers in clothing. Diverse crops meant year-round employment. He believed that economic evolution would bring ever more minute divisions of land, with efficient, garden-like utilization of the land, and a gradual diminution of differences between rural and village life, between farming and manufacturing. Truly scientific farms might occupy little more land than a cotton mill or a coal mine. He welcomed continuous subdivisions of land, insisted on individual ownership above everything else, but believed that in a free and developing economy such division would stop short of economically inefficient plots, simply because his balanced economy would always provide profitable vocational opportunities in manufacturing or services.[14]

Carey had the same proprietary image of what he called iron farmers and also of cotton processors, an image that seemed both innocent and anachronistic in the years after the Civil War. In his idealized conception of a protected American economy, all workers would be independent and always in some sense would work for themselves. Every male worker would either be a proprietor or working toward ownership. Ownership was a prerequisite of free association. In a cohesive and growing but decentralized and free economy, individual ownership, even the achievement of great wealth, was in no way threatening to others, no occasion for jealousy and class conflict, as it was either on the meager frontiers or in the centralized collectivities of England. Americans competed with nature, not against each other. In a protected, balanced economy, affluent entrepreneurs would gain from growth but never at the rate of competing small businessmen, whose very survival was threatened by so-called "free trade." In America everyone was a capitalist, building his own large or small savings bank. Americans worked not because of the whip of need but because of the pull of soaring hopes. This meant free Americans exhibited non-Malthusian moral qualities appropriate to prosperous communities—liberality, responsibility, honesty, benevolence, self-control, pacifism, confidence in the future. Where men enjoyed such freedom, women were likewise free and valued, enjoyed the right to choose their own husbands, expected fidelity and honor in marriage, and reigned as complete mistresses of their own castles, blessed with numerous household conveniences. Children were regarded as a blessing, valued by parents, trusted as valuable friends, and provided a free education before they assumed an adult vocation.[15]

How can one square this vision with the early factory system in America? Carey had no problem, but one has to ask if he really described a developing reality or only his own ideal. Judgment here depends upon perspective, for the reports and estimates on early American mills ranged between extremes of celebration and condemnation. Carey was the extreme celebrant. He seemed to find exactly what he wanted to find. To Carey, at least until the disillusioned last years of his life, the small shops of Philadelphia, the nearby coal mines, the ironworks dotting the valleys of western Pennsylvania, the village banks, and even the large cotton mills of New England all bore absolutely no comparison to the terrible factories in the financial centers of England. However he gathered his data, he always seemed to assume that the mills in New England were owned by local farmers, by town mechanics, or even in part by female operatives. As he argued, the "great merchants, the little capitalist, the merchant, the foundry-master, the engineer, the workman, and the girl who tends a loom, divide among themselves the ownership of the great mill. . . ." There workers exchanged labor for labor, with no cheating. He followed Toqueville in denying that America had great men, and rejoiced that America would never suffer great cities. As much as a farm, the shop or mill was a savings bank for local citizens, one means of building up socially beneficial capital. Such mills, almost alone, provided the best avenue of redemption for the South, and only they could solve the slavery problem.

Carey never stopped extolling all the beneficial effects of local manufacturing. He assumed that the workers were grateful for the opportunity to work in local factories, particularly young men who otherwise would have had to flee to the wild West. Always his image was one of small, manageable, personal firms (not far from the truth in the middle period),

locally owned and managed (less often true), and more nearly cooperatives than investment vehicles (scarcely ever true). At times he echoed
the idealism of Robert Owen, as, for instance, in his idealized portrait of
small-town banks. He assumed that most people who needed and used a
bank did not deposit their money (a form of loan) but instead bought its
stock. In a persuasive economic argument, he pointed to the stabilizing
influence of bank discounts and bank notes extended on the basis of bank
capital rather than on vulnerable, recallable demand deposits. In a sense,
he conceived of banks as credit unions, just as his factories were producers' cooperatives. Both came close to the one frontier institution he
praised: the "bee," as in a quilting bee. This primitive form of cooperation, he said, climaxed in the corporation, in the final realization of
self-help in unity.[16]

Carey believed almost all warfare originated in callous colonialism. An
imperial type of economy, with its metropolitan centers of control and
outlying sources of raw produce, depreciated human life. Malthus, an
apologist for such an economic system, typically blamed too many people, not a lack of balanced economic development, for the impoverishment of places like Ireland or India. When in a contrived colonial system
surplus people lose even economic value, then war becomes an appealing
policy option. It is a preferred means of maintaining colonial subservi-
ence and low resource prices. But when men are valuable, as they are in
intensively developed communities, the costs of war become prohibitive.
Also, local development leads to high living standards that undercut
expansionist motives. There war occurs, if at all, only in defense either of
home territory or, as in the later American Civil War, of an attained level
of association or federative unity against an expansive, class-divisive,
colonial-style economy, typified by both Britain and the allied southern
plantation system. Even for citizens who do not have to fight wars of
expansion, in India or against Mexicans and Indians, the high taxes
needed to maintain a military establishment are a direct drain on real
wages. Economically, a large army is equivalent to a large class of citizens
living on the dole.[17]

This analysis made even clearer the needed answers for the American
South. The colonial agricultural pattern of that region, tied to England,
had to be broken. Such agriculture, and the exhausted soils it engendered, caused slavery. Under protection, cotton factories could spring up
all over the South. These new markets would reverse the southern thirst
for expansion to the Southwest, make slaves more valuable and also
restrict them to existing slave states, and begin the gradual process toward
emancipation. A slave, anywhere, was one who had to work at a master's
bidding and accept whatever wages a master offered. Such slavery was the

certain result of a centralized factory system, of great manufacturing and trading elites, detached from distant agricultural suppliers. Economic arrangements were much more critical in maintaining slavery than were political institutions. People in despotic countries with balanced economies moved toward freedom, as in Russia. People under free constitutions, as in Britain, moved toward slavery because they did not merge manufacturing and agriculture, because producers and consumers did not live side by side. In Britain the people increasingly knew only the "despotism of the spindle and the loom," while ever less independent American farmers suffered the despotism of low commodity prices dictated by forces beyond their control. And while our farmers suffered, great trading cities such as New York grew apace, providing further evidence that we were on the way to duplicating the British system. Even our surviving manufacturing tended toward urban centralization and narrow bureaucratic management, or more power to a few and slavery for the many.[18]

In 1858 Carey completed his three-volume *Principles of Social Science*. He now tried to place his virtually unchanged political economy in a much more universal context. He wrote at a time when all his early hopes seemed betrayed. Democratic administrations consistently implemented policies that were the very opposite of what he deemed necessary, policies that favored free trade, territorial expansion, sparser populations, and appeasement of southern slave owners. Largely because of low tariffs, Carey believed he was witnessing for the United States "a decline more rapid, and more pervading, than is recorded in the history of any country of the world." He sounded ever more like John Taylor, as he continuously lamented the high cost of government, the increasing power of private interests, the incompetence and corruption of office holders, and the dictatorial power of presidents. He decried the overriding of the Missouri Compromise, the violation of Indian treaties in continental expansion, and the likelihood of new imperial wars to feed the slave interests. He lamented that our legislatures increasingly sold economic privileges for power, as in large land grants to navigation and railroad companies. Instead of a nation of small firms, clustered in local communities, he witnessed ever greater centralization in large cities, the obverse and logical complement of a dispersed and unscientific agriculture. In despair, Carey anticipated an early dissolution of the Union.[19]

Such looming disasters surely made it even more imperative that Americans heed the prophetic admonitions of its most notable Jeremiah. Prophets speak for God. Now, in a sense, Carey tried to add the highest authority to his policy advocacy. As he matured his political economy, he came to realize that its laws rested within the larger context of physical law. One great system of law governed all phenomena, from material particles to human societies. Carey even claimed for himself the stature of the great physical scientists of the past. He would finally clarify the universality of all laws and show their exact implications for man. What he actually did, after all his boasting, was add some persuasive physical analogies to his system, analogies that he mistakenly acclaimed as cosmic identities.

Closely following Comte, Carey offered a quite sophisticated theory of scientific method. Logic and mathematics were tools of a mature positive science, not components of it. Historically, such a science first developed at the level of matter and only now began to encompass man. He stressed the continuum from physics to chemistry to physiology to biology and finally to sociology. Each higher stage overlapped and incorporated those below it. All branches had their roots in matter and its uniformities. In all areas of inquiry scientists had one method; they began with hypotheses, deductively developed them, and then moved to observational verification. Too often economists, such as Ricardo, had stopped short of the final step, leaving only coherent and abstract deductive systems with no more empirical truth-value than a system of logic. Carey promised to rectify these errors and in the process add greater conceptual precision to an area of science so far distinguished only by the fervor of its contending schools. American social scientists, instead of striking out anew, had all too often borrowed their purported "laws" from Europe, laws formulated by men who were beholden to monarchs and whose self-interest was served by cheap labor systems. Not surprisingly, Carey's final and perfected system featured his own "law" of human evolution, which showed how mankind moved from sparse and infertile hilltops down to rich valleys, there to develop self-sufficient and prosperous communities.[20]

Carey was most original in his theories about man. In general, he drew upon early evolutionary theories, anticipated or paralleled much of Spencer's sociology, and anticipated several themes in John Dewey. In his last book he used Darwin's *Descent of Man* as a source for his own views. Carey saw man's roots in matter, but at the level of organization at which it attained its most complex order and achieved its most refined functions. He acknowledged God's creation of matter, but otherwise offered a completely naturalistic yet nonreductionist account of human uniqueness. Like John Fiske later, Carey noted man's extended infancy, his comparative lack of instincts, his early need for parental care, and the critical responsibility of society for his developed moral standards. By necessity, man was more social than any other animal. Language was the key to his distinctiveness, and he could learn language only in a social context. Without other people, and thus without language, a child never learned to think, to use concepts, to draw upon a cultural inheritance. Without thought, he remained more helpless than beasts. In fact, Carey would not assign the label *man* to an organism lacking language, since language was the essential element in the definition of humanity.[21]

Typically, Carey tied man's need for association to physical law. For man, association was a law of molecular gravitation. Just as the more molecules collected in one place, the greater the attractive force, so for man. Carey believed this social gravitation accounted for the powerful lure of great cities. But in molecules, and in heavenly bodies, gravitation only balanced off centrifugal forces, which otherwise would have led to the infinite dispersion of individual units. In society as in physics, the ideal was an equilibrium between outward-pushing imperatives and the attractive lure of great centers. Small local clusters provided the best resistance against great cities. These made possible true individualism and freedom, a freedom meaningless in the context of cosmic isolation and impossible in the context of centralized control. Once again, by using some rather dubious physical analogies, Carey endorsed his earlier insights into the subtle interaction of society and individuals. Only in groups, where options multiply and where variant human talents alone find expression, can one be free. Only in a social context, only in the mutually beneficial association of differences, can dissimilar parts function at all. This was a suggestive organic metaphor. Economically, only clusters of associated people allow occupational specialization, and with it a fulfillment in work never present in primitive or simple societies with few people and few options. But of course social interdependence always raises the specters of centralized control, of decision making by a few for the many, and of a loss of humanity on the part of those controlled from above. Carey tried to define and defend an individualism that thrived on the tension between those two poles, and which became richer as smooth social interactivity increased. Typically, he used the analogy of low friction in celebrating this.[22]

In such a cosmic context, man's evolution assumed a slightly different meaning than it had earlier in Carey's system. As before, human progress depended on population increase. More people in the same space allowed richer association and an increasing power to control events. But now he stressed the physical implications. Change became ever more rapid as social motion increased. This involved a great natural principle—the more motion in a system the higher its form. In evolution, matter moved from simple inanimate forms to organic species and on to the highest form—man. Each ascending form retained all elemental properties and thus remained subject to all the laws of matter. In human societies, at the level of organization at which mind was most active, the process continued, with ever more heterogeneous clusters, more motion, and more rapid changes in the form of social institutions. As man developed rich social institutions locally, he was better able to resist the gravitational pull of centralized cities. It was clear to Carey that human progress entailed ever more nonsubordinating or cooperative association, and less isolation or centralized dependency, or a scheme reminiscent of Spencer's.[23]

Carey's new cosmic perspective reinforced all his old loyalties. Traders now became the outright parasites claimed by Owenite socialists. They added some value to goods by moving them, but devalued man himself. With the support of his physical analogies, he again stressed the importance of compact development, of keeping and using manure, and of complex industrial recycling. As he defended his intensive model of development he found a new measure of economic maturity—the convergence of prices for raw produce and highly processed or refined goods. In an exploited, colonial economy, provincial farmers or miners usually exchanged approximately twelve hours of their labor for one hour of manufacturing labor. The other eleven-twelfths of lost value went partly to pay the higher transport cost of bulky materials, but mainly to various middlemen. Conversely, a balanced economy meant equal exchanges of labor, or similar prices in terms of labor inputs for farmers and manufacturers. He also foresaw a larger proportion of labor devoted to agriculture and mining in a mature economy, or in what he defined as the broad base of any rational economy. This would reflect the enormous efficiency of manufacturing, the increased demand for raw produce, and the labor continuously needed to replenish nature, and not any inherent inefficiency in agriculture or extractive industries. Convergent, relatively higher food and fiber and mineral prices alone made possible a scientific agriculture, and also created in the population at the base of the pyramid a high demand for manufactured goods. Unfortunately, in the United States of 1858 prices of raw produce were ever lower, land values down, soils more exhausted, and barbarism in the offing.[24]

Of all forms of what he called agriculture, Carey most valued mining. He continuously praised the coal and iron industries of Pennsylvania. More than any other products, these allowed man to substitute mental control for physical prowess. Both minerals were as plentiful as the air we breathe. The coal mined by one man could do the work of a thousand arms. The United States had more mineral power than any other country, yet had developed little of it. Railroad companies even purchased most of their iron rails from the "merchant princes" of England. Carey looked forward to the day when domestic iron would replace wood in buildings, lessening the danger of fire and the cost of insurance.[25]

Still an enemy of dualisms, Carey now tried to rout a final one—that between consumption and production. They blend into each other. What is consumption from one perspective (a manufacturer's use of raw materials) is production in another. There is no final consumption in man's endless rearrangement of natural events. Even eating is the production of manure. Man originates no matter and no motion. The goal of a mature economy is neither production nor consumption, but greater rapidity of motion or circulation. Even man himself is, from one perspective, a production, and the best of all. He results from redirected natural energies that begin with conception and continue through the rearing of a child.[26]

Carey had long argued that the more people the better, seemingly without limit. He now acknowledged theoretical outer limits, and finally engaged the population issue. Unlimited human fertility would eventually so overcrowd the earth as to make life unbearable if not unsupportable. Was this the ultimate outcome? Was God so evil as to create the earth and man with some devilish outcome of scarcity and class conflict? Or did He so create man as to fit him into a larger natural ecology? The questions begged the expected "No" answers, but how limit births short of vice or starvation or cruel and inhumane sexual restraint? Carey had an easy answer. Fertility is not a fixed law in man but culturally specific and contextually variant. God so formed man that high fertility attends only one stage of society—the low skills of a politically secure frontier stage of development. In more civilized societies fertility decreases. In part this is culturally based, tied to changed human preferences. Sexual intercourse, often the only available mode of gratification in backward societies, competes in advanced societies with other gratifications, and thus takes place less frequently. Slowly, the "real" man develops, and he enjoys the higher intellectual and spiritual gratifications made possible by increased association.[27]

To these cultural determinants, Carey added a purely physiological regulator. He would have no enforced celibacy, which caused bad health. But organic laws tied to divine providence nevertheless regulated both male sexual ardor and sperm count. He appealed to a popular nineteenth-century physiological theory—the body is a repository of various vital and interrelated energies. The net amount of energy is genetically fixed, but in males it flows to various organs in quite variant patterns, yet short of the gross distortion of disease. It seemed to Carey that sexual energy had an inverse relationship to nervous energy, and that each curtailed the other. Muscular activities stimulate ardor; cerebral ones inhibit it. In women, the reproductive organs always had a large role and seemingly diminished intellectual vitality. Since nobler faculties, which require a careful culture to develop at all, involved nervous energy, men in advanced civilizations effectively subordinated sexual passion. Carey followed early findings in physical anthropology, including cranial measurements, to fit this thesis to individuals and races, arguing that large-skulled people had reduced fertility. Who, he asked, could doubt that men of brilliance were unprolific? He cited European nobility and even American presidents to make his point, George Washinton being a prime exemplar. Thus, nature took care of population even as progress occurred. Carey based his racial theories on his demographic theory. He held in low esteem all pastoral, scattered, nomadic peoples, and rarely said a good word for the American Indians. Such primitive types would, like many lower animals and the wilderness itself, become extinct in the course of evolution. Even pure air required a diminution of the number of animals, as people replaced animals in the balanced cycle of oxygen and carbon dioxide.[28]

By the time he wrote *Social Science*, Carey desired an extensive economic role for government. A good government often needs to provide a wide spectrum of services. It needs to regulate, innovate, incite, although never control. It is the referee of economic activity, the coordinator of movement, the promoter of increased association. He compared government to a joint stock company, with limited liability, open to all, and committed to the common interest. A government is the head of an organic society and must nourish manufacturing by guiding people into certain employments. Laissez-faire meant governmental abdication. A coordinating government seeks economic balance and at times has to frustrate private choice. For example, it should discourage too many middlemen. The ideal end of government guidance was a degree of association so great that no classes and no conflicts survived in a society without separable profits and wages, without rents or interest, without the buying and selling of labor, or one in which everyone was a capitalist and a laborer alike, and all were bound in the mutuality of voluntary cooperation.[29]

Even more significant, Carey tried to make consistent his rather technical and often contradictory views on money and credit. He thus oriented himself toward the final inflationary theories he embraced after the Civil War. He saw three types of exchange (or really change) undergirding a developed economy—changes in form, in place, and in ownership. Each required tools. Money aided in the infinitely varied changes of ownership just as ships or trains served transportation or machines aided manufacturing. Money allowed the minute divisions and combinations of services in a modern economy, as in the hundred minute portions of labor sold in a single newspaper. Yet, as Carey frequently admitted, most of these exchanges could take place through credit arrangements, by purely paper transfers. He even welcomed the degree of local trust that could virtually eliminate the need for circulating money. Nonetheless, Carey insisted upon not only the importance of money as a measure or standard of value, but the need for large quantities of money. He often seemed to confuse the amount of money, defined as specie, with the total circulation or effective money supply.

In effect, Carey made money a type of productive capital, although a quite distinct class of capital. To gain extra money in a country was equivalent to gaining railroads or foundries. Money was the lubricant that kept an economy moving smoothly and rapidly, without periodic break-downs. His position was close to the mercantilist one, and in fact Carey now identified himself as a disciple of the great Colbert. Unlike the British economists, he insisted upon favorable trade balances and the steady accumulation of more gold and silver. Net losses of specie through exports could slow the circulation of money and lead to a depression. So long as the money supply increased, monetary prices would remain stable or slowly increase, interest rates decline, credit use increase, wages rise, and economic activity greatly expand. Yet Carey had to qualify such a monetary theory of growth. He acknowledged that the quantity of money was no more important than its rate of circulation, and that credit instruments could expand the effective money supply many times over. What he really argued for, behind his strange and lingering loyalty to specie, was either a steady growth of the total circulation, or an increased tempo of circulation, or both.[30]

Like Malthus and Colton, Carey was always a mild inflationist. That is, he welcomed very gradual and steady monetary price increases as a natural aspect of a growth economy. The money or credit expansion underlying such inflation served distributive justice by increasing economic equality. Just as Carey noted how improved productive tech-niques slowly diminished the value of older capital, so he also noted a normal decline in the value of money (the cost of producing gold and silver also declined through time). Cheaper and more plentiful money, documented by lower interest rates, hurt only creditors. Lower monetary values helped shift more of the national wealth to wages, and also made it easier for farmers and small businessmen to acquire capital and thereby offer more effective competition to large capitalists. The fruits of normal inflation thus all lay on the side of increased economic activity.

Deflation, or a decline in circulating money or credit, always meant a slowdown in economic activity. As interest rates rose, the cost of doing business went up; the rate of profit necessary to sustain investment rose; small entrepreneurs were squeezed out; and production and employment declined. Only creditors gained, and Carey had little concern for them. He never liked the cautious "saving mentality." One should use his money, be his own investor. Apparently Carey assumed that a growing supply of specie was necessary to gain public acceptance of various credit devices, such as bank notes or private checks. He certainly applauded these, and saw no danger at all in credit expansion, provided it reflected a realistic public demand and need for it, not merely a deliberate and artificially stimulated demand fostered by large bankers. Unlike most economists of his day, he denied that bank notes or other credit instru-

ments drove specie from the country. Of course, they drove less convenient specie from circulation. But increased economic activity in an expanding economy insured productive efficiency, trade balances, and the
import of specie, whether for use as money or as consumer goods. Specie
always flowed to economically strong countries, those with the most to
sell at the best prices.[31]

In 1858 Carey first stressed the difference between great banks, whose
selfish power he feared, and small-town banks, whose responsible services insured a steady rise in money-credit and either stable or improving
prices for goods. Even the evils of large banks reflected a failure to enact
protective tariffs. In periods of low tariff and cheap foreign goods, specie
did flow to Britain. The aftermath was bank failures, loss of confidence,
the hoarding of money, and either economic stagnation or depression.
After 1836, federal tariff reductions assured such a loss of specie, while
Democratic administrations increasingly warred against compensatory
credit expansion through local bank-note issues. As a result, small banks
failed while the large banks of New York City gained a near-monopoly.
These large city banks could manipulate the money supply and continue
periodic speculative booms and busts.[32]

By 1860 national events finally conspired in Carey's favor. He had
helped steer the new Republican Party toward protection. The Lincoln
administration supported a new tariff bill that pleased Carey on most
counts. Even the Civil War won his fullest support. Unlike most wars, it
was not a war for any type of imperial glory. It was a people's war, fought
for national unity, to destroy slavery, to overcome the political policies
that came in the wake of the southern plantation system. From serving as
a prophet of doom, Carey temporarily shifted roles. In published letters
to congressmen, cabinet officers, and even presidents, or in articles and
speeches, he tried to keep the ship of state on course. He failed. Soon
after the war ended he sensed major, even calamitous shifts of direction,
and the misuse of the very policies he had so long advocated. As an old
man, Carey became a caustic, even radical, social critic.

The Civil War brought a type of economic boom. Carey believed it
encouraged not only growth in productivity but even higher living standards. Why? Carey would not accept the "absurd" demand theories of
Malthus and Raymond. He denied any essential role to government war
purchases, since these led to a form of waste and a net drag on the
economy. Without all the waste of war and yet with a comparable level of
economic activity, the economy would have supported a much higher
living standard in 1865. Thus, not government demand but an overall
higher level of economic activity explained the boom. As usual, Carey so
linked supply and demand as to treat them as a single entity, which he
usually called circulation or motion. But even if government demand did

not cause the economic miracle, government policies did sustain it. The government finally assumed its proper coordinating role. Specifically, it first protected us from British competition and thereby stimulated the manufacturing required for national self-sufficiency. Then it provided the oil of increased circulation—a plentiful and growing supply of money. Given a continuation of such policies the boom should not only have continued after the war but accelerated, since the waste of war could then be translated into new capital goods. But it did not happen that way. War's end meant economic decline, even a threat of depression.[33]

By 1866 Carey had joined the cause of protection with that of deliberate inflation. Zealously he fought against any lowered tariffs or deflationary currency policies. The latter involved the greenback issue, and later led Carey into the Greenback Party. During the Civil War the Lincoln administration had to borrow much of the cost of the war. The difficulty it had in selling bonds for specie, at least at anything close to decent interest rates, led to an old strategy—the printing of fiat money, or circulating notes made legal tender by law but not redeemable in specie. These greenbacks, as they were popularly called, depreciated with the adverse fortunes of war. Although the United States never officially devalued its dollar by changing its legal gold content, the greenbacks had the same effect on domestic prices as devaluation. They raised prices as they effectively lowered the gold content of circulating dollars. But since foreign countries continued to demand gold for their exports, the "dollar" of international exchange remained the gold dollar. Carey saw one obvious policy implication of such de facto devaluation. It raised the effective tariff rate. Just as 20 percent duties raised the cost of linen by that much over the official British price, so the effect of 20 percent dollar devaluation effectively doubled the hurdle faced by British imports. A linen scarf that sold for the equivalent of a dollar (gold standard) in England, now sold for $1.40 (fiat money) in the United States. The greenbacks also related to protection in another way. Should the government decide to redeem the greenbacks, that is, to pay all its domestic debts in gold, it either had to tax to get the gold or somehow secure it from abroad. The most likely political ploy was higher tariff collections on imports. Ironically, larger tariff revenues meant lower tariff rates, for only this would insure a volume sufficient to yield significant revenue. Thus, the fates of high protection and plentiful monetary supplies, the twin pillars of Carey's economic model, were inseparably married to each other.

Without acknowledgment, Carey finally accepted the counter-cyclical policies of Malthus and Daniel Raymond. To sustain the wartime boom he believed the United States had to keep up the high level of circulation. This entailed expansionist policies, and particularly a continued increase in monetary supplies. At the very least, the government courted disaster if it adopted the deflationary policies that were increasingly popular, even orthodox, in the Republican Party. Such policies always involved redemption of the greenbacks and repayment of all government debts in specie, even when bonds did not specify repayment in gold. These policies, if adopted, almost required the federal government to raise taxes, push up interest rates, or lower selected tariffs to gain increased tariff revenue, policies all anathema to Carey. They threatened lower prices and wages for farmers and mechanics, unfair and even disastrous penalties on debtors, new hurdles to capital formation, bankruptcy for new manufacturers, and an inevitable decline in economic activity, if not a deep depression.

Vainly, after 1866, Carey begged officials in Washington to lower taxes for producers, to postpone specie payments on the debt, to pay at most only the interest on the debt, thereby stimulating a lagging economy. And he wanted the government to issue more fiat money, if needed, not retire the existing notes. Postwar needs, particularly in the South, meant a growing need for money, and short of issuing greenbacks the government could increase the money supply only by self-defeating, credit-depressing policies. In effect, Carey wanted future economic growth to pay off the postponed debt. In 1866 the circulation in America, he believed, was only half that in Britain, as farmers burned corn and wealthy capitalists rejoiced in receiving twofold returns on wartime loans. The United States had adopted the unfair policy of supporting a gold dollar, which largely benefited foreign creditors or wealthy domestic owners of the national debt, but in order to do this had laid siege on the prices and the incomes of farmers and laborers. Why not maintain stable commondity prices, encourage economic expansion, and let gold and creditors bear the burden, if there had to be a burden at all?[34]

The greenback issue taught Carey a lesson. Before, he had tied credit expansion to supplies of specie. Now he wanted government to be the final arbiter of circulation regardless of specie. Once again, he advocated a larger economic role for government. During the war gold fled the country to pay for necessary war-related imports. In this context, only greenbacks saved the economy by assuring an increased but responsible circulation. Government issues proved more responsive to actual need, and more stabilizing, than private bank notes. Carey desired the slight inflation that paralleled a growing circulation. But he did not want an unmoored, ever-shifting dollar, and deplored the insecurity caused by varying gold prices during the war. But fiat money, responsive to the needs of the public, did not of necessity lead to any devaluation. In fact, Carey attributed the wartime devaluation, not to the quantity of greenbacks issued, but to an over-expansion of bank credit tied to vulnerable deposits and often deliberately manipulated by large city banks. Such bankers stimulated credit expansion only to set a trap for debtors in a later retirement of loans. So long as the government used fiat notes to pay for goods and services, he anticipated no speculation on their value and expected them to remain at par in relation to gold. Literally, such notes were as good as gold. Instead of credit expansion through private banking, with all the control in the selfish hands of a few private bankers, the government could do it with its own notes and in ways calculated to stimulate investment and increased industry. Such notes could be as manna to an economy, and work only to the good, whereas private bank issues were too often like gas, which wildly inflated an economy without public controls and in behalf of no public ends.[35]

Carey not only lost on the greenback issue and subsequently left the Republican Party, but also became increasingly disillusioned with the whole tendency of economic policy after the war. As so often before, his disillusionment reflected local and private concerns. It began in part with postwar challenges within the Grant Administration to certain high duties, particularly those on iron. Carey's favorite industry seemed threatened. He called for the ironmasters to strike; they should refuse to maintain their furnaces, and force Congress to live up to its implied commitment—the level of continued protection necessary to make their business profitable. He also found that former allies on the tariff issue had not really embraced his protectionist rationale. For example, New England cotton mill owners wanted protection from British competition but at the same time wanted cheap raw materials, such as coal and iron and cotton. Railroad companies wanted the cheapest rails, whether domestic or foreign.

As Carey should have realized all along, most producers looked out for their own interest and never subscribed to lofty principles except when such principles also served their self-interest. Nonetheless, he felt betrayed by those who would now desert iron. It was, he believed, the most important manufacture in America. The best test of a developing civilization, he now declared, was iron consumption (earlier it had been manure retention or agricultural prices). When Americans imported British iron, they really imported food (the argument of Calvin Colton), for iron products reflected the food that had nourished workers as they manufactured it. It was simply food at a later stage in the consumption-production chain. Thus, he vainly argued with railroad executives that the use of iron rose only when prices for iron were high. His subtle point: that a thriving domestic iron production, based on high prices, created a larger domestic market for farmers, and through them stimulated a dramatically increased market both for railroad transport and for iron products. But the acceptance of such logic, the implementation of such policies, depended on a large, national viewpoint. Such acceptance required an organic perspective, a sense of community, a renunciation of selfish and short-term gains for one section or sector. The Civil War was supposed to end all such divisions; it was fought on behalf of union and harmony. Carey could only vainly ask: What happened?[36]

His answer was simple but despairing. A few men in the North, either through malice or short-sightedness, had betrayed the goals of the war. In 1861, when the Republicans assumed control of the government, they avowedly represented the working people of the North. This was clear from their platform, from their tariff protection for American laborers, from war-time monetary policies, even from an eight-hour-day law for government workers. But as soon as the war ended, the party swung its support to wealthy capitalists, to the few with fixed incomes or outstanding loans. By debt retirement and the early resumption of specie payments, Congress assessed up to 50 percent penalties on debtors, farmers, miners, and mechanics. Small entrepreneurs, who borrowed cheap dollars to get a start (so wonderful the opportunity) now faced bankruptcy as their debts came due.

Just as significant, Republican monetary policies clearly favored the Northeast, the area with most creditors and bankers, and hurt the South and West, the region of debtors. From being a party opposed to classes and sections, the Republicans were on the way to becoming a party of one class and one section. They threatened the precious money of the common people, yet catered to the paper of Wall Street, to a money-lending aristocracy. They favored high interest rates and unemployment so long as the rich grew richer. Carey even repudiated his formerly beloved capitalists of Lowell and Boston. They had, somehow, become "great capitalists," and behaved surprisingly like those of London and Liverpool. Instead of serving as allies of farmers and workingmen, they were allied with gold and with British imperialism and oppressed the working classes. New Englanders, smug in their own well-being, now joined with New York City to control national banking and to exercise centralized financial control over the whole country. They had no concern at all for the welfare of Carey's extractive and agricultural industries. They did not seem to care about the West or the South. They even opposed competitive southern manufacturing, and did not want a revived and equal South but only a cheap source of raw materials. Already, New England and New York had moved from commerce to trading, and threatened to treat the rest of the country as their colonies, to practice a familiar variety of centralization and colonialism almost as sinister as that earlier imposed by Britain.[37]

Carey did not live out his last years mired in such disillusionment. His mood fluctuated. In 1872, in his last book, he generally saw a bright future for the United States, Germany, and Russia. At least the Civil War had achieved an enduring policy of protection; we did have a national and very productive economy. Who could deny it in the years after 1865? But Carey, again prophetically, appreciated the changed problems of public policy such economic achievement posed. Issues of distribution, of fairness, of humane outcomes had now become all-important. His idealized, almost communal model for an American economy seemed ever less realistic. The large factories of America no longer seemed very different from those of England. Who, by 1879, the year of his death, could image typical American banks as local money shops? Were American farmers honored and respected? Was agriculture scientific? Did anyone heed the hard logic of manure? Who could believe that the corporate form was the final, emergent expression of voluntary association? And would all Americans really attain proprietary status and move closer to economic equality? Would America really be able to resist the lure of big cities, with their centralized control, or to pass up the imperial glory made possible by its new wealth and power? Carey nourished profound doubts, and for good reason. As a perceptive prophet he lived too long. Unlike Moses, he was able to explore all the dark corners of his promised land.

Afterword

Henry C. Carey, unlike most of the other economists in this book, lived well into the post–Civil War era. But he did his most creative work in political economy between 1835 and 1853. He was fully part of the first generation of American economists, of those who matured their theoretical systems between 1820 and about 1850. Carey had more fervent disciples than any of his American predecessors. He became something of a cult figure to many businessmen, politicians, and journalists. He gained fame in Germany and merited a detailed refutation from John Stuart Mill. A few young American economists adopted his system; one tried to reduce it all to a simplified textbook. Yet Carey's inverted Ricardian system, so idiosyncratic in detail and lacking any academic base, proved to be a dead end in the development of modern economic thought.

After 1865, most political economists sought and found academic posts. This slowly changed the discipline and altered the kind of people attracted to it. Of course, many of America's ablest early economists held academic appointments, among them, Cooper, Tucker, Vethake, and Wayland. As college presidents they were prominent public figures, and Cooper and Tucker also dabbled in politics. None taught political economy full-time. Not until after the Civil War would any university support a separate economics department or fund fully specialized economics professorships. But eventually most economists would depend on an academic salary, a hard fact that narrowed the range of acceptable theoretical deviance but finally opened up opportunities for young men who were not part of an established gentry. The technical content of an increasingly specialized discipline, plus the intimidating role of scholarly credentials, made it increasingly difficult for businessmen, lawyers, or journalists to gain an expert audience or possibly even a prestige publisher for their economic theories, although Henry George would later be one dramatic exception to this rule. With these changes, one senses a loss of variety and also a diminution in new and daring systems or models.

This does not mean that a narrow, monolithic orthodoxy came to prevail among academic economists. Later academic reformers, such as Richard T. Ely, helped nourish a widely accepted caricature of a reigning, hidebound laissez-faire school that completely dominated university economics from 1850 to 1885. What is true is that mild versions of Ricardian theory, usually qualified by Say's emphasis upon a harmony of classes and interests, seemed persuasive to a majority of academic economists. Given the prestige and eloquence of John Stuart Mill, his 1848 text provided a clinching argument for the validity of the Ricardian approach. In this sense, a majority of American economists remained in the tradition of the mild and conventional Frances Wayland, not that of the acerbic and pessimistic George Tucker. Not only was Wayland's text widely used in colleges but a popularized version won wide acceptance in secondary schools. Most other popularizations were in the same vein. But to suggest such a consensus is to conceal all the subtleties of economic analysis, and thus to overlook the fascinating array of questions still argued within the Ricardian tradition. It is also to discount the dissenting mavericks who continued to toss brickbats at Ricardo, even if now only from the periphery of a profession.

From a present perspective, the second generation of academic economists, those who matured in the Civil War and Reconstruction periods, make up a forgotten generation. Most historians seem to view William Graham Sumner as the commanding general of a type of insensitive and inflexible orthodoxy. Sumner was an able popularizer of Ricardian theory, and often brilliant in applying it to policy debates, yet he contributed little to economic theory. The men who most advanced the discipline, who finally achieved a level of technical skill comparable to their English contemporaries, lacked Sumner's flair or notoriety. Certainly such economists as Charles Dunbar of Harvard, Arthur Perry of Williams, or J. Laurence Laughlin of Chicago are no longer household names. Even Simon Newcomb of Johns Hopkins, who first introduced the marginal utility theory and mathematical methods of Stanley Jevons to American audiences, is today best remembered for his primary professional commitment—in physics. Francis A. Walker of Harvard, a theorist much too eclectic to fit any Ricardian mold, is usually remembered not for his theoretical innovations, but for being the first president of the American Economics Association. Largely in such hands as these rested the fate of serious economic inquiry in America.

Even before Carey's death in 1879, a group of American students were in Germany eagerly absorbing new approaches to economic analysis. John Bates Clark, Richard T. Ely, Simon Patten, and others came home with a new, more historical outlook. They emphasized a nongeneralizable cultural context, distrusted overly abstract models, and often tried to integrate empirical and descriptive studies with their ethical goals. Like Daniel Raymond at the very beginnings of serious economic inquiry in America, they recognized the elements of political choice involved in basic property arrangements, and thus essayed a very broad area of government responsibility for the functioning of a national economy. In their emphasis on the positive state, and in their openness to increased government regulation, they revived some of the dominating concerns of such Whig economists as Colton, Phillips, and Carey. But because of their sharp and polemical attacks on laissez-faire orthodoxy, one can mistakenly infer both an overly sharp contrast between them and American Ricardians or too much uniformity in their own doctrines. Clark, for example, incorporated much classical analysis into his work, and even Ely later made use of marginal utility theory. In their early crusade for what in 1885 eventuated in the American Economic Association, they seemed to launch a veritable crusade against their orthodox elders. But very shortly the new Association divested itself of any doctrinal stance and welcomed academic economists from every camp. However we group those youthful insurgents, we still find internal tensions and doctrinal diversity. This is even more true for their most brilliant successors, the so-called institutionalists. Despite some shared assumptions about method, the perverse and brilliant work of Thorstein Veblen was far removed from the careful and technically proficient analysis of Wesley Claire Mitchell or from the active but accommodating public advocacy of John R. Commons.

Neither the historical school nor the major institutionalists emphasized the countercyclical fiscal and monetary theories of Malthus and Raymond. Instead, they envisioned a much more direct governmental role. Of course, Carey's late emphasis on monetary inflation continued to have support, often with a vengeance, from Greenbackers and Populists. Only much later, with the latter-day Malthusian theories of Lord Keynes, did countercyclical fiscal policies gain not only respectability but for a time after World War II an intimidating dominance.

The agrarian cause fared well in the decades after the Civil War. The presuppositions and the moral goals of a Skidmore or a George Henry Evans, which still awaited full and systematic theoretical development, gained this and more in *Progress and Poverty*. Henry George defied classification. The consummate layman, a pariah among professionals, he exerted greater influence worldwide than any other contemporary American economist. Measured by influence, and not technical proficiency, he came closer to the status of the great economic trinity (Smith, Ricardo, and Marx) than did Tucker, Carey, Veblen, or Mitchell. Sometimes he displayed great analytical skill; at other times he embraced near-nostrums. But as Marx had explored the crucial moral implications of the Ricardian model for a developing and exploited European proletariat, so George explored its implications for the beleaguered proprietors of America. And, at the very least, he did accept the formal and technical requirements of economic analysis, which was much less true for early American popularizers of Marx, such as Lawrence Gronlund and Edward Bellamy.

Lest this sketchy preview of future developments in economic theory be misleading, I should say that most parallels between pre-Civil War economists and later schools are partial at best. The only compelling continuity is one of diversity, complexity, and richness. I have been unable to identify in the pre-Civil War period anything close to a distinctive American tradition in political economy. Except for a common commitment to economic growth and to a proprietary society, our first economists scarcely agreed on any beliefs or values. I also doubt if many post-war American economists turned to the early American economists for either doctrines or inspiration. Influential European economists continued to determine the theoretical fashions in America. When McVickar first introduced the Ricardian model to Americans in 1825, he dutifully surveyed earlier American economic thought but largely in order to judge how well it anticipated Ricardo. Sixty years later, when Richard T. Ely encouraged two of his students—Woodrow Wilson and Davis R. Dewey—to begin a major but never completed history of American economic thought, he hoped to find a native, anticlassical position to vindicate doctrines he had borrowed from German mentors. Once again, the American past was more a usable weapon than a living tradition.

It is also easy, and for me very tempting, to exaggerate the policy impact of our first economists. Most were men of affairs. They either held political office or had close friends within government or in one of the political parties. Henry C. Carey tried to be a one-man Council of Economic Advisors. At times he almost bombarded congressmen, cabinet members, and even presidents with detailed letters or extended policy proclamations. Economists typically sent copies of their books and articles to congressmen and often joined in a continuing dialogue with friendly politicians. Yet, I doubt that arguments drawn from one or another system of political economy had much to do with the basic policy preferences of politicians. I doubt if they serve this role today. Had all the economists of 1840 agreed with each other, had they achieved a solid phalanx of economic doctrine, they might have persuaded laymen to accept their prescriptions. But in fact they variously reflected the whole range of economic beliefs and preferences held by politicians and voters.

Thus, like-minded politicians and economists found each other and freely used each other. Every political preference, including the most radical, eventually gained the flattering support of some economic theory. This meant a quite limited and subtle role for theoreticians. They provided excellent ammunition for sympathetic policy makers, but guided policy only to the limited extent that their rationalizations influenced, not the overall direction of policy, but its detailed implementation.

The actual political record backs up this modest evaluation. I have spent months reading congressional debates on economic issues between 1820 and 1850. This meant reading most of the debates, for economic policy issues dominated. On the whole, congressmen were sophisticated consumers of even technical economic theory. In specialized areas of responsibility, such as land policy or banking, or on such pervasive issues as the tariff, they read widely and accumulated all the economic data they could find. If anything, the wealth of pro- and anti-tariff arguments offered by congressmen excelled in subtlety those offered by economists. On any specialized issue a layman could usually gain full equality with experts. Frequently congressmen cited or quoted from political economists, although they tended to quote Smith or McCulloch more often than American economists. However, one can easily identify points of view either directly or indirectly drawn from the writings of our native economists. In particular, one finds themes or even phrases borrowed from such polemical writers as Taylor, Gouge, or Colton. But politicians always picked theories to fit their political needs. They were selective consumers. They did not feel obliged to be consistent or to subscribe to any full system or model. Such logical and holistic commitments, more than doctrines or technical proficiency, separated political economists from interested laymen.

Such disclaimers could continue. For example, I doubt that the ablest political economists, or their most serious books or articles, had much direct impact on popular economic assumptions. Most often our economists shared these assumptions. The long-term influence of our most innovative economists depended upon the degree to which their theories fed into and helped shape the growing descipline. I have conceded that this influence was very limited, and in most cases not a necessary condition for future theoretical development even in America. Thus, I have written a book about a few intellectuals who founded a major new discipline but were incapable of controlling its future development, and who had limited success in using their expert knowledge to guide public policy. So be it. Such problems of direct influence, of impact upon large populations, of winning political strategies, even of control over the direction taken by a discipline, relate not at all to my purposes in writing this book.

The history of economic theory is a part of the larger history of moral philosophy. It is an essential part of the larger story of man's effort to understand himself, in the context of his environment, in order to direct events and choices in behalf of widespread personal happiness and fulfillment. The best reason for confronting historical examples of this effort is to support and guide our own moral engagement. All moral issues involve issues of fact and of taste, of means and ends. By the definition of our earliest experts, political economy largely involved one side of this pair—matters of fact, or the means necessary for achieving previously accepted goals. This did not in any way diminish its importance or segregate it from the ongoing process of criticizing ends and purposes. From Malthus on, political economists noted that economic knowledge should clarify the limits of the possible, dissipate utopian illusions, and in this way make a vital contribution to the valuative side of economic development. They believed it foolish for economists, or anyone else, to sever their beliefs about facts and relationships from matters of taste and preference. The best possible reason for engaging in any empirical inquiry, in natural or moral philosophy, was in response to some human dilemma or problem, or at least in the firm expectation that one's finding would help solve future even as if yet unanticipated problems.

Whether or not our first economists had great influence on their contemporaries or on immediate successors is an empirical issue worth noting by an intellectual historian. But it is of little import in guiding his selection of a subject. The ultimate impact of past beliefs is always an open issue. The living past, the only one worth our efforts to recapture it, is any past that engages our present concerns. If a few gifted thinkers from any past age deserve extended and rigorous historical treatment, it is not so much because of their significance in their own age as because of their significance in our age. If we recognize their significance, then very often even the losers in the past finally win a victory in our present. Our first economists engaged issues that are still current, wrestled with major policy issues that we have to confront today. They often either struggled with these issues for the first time, approached them from completely new perspectives, or confronted them with new but still relatively simple and comprehensible analytical tools. Their social environment was less complex than ours. Daniel Raymond suggested that the very openness of America, the absence of deeply entrenched institutions, made it a peculiarly useful laboratory for clarifying economic theory. I agree. Thus our first economists, often because of their disagreements, their wide-ranging theoretical differences, offer present Americans a peculiarly revealing, often poignant, insight into themselves.

NOTES

3. John Taylor

1. Taylor, *Construction Construed and Constitutions Vindicated* (Richmond: Shepherd and Pollard, 1820), p. 206 (henceforth cited as *CC*); Taylor, *An Inquiry Into the Principles and Policy of the Government of the United States* (New Haven: Yale University Press, 1950), pp. 543–44 (henceforth cited as *Inquiry*).

2. Taylor is now an "in" subject. The volume of literature about him is ballooning. Yet I find none of it very helpful in unravelling his economic beliefs. So far we have no adequate personal biography. I largely discount Henry H. Simms's outdated and unimaginative effort: *Life of John Taylor: The Story of a Brilliant Leader in the Early Virginia State Rights School* (Richmond: William Byrd Press, 1932). Although simplistic and much out of date, Eugene T. Mudge's *The Social Philosophy of John Taylor of Caroline* (New York: Columbia University, 1939) does include a chapter on what the author calls Taylor's agrarianism (see pp. 151–208). In a recent, tedious, but perceptive topical study, Charles W. Hill attends largely to Taylor's political thought, but has brief sections on funding, banking, and corporations: *The Political Theory of John Taylor of Caroline* (Rutherford, N.J.: Fairleigh Dickinson University Press, 1977), pp. 110–19. Hill also begins his book with a thorough and very enlightening bibliographic essay.

3. *Inquiry*, p. 298; *CC*, pp. 28–29.

4. *Inquiry*, p. 124.

5. *Inquiry*, pp. 128–29; Taylor, *New Views of the Constitution of the United States* (Washington City: Way and Gideon, 1823), p. 270; Taylor, *Arator: Being a Series of Agricultural Essays, Practical and Political* (Georgetown, D.C.: J. M. and J. B. Carter, 1813), p. 12.

6. *Inquiry*, pp. 484–86; *Arator*, p. 43.

7. *Arator*, p. 41; *New Views*, p. 268; *CC*, p. 11.

8. *CC*, p. 11; *Inquiry*, pp. 60, 298, 488.

9. Taylor, *Tyranny Unmasked* (Washington City: Davis and Force, 1822), p. 192; *Arator*, p. 45; *CC*, p. 248; James C. Hite and Ellen J. Hall, "The Reactionary Evolution of Economic Thought in Antebellum Virginia," *The Virginia Magazine of History and Biography* 80 (October 1972): 478–79.

10. *Tyranny Unmasked*, p. 194; *Arator*, pp. 24, 25, 40, 42, 51.

11. *Arator*, pp. 17, 38, 45, 59; *Inquiry*, p. 245.

12. *CC*, pp. 207, 240; *Inquiry*, pp. 249, 253, 308.

13. *CC*, p. 208; *Tyranny Unmasked*, p. 196.

14. *CC*, pp. 4–5, 229, 251.

15. *Tyranny Unmasked*, pp. 195–98; *Inquiry*, p. 489.

16. *CC*, pp. 15, 234, 238; *Tyranny Unmasked*, pp. 147, 217.

17. *Inquiry*, pp. 43, 262, 299; *Arator*, p. 42; *CC*, p. 15.

18. *Inquiry*, pp. 59, 246–47, 251, 255, 484, 493.

19. Ibid., pp. 230–64.
20. Ibid., pp. 83, 86, 242, 346, 347, 546–47; *CC*, pp. 12–13, 88, 90, 95, 187, 191–99, 320.
21. *Inquiry*, pp. 323, 344; *Tyranny Unmasked*, p. 125; *CC*, p. 246.
22. *Tyranny Unmasked*, p. 227; *Inquiry*, pp. 316–23.
23. *CC*, pp. 337–38.
24. *Inquiry*, pp. 267–316.
25. Ibid., pp. 318–19.
26. *Tyranny Unmasked*, pp. 86–94.
27. Ibid., pp. 123–25.
28. Ibid., pp. 136–41, 195–96.
29. *New Views*, p. 277; *CC*, p. 293; *Inquiry*, p. 317.
30. *Arator*, pp. 68–74.
31. Ibid., pp. 65, 74, 135.
32. *CC*, pp. 293–314; *New Views*, p. 276.

4. Daniel Raymond

1. These biographical details come from Kenneth V. Lundberg, "Daniel Raymond: Early American Economist," Ph.D. dissertation, University of Wisconsin, 1953. This dissertation remains the fullest and most sophisticated study of Raymond, both as a person and as an economist. It is much more reliable and thorough than an older, published monograph: Charles P. Neill, *Daniel Raymond: An Early Chapter in the History of Economic Theory in the United States* (Baltimore: Johns Hopkins University Press, 1897). Ernest Teilhac, in *Pioneers of American Economic Thought in the Nineteenth Century*, translated by E. A. J. Johnson (New York: Russell and Russell, 1967), devotes one of three chapters to Raymond.

2. Daniel Raymond, *The Elements of Constitutional Law and of Political Economy*, 4th ed. (Baltimore: Cushing and Brother, 1840), pp. 13–20, 21–23.
3. Ibid., pp. 25–28.
4. Ibid., pp. 33–44.
5. Ibid., pp. 29–32.
6. Daniel Raymond, *Thoughts on Political Economy* (Baltimore: Fielding Lucas, 1820), p. 41; Raymond, *The Elements of Political Economy*, 2 vols. (Baltimore: F. Lucas, Jun. and E. J. Coale, 1823), I, p. 71; II., 395–400.
7. Ibid., I, 23, 25; II, 10–11; Raymond, *Elements of Constitutional Law and of Political Economy*, pp. 68–70.
8. Raymond, *Thoughts on Political Economy*, pp. 50, 57, 70, 73, 165.
9. *Elements of Political Economy*, I, pp. 9, 32–54.
10. Ibid., pp. 168, 226.
11. Ibid., II, pp. 8–11, 113.
12. Ibid., pp. 10–11, 113.
13. Ibid., pp. 69–70.
14. Ibid., pp. 14–17.
15. Ibid., pp. 22–23, 26–27, 30–34, 80–82.
16. Ibid., pp. 30–48.
17. Ibid., I, pp. 62–65.
18. Ibid., pp. 71–72.
19. Ibid., pp. 119–38, 149; Ibid., II, pp. 38–39, 48–49.

20. Ibid., pp. 20–21, 111.

21. Ibid., pp. 91–95.

22. Ibid., pp. 91–103.

23. Ibid., pp. 149, 107–11, 198–99.

24. Ibid., I, pp. 182–89, 192–94, 198.

25. Ibid., pp. 201–3.

26. Ibid., pp. 204–6, 209, 216, 261.

27. Ibid., pp. 215–20.

28. Ibid., pp. 210–12, 214, 261–70; *Elements of Constitutional Law and of Political Economy*, pp. 147–49.

29. *Elements of Political Economy*, I, pp. 162–63, and passim.

30. Ibid., II, pp. 158–62, 327.

31. Ibid., p. 320.

32. Ibid., pp. 256–80, 317–31.

33. Ibid., p. 335.

34. Ibid., pp. 333–53.

35. Ibid., pp. 295–303.

36. Ibid., pp. 197–202.

37. Ibid., pp. 207–13, 228.

38. Ibid., pp. 230–38.

39. Ibid., pp. 240–41.

40. *The American System* (Baltimore: Lucas and Deaver, 1828), pp. 5–26; Gary Hull, "The Prospect for Man in Early American Economic Thought" (Ph.D. dissertation, University of Maryland, 1969), pp. 75–77.

41. *Elements of Political Economy*, I, pp. 65–67, 230–34.

42. Ibid., pp. 235–40, 243, 245, 251.

43. Ibid., pp. 243–50.

44. Ibid., II, pp. 126–28.

45. Ibid., pp. 129–39.

46. Ibid., pp. 139–49.

47. Ibid., pp. 154–57, 171–72.

48. Ibid., pp. 163–67, 176–80.

49. Ibid., pp. 171.

50. Ibid., pp. 117–19.

51. Ibid., pp. 119–20.

52. Ibid., pp. 120–23.

53. *Elements of Constitutional Law and of Political Economy*, pp. 273–76.

54. Daniel Raymond, *The Missouri Question* (Baltimore: Schaeffer & Mound, 1819), pp. 5–7; *Elements of Constitutional Law and of Political Economy*, p. 124.

55. *Elements of Political Economy*, I, pp. 17–21, 54; *The Missouri Question*, pp. 9–13.

56. *Elements of Political Economy*, II, pp. 356–69; *The Missouri Question*, pp. 5, 12–39.

5. Ricardo Domesticated

1. For a sympathetic portrait of McVickar, see Joseph Dorfman and Rexford G. Tugwell, *Early American Policy, Six Columbia Contributors* (New York: Columbia University Press, 1960), pp. 99–154.

2. John McVickar, *Outlines of Political Economy*, introduction by Joseph Dorfman (New York: Augustus M. Kelley, 1966), pp. 15, 48, 49, 64, 88, 90, 98, 104.

3. Ibid., pp. 100–102.

4. Ibid., pp. 166–73.

5. Ibid., pp. 187–88.

6. Samuel P. Newman, *Elements of Political Economy* (Andover: Gould and Newman, 1835), pp. iii–iv.

7. Ibid., pp. 13–35.

8. Ibid., pp. 57–65, 70–74, 213–17, 319–20.

9. Ibid., pp. 120–37, 234–76.

10. See D. H. Meyer, *The Instructed Conscience* (Philadelphia: University of Pennsylvania Press, 1972), pp. 13–15; and Michael J. L. O'Connor, *Origins of Academic Economics in the United States* (New York: Columbia University Press, 1944), p. 17, 172–74.

11. Francis Wayland, *The Elements of Moral Science* (Cambridge: Harvard University Press, 1963, a reprint of the original 1837 edition), pp. 30–47.

12. Ibid., pp. 210–15; Francis Wayland, *The Elements of Political Economy* (New York: Leavitt, Lord and Co., 1837), pp. 111–15, 123, 124.

13. Wayland, *Elements of Political Economy*, pp. 108–11.

14. Ibid., pp. 28–33, 48, 53–54, 72, 90, 132–37.

15. Ibid., pp. 96–103, 105.

16. Ibid., pp. 140–61.

17. Ibid., pp. 5–6, 168, 179.

18. Ibid., pp. 326–46.

19. Ibid., pp. 380–406.

20. Ibid., pp. 222–318.

21. Ibid., pp. 341–42, 442–49, 406.

22. Joseph Dorfman and Rexford G. Tugwell, "Henry Vethake, Jacksonian Ricardian," an introduction to the reprint of Vethake's *The Principles of Political Economy*, 2d ed. (New York: Augustus M. Kelley, 1971), pp. 5–54; Gary Hull, "The Prospect for Man in Early American Economic Thought," Ph.D. dissertation, University of Maryland, 1968, pp. 174–77.

23. Vethake, *The Principles*, 2d ed., pp. 402–6.

24. Ibid., p. 37.

25. Ibid., pp. 40–49.

26. Ibid., pp. 50–67, 80–83.

27. Ibid., pp. 68–72.

28. Ibid., pp. 85–97.

29. Ibid., p. 99.

30. Ibid., pp. 99–100.

31. Ibid., pp. 107–27.

32. Ibid., pp. 153–211.

33. Ibid., pp. 218–43.

34. Ibid., pp. 244–56.

35. Ibid., pp. 257–75.

36. Ibid., pp. 275–94.

37. Ibid., pp. 302–24, 334–55.

38. Ibid., pp. 325–31.

39. Ibid., pp. 343–55.

40. Ibid., pp. 380–401.

6. Three Southerners

1. Jacob N. Cardozo, *Notes on Political Economy* (Charleston: A. E. Mille, 1826), pp. ii-iii; also see Melvin M. Leiman, *Jacob N. Cardozo, Economic Thought in the Antebellum South* (New York: Columbia University Press, 1966), which I believe is the most sophisticated monograph yet written about an early American economist.

2. *Notes*, pp. 7–10.

3. Ibid., pp. 12–13, 17–18, 36, 51.

4. Ibid., pp. 26–30, 123.

5. Ibid., pp. 39–43, 47, 51, 54.

6. Ibid., pp. 54, 56–57.

7. Ibid., pp. 75–90.

8. Ibid., pp. 77–80.

9. For details on Cooper's fascinating life, see Dumas Malone, *The Public Life of Thomas Cooper*, 1783–1839 (New Haven: Yale University Press, 1926).

10. Thomas Cooper, *Lectures on the Elements of Political Economy*, 2d ed. (1830), reprint introduced by Joseph Dorfman (New York: Augustus M. Kelley, 1971), pp. 8–30, 61.

11. Ibid., pp. 64, 360–62.

12. Ibid., pp. 363–66.

13. Ibid., pp. 64–71, 100, 270.

14. Ibid., pp. 72–78, 99.

15. Ibid., pp. 80–98.

16. Ibid., pp. 100–103.

17. Ibid., pp. 104–5, 274–81.

18. Ibid., pp. 106–11.

19. Ibid., pp. 116–19.

20. Ibid., pp. 129–37, 193–97, 213–15.

21. Ibid., pp. 139–79.

22. Ibid., pp. 254–71.

23. Ibid., pp. 217–53.

24. Ibid., pp. 211, 348.

25. Ibid., pp. 302–43.

26. Ibid., pp. 349–54, 356–57, 365.

27. Ibid., pp. 357–58.

28. Tipton R. Snavely, in *George Tucker as Political Economist* (Charlottesville, Va.: University of Virginia Press, 1964), provides biographical details and a simplified summary of Tucker's contributions to political economy; for Tucker's literary achievements, see Robert C. McLean, *George Tucker, Moral Philosopher and Man of Letters* (Chapel Hill: University of North Carolina Press, 1961).

29. George Tucker, *Essays on Various Subjects of Taste, Morals, and National Policy*, by a Citizen of Virginia (Georgetown: Joseph Milligan, 1822), pp. 305–21.

30. George Tucker, *The Laws of Wages, Profits, and Rent, Investigated* (Philadelphia: E. L. Carey & A. Hart, 1837), pp. 2–7.

31. Ibid., pp. 7–21.

32. Ibid., pp. 53–54; *George Tucker, Political Economy for the People* (Philadelphia: C. Sherman & Son, 1859, reprinted by Augustus M. Kelley, New York, 1970), pp. 45, 53.

33. *Laws*, pp. 30–33.

34. Ibid., p. 71.
35. Ibid., pp. 66–67.
36. Ibid., pp. 33–42.
37. Ibid., p. 42.
38. Ibid., pp. 98–103, 124–31.
39. Ibid., pp. 47–49; *Political Economy for the People*, pp. 85–87.
40. *Essays on Various Subjects*, p. 19; *Laws*, pp. 79–81, 120, 212, 224–25.
41. *Essays on Various Subjects*, pp. 128–56; George Tucker, *The Theory of Money and Banks* (Boston: Charles C. Little and James Brown, 1839), pp. 141–42.
42. *Theory of Money and Banks*, pp. 3–29.
43. Ibid., pp. 33–42.
44. Ibid., pp. 122–43, 173–82.
45. Ibid., pp. 191–99.
46. Ibid., pp. 183–89, 234, 240–59, 273–88, 328.
47. Ibid., pp. 204–31.

7. Protectionists

1. See Hamilton's "Report Relative to a Provision for the Support of Public Credit," in Jacob E. Cooke, ed., *The Reports of Alexander Hamilton* (New York: Harper, 1964), pp. 1–45.
2. "Report on Manufactures," Ibid., pp. 115–205.
3. Matthew Carey, *Essays on Political Economy* (Philadelphia: H. C. Carey and Lea, 1822).
4. *Dictionary of American Biography*, XIV, pp. 547–48; Willard Phillips, *Propositions Concerning Protection and Free Trade* (Boston: Little and Brown, 1850), p. iv.
5. Willard Phillips, *A Manual of Political Economy* (Boston: Hilliard, Gray, Little, and Wilkins, 1828), pp. v-vi, 9–13, 34.
6. Ibid., pp. 14–54, 95–97.
7. Ibid., pp. 58–62, 64–67, 73–82.
8. Ibid., pp. 84–93, 94–95, 113.
9. Ibid., pp. 107–20, 122–23.
10. Ibid., pp. 127–29.
11. Ibid., pp. 127–59.
12. Ibid., pp. 165–209.
13. *Propositions Concerning Protection and Free Trade*, pp. iv, 2, 16, 20.
14. Ibid., pp. 2–19.
15. This list appeared in Ibid., pp. 21–22, but provides a framework for the arguments in the rest of the book.
16. Ibid., pp. 48–55.
17. Ibid., pp. 80–84.
18. Ibid., pp. 86–116.
19. Ibid., pp. 118–21.
20. Ibid., pp. 128–57.
21. Ibid., pp. 178–217.
22. *Dictionary of American Biography*, IV, 320–21.
23. Calvin Colton, *Public Economy of the United States* (New York: A. S. Barnes, 1848), pp. 27–41.

24. Ibid., pp. 61–62, 69–71, 90–97.
25. Ibid., pp. 152–62, 165–68, 299–300, 359.
26. Ibid., pp. 284, 165.
27. Ibid., pp. 155, 180–81, 289.
28. Ibid., pp. 284–85, 286–88.
29. Ibid., pp. 274–76.
30. Ibid., pp. 289–93, 317–19.
31. Ibid., pp. 178, 407–9.
32. Ibid., pp. 342–45.
33. Ibid., pp. 481–501.
34. Ibid., pp. 200–29.
35. Ibid., pp. 240–59.
36. Ibid., pp. 351–53, 356–59, 387–88.

8. Jacksonians

1. *Dictionary of American Biography*, XVI, 551.
2. Theodore Sedgwick, *Public and Private Economy* (New York: Harpers, 1836), I, pp. 13–22, 25, 40.
3. Ibid., pp. 41–70.
4. Ibid., pp. 23, 25–26.
5. Ibid., pp. 72–75.
6. Ibid., pp. 77–87.
7. Ibid., pp. 89–113.
8. Ibid., pp. 175–217.
9. Ibid., II (New York: Harpers, 1838), pp. 87–88; most of Volume II relates to self-help strategies for the poor.
10. Ibid., I, pp. 256–63.
11. Benjamin G. Rader, "William M. Gouge, Jacksonian Economic Theorist," *Pennsylvania History* 30 (1963): 443–53; Gary Hull, *The Prospect for Man in Early American Economic Thought*, Ph.D. dissertation, University of Maryland, 1968, pp. 242–43; Joseph Dorfman, "William M. Gouge and the Formation of Orthodox American Monetary Policy," an Introduction to a reprinted edition of William M. Gouge, *A Short History of Paper Money and Banking in the United States and* etc. (Philadelphia, 1833, reprinted by Augustus M. Kelley, New York, 1968), pp. 5–26. The whole issue of banking in the Jacksonian era is treated extensively by Bray Hammond, *Banks and Politics in America from the Revolution to the Civil War* (Princeton: Princeton University Press, 1957), and by Sr. M. Grace Madeleine, *Monetary and Banking Theories of Jacksonian Democracy* (Philadelphia: The Dolphin Press, 1943).
12. William M. Gouge, *A Short History of Paper Money and Banking in the United States* (1833 edition as reprinted by Augustus M. Kelley), pp. 26–33, 62–63.
13. Ibid., pp. 34–39.
14. Ibid., pp. 53–61.
15. Ibid., pp. 41–44.
16. Ibid.
17. Ibid., pp. 41–42.
18. Ibid., pp. 78–83, 133–34.
19. For Jackson's veto, see James D. Richardson, ed., *A Compilation of the*

Messages and Papers of the Presidents, 1789–1902 (Bureau of National Literature and Art, 1904), pp. 576–91; Hammond, *Banks and Politics*, pp. 278–79, 283–84, 325.

20. Gouge, *A Short History*, pp. 67–68, 70–75.

21. Ibid., pp. 90–94.

22. Ibid., pp. 94–99.

23. Ibid., pp. 45–52, 101–5.

24. Ibid., pp. 117–22.

25. *Dictionary of American Biography*, XV, pp. 325–326.

26. Condy Raguet, *The Principles of Free Trade* (Philadelphia: Carey, Lea, and Blanchard, 1835), pp. 11, 13, 19, 156–57, 166, 268–70, 280.

27. Ibid., pp. v, 47, 151–52.

28. Ibid., pp. 37–47, 55, 149–50.

29. Condy Raguet, *A Treatise on Currency and Banking* (Philadelphia: Grigg & Elliott, 1839), pp. 182–201.

30. Ibid., pp. 1–38.

31. Ibid., pp. 51–62.

32. Ibid., pp. 72–76, 80–84, 169–70.

33. Ibid., pp. 142–46.

34. Ibid., pp. 95–104.

35. Ibid., pp. 106, 111–17, 121–31, 157–66.

36. Ibid., pp. 175–77.

37. Ibid., pp. 108–10.

38. Ibid., pp. 212–14.

9. Agrarians

1. William B. Scott, *In Pursuit of Happiness: American Conceptions of Property, from the Seventeenth to the Twentieth Century* (Bloomington: Indiana University Press, 1977), pp. 13–20.

2. For the life of Spence, see Olive D. Rudkin, *Thomas Spence and His Connections* (New York: Augustus M. Kelley, 1966 reprint of 1927 original edition). Additional information is in P. M. Kemp-Ashrof, "Introduction" to "The Selected Writings of Thomas Spence," a Supplement to *Essays in Honour of William Gallacher* (Berlin: Humboldt University, 1966), pp. 268–71.

3. Thomas Spence, "The Real Rights of Man," in *The Pioneers of Land Reform* (London: G. Bell and Sons, 1920), pp. 5–16.

4. Thomas Spence, "The History of Crusonia, or Robinson Crusoe's Island," in *Essays in Honour of Willliam Gallacher*, pp. 297–307.

5. In *Essays in Honour of William Gallacher*, "The End of Oppression," pp. 310–16; "The Right of Infants," pp. 327–36.

6. Thomas Paine, "Agrarian Justice," in *The Pioneers of Land Reform*, pp. 179–82.

7. Ibid., pp. 187–206.

8. William Ogilvie, "The Right of Property in Land," in *The Pioneers of Land Reform*, pp. viii-ix, 29–45, 64–166.

9. Langton Byllesby, *Observations on the Sources and Effects of Unequal Wealth* (New York, 1826), pp. 30, 32–44.

10. Ibid., pp. 42–82.

11. Ibid., pp. 82–1291.

12. Louis H. Arky, "The Mechanic's Union of Trade Associations and the Formation of the Philadelphia Working Men's Movement, " *The Pennsylvania Magazine of History and Biography* 76 (April, 1952): 142–76.

13. John R. Commons, Ulrich B. Phillips, Eugene A. Gilmore, Helen L. Sumner, and John B. Andrews, eds., *A Documentary History of American Industrial Society*, Vol. 5 (Cleveland: Arthur H. Clark, 1910), pp. 85–93, 124–29.

14. Thomas Skidmore, *The Rights of Man to Property* (New York: Burt Franklin, 1829), pp. 11–26.

15. Ibid., pp. 28–82.

16. Ibid., pp. 83–145.

17. Ibid., pp. 143, 146, 159, 160–61, 172.

18. Stephen Simpson, *The Working Man's Manual: A New Theory of Political Economy* (Philadelphia: Thomas L. Bonsal, 1831), pp. 6–52.

19. Ibid., pp. 53–225.

20. The "Report" of the Committee of Fifty, and the details about the founding of the New York Working Men's Party are in *The Working Man's Advocate*, October 31, 1829; also see Edward Pessen, *Most Uncommon Jacksonians, the Radical Leaders of the Early Labor Movement* (Albany: State University of New York Press, 1967), pp. 9–33.

21. *The Working Man's Advocate*, Oct. 31, Nov. 7, Nov. 14, Nov. 21, Nov. 28, 1829.

22. Ibid., Oct. 31 and Nov. 14, 1829; John R. Commons et al., *History of Labour in the United States*, 4 vols. (New York: 1918–1935), Vol. 1, p. 302; Walter Hugins, *Jacksonian Democracy and the Working Class: A Study of the New York Workingmen's Movement, 1829–1837* (Stanford: Stanford University Press, 1960), pp. 53–54.

23. Frederick W. Evans, *Autobiography of a Shaker* (1888 edition reprinted in Philadelphia: Porcupine Press, 1972), pp. 2–12, 16–25; Lewis Masquerier, *Sociology: or the Reconstruction of Society, Government, and Property* (By author, 1877, but reprinted by Greenwood Press, 1970), pp. 93–99, 162; Helen Sara Zahler, *Eastern Workingmen and National Land Policy* (New York: Columbia University Press, 1941), pp. 19–20.

24. *The Working Man's Advocate*, Nov. 14, Nov. 21, Nov. 28, Dec. 5, 1829; July 14, 1830; Aug. 7, 1832.

25. Ibid., Mar. 5, 1830; July 30, 1831; Apr. 21, 1832; Nov. 30, Dec. 6, Dec. 14, and Dec. 21, 1833; May 15, Aug. 30, Oct. 4, 1834; Jan. 3 and 10, Feb. 21, May 16, June 20, June 27, Aug. 29, 1835.

26. Ibid., Sept. 5, Sept. 12, Sept. 19, Oct. 17, Oct. 24, Nov. 21, 1835; Zahler, *Eastern Workingmen*, pp. 29–30.

27. *The Working Man's Advocate* (Series 2), March 23, 1844.

28. Ibid.

29. Ibid., Mar. 23 and Mar. 30, 1844; Feb. 22 and Sept. 7, 1845.

30. Ibid., Mar. 30, May 4, Oct. 12, 1844.

31. Commons et al., *Documentary History*, Vol. 8, pp. 22–24; Zahler, *Eastern Workingmen*, pp. 63–67; *Young America*, April 29, 1848.

32. *The Working Man's Advocate*, Apr. 6, Apr. 20, July 20, July 27, 1844.

33. Ibid., July 6, July 20, and July 27, 1844; *Young America*, Apr. 29, 1848.

34. *The Working Man's Advocate*, Aug. 6, 1844.

35. Zahler, *Eastern Workingmen*, pp. 81–108.

36. *The Working Man's Advocate*, Nov. 23, 1844; a selection of NRA songs is included in Zahler, *Eastern Workingmen*, Appendix I, pp. 203–6, and in John

Pickering, *The Working Man's Political Economy* (reprint of 1847 edition, New York: Arno Press, 1971), pp. 194–206. Other poems and songs appeared periodically in the *Advocate*.

37. *The Working Man's Advocate*, Nov. 16 and Nov. 23, 1844.

38. See Josiah Warren, *Equitable Commerce: A New Development of Principles* (New York: Fowler and Wells, 1852).

39. John Campbell, *A Theory of Equality; or, the Way to Make Every Man Act Honestly* (Philadelphia: John D. Perry, 1848); Joseph Dorfman, *The Economic Mind in American Civilization, 1606–1865* (New York: Viking Press, 1946), II, pp. 671–73, 685, 692–93.

40. Pickering, *Working Man's Political Economy*, pp. 3-12.

41. Ibid., pp. 15–26.

42. Ibid., pp. 50–51.

43. Ibid., pp. 56–68.

44. Ibid., pp. 95–164.

45. This pamphlet is in Zahler, *Eastern Workingmen*, Appendix II, pp. 207–8.

46. *Congressional Globe*, VI (25th Congress, 2nd Session, 1837–1838), Appendix, pp. 492–93.

47. Ibid., XV (29th Congress, 1st Session, 1845), Appendix, p. 806.

48. Isaac P. Walker of Wisconsin was most active in supporting agrarian homestead bills in the Senate. In the House, the first support for agrarian legislation came from the radical abolitionist and later Free Soiler, George Julian of Ohio. Other supporters were William R. Sapp, a Whig from Ohio; Galusha A. Grow, a free soil Democrat from Pennsylvania; and, of course, Gerret Smith of New York.

10. The Abolition of Rent

1. The most useful study of Carey remains unpublished: Rodney J. Morrison, "Protection and Development: A Nineteenth Century View," Ph.D. dissertation, University of Wisconsin, 1965; also see A. D. H. Kaplan, *Henry Charles Carey: A Study in American Economic Thought* (Baltimore: The Johns Hopkins Studies in Historical and Political Science*, Series 49, No. 4, 1931.

2. Henry C. Carey, *Essay on the Rate of Wages, Etc.* (Philadelphia: Carey, Lea & Blanchard, 1835), pp. 230–31.

3. Ibid., pp. 7–10, 15–17.

4. Ibid., pp. 15–23.

5. Ibid., pp. 15–18, 24–26, 29.

6. Ibid., pp. 54, 80, 84, 95, 130–31, 134, 145–49, 172, ·181.

7. Henry C. Carey, *Principles of Political Economy*, 3 volumes (Philadelphia: Carey, Lee & Blanchard, 1837), I, pp. 8–18.

8. Ibid., I, pp. 20–26; also see John R. Turner, *The Ricardian Rent Theory in Early American Economics* (New York: New York University Press, 1921), pp. 110–42.

9. *Principles*, I, pp. 27–50.

10. Ibid., pp. 55–56.

11. Ibid., pp. 73–74.

12. Ibid., pp. 238.

13. Ibid., pp. 97–99, 107–109, 114–116; Ibid., II, pp. 15, 18–19.

14. Ibid., I, p. 143.

15. Ibid., pp. 294–333.

16. Ibid., II, pp. 11–13.

17. Ibid., pp. 39–245, 304–93.

18. Ibid., III, pp. 102–5, 115, 196–207.

19. Henry C. Carey, *The Credit System in France, Great Britain and the United States* (Philadelphia: Carey, Lea & Blanchard, 1838), pp. 3–7.

20. Ibid., pp. 8–25, 111–17.

21. Ibid., pp. 42–51, 111, 117–19.

11. Down from the Hills

1. Henry C. Carey, *The Past, The Present, and The Future* (New York: Reprint by Augustus M. Kelley, 1967), pp. 6–15.

2. Ibid., p. 75.

3. Ibid., pp. 83, 95–99.

4. Ibid., pp. 110–12, 128–33, and endlessly in all Carey's subsequent writing.

5. Ibid., pp. 101–2, 110; Henry C. Carey, *The Slave Trade, Domestic and Foreign* (Philadelphia: Henry Carey Baird, 1853), pp. 101–2; Henry C. Carey, *Principles of Social Science*, 3 vols. (Philadelphia: J. B. Lippincott and Co., 1858), I, pp. 272–81, 337; II, pp. 29–31, 212, 214–15.

6. *The Slave Trade*, pp. 113–14; *Social Science*, II, p. 99; and endlessly in all Carey's later books and articles.

7. *Social Science*, II, p. 250; Henry C. Carey, *The Harmony of Interests. Agricultural, Manufacturing, and Commercial*, in *Miscellaneous Works* (Philadelphia: Henry Carey Baird, 1872), pp. 198, 202–3.

8. *Slave Trade*, pp. 36, 101–2; *Harmony of Interests*, pp. 54–60.

9. *Harmony of Interests*, pp. 464–70; *Social Science*, I, p. 408; III, pp. 446–53.

10. *Harmony of Interests*, pp. 46–49.

11. Germans appreciated Carey's views. They translated and published his books, and even wrote the earliest and even yet the most thorough analyses of his economic model.

12. *Past, Present, and Future*, p. 324; *The Slave Trade*, pp. 114, 209–93; *Harmony of Interests*, pp. 210–11; *Social Science*, I, pp. 420–25.

13. Henry C. Carey, *The Unity of Law, as Exhibited in the Relations of Physical, Social, Mental, and Moral Science* (Philadelphia: Henry Carey Baird, 1872), pp. 240–49, 257–58, 261–62, 268, 273, 285, 287, 289, 314–44, 368–69, 370–71, and in Appendix F, "The Proletariat," pp. 406–10.

14. *Past, Present, and Future*, pp. 137–45.

15. Ibid., pp. 152–53, 249–60, 261–75, 426; *Harmony of Interests*, p. 216.

16. *Past, Present, and Future*, pp. 159–64, 228, 441–45; *Social Science*, II, pp. 178–79, 422; *Harmony of Interests*, pp. 43–45, 214–15.

17. *Harmony of Interests*, pp. 193–97, 215; *Social Science*, I, pp. 428, 437.

18. *Slave Trade*, pp. 363, 368, 378–80, 396–97.

19. *Social Science*, II, pp. 257–63.

20. Ibid., I, pp. 9–39; *Unity of Law*, pp. 33–76.

21. *Social Science*, I, pp. 41–44; *Unity of Law*, pp. 159–61, 172–73.

22. *Social Science*, I, pp. 42–56, 198–204.

23. Ibid., pp. 64–92, 231; *Unity of Law*, pp. 77–115, 157, 159.

24. *Social Science*, I, pp. 260–63; II, pp. 24–25, 192–95, 228–30.

25. Ibid., II, pp. 207–10, 247.

26. Ibid., III, pp. 18–21.

27. Ibid., pp. 264–94.

28. Ibid., pp. 296–310, 319.

29. Ibid., pp. 411–44.

30. Ibid., II, pp. 293–98, 329–39.

31. Ibid., pp. 344–61.

32. Ibid., pp. 369–442.

33. Henry C. Carey, "Review of the Decade, 1857–67," in *Miscellaneous Papers*, pp. 19–21.

34. "The Currency Question," *Miscellaneous Papers*, pp. 29–32; "The Public Debt, Local and National," a Letter to David A. Wells, 1866, in *Miscellaneous Papers*, pp. 10–15; "Contraction or Expansion? Repudiation or Resumption?", a Letter to Hugh McCulloch, 1866, *Miscellaneous Papers*, pp. 3–5, 25–27; "Our Future," 1869, in *Miscellaneous Papers*, pp. 1–2.

35. "The Currency Question," pp. 3–25.

36. "Review of the Report of the Honorable D. A. Wells," 1869, in *Miscellaneous Papers*, pp. 14–28.

37. "Review of the Decade, 1857–67," pp. 39–55.

INDEX